Our United States History

BOOK 1
Beginnings Through Reconstruction

by Hilarie Staton

EDUCATIONAL DESIGN, INC.   EDI 297

Our United States History, Book 1, Beginning Through Recognition
297
ISBN-10: 0-87694-459-4
ISBN-13: 978-0-87694-459-2

Author: Hilarie Staton
Cover Illustration: Joe Staton

Triumph Learning® 136 Madison Avenue, 7th Floor, New York, NY 10016
A Haights Cross Communications, Inc. company

Printed in the United States of America.

10 9 8 7 6

TABLE OF CONTENTS

LEARNING WITH THIS BOOK

When I began writing this book, I wanted to use the best instructional techniques I could find. Now, after it is done, I look back with pride at those that I have chosen. They continue to be important techniques to help all students learn content in the best way possible.

First, I decided to put an emphasis on what happens before students read the text. This is to activate what they already know (including how the chapter they are studying ties into other chapters) and to teach them important concepts before they read the chapter.

The newest research shows that previewing the chapter is a very effective learning strategy, but also that most students do not automatically do this. One effective strategy for previewing is to read the chapter's title, section headings, smaller headings, and captions. Students can then discuss these or write questions they think will be answered in each section. This can be done by small groups or by the class as a whole. Any way previewing is done creates an active involvement with the chapter and the content BEFORE the chapter is read. This gives students a frame of reference with which to understand what they are reading.

There are many effective reading strategies that can be encouraged. Different sections of this text lend themselves to paraphrasing, summarizing, and visualizing. Other strategies, such as asking questions or taking notes, can be taught for more general use. You choose the appropriate strategy for your students and the section, but be sure to first teach the strategy, model it, and encourage the students to use it often—not only in this text, but with other books as well.

You may also wish to read historical literature so you can give your students a sense of how history is filled with people of all kinds, striving to solve all kinds of problems. In my adolescent years I read a great deal of historical fiction, which helped create my love of history. I highly recommend doing so and sharing it with your class, whether you have them read it orally or silently, from picture books or thick tomes. It provides the flavor which a textbook does not have.

After students have read, include activities that will help them put what they have learned into

perspective. Tie the information into science, art, and literature. Have students communicate what they have learned by writing, chart- and graph-making, pictures, or in oral presentations. Discuss the ideas and help students predict what will (what historically did) happen next. This will naturally lead into previewing the next chapter.

Its not all here. I couldn't include everything. And, above all, research has shown us that effective teaching is much more important than a decent textbook.

Good luck!

INTRODUCTION

When I began writing this book, I thought that it would be easy. I thought I would find historical facts and write them down. Once I started, though, I learned that a historian's job is not so simple.

I had to use many sources. I read books—including textbooks—and magazines by historians. I also used original source material, which are written records by people who had actually lived through some historical event. An example of original source material are the journals, like diaries, many women kept as they crossed the plains in covered wagons. Another example are old newspapers, which I read to find out how people saw the times in which they lived.

I had to use information from other experts besides historians. I read books and articles by geologists, who are scientists who study the earth. Archaeologists, who learn about ancient people by studying what they have left behind, helped me understand cultures like the Aztecs. I read books by economists to learn about work, banks, and trade. I learned from sociologists, who study different groups and types of people, like women or African Americans. Political scientists helped me understand how our government works.

Even once I had the facts, I still had many problems to solve. One problem was that not every historian agrees on what happened and why. Older books said different things than newer books do. Some did this because new facts were uncovered, like the Viking ruins in Canada. But also, historians use their own ideas to look at the past. For example, historians today write about slavery in a different way than did historians who lived before the Civil War and who believed in slavery.

As I thought about all the facts I had found, I realized I had to make them fit together into an exciting story. I wanted to tell the story of the many people who came to this continent, from the first Asians migrating over the land bridge to the Russians who came yesterday. They have all changed the land and been changed by it.

When I started to tell this story, I realized I had too much information. I had to leave out many things and cut down my description of some very exciting events.

Sometimes while researching and writing, I got angry at someone for doing stupid things that would cause trouble, like President Andrew Johnson during Reconstruction. I got angry at governments, wars, and everyday people who treated others badly. But I also became excited about how people reacted to new ideas, how these ideas changed life, and the possibilities for the future. I learned what history really is and became involved in America's story. I hope you will, too.

Hilarie Staton

1

THE LAND AND T

*L*ong before the American Revolution, before the British and French and Spanish planted colonies in what would later become the United States, even before Europeans first discovered the New World, there were Americans and American history.

12,000 years or more ago, people came to America from Asia. Traveling on foot, they crossed over a "land bridge," which at that time connected Asia and Alaska. From there, they spread all throughout North and South America, creating dozens of different cultures. Some of these cultures were as complex and widespread as ancient Egypt or Rome. The story of America starts with these first Americans.

To understand their story, though, you have to understand something about the lands they lived in. The people who settled in the northeast forests or southwest deserts did not live the same way as their ancestors who had crossed into frozen Alaska. Their homes were different. Their clothes and tools were different. Their foods were different. Even how they got along with each other or with nearby people was different. Because human beings adapt to their environments, you have to understand their environments to understand them.

CHAPTER 1

THE LAND

Our history begins with the land. It was here before the first Native Americans and before the first European settlers. When people arrived, the land shaped the way they lived. It still shapes the way that we live today.

The quickest way to become familiar with the land that is now the United States is to take an imaginary trip across it. We will travel through six great regions. Each one has its own **natural environment**. The natural environment of a region includes its geography, its climate, and its common plants and animals. As we travel, you will see how people have learned to fit into the natural environment of each region.

To understand our history, you must first understand the land.

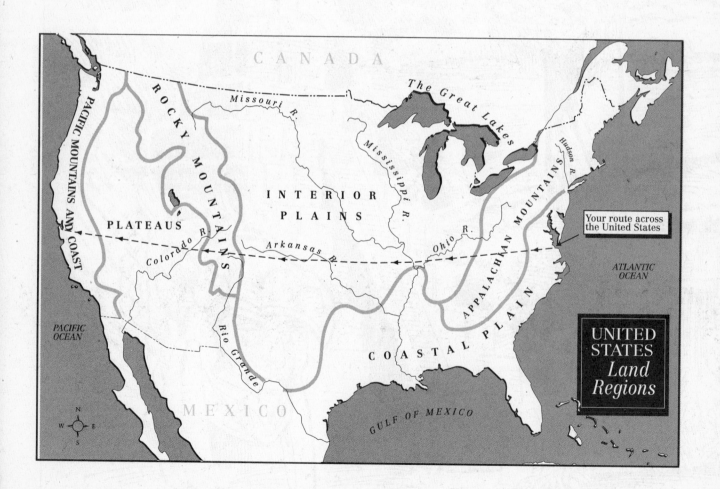

UNITED STATES *Land Regions*

BEFORE YOU READ

Sections in This Chapter

1. The East
2. The Interior
3. The West

Reading a Map

Use the map on the opposite page to answer the following questions. The compass and labels can help you locate the information you need.

1. If you take a trip from the Atlantic Ocean to the Pacific Ocean, in what direction will you travel?

2. If you travel on the route marked on the map, what type of land will you cross in the center of the United States?

3. What large mountain regions does your route cross?

4. List two rivers your route crosses.

5. What direction would you have to travel from your route to get to the Gulf of Mexico?

6. What direction would you have to travel from your route to get to the Great Lakes?

7. Which of the following will you cross on this route: the Hudson River, the Appalachian Mountains, the Mississippi River, the Rocky Mountains, the Pacific Coast mountain ranges, the Colorado River?

8. Choose two geographic regions or areas shown on the map. For each region, list all the facts you know or can figure out from the map.

Understanding a Key Concept:
NATURAL ENVIRONMENT

The **natural environment** of an area is <u>everything</u> from nature that is found in the area. It includes the land, water, climate, plants, and animals that are found there. It does not include things made by people, like buildings or cars.

Separate the following things into two lists. One list should have things that are part of a natural environment. The other list should have things that are NOT part of a natural environment.

pine trees, clothes, houses, soil, river, rain, boats, roads, raccoons, zoos, mountains, wooden furniture, oceans, fish, flowers, trains

Now add three more things that can be found in a natural environment.

Using What You Already Know

For each geography term below, list at least five things that you already know about it. One is done for you.

1. mountains
   higher than hills, steep and rocky, snow on top, hard to climb, often covered with forests

2. ocean

3. coast

4. valley

5. river

6. lake

7. harbor

8. island

1. THE EAST

Main Ideas

Think about the following Main Idea questions as you read this section.

1. What geographic features helped make the Northeast, but not the Southeast, a shipping area?

2. Why was the Coastal Plain an important farming region for both Native Americans and European settlers?

3. What effect did the Appalachian Mountains have on the European move west?

THE ATLANTIC COAST

The Beach

Imagine we are standing on a wide, sandy beach in Virginia, at the beginning of our journey across the United States. We are about halfway between the Canadian border and the Gulf of Mexico. As we face west, the broad Atlantic Ocean is at our back. Much of the Atlantic Coast to our north and south is a sandy beach like this. Sometimes the beach is on the mainland. Sometimes it is on sandy islands lying a few miles off the shore.

Bays and Rivers

North of where we are standing, arms of the ocean reach inland to form many bays and harbors. The largest bays are long, deep ones like Chesapeake Bay and Delaware Bay. The deep harbors, like the harbors of Boston and New York, are safe places for ships to stop. A few rivers, like the Hudson River and the Delaware River, are so deep that ships can travel up them for long distances.

To the south, though, there are no deep bays or rivers, although there are many shallow ones. They are too shallow for ships to travel very far inland.

Because of their natural environments, the coastal cities of the Northeast, but not the Southeast, became the great shipping centers of eastern America.

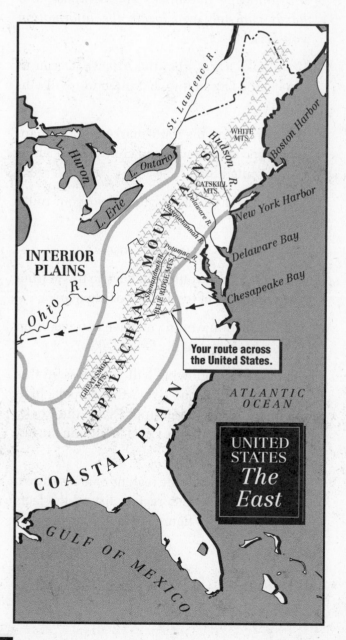

Your route across the United States.

THE COASTAL PLAIN

The Plain from New Jersey to Texas

As we begin our journey west, we cross a flat land, or **plain**, called the **Coastal Plain**. The Coastal Plain runs along the Atlantic Coast from New Jersey to Florida and all along the Gulf of Mexico. In New Jersey, the Coastal Plain is only a narrow band of land, but it is hundreds of miles wide further south. Many rivers cut through it to the sea.

In most places, the weather of the Coastal Plain is mild and it rains often. Because trees and other plants do well in this environment the Coastal Plain was once covered with deep forests. The climate is also good for growing food crops. Native Americans cleared land to grow beans, corn, and squash. Later, Europeans cut down nearly all the forests. Most of the Coastal Plain then became farmland where people grew food, tobacco, and cotton.

Not all of the coastal plain is good for growing crops, however. In some places, especially in the South near the coast, the land is so flat that water does not drain away. Here we find great swamps that cannot be farmed. Away from the rivers, much of the soil is clay. This, too, is hard to farm.

New England

North of New Jersey, in New England, there is no real Coastal Plain. The land becomes rocky and hilly just inland at the coast. This area has longer, colder winters and a shorter spring and summer than further south, making its natural environment not as good for crops. Many of the region's farmers instead raise dairy cattle.

THE APPALACHIAN MOUNTAINS

The Mountains

As we continue moving west, the land changes. About a hundred miles from the coast we enter a region of rolling hills, and then higher mountains. These are the **Appalachian Mountains**, the first of three mountain chains in the United States.

The Appalachians begin as rocky hills in Canada. They stretch south in a chain of mountains all the way to Georgia. Smaller groups of mountains, or **ranges**, make up the chain. Some of the main ranges are the White Mountains of New England, the Catskills of New York, the Blue Ridge of Virginia, and the Great Smoky Mountains of North Carolina and Tennessee.

The Appalachian Mountains are not very high. The highest is about 6,700 feet above sea level. The chain is wide, though. In some places it is more than 300 miles wide, covered with forests, and very rugged. It is not easy to walk over these mountains. Native Americans lived in and around the Appalachians, but the mountains stopped early European settlers from moving west.

The Valleys

The mountains themselves are hard to live on. But between the mountain ranges, there are long valleys with rich soil that is good for farming. These valleys were carved by rivers that still run through them. Among the largest valleys are those along the Hudson River, the Delaware River, and the Shenandoah River. In these valleys, Native Americans and, later, Europeans made their homes.

SECTION REVIEW

Can you answer these Main Idea questions?

1. What geographic features helped make the Northeast, but not the Southeast, a shipping area?

2. Why was the Coastal Plain an important farming region to both Native Americans and European settlers?

3. What effect did the Appalachian Mountains have on the European move west?

Can you locate and describe these places?

the Atlantic Coast, the Appalachian Mountains, the Coastal Plain, the Hudson River

2. THE INTERIOR

Main Ideas

Think about the following Main Idea questions as you read this section:

1. Why are the Mississippi River, the Great Lakes, and the Saint Lawrence River important to the people living on the Interior Plains?

2. How are the Prairie and the Great Plains alike? In what ways are they different?

3. How are the Rocky Mountains different from the Appalachians?

THE INTERIOR PLAINS

When we finally cross the Appalachians, we are at the beginning of a huge region of flat land and low hills. As far as you can see, the land rolls on and on and on without a real mountain. These plains stretch for a thousand miles across the center of the North American continent, from the Appalachians to the Rocky Mountains. They reach from the Arctic Ocean north of Canada to the Gulf of Mexico. This region is known as the **Interior Plains**.

The eastern part of the Interior Plains is a region of trees and rich land. Long before Europeans came here, Native Americans farmed this land. They built villages and large towns, some with thousands of people. Today, this is still a region of farms

The Mississippi River

After several hundred miles, we come to the greatest river on this continent, the mighty, mile-wide **Mississippi**. The river begins almost at the Canadian border and flows south all the way to the Gulf of Mexico. The Mississippi has always been a route for boats of all kinds. Native American canoes and dugouts traveled up and down it. Later came the steamboats of European settlers.

The Mississippi Valley is a place where many people have settled. Native Americans had large towns along the river. Today, some of our greatest cities lie along it: Minneapolis and St. Paul in Minnesota, St. Louis in Missouri, Memphis in Tennessee, and New Orleans in Louisiana. On both sides of the river is the richest soil in the country—perfect for farming.

The Great Lakes

Far to the north of our route across the country, the Mississippi just misses joining the five **Great Lakes:** Lake Superior, Lake Michigan, Lake Huron, Lake Erie, and Lake Ontario. They form the largest chain of freshwater lakes in the world. From Lake Ontario, the Saint Lawrence River flows to the Atlantic Ocean. The lakes and the river form a waterway that carries goods from the Interior Plains to the Atlantic Ocean and then to the rest of the world. This waterway is a major transportation route from the Interior Plains to the Atlantic Ocean, just as the Mississippi River is to the Gulf of Mexico.

The Interior Highlands

After we cross the Mississippi, we travel through a small region of low, wooded mountains. They seem like an island of rolling Appalachian hills set down in the middle of the flatlands. These are the **Interior Highlands**—the Ozark and Ouachita (WASH uh tuh) Mountains of Missouri and Arkansas.

The Prairie

We soon move out of the hills onto the plains again. The environment changes, and the trees become fewer. We are in a grassy land known as the **Prairie**. Once the Prairie was covered with grass taller than a human being. Its roots formed a deep tangled web called **sod**. Hardworking farmers called "sodbusters" broke through the

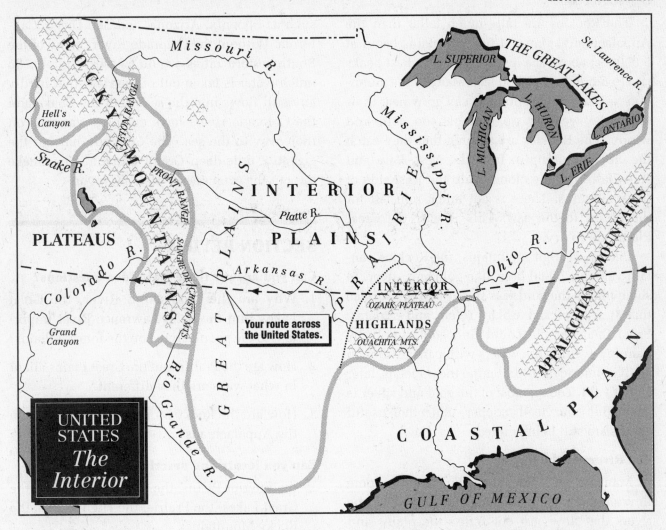

United States: The Interior map. Labels include: ROCKY MOUNTAINS, Missouri R., THE GREAT LAKES, L. SUPERIOR, St. Lawrence R., TETON RANGE, Hell's Canyon, L. MICHIGAN, L. HURON, L. ONTARIO, Snake R., FRONT RANGE, Mississippi R., L. ERIE, INTERIOR PLAINS, PLATEAUS, Platte R., SANGRE DE CRISTO MTS., APPALACHIAN MOUNTAINS, Colorado R., Arkansas R., Ohio R., PRAIRIE, GREAT PLAINS, Your route across the United States., INTERIOR HIGHLANDS, OZARK PLATEAU, OUACHITA MTS., Grand Canyon, Rio Grande R., COASTAL PLAIN, UNITED STATES The Interior, GULF OF MEXICO.

sod to plant crops. Today, farmers grow so much grain here that the area is called the "Breadbasket of America."

The Great Plains

We have now traveled halfway across the North American continent. There is much less rainfall here than back east. The grass becomes much shorter, and the land starts to rise. The rise is slow—only a few feet in a mile. You hardly notice it. But after several hundred miles, the land is almost as high above sea level as the tops of the Appalachians. Yet it still seems flat. This region is called the **Great Plains** or the **High Plains**. Millions of buffalo once lived here, as did the Native Americans who hunted them. Later, cowboys raised huge herds of beef cattle on the plains, for the climate is too dry for most crops to grow. Today, some of this land is still used for grazing cattle. On other parts wheat is grown, with water pumped from deep underground.

THE ROCKY MOUNTAINS

The Ranges of the Rockies

Suddenly, the Great Plains end. The huge wall of the **Rocky Mountains** rises in front of us. This great mountain chain runs from Alaska through Canada and the United States to northern New Mexico. Like the Appalachians, it is made up of many ranges: the Alaska Range, the Tetons of Wyoming, the Front Range of Colorado, the Sangre de Cristo of New Mexico, and many others.

The Rockies are tall—much taller than the Appalachians. Many of the mountains begin at 5,000 feet above sea level, and the highest peaks rise to more than 14,000 feet. Many of the mountains are so tall that no trees can grow near their tops—the weather up there is too cold and windy. The Rockies are so high that they catch the clouds coming in from the west. Rain and snow fall from the clouds onto the west side of the mountains. There is not much rain left for the plains to the east. This is why the Great Plains are so dry.

Like most high mountains, the Rockies contain valuable metal ores, like gold and silver. In some places the gold was so close to the surface that it was picked up by rivers and streams. From them people could find gold simply by panning—sifting the waters with pans. Although Native Americans didn't mine these metals, later settlers did. Today, most of the gold and silver is gone. But zinc, lead, copper, and other useful metals are still being mined.

The Rivers of the Rockies

Many rivers flow out of the Rockies. Some flow east, others west and south. Most of the rivers that flow east cut across the plains and empty into the Mississippi River. These include some of America's longest rivers, such as the Missouri River, the Platte River, and the Arkansas River. In spite of all the rivers which flow through it, the High Plains are so dry that some of the smaller rivers disappear for months at a time. One of the larger rivers that flows south from the Rockies, the Rio Grande, later turns southeast and forms part of the border between the United States and Mexico. It then empties into the Gulf of Mexico.

Two great rivers flow west from the Rockies. In the north, the Snake River joins the Columbia River, which flows down from Canada, and together they empty into the Pacific Ocean. In the south, the Colorado River flows into the Gulf of California. The Colorado's water is used to grow crops and to supply the needs of people in cities such as Phoenix, Arizona, and San Diego, California. Without the Colorado River, many of the Southwestern cities would be very thirsty. So much water is taken out of the river that hardly any still flows into the sea. Both the Snake and the Colorado rivers have cut huge **canyons** on their way to the sea. The Colorado has cut the gigantic, mile-deep Grand Canyon. The Snake has cut the even deeper Hell's Canyon.

SECTION REVIEW

Can you answer these Main Idea questions?

1. Why are the Mississippi River, the Great Lakes, and the Saint Lawrence River important to the people living on the Interior Plains?

2. How are the Prairie and the Great Plains alike? In what ways are they different?

3. How are the Rocky Mountains different from the Appalachians?

Can you locate and describe these places?

the Interior Plains, the Mississippi River, the Great Lakes, the Prairie, the High Plains, the Rocky Mountains

3. THE WEST

Main Ideas

Think about the following Main Idea questions as you read this selection:

1. Why isn't much farming done on the Colorado Plateau and in the Great Basin?

2. Where do you find great forests in the regions west of the Rockies?

3. How do the northern regions of the West differ from the southern regions?

THE PLATEAUS

The Colorado Plateau

After crossing the Rockies, we come to a region where the land is flat but still high. We are between 5,000 and 10,000 feet above sea level. A high flatland like this is known as a **plateau**. We are at the northern edge of the **Colorado Plateau**, named for the Colorado River that flows through it. This dry plateau is a land of flat-topped hills, called **mesas.** The region's few rivers and streams have cut many canyons deep into the red rock. The gigantic Grand Canyon in Arizona was cut by the **Colorado River.** It is the best-known canyon in the world, but there are many others as well.

The Great Basin

When we come to western Utah and Nevada, the high Colorado Plateau drops to a lower, different kind of plateau. This is a desert land, hot in summer and cold in winter. It has many small but high mountain ranges. In this environment, streams dry up or flow into lakes so salty you cannot drink from them. Small, scattered bushes called sagebrush cover the ground. This area is called the **Great Basin**. Few Native Americans lived in this desert environment, and many later settlers died trying to cross it. Even today, not many people live there.

The Southwestern Deserts

In the south are hotter, drier deserts where cactus grows instead of sagebrush. These deserts cover much of southern Arizona and California, right into Mexico. The lowest area in the United States, Death Valley, is in this region. It is 282 feet *below* sea level.

The Columbia Plateau

Far to the north of our cross-country route is still another plateau, the **Columbia Plateau,** named for the Columbia River which runs through it. It covers the eastern part of Washington state and Oregon and the southern part of Idaho.

THE PACIFIC MOUNTAINS AND THE PACIFIC COAST

The Sierra Nevada and the Cascades

When we reach California, the Great Basin ends. Here the last of the three great American mountain chains rises into the sky. This is the **Sierra Nevada** (Spanish for "Snowy Mountains"). Farther north, it joins another great range, the **Cascades,** which reaches almost to the Pacific coast. The Cascades contain many volcanoes. Some are dead, but others, like Mt. St. Helens, are very much alive. Still others, like the huge Mt. Rainier, may only be sleeping. Both the Sierra Nevada and the Cascades are high mountains covered with thick forests. Some of their peaks are as tall as the tallest peaks in the Rockies. One, Mt. Whitney in the Sierra Nevada, is the highest mountain in the United States outside Alaska.

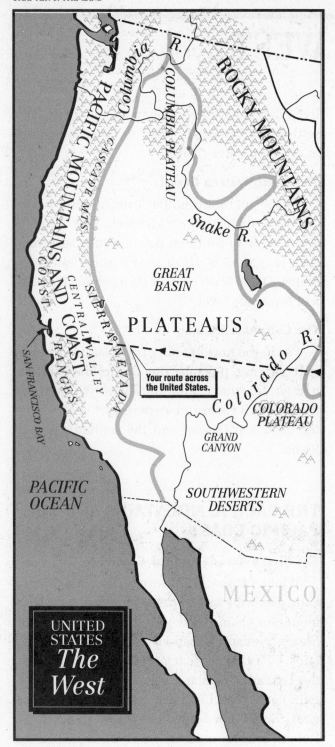

UNITED
STATES
*The
West*

The Central Valley and the Coast Ranges

Once across the Sierra Nevada, we drop into the 50-mile-wide **Central Valley** of California, which is one of the richest farm regions of the world. Along its western edge are ranges of lower mountains, the **Coast Ranges**. These mountains border the Pacific Ocean from Mexico all the way to Canada. South of our route they are dry, and low bushes grow on them. In the north, however, the mountains get plenty of rain, and the temperature is mild. Thick rain forests grow there. Most of America's lumber comes from the forests of the northern Coast Ranges and the Cascades. The world's tallest trees, the redwoods, grow in forests of the Coast Ranges near our route.

The Pacific Coast

In many places along the Pacific coast, the mountains reach down to the sea. Rocks line the shore instead of sandy beaches. This rough coast has only a few bays where ships can stop. One such bay is where we end our journey: deep San Francisco Bay. From a beach in Virginia to San Francisco Bay, our journey has covered more than 2,500 miles.

ALASKA AND HAWAII

Alaska

Our journey has taken us across a continent. But there are still two more regions in the United States. If we look north from San Francisco, we can imagine the distant state of Alaska. The Pacific Mountains and the Rocky Mountains both end in Alaska. These northern ranges contain both active volcanos and the highest mountains in North America. Alaska also has low rolling hills, broad river valleys, and glaciers, which are large masses of slowly moving ice. Alaska's Arctic Coastal Plain is frozen for 1,000 feet down, and only the surface thaws in the summer. Small plants, like grasses, are the only ones that can grow in this harsh environment.

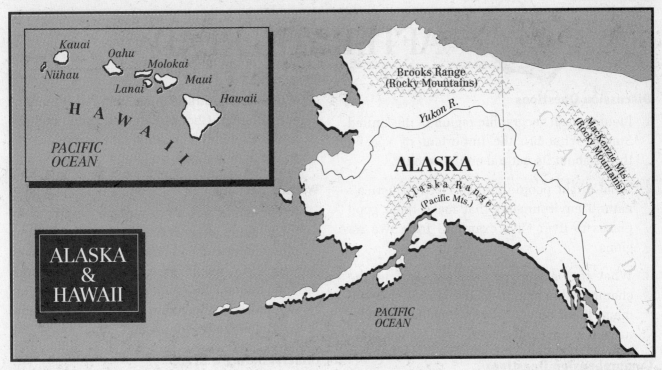

ALASKA & HAWAII

Hawaii

If we look west from San Francisco across the peaceful blue Pacific Ocean, we are looking toward our 50th state: Hawaii. Hawaii is made up of 132 islands, but people live on only 7 of them. The Hawaiian Islands are almost 2,400 miles from the Pacific Coast. All of them were formed by undersea volcanoes, some of which are still active. The temperature in Hawaii stays warm all year, but rainfall varies. Some places in the islands receive only 10 inches a year, while others get more than 300. In places where there is a lot of rain, tropical plants and trees grow in the rich soil. On some islands, crops like pineapples and sugar cane are grown.

America's many regions are all different from one another. Each region has offered its own set of challenges and opportunities to the people who have lived there. America's geography and its many natural environments have helped to shape its history. They continue to shape our lives today.

SECTION REVIEW

Can you answer these Main Idea questions?

1. Why isn't much farming done in the Colorado Plateau and in the Great Basin?

2. Where do you find great forests in the regions west of the Rockies?

3. How do the northern regions of the West differ from the southern regions?

Can you locate and describe these places?

the Plateaus, the Sierra Nevada, the Cascades, the Central Valley of California, the Coast Ranges, Hawaii, Alaska, the Colorado River

AFTER YOU READ

Discussion Questions

1. Identify each geographic region in the United States. What are the important or special things about its natural environment?

2. What might people find in North America's natural environments that make them good places to live? Give examples from two regions.

3. What region do you live in? Add to the chapter's description of its natural environment. What do you like and dislike about its natural environment?

Comprehension Questions

1. Create a chart which includes the seven geographic regions. List each region in the first column of your chart. List facts about the natural environment of that region in the second column. Include information about the land, water, climate, plants, and animals. One region has been started for you.

REGION	NATURAL ENVIRONMENT
Atlantic Coast	sandy beaches, bays

2. When you contrast things, you tell how they are different. Choose two geographic regions of the United States. Contrast these two areas in a few sentences.

Writing Activity

If you could live in any place described in this chapter, where would it be? Picture that place in your mind. List words and phrases which you would use to describe the place. Then write a few sentences telling why you would like to live there. Use the chapter and your chart at left for ideas.

Understanding a Graph

Using the graph below, determine which city has the highest average temperature and which has the lowest. In which month is the highest temperature found? The lowest temperature?

Average temperatures in Phoenix, San Francisco, and Boston for January, April, July, and October.

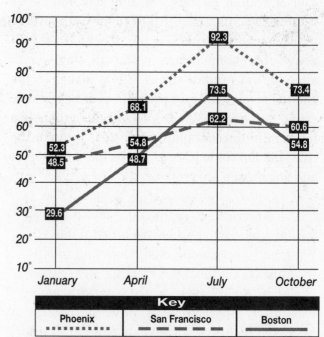

MAP OF RAINFALL IN NORTH AMERICA

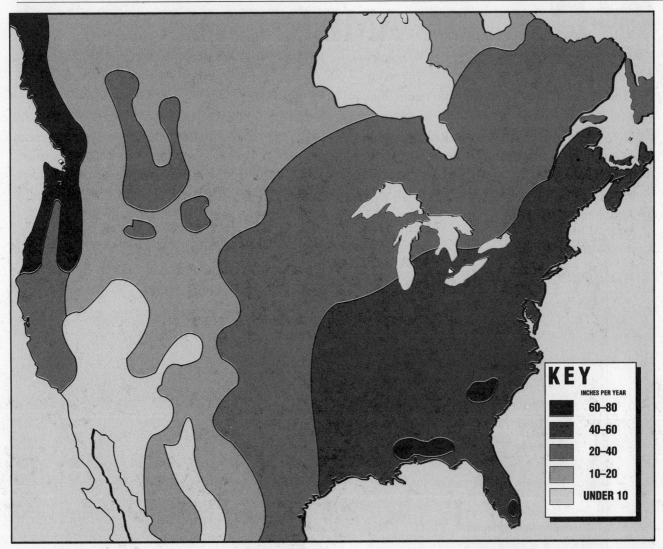

KEY

INCHES PER YEAR

■	60–80
■	40–60
■	20–40
■	10–20
□	UNDER 10

What kind of shelter and clothing are appropriate? Should people hunt or farm or both? How many people can live in a given area? These are questions that can only be answered by taking into account the natural environment.

There are many features of the natural environment which influence how people will live. One of the most important is **precipitation**, or how much it rains. The amount of rain determines what kinds of plants will grow, and what animals (and how many animals) will live somewhere. Generally speaking, if there is more rain, there will be more living things—plants, animals, and people—in a place.

As you can see from the map above, different sections of the United States get different amounts of rain. Compare this map with the maps on pages 6, 9, and 12. Which regions of the country get the most rain? The least? Why do you think this is so—what features do you think influence how much rain an area gets? (A hint: two features involve distance, either across or up.)

When you can answer questions like these, you will be on your way to understanding how geography affects the natural environment and the way people live.

CHAPTER 2

THE FIRST AMERICANS

First came the land. The people came later—no one knows exactly when. We do know that people have lived on the American continents for thousands of years. But there are no written records to tell us what happened here thousands of years ago. What we know comes from scientists who study the past.

This chapter tells some of the things that scientists have discovered. But we don't know the whole story of how the ancient Americans came here or how they lived. A lot of important information is still missing, and scientists continue to discover new information about the people who lived here long ago.

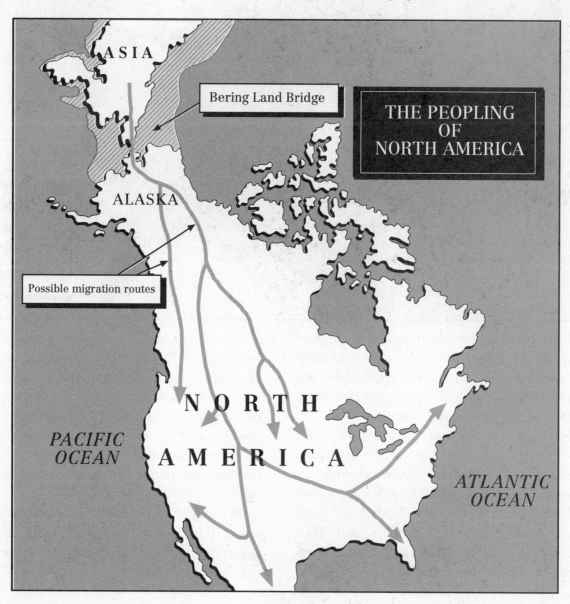

ASIA

Bering Land Bridge

THE PEOPLING OF NORTH AMERICA

ALASKA

Possible migration routes

NORTH AMERICA

PACIFIC OCEAN

ATLANTIC OCEAN

BEFORE YOU READ

Sections in This Chapter
1. People Come to America
2. Central and South American Civilizations
3. Complex Cultures in North America

Reading a Map

Study the map on the opposite page. It shows the possible routes used by people who moved into the Americas. Use it to answer the following questions.

1. People walked to Alaska over a land bridge. What two continents did the land bridge connect? What continent did the people come from?

2. On a map of the modern world, find the area where the land bridge was. Why can't people travel over the land bridge today?

3. In what direction did people travel over the land bridge? In what directions did they travel after they reached North America?

4. Do you think all of the people who came to North America stayed together? What information on the map supports your answer?

5. Do you think the people that settled in desert areas lived the same way as those that settled in the forests? Use facts from geography to support your opinion.

Understanding a Key Concept: CULTURE

A group's **culture** is its way of life. A group's culture includes what the group knows and believes, its laws, the things its people use, how they get their food, how they prepare it, and many other things.

The following things are part of any culture. Write them across the top of a sheet of paper.

Food, Beliefs, Buildings, Transportation, Tools

On the following list are a number of items that were part of Native American cultures. Write each item under the category to which it belongs. For example, you would write corn under "Food" because it was used as food. Then add at least three other items to your chart that you think were part of some Native American cultures.

corn, pueblos (apartment houses), wild plants, spears, stone roads, the world is filled with spirits, canoes, deer, bows and arrows, walking, stones for cutting, people should respect the land, stone temples, bowls, tipis or tepees (skin tents), bone needles

Using What You Already Know

The **environment** includes the land, weather, plants, and animals.

The parts of the environment that people can use, like water or gold, are called **natural resources**.

A clay bowl shows how Native Americans used a resource, clay, to create something in their culture, a bowl.

Choose three natural resources from the list below. Write a sentence describing something that a person might make with each one. For example, you might write:

The skins of deer can be made into clothes.

Here is the list:

deer, clay, buffalo, trees, stones, gold

1. PEOPLE COME TO AMERICA

Main Ideas

Think about the following Main Idea questions as you read this section.

1. How and why did people move from Asia to North America?

2. Why did Native American groups develop different cultures?

3. How did agriculture change the way of life of hunter-gatherers?

THE FIRST NATIVE AMERICANS

People from Asia Cross a Land Bridge into America

Geologists (jee OL uh jists) are scientists who study the earth. They tell us that thousands of years ago, the climate of the earth was much colder than it is today. Ice a mile thick covered much of northern Europe, Asia, and North America. This time is called the **Ice Age**.

Because all this ice contained so much water, there was less water in the ocean. The ocean was more than 300 feet lower than it is today. Some of what is now the sea floor was dry land. A large, flat area, called a **land bridge**, connected Asia and North America. It was a broad, flat plain a thousand miles wide, filled with huge herds of animals.

About 12,000 years ago, most of the ice melted. The oceans filled up again. Today, the land bridge is under water except for a few islands.

At the time of the Ice Age and the land bridge, there were no people in America. There were people living in Asia, however. Sometime between 12,000 and 30,000 years ago, groups of Asian people moved onto the land bridge. There they hunted deer and moose. They also hunted

animals that no longer exist, like huge woolly elephants called mammoths and buffalo with horns seven feet across.

Some of these people crossed into Alaska. They were the first Americans, the first people to live in the Western Hemisphere. Scientists believe they were the earliest ancestors of today's Indians. They were the first **Native Americans**.

The Three Asian Migrations into America

The newcomers did not stop when they entered Alaska. Their descendants spread all through America. After thousands of years, there were people living everywhere from Alaska to the southern tip of South America.

When people move from one region to settle in another, it is called a **migration**. There were probably three different migrations into America. The people in the first were the ancestors of nearly all the Indians in North and South America. The second migration was smaller. It contained the ancestors of those Indians who call themselves the Diné or Dene. They are the Indian peoples of Alaska and northwestern Canada, and the Apache and Navajo Indians of the southwestern United States. The people in the third and last migration probably came by boat after the land bridge was under water. They were the ancestors of the Inuit, or Eskimos, of the cold north of Alaska and Canada.

EARLY NATIVE AMERICAN LIFE

The Earliest Americans were Big-Animal Hunters

Archaeologists (ark ee OL uh jists) are scientists who dig up and study the things left by people who lived long ago. From their studies, we know that the earliest Americans lived mostly by hunting big Ice Age animals. They didn't live in villages or towns. They moved from place to place. That way, they didn't run out of animals to hunt. Their main hunting weapon was the spear. They used a special throwing stick to give their spears extra power and speed. They didn't use bows and arrows, which were invented much later.

Native Americans Become Hunters and Gatherers

By about 8,000 years ago, all the huge animals of the Ice Age had died out. Native Americans had to change their way of getting food. They became **hunters and gatherers**. They hunted smaller animals and gathered wild plants to eat.

GROUPS BECOME DIFFERENT

Early Native Americans Develop Different Cultures

As time passed, groups of Native Americans settled in different parts of the country. They became very different from each other. They developed different ways of life, or cultures.

Anthropologists (an thruh POL uh jists) are scientists who study people's **cultures**—their daily lives, their beliefs, their traditions, and their languages. These studies help explain why Native Americans developed so many different cultures.

One reason was that each group's environment contained different **natural resources**. Natural resources are all the things in the natural environment that people use to meet their needs and wants.

Anthropologists point out that every group's culture is based on the natural resources found where that group lives. Groups with different natural resources develop different cultures. For example, Native Americans built their homes with building materials from their environment. The Pueblo Indians of the Southwest used the natural resources they had—clay, stone, and wood—to create cool apartment houses in the hot desert. The Plains Indians made portable skin tipis from the hides of the buffalo they hunted. The Indians of the Northeast built long houses made of wood and bark from the thick forests where they lived. From each type of house, we can tell whether the people that built it were settled or whether they moved around a lot.

Many Languages, Many Tribes

The speech of the different groups changed, too. The earliest Americans split into hundreds of different groups, or **tribes,** each with its own language. In what is now the United States, Native American tribes spoke almost 300 different languages. More than 100 of these languages are still spoken today.

Early Americans hunting a mammoth. Such hunts were often almost as dangerous for the hunters as for their prey. The man in front is using a throwing stick, called an atlatl, as is the man to his right, who has just thrown his spear.

A Hawaiian canoe. Such canoes could be either sailed or paddled, and were very seaworthy. Canoes like this one carried ancient Polynesians thousands of miles across the Pacific to Hawaii and many other islands.

Tribes did not always stay in one place. Wars, climate changes, crowding, and the lack of food caused some tribes to move. Sometimes, only part of a tribe moved, creating a new tribe. One way that anthropologists trace related tribes is by their language. For example, the Navajos of Arizona and New Mexico speak a language like that of the Kutchin people in northern Alaska. Two thousand years ago they were probably all part of the same tribe with the same culture. The ancestors of the Navajos moved south. Now they live thousands of miles apart and have very different cultures.

The Development of Agriculture

Tribes learned from other tribes. They traded with each other and borrowed ideas from each other. Indians in Mexico and Peru discovered **agriculture**, or farming. They learned how to plant and grow food crops. Knowledge of these crops spread from one tribe to another. When Europeans first arrived in America, Native Americans from Canada to Argentina in South America were growing corn, beans, squash, and other crops.

The Sea Migrations of the Hawaiians

One group of Native Americans has a very different history from all others. The native people of the island state of Hawaii are not Indians or Eskimos. They belong to a group of people called Polynesians (pol uh NEE zhuns). Polynesians are the native people of islands in the central and south Pacific Ocean.

The ancestors of the Polynesians left southeast Asia in canoes, probably about 5,000 years ago. For thousands of years, their descendants migrated from island to island, moving far out into the Pacific. The Hawaiian Islands were one of the last group of islands they settled. The first Polynesians reached Hawaii more than 1,500 years ago. Their descendents are the Native Hawaiians of today.

SECTION REVIEW

Can you answer these Main Idea questions?

1. How and why did people move from Asia to North America?

2. Why did Native American groups develop different cultures?

3. How did agriculture change the way of life of hunter-gatherers?

Can you define the following terms?

land bridge, migration, tribes, cultures, agriculture

Can you identify the following people?

Native Americans, hunters and gatherers, geologists

2. CENTRAL AND SOUTH AMERICAN CIVILIZATIONS

Main Ideas

Think about the following Main Idea questions as you read this section.

1. Why are the Maya and the Aztec considered great civilizations?

2. How did people in Peru adapt, or change, to fit their environment?

3. Who or what destroyed the Aztec and Inca civilizations?

A culture with many people and a very complex organization and government is called a **civilization**. Several Native American civilizations grew up in both North and South America. One great civilization was in southern Mexico and neighboring Central America. Another was in Peru in South America.

CIVILIZATIONS IN MEXICO: THE MAYAS AND AZTECS

Agriculture Makes Civilization Possible

In both Mexico and Peru, agriculture allowed the Indians to develop complex cultures. Farming people could settle and work together in one place instead of moving around to search for food.

About 6,000 years ago Indians in Mexico developed corn from a kind of wild grass. They also

The Maya stone carving at right shows Lord Pacal, a Mayan noble, being crowned ruler by his mother. Such carvings often served as records of important events. ▶

discovered how to grow beans, squash, tomatoes, and other vegetables. More and more people settled in villages and became farmers.

Then, beginning about 3,500 years ago, these Indian farmers of Mexico created one of the world's great civilizations. Over the next 3,000 years they built religious centers that grew into cities containing stone temples and pyramids—some bigger than the famous pyramids of Egypt. They carved giant stone statues of their gods and their kings. They studied the movements of the sun, moon, and stars. They developed systems of writing and wrote books. They created wonderful works of art.

Mexican civilization was the work of many different peoples in Mexico and Central America. The best known are the **Mayas** and the **Aztecs**.

21

The Mayas

The Mayas lived in southern Mexico and Guatemala. The early Mayas learned how to plant corn in fields, instead of having to gather wild corn. This saved time, which they used to begin building cities, studying the stars, and creating beautiful art.

Beginning about 200 B.C., they built hundreds of cities and religious centers in the rain forest and in the dry lands farther north. The cities were ruled by rich, powerful lords who were constantly at war with each other. Mayan artists carved statues and built temples to celebrate important happenings in the lives of the rulers as well as for great religious events. The temples they built were huge stone pyramids. No animals or carts with wheels were used in the construction—it was all done by people.

The Maya also built and used a special building to watch the stars and the moon. They then used this information to make a calendar that was better than the one used in Europe at that time. They also developed an excellent way of doing math.

For 1,500 years the Mayas were among the world's finest artists, scientists, and builders. But then most Maya left their cities. No one knows why. For hundreds of years, many of these cities were covered by the rainforest. Archaeologists and other historians are now studying those places to learn about how the Maya lived.

The Aztecs

The Aztecs rose to power much later than the Mayas, about 1400 A.D. At first, they were a wandering, warlike tribe. Later, they settled in a

 The Aztec capital city of Tenochtitlán. Religion was very important to the Aztecs, as can be seen from the city's layout: the huge pyramids were temples, and the many smaller platforms in the foreground were used in religious rituals as well.

high valley in central Mexico. There, in the marshes of a lake, they built a beautiful capital city filled with huge painted temples, palaces, and canals. The Aztec made artificial islands in the lake on which to grow crops. Farmers lived in huts on these islands and grew corn to feed the people who lived in the capital .

By 1500 A.D., the Aztecs had become the most powerful people in Mexico. They conquered many other cities and forced them to send food, slaves, and other goods to the Aztec capital.

The Aztecs had a complex civilization. They loved flowers and poetry. Yet their religion, like that of most Mexican tribes, was based on human sacrifice. The Aztecs believed that human blood gave strength to their gods and kept the world from being destroyed. They even fought special wars to capture people to kill for their gods.

The Spanish Destroy the Aztec and Maya Civilizations

The civilizations of Mexico lasted until the Spanish came to the New World. The Aztecs and Mayas could not stand up against Spanish steel swords, guns, armor, and horses.

The Aztecs were conquered after only a few battles and their civilization destroyed. The Spanish built a new city, Mexico City, on the ruins of the Aztec capital. Today it is the largest city in North, South, or Central America.

When the Spanish came, the Mayas were no longer a powerful people. Most of their great cities were empty. Yet it still took 200 years for the Spanish to conquer them all. Maya uprisings continued until 1910. Today, two million Mayas live in Mexico and Central America. People come to their land from all over the world to see the magnificent ruins of the great Maya cities and temples.

CIVILIZATION IN PERU: THE INCAS

Civilization Begins in Peru

Civilization may have begun in South America, in Peru, even earlier than it did in Mexico. As in Mexico, agriculture made a complex culture possible. The Peruvian Indians developed the potato, the sweet potato, and other root crops. Later, they learned from northern neighbors how to grow corn and beans.

Much of Peru is desert, so the Peruvians built canals to bring water to their crops. They even learned to grow crops on the steep sides of the Andes Mountains, the second highest range of mountains on earth. The Pacific Ocean off the coast of Peru is one of the world's richest fishing areas, and so coastal Peruvians also became fishermen.

The Rise of the Incas

Peru had been the home of various civilizations for more than 3,000 years when the Incas rose to power.

The Incas started out as a small tribe who lived high in the Andes. At about the same time as the Aztecs, they started to conquer their neighbors. By the year 1500 A.D., the Incas ruled the largest empire in America. It stretched more than 2,000 miles along the west side of South America. It included most of the present-day countries of Ecuador, Peru, Chile, and Bolivia.

The Incas were great builders. They built wonderful roads in the mountains, bridges hanging across rivers, and giant forts. These forts were made of huge, carefully cut stone blocks. Some of the blocks weighed more than 60 tons! The Incas were also great artists. They made beautiful things in gold. The walls of their main temple were covered with thick gold plates, and inside was a garden made entirely of gold. It had gold plants, gold animals, gold gardeners, and even gold clumps of earth.

Strangely, the Incas thought they were the only civilized people in the world. They did not know about the Aztecs and Mayas, and the Aztecs and Mayas had never heard of the Incas. And, of course, before 1492 nobody in the Americas had ever heard of Europeans, Africans, or Asians.

The Incas were master builders. For example, they built rope bridges, very similar to modern suspension bridges in concept, to cross deep river gorges. Bridges such as the one below are still in use in the Andes today. ▼

The Spanish Conquer the Incas

The Spanish arrived in Peru about 10 years after they arrived in Mexico. They conquered the Incas even more easily than they had conquered the Aztecs. The Incas worshiped their emperor like a god. When the Spanish took him prisoner by surprise, the Incas had no leader. The Spanish became the rulers of Peru. They destroyed the Inca civilization, just as they had destroyed the civilizations of the Aztecs and Mayas.

SECTION REVIEW

Can you answer these Main Idea questions?

1. Why are the Maya and the Aztec considered great civilizations?

2. How did people in Peru adapt, or change, to fit their environment?

3. Who or what destroyed the Aztec and Inca civilizations?

Can you describe the following cultures?

Maya, Aztec, Inca

3. COMPLEX CULTURES IN NORTH AMERICA

Main Ideas

Think about the following Main Idea questions as you read this section.

1. Why did the different Mound Builder cultures build mounds?

2. In what ways did the Anasazi adapt to their environment?

3. How have modern people learned about the Anasazi and Mound Builder cultures?

COMPLEX CULTURES IN THE EAST

The Mound Builders

Complex cultures in what is now the United States began about 500 B.C. At that time, people in southern Ohio began burying their chiefs under great mounds of earth. Anthropologists, scientists who study cultures, call these people the **Mound Builders**. Their mounds were neatly built, with flat or dome-shaped tops. Tools and jewelry were buried in the mound with the dead person, and the mound was often surrounded by raised circular designs in earth.

The Mound Builder culture spread. By 300 A.D., Mound Builder cultures covered most of the United States between the Appalachian Mountains and the Great Plains. Then, shortly before 500 A.D., mound building came to an end. No one knows why.

The Temple Mound Builders

A few hundred years later, after 800 A.D., another mound-building culture grew up in the Mississippi River Valley. The new mounds were bigger than before. The largest one was the size of 16 football fields and stood 100 feet high.

These mounds were not just tombs for the dead. Temples and public buildings were built on top of them. For this reason, the Indians of this culture are called **Temple Mound Builders**. They are also known as **Mississippians**, since their main population centers were near the Mississippi River. Their largest city was in southern Illinois. More than 10,000 people lived in it.

A new, better kind of corn which could feed more people than the old kind, made the Temple Mound Builder culture possible. Corn became the main Indian crop. The Temple Mound Builders also used another new invention—the bow and arrow. They used it both to hunt and as a weapon of war.

By the time Europeans came, the Temple Mound Building culture had come to an end. Only one Temple Mound Building tribe, the Natchez of Mississippi, still kept some of the old ways. Everywhere else the people had stopped building mounds and had gone back to living in small villages. No one knows why this happened. It is one of the mysteries of American history.

COMPLEX CULTURES IN THE SOUTHWEST

Early Southwestern Cultures

Far to the west of the Temple Mound Builders was another important group of Indian cultures. They grew up in the desert lands of the Southwest, mostly in Arizona and New Mexico. Like most other complex cultures, this one was made possible by agriculture. Since there is very little rain in the Southwest, in many places the people had to bring water to their fields from nearby rivers or mountain streams.

An Anasazi pueblo. Such a pueblo was similar to a modern apartment building, with many different families living side-by-side in separate "apartments."

They built canals, small dams, and ditches to water their crops. They traded with the Indians of Mexico and borrowed ideas from them for pottery and clothing.

The Anasazi

One important Southwestern culture was the **Anasazi** (an uh SAHZ ee) culture. About 800 A.D., the Anasazi people started building villages called **pueblos** (PWEB loz). The houses in an Anasazi pueblo were joined together into large buildings. Often these were three or more stories high. Families lived in these buildings the way people live in apartments today. Some of the Anasazi pueblos were very large. One of the largest contained 800 rooms and was 5 stories high. For protection, many Anasazi pueblos were built inside large cracks in the cliff walls of canyons. For this reason, the Anasazi are sometimes called "Cliff-Dwellers."

The End of Anasazi Culture

Around the year 1300 A.D., the Anasazi left their pueblos. Archaeologists are not sure why. They know that from 1275 to 1300 a terrible dry period struck the area. For nearly 25 years hardly any rain fell. Perhaps the Anasazi could not grow crops. Perhaps the pueblos started fighting each other. Other tribes may have attacked them. They may even have used up all the trees nearby that their culture depended on for fuel and building material.

In any case, they left their canyon homes. Archaeologists believe that many moved east to the Rio Grande River in northern New Mexico. There they built new, smaller pueblos. Their descendants are the Pueblo Indians who live there today. The ruins of the old Anasazi pueblos can still be visited in many Southwestern National Parks.

From the Ice Age to about the year 1500, the history of America was separate from the history of the rest of the world. Native Americans spread over two continents and split into many different tribes. Some developed agriculture. Great cultures like the Aztecs, Mayas, Incas, Temple Mound Builders, and Anasazi developed long before the first people from Europe and Africa came to America.

SECTION REVIEW

Can you answer these Main Idea questions?

1. Why did the different Mound Builder cultures build mounds?

2. In what ways did the Anasazi adapt to their environment?

3. How have modern people learned about the Anasazi and Mound Builder cultures?

Can you describe these cultures?

Mound Builders, Mississippians, Anasazi

Can you describe what these scientists study?

archeologist, anthropologist

AFTER YOU READ

NORTH AMERICANS

Discussion Questions

1. How do scientists know that the cultures of the first people in America were different from the cultures of people today?

2. In what ways was the culture of the North American Mound Builders like the culture of the Aztecs? In what ways was it different?

3. In what ways did the geography and natural resources of the Incas and the Anasazi affect their cultures?

4. What part of the Aztec culture would you like to learn more about?

Comprehension Questions

I. **Sequence** is the order in which events happen. The sentences in each set below are out of order. Read each set carefully and decide the correct sequence. Rewrite each set so the sentences are in the order in which they happened.

1. A land bridge connected North America and Asia.

   The Ice Age made the ocean level fall.

   People from Asia crossed the land bridge.

2. Most people living in North America were hunters.

   Large cities and complex cultures developed in North America.

   Agriculture was discovered.

3. The Maya built huge stone temples.

   Archaeologists found the ruins of Mayan cities.

   The Spanish conquered the Aztec empire.

4. The Mississippian culture began.

   The early Mound Builders raised great mounds of earth.

   The Anasazi left their canyon pueblos and founded new ones.

II. When you **categorize**, you put items into the groups where they belong. Make three columns on your paper. Write one of the following cultures in each column.

Early Hunter-gatherers   Aztecs

Mound Builders

Categorize the following cultural details by writing them under the culture that had them. If they have a *, they will fit in more than one culture.

built mounds, large capital city, used canals, used slaves, circular designs in earth, no cities, no farms, wrote poetry, grew corn*, used bow and arrow, believed in human sacrifice, civilization destroyed by Spanish, built palaces, built public buildings, traveled all the time, ate mostly wild plants and small wild animals.

After you have completed your categories, decide which of the three cultures was the most complex. Write two sentences that tell your opinion. Support your opinion with facts from the chart.

Writing Activity

Several ancient Native American cultures have been described in this chapter. If you could go back in time, which one would you most like to visit? Write a short paragraph to tell why you would like to visit it and what you would like to see there.

CHAPTER 3

NATIVE NORTH AMERICANS

American history begins with Native Americans. But Native American tribes were very different from each other. The part of North America that became Canada and the United States is very large, and hundreds of different Native American tribes lived there. Each tribe followed its own way of life and had its own ways of dealing with the environment.

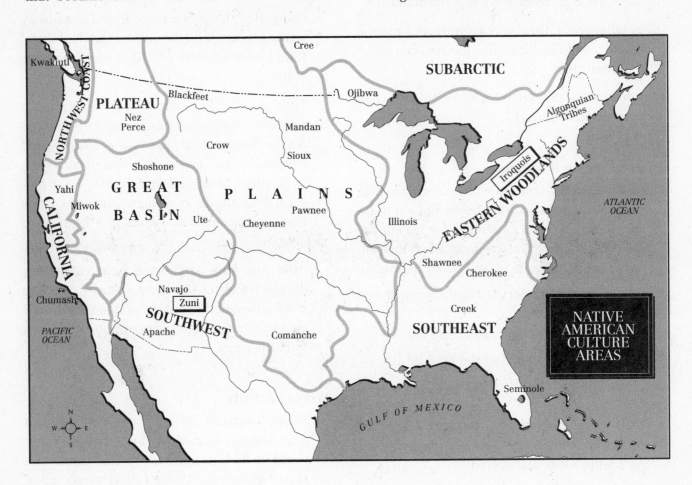

NATIVE AMERICAN CULTURE AREAS

BEFORE YOU READ

Sections in This Chapter

1. Native American Culture Areas
2. The Zuni of New Mexico
3. The Iroquois of New York
4. The Coming of the Europeans

Reading a Map

Use the map on the opposite page to answer the following questions.

1. What does this map show? (HINT—Read the map's title.)

2. List the nine North American culture areas shown on this map. (The tenth culture area, the Arctic, is further to the north.)

3. In what culture area were the Zuni Indians located?

4. Compare this map with the map at the front of Chapter 1. What type of land is located where the Zuni lived?

5. In what culture area were the Iroquois Indians found?

6. What type of natural environment did the Iroquois live in?

Understanding a Key Concept: FAMILIES AND CLANS

Families are an important part of every culture. In many Native American cultures, groups of related families formed **clans**. Clans included close family members, like sisters. They also included members of very distantly related families. Clans had names, for example, "Badger clan" or "Dogwood clan." These clans played an important part in everyday life.

1. Who are your close family members?

2. Could a mother and daughter be in the same clan? Why?

3. Clan members may get together at special times. Are there any special times when you get together with family members who don't live with you?

4. Clan members are not allowed to marry each other. List some people that you would not be allowed to marry.

5. How do you think clan members would treat a stranger from their clan who was visiting, but whom they had never met?

Using What You Already Know

People use their environment and its natural resources to meet their basic needs. Basic needs include food, shelter, and water. Answer each question by telling how these people might fill their needs in that environment. One is done for you.

1. What natural resources might people living in forests use for shelter? *They might use trees to build houses.*

2. What natural resources might people living in deserts use for food?

3. What important natural resources are scarce for people living in a dry, desert area?

4. What might people do to make living in desert areas easier?

5. What important natural resources are plentiful for people living in a forest?

1. NATIVE AMERICAN CULTURE AREAS

Main Ideas

Think about the following Main Idea questions as you read this section.

1. What are each of the Native American culture areas named for?

2. How did the Native Americans of each culture area use their environment to get food and shelter?

Native American tribes that lived in the same environment used the same resources. They often had similar cultures, even though they might not be closely related. For this reason, anthropologists often group Native American tribes according to the region of the country, or **culture area**, they lived in. Anthropologists divide North America north of Mexico into ten Native American culture areas.

1. THE EASTERN WOODLANDS CULTURE AREA

The Eastern Woodlands Culture Area went from the Atlantic Coast to the Mississippi Valley, and from the Great Lakes south to Kentucky and Virginia. The people of this area were farmers, hunters, and gatherers.

Many Woodland people lived in villages for part of the year and moved about during the rest of the year. In the spring, groups came together and planted crops, then split up into smaller bands during the summer to hunt and to gather wild plants. In the fall, they returned to harvest their crops, then split up again to hunt deer and other wild animals until spring. Other Woodland tribes stayed in their villages all year. The

many trees gave the Woodland tribes plenty of wood for shelter, tools, and fuel.

The Algonquian and Iroquois Indians who met the early French, Dutch, and English settlers lived in this culture area. Further west were the Ojibwa, the Shawnee, the Illinois, and many other Woodland tribes.

2. THE SOUTHEAST CULTURE AREA

The Southeast Culture Area was the rest of the United States east of the Mississippi. The people there were also hunters and farmers. Sometimes the Southeast and the Eastern Woodlands are thought of as a single culture area.

Many Southeastern tribes lived in towns, and a few were ruled by powerful chiefs whose word was law. Among the tribes in the Southeast are the Cherokee, Creek, and Seminole.

 A Creek Indian village included a large round town house used for meetings, and smaller houses where the people lived. In the background is a playing field for a Native American game similar to lacrosse.

3. THE PLAINS CULTURE AREA

The Plains Culture Area stretched from Texas north into Canada, and from the Mississippi Valley west to the Rockies. Before Europeans came, most Plains tribes lived in farming villages on the eastern prairies and along the Missouri River. Among these prairie tribes were the Pawnee and the Mandan. Hardly any people lived on the dry, short-grass high plains further west, where huge herds of buffalo grazed.

Then the Plains tribes got horses and guns from the Europeans, and Plains life changed. Horses and guns made it easier to hunt buffalo. Some tribes moved out onto the high plains and followed the buffalo herds. They came to depend on the buffalo for nearly all their needs. Among these tribes are the Sioux, the Blackfeet, the Crow, the Cheyenne, and the Comanche.

4. THE PLATEAU CULTURE AREA

The Plateau Culture Area was located on the plateau of the Columbia River in the Far West. It stretched between the northern Rockies and the Cascade Mountains. The Plateau people lived in villages. They did not grow food crops, but instead gathered wild roots, caught fish, and hunted animals. Later, they got horses from the Plains tribes. Some tribes, like the Nez Perce, became the finest horse trainers and breeders in the West.

5. THE GREAT BASIN CULTURE AREA

The Great Basin Culture Area was in the mountains and deserts between California and the Rockies, and between the Columbia Plateau and the Colorado River. The Indians of the Great Basin were gatherers who lived in small bands and ate roots, berries, and small animals. Some Rocky Mountain tribes moved east out onto the Plains after they got horses. These tribes included the Ute (YOOT) of Colorado and the Shoshone (shuh SHOH nee) of Wyoming.

6. THE SOUTHWEST CULTURE AREA

The Southwest Culture Area was the Colorado Plateau and the deserts to the south of it. Three very different groups of people lived there: the farming people of the Pueblo villages; the desert farmers of western Arizona; and the wandering and raiding Apaches and Navajos. When Europeans brought sheep to America, the Navajos became sheep herders. Today they are the largest tribe in the United States.

7. THE CALIFORNIA CULTURE AREA

The California Culture Area was the home of more than 250 village tribes, speaking more than 100 different languages. Each tiny tribe lived in its own small area. The Californians had no agriculture, but lived by hunting and gathering. Their most important food was acorns, which they ground into flour and either boiled like oatmeal or baked into bread. The land was so rich that California had the largest Indian population in the United States. The Chumash, the Yahi, and the Miwok were some of the many California tribes.

8. THE NORTHWEST COAST CULTURE AREA

The Northwest Coast Culture Area was along the Pacific coast from Oregon to Alaska. In this area, the climate is rainy and mild. Forests of huge trees come down to the shore, and the sea and rivers are filled with fish. Northwest Coast people lived mostly on river salmon and on food from the sea—fish, shellfish, sea lions, and whales. They also gathered plants, berries, and roots to eat.

The Northwest Coast people were unusual because they had a rich and complex culture without agriculture. They are famous for their wood build-

A Tlingit chief in ceremonial clothing and headdress. The totem pole behind him would have stood in front of his house. It shows animals and people who are important in his family's legendary history. ▶

ings and their art. They carved and painted tall wooden totem poles, the wood fronts of their houses, giant dugout canoes, wooden boxes, and masks with moving parts. The Tlingit, (KLINK it) the Haida (HI duh), and the Kwakiutl (kwok YOOTL) were three of the tribes in this culture area.

9. THE SUBARCTIC CULTURE AREA

The Subarctic Culture Area stretched across most of northern and central Canada and Alaska. The climate is very cold, and most of the area is covered by forests of fir and spruce trees containing many lakes and swamps. Treeless land called tundra is in the far north. Indians in the Subarctic lived in small family groups. They hunted caribou (a kind of reindeer), moose, and other northern animals. The climate was too cold for agriculture, and wild berries were the main plant food. Life in the Subarctic was hard, and starvation was common. When Europeans arrived, many of the Subarctic people trapped fur animals to trade with them. The Kutchin of Alaska and the Chipewyan and Cree of Canada lived in this culture area.

10. THE ARCTIC CULTURE AREA

The Arctic Culture Area was the cold coastal land along the northern edge of Canada and Alaska. It was the home of the Inuit (IN yuh wuht), or Eskimos, and the Aleut (al ee OOT) of the Aleutian (uh LOO shun) Islands. They hunted land animals like caribou and large sea animals like whales and seals. They ate hardly any plant food, since few plants grow so far north. In Canada, but not in Alaska, Inuit families sometimes built igloos (houses) from blocks of snow. Until recently many Inuit families lived much as their ancestors did.

SECTION REVIEW

Can you answer these Main Idea questions?

1. What are each of the Native American culture areas named for?

2. How did the Native Americans of each culture area use their environment to get food and shelter?

Can you locate and describe each of the ten Native American culture areas in North America?

2. THE ZUNI OF NEW MEXICO

Main Ideas

Think about the following Main Idea questions as you read this section.

1. How did the Zuni use their environment for their homes and agriculture? How did they change it?

2. What were the different roles men and women had in Zuni family, clan, and religious life?

3. What ideas were especially important to the Zuni?

The Zuni of New Mexico and the Iroquois of New York State are examples of different Native American tribes living in different culture areas. Both were among the first Native American peoples that the Europeans met when they came to this land. Both tribes were farmers and hunters, and in both tribes women held a large amount of power. Aside from that, they were as different as Arabs and Japanese.

PUEBLO VILLAGES AND HOMES

The Pueblo Indians

The Zuni lived in the hot, dry Southwest, in what is now western New Mexico. They lived in apartment-house towns, like several other tribes in the Southwest. The Spanish called these Indian apartment-house towns **pueblos**, from the Spanish word for a village. They called the Zuni and other tribes who lived in towns **Pueblo Indians.**

All the Pueblo Indians had similar ways of life, but they were not all closely related. The Zuni language, for example, was not like any other Pueblo language.

Apartment-House Towns

At the time the Spanish first saw the Zuni, there were six Zuni villages. They were built near running water at the foot of a flat-topped mountain, or mesa, called Corn Mountain. Sometimes, when the Zuni were raided by the Apaches or attacked by the Spanish, they hid on Corn Mountain.

Each Zuni village contained buildings made of stone covered with **adobe** (a kind of clay). The buildings were grouped around open areas. Some buildings were five stories tall, but most had only two stories.

Each building contained many apartments, and each apartment had several rooms. Ladders were used to get to the higher apartments. Inside doorways connected all the apartments on a floor. The doors were low and the windows small. This kept the rooms cool in summer and made them easy to heat in winter. There were no closets. Things were hung from poles along the ceiling. One inside room was used to store food. If a family ran out of space, they built new rooms onto their apartment.

ZUNI FAMILY AND CLAN LIFE

The Importance of Women

The Zuni family was centered on the women. The family that shared an apartment was made up of women who were related, their husbands, and their children. When a man got married, he moved in with his wife's family. If something happened to her, he returned to his mother's house.

The Zuni women owned the fields and gardens, just as they owned the pueblo apartments.

The end of the Zuni festival of Shalako, when the figures of the kachinas appear in the village. The Zuni believed that the Kachinas were disembodied spirits living in their own world for part of the year, but visiting the Zuni village for several months in early winter.

The crops, too, were jointly owned by all of the women in a household.

The Duties of Family Members

Each member of a Zuni family had different duties. Zuni women tended small gardens of onions, chili peppers, and tomatoes. They also gathered wild nuts, herbs, and berries. Zuni men built houses, hunted, and worked in the fields where they grew the main crops—corn, squash, and beans. Children worked with their parents from an early age.

Clan Life

Zuni families were organized into large family groups, or clans. The members of a clan were all related through the women. A clan member was not permitted to marry anyone from his or her clan.

Clan members did many things together. They worked together to build houses and take care of the fields. Each clan also had its own ceremonies, which were kept secret from other clans.

ZUNI FARMING, ART, AND TRADE

Catching Water for Farming

The Zuni were careful farmers. To protect their crops from the wind, they built low walls around their gardens and planted rows of sagebrush near their fields. The streams were dry much of the time, so the Zuni developed a way of watering their crops with the water from distant thunderstorms.

In the Southwest, thunderstorms are heavy but short. The rainwater rushes off higher ground into dry stream beds, flows away, and quickly disappears. Zuni farmers built dams in their fields to catch some of this water and the soil it carried. The trapped water soaked into the ground, and crops were planted in the moist soil. Other dams, canals, and wooden pipes brought water from later storms to the crops.

Storage Rooms for Crops

Because crops would not grow in very dry

years, the Zuni kept a two-year supply of food in special storage rooms. The rooms were sealed so that rats and other small animals couldn't get in and eat the corn.

The Zuni people say, "The land is our church. It's like a sacred building." They worked with nature and treated the land with reverence. The entire landscape was holy, and the Zuni treated it with the same respect that they showed to their families.

Art and Trade

Much of the tribe's time was spent making sure everybody had enough to eat. But the Zuni also made beautiful pottery and wove cloth. They traveled to a lake where they collected salt, which they traded to the Hopi, another Pueblo tribe. The Hopis traded the cotton they grew for the salt. The Zuni also traded with tribes in Mexico.

ZUNI RELIGION AND SOCIAL LIFE

The Zuni Gods

Zuni religion was an important part of their daily life. The Zuni spent about half their time in religious activities.

Men were in charge of religious matters. They met in special buildings, called **kivas**. Zuni ceremonies included song, dance, poetry, and stories. For these ceremonies, men dressed up as **kachinas**, the Zuni gods and holy spirits. Dolls shaped like the kachinas were given to children to teach them about their religion. Four Zuni priests were in charge of the pueblo's religious life. They also appointed officers who made other tribal decisions.

Shalako, the Major Zuni Religious Festival

The major religious festival of the Zunis was called **Shalako**. It took place in November and December, and it lasted forty-nine days. At the end of Shalako, giant masked figures of the gods appeared in the villages. Ceremonies, dancing, and feasting continued all night.

Shalako is still celebrated every year at Zuni Pueblo. When the pueblo permits visitors, people come from miles around to see Shalako and to take part in the feasting.

The Importance of the Group

The Zuni's beliefs shaped their behavior. Zunis believed that the group—family or clan or village—was more important than the individual. Being first or best was not as important as being a good family or tribal member. The Zuni believed that what one person did affected the whole tribe. Acting wrong could cause illness, drought, or other problems for everyone. Each Zuni followed the rules to protect the tribe and family. Every decision was thought out very carefully, so no harm would come to anyone.

THE ZUNI TODAY

The Zuni have lived in the same area for about 800 years. Today, only one Zuni town of about 6,000 people is at the bottom of Corn Mountain. The other villages have been empty for many years. The Zuni are still the largest Pueblo tribe, however. They have kept much of their old way of life, although today they raise sheep instead of hunting. Their homes are more modern, with electricity and television. But their beliefs have changed very little. Their religion, family, and tribe are still the center of their lives.

SECTION REVIEW

Can you answer these Main Idea questions?

1. How did the Zuni use their environment for their homes and agriculture? How did they change it?

2. What were the different roles men and women had in Zuni family, clan, and religious life?

3. What ideas were especially important to the Zuni?

Can you identify this place?

New Mexico

Can you identify these people?

Pueblo Indians, Zunis

Can you define these words?

adobe, clan

3. THE IROQUOIS OF NEW YORK

Main Ideas

Think about the following Main Idea questions as you read this section.

1. How did the Iroquois use the natural resources in their environment to meet their basic needs?

2. What facts support the idea that war was an important part of Iroquois life?

3. How did the League of the Five Nations change life for the Iroquois tribes?

THE FIVE NATIONS

The Iroquois Tribes

The Iroquois were the most powerful people of the Eastern Woodlands culture area. They lived in the forests of New York State, far from the desert lands of the Zuni. Five different Iroquois tribes settled near the Finger Lakes and in the Mohawk Valley. From west to east, they were the Senecas (SEN uh kuh), Cayugas (kee OO guh), Onondagas (ahn uhn DAH guh), Oneidas (oh NYE duh), and Mohawks. Together they are called the **Five Nations**.

The thick forests of the Eastern Woodlands provided the Iroquois with resources for food, tools, and shelter. The Iroquois began as hunter-gatherers who moved around a lot. When they began growing corn, beans, and squash, they settled in one place. They traded with other tribes for flint, dried fish, and furs.

THE LIFE OF THE LONGHOUSE

The Longhouse and the Family

Iroquois towns were built along streams and rivers. Tall walls of pointed logs surrounded each town. The Iroquois homes, called **longhouses**,

Everyone in an Iroquois village lived in a longhouse. Longhouse villages were not permanent. After ten or twenty years, the surrounding land would be exhausted and firewood scarce. The village would then be abandoned in stages and a new village built nearby.

were made of a frame of poles covered with elm bark. Some longhouses were more than 60 feet long. Several related families lived in each one. A hallway ran down the middle, and there were small rooms on each side. Sleeping platforms in each room were covered with tree branches and furs. These homes were so important to Iroquois life that the Iroquois called themselves "People of the Longhouse."

Like the Zuni, the Iroquois families were organized into clans. Iroquois clans (all related people, even distant relatives) cut across tribal lines. When a Seneca warrior traveled, he was sure of a good welcome by his clan in the Mohawk tribe.

The Importance of Women

Iroquois women ran much of Iroquois society. They owned the property. They settled disagreements. They chose the chiefs, and they could fire a chief if he wasn't doing a good job. They did much of the daily work, too. They made the wooden tools, baskets, and leather items. The women in a longhouse jointly owned the tools and land. They grew the crops while the men hunted, traded, or fought.

Iroquois men cleared the land for the fields, but they didn't need to build dams or canals the way Zuni men did. Usually there was plenty of rain and stream water.

A Society for Curing Diseases

The Iroquois believed in a supreme God. They also believed in less powerful spirits. They believed, for example, that illness was caused by evil disease spirits. Each tribe had several groups, or "societies," whose job was to prevent illness in the tribe and to cure sick people.

One of the most important of these societies was called the False Face Society. Members wore carved and painted wooden masks with twisted, frightening features. Although they looked horrible, the masks were the faces of friendly spirits who could cure disease by frightening the disease spirits away. To cure a patient, several members of the society, wearing False Face masks, danced around the sick person and shook rattles made from turtle shells.

THE WARS OF THE IROQUOIS

Iroquois Men—Fighters and Warriors

One reason that the Iroquois women were in charge in the village was that the men were often away hunting, trading, or fighting. Unlike the peaceful Zuni, the Iroquois were often at war with their neighbors. Other tribes feared them because they were such fierce fighters.

Wars for Furs

Many Iroquois wars were fought after white men came to America and started trading with the Indians for furs. To gain control of the fur trade, the Iroquois destroyed many of the tribes around them. Some of their raiding parties went as far west as Illinois. They captured and killed many of their enemies, but younger captives were often adopted as members of the Iroquois tribes.

THE GREAT LAW OF PEACE

The Message of the Peacemaker

At one time the five New York Iroquois tribes were at war with each other. But sometime between 1450 and 1570, before Europeans came, they formed the League of the Five Nations.

The Iroquois themselves say that the idea began with a leader whom they call "The Peacemaker." He was from a nearby tribe, the Hurons. He preached that all tribes should join together in peace. But the Hurons would not listen to him, so he took his message to the New York Iroquois tribes, who were fighting with each other.

The Peacemaker's message moved from tribe to tribe. A woman named Jigonsaseh (jig uhn SAS uh), called "The Mother of Nations," carried it. So did a man named Aionwatha (sometimes called Hiawatha), who was a great speaker.

The Iroquois say that Aionwatha calmed an evil chief who had snakes growing out of his hair with a song of peace. The Mother of Nations suggested that the chief should be made the head chief when the tribes joined together. The five Iroquois tribes met together and agreed to follow the Peacemaker's "Great Law of Peace."

The First Constitution in America

The Great Law was a kind of constitution—a set of basic laws that set up a government. It was the first known constitution in what is now the United States. Under the Great Law, each tribe kept its own government and its own family and clan rules. But it also had special duties to do for the League. This kind of government is called a **confederacy**.

Once a year, a council of chiefs from the different tribes met to discuss League matters. The council was chosen by women, just as the first chief had been chosen by the Mother of Nations. Each tribe had a different number of members on the council, but only one vote. All the tribes had to agree to a decision. Wars were decided and fought by the League as a whole, not by single tribes. No fights were allowed among member tribes. Any tribe was welcome to join if it agreed to the League's rules.

The Tuscarora Join the League

The Iroquois believed that when people everywhere joined their League, there would be peace all over the world. They even asked their enemies the French to join their League. The French didn't, but several other Indian tribes did.

The most important tribe to join the League was the Tuscarora (tus kuh ROR uh). This tribe from North Carolina spoke an Iroquois language. In 1715, the Tuscaroras lost a war with the English colonists who wanted their land. The tribe traveled north and joined their Five Nations relatives. They were welcomed into the League, which then became the League of the Six Nations.

The Iroquois and Europeans

When Europeans came to America, the Iroquois traded with the Dutch. Later they became allies and trading partners with the English and enemies of the French. In many wars Iroquois warriors helped protect the English colonies from the French. Without this protection, the United States as we know it might never have come into being. And the ideas behind the Iroquois Confederacy may have influenced the Americans who developed the first government for the United States. That first U.S. government was also a confederacy.

The Iroquois Today

The Iroquois League broke up during the American Revolution. Most of the Iroquois fought on the British side, while the Oneidas and Tuscaroras supported the American colonists. After the war, some of the Iroquois moved to Canada, while others moved west. The rest remained in New York State, where they still live today.

The Iroquois are famous as expert steel and iron workers. They seem to have no fear of heights, and so are valuable workers in building skyscrapers and bridges. They are the third largest Native American group in North America (after the Navajo and Sioux). Both in Canada and the United States, they remain fiercely proud of their tribes and their history, and they fight any attempt to take away their tribal lands or tribal rights.

SECTION REVIEW

Can you answer these Main Idea questions?

1. How did the Iroquois use the natural resources in their environment to meet their basic needs?

2. What facts support the idea that war was an important part of Iroquois life?

3. How did the League of the Five Nations change life for the Iroquois tribes?

Can you identify this place?
New York

Can you identify these people?
The Peacemaker, Jigonsaseh, Aionwatha

Can you define these words?
confederacy, longhouses

4. THE COMING OF THE EUROPEANS

Main Ideas

Think about the following Main Idea questions as you read this section.

1. How did life change for Native Americans after Europeans arrived in North America?

2. What cultural and technological differences allowed the Europeans to defeat Native Americans?

3. How have Native Americans contributed to our lives today?

THE IMPACT OF EUROPEANS ON NATIVE AMERICANS

The Destruction of Native American Cultures

Native Americans and Europeans did not know about each other before Columbus arrived here in 1492. But in the years after 1492, every Native American culture was changed or destroyed by the newcomers from Europe. Millions of Native Americans died. Europeans took over the land. They created new and powerful cultures in America that were based on European ways of doing things.

We do not know how many Native Americans lived in what is now the United States when the Europeans came. Guesses range from one million to ten million people. But by 1900 there were fewer than 120 thousand.

Why did this happen? The most important reason was **disease**. European diseases killed more Indians than European guns did. Perhaps 95 percent of Native Americans died from European illnesses. Diseases spread so quickly that millions of Indians died before they even saw a European. The worst diseases were smallpox and measles.

The second reason was **technology**. Technology is things made by people or ways of doing things that make life easier for people. Native American technology could not fight successfully against the technology of Europe. Native Americans did not have metal tools or complex machines. They had no vehicles with wheels, and no strong animals like horses or oxen to do work for them. They couldn't defeat the Europeans, who had swords, armor, guns, horses, and large ships.

Technology Changes Native American Life

Many Native American people quickly learned to use European technology. They learned to use iron tools. They learned to shoot guns, but not to make them. In the West, Indians became skilled riders of the horses the Europeans brought. One tribe, the Navajo, learned how to raise sheep. Nearly all tribes traded for many useful European goods, such as iron kettles, blankets, and beads to decorate their clothing. Unfortunately, many also learned about getting drunk on alcohol.

Differences Between Indian and European Views of the World

European and Native American cultures and ideas were very different. For example, Europeans and Native Americans could not understand each others' views about nature and the land. Native Americans felt a close relationship to the land they lived on and to the animals they hunted. They felt that no person could own the land, for it belonged to all. Europeans believed they had the right to take whatever they needed from nature in order to get rich or to make a better life for themselves. Europeans also believed that individuals could own land, and that the owner had the right to do whatever he or she wanted with it.

Europeans believed that they were naturally better than the Indians. They believed that they had a right to take over Native American lands, to make Native Americans into slaves, and to destroy the Native American ways of life.

NATIVE AMERICANS TODAY

The Revival of Native American Culture

Native American life and culture was at its lowest point around 1900. White people were calling Indians "the vanishing Americans." Today, the number of Native Americans in the United States has climbed from 120 thousand to about two million, and Native American culture is making a comeback

Today Native Americans have won back many of the rights that were taken away from them. They have their own tribal governments. They have the right to vote, and they are full citizens of the United States.

They celebrate traditional ceremonies that were once against the law. Traditional Native American music and dance are popular. All across the country people from many different tribes come together in festivals of Native American music and dance called **powwows**. At a powwow, men and women dress in traditional dance costumes and compete for prizes in different traditional dance styles.

Problems of Native American Life

Nevertheless, Native Americans are still among the poorest people in the country. They have the shortest lives, the worst housing, the highest school dropout rate, and the highest unemployment. In every part of the United States Native Americans are struggling to overcome these obstacles. But it is a hard fight.

Native Americans have joined their old cultures with modern American culture. They have fought and died for the United States in every American war. They produce beautiful, unique art and literature. They are leaders in the environmental movement, which tries to keep the land from being destroyed to build cities, factories, highways, and farms. They know they can't go back, but many of them are working to make their future a better one.

THE IMPACT OF NATIVE AMERICANS ON THE WORLD

Native American Gifts to the World

Native American gifts to the rest of the world have been enormous. Almost half the crops that are grown today throughout the world were first developed and grown by Indians. Native American foods include turkey, corn, potatoes, sweet potatoes, tomatoes, chili peppers and sweet peppers, most kinds of beans, squash, peanuts, and chocolate.

Native Americans discovered many medicines. Quinine fights the disease malaria, and coca is used in many painkillers. The cotton grown in the United States comes from types first grown by Indians. Rubber and the chicle used in chewing gum are both Indian discoveries.

We still use many products of Native American technology. Their inventions include moccasins,

Important Crops Native to the Americas

CACAO
(chocolate)

PEANUTS

MAIZE
(corn)

POTATOES

TOMATOES

toboggans, hammocks, canoes, snowshoes, parkas, ponchos, and even the game of lacrosse.

Native American products changed European ways of life, too. Indian gold and silver changed European history by making Spain and other European nations rich and powerful. Some European people, like the Irish and the Italians, came to depend on Native American foods like potatoes and tomatoes. Europeans drank American chocolate, smoked American tobacco, and wore hats made from American beaver fur.

Native American Names

Native American names cover our land. We use Indian names for many states, like Massachusetts, Texas, and Oregon. We use Indian names for cities, like Chicago and Seattle. Rivers, lakes, and mountains have Indian names: Mississippi River, Lake Ontario, and the Adirondack Mountains.

Native American Ideas

Native American ideas of freedom and democracy inspired the people in both Europe and America who were struggling against all-powerful kings and rich nobles. The Iroquois Confederacy may have been one of the models used by the 13 colonies in America when they were forming a new nation—the United States.

Native Americans continue to teach us respect for the land. European settlers and their descendents destroyed American rain forests, grasslands, and forests and replaced them with farms. These farms grow enough food to feed people in America and all over the world. But we have lost many of the animals, trees, and plants that once covered the Americas.

For years, people didn't pay attention to what they were doing to the land in their search for a better life. But today, people who work to save the natural environment are guided by Native American ideas of harmony with nature and respect for all living things.

Native American cultures and people were changed and sometimes destroyed by the Europeans. But the Europeans were also changed by the land, people, and resources they found in America. The rest of American history is the story of what happened to both peoples—the people already in America and the people who came to America from all parts of the world. They have both made America what it is today.

SECTION REVIEW

Can you answer these Main Idea questions?

1. How did life change for Native Americans after Europeans arrived in North America?

2. What cultural and technological differences allowed the Europeans to defeat Native Americans?

3. How have Native Americans contributed to our lives today?

Can you define these words?

disease, technology

AFTER YOU READ

Discussion Questions

1. How did the environment affect the way people lived in each of the culture areas?

2. What was the purpose of the League of the Five Nations?

3. Compare farming in the Zuni culture to farming in the Iroquois culture.

4. What Indian tribes lived in your area before the Europeans came? What culture area did they belong to? Tell about their culture.

Comprehension Questions

To compare and contrast two things, you must describe what is the same and what is different about them. One way to decide what is the same and what is different is to make a chart.

Make a chart like the one below listing facts about the Zuni and Iroquois cultures. Then answer the questions.

	IROQUOIS	ZUNI
Natural Environment		
Homes		
Food		
Government		
Women's Role		
Men's Role		

Now use your chart to compare and contrast the two cultures:

1. What are two ways in which the Zuni culture and the Iroquois culture were similar?

2. What are two ways in which the Zuni culture and the Iroquois culture were different?

3. Write two sentences for each statement below, either agreeing or disagreeing with it. Tell whether the facts on your chart support the statement. Give examples from the chart to support your ideas.

   a. Native American cultures had nothing in common.

   b. All Native American cultures used natural resources in the same way.

   c. Native American cultures were different, but had some similarities.

Writing Activity

Pretend you are a Zuni or an Iroquois Indian. Write a short paragraph which tells about your village. In your first sentence tell who you are. Then describe the natural environment in which you live. Finally, tell at least three different things about your village. Use your chart for details.

What's in a Picture

Look at the two-page illustration at the beginning of this unit, on pages 2–3. The people or things listed below are shown in the illustration. Try to identify which is which.

Iroquois Village Mayan Temple
Aztec Warrior Zuni Pueblo
Early North Americans

EXPLORING

Native Americans may have been the first Americans, but they certainly were not the last. Today, America is home to people from all over the world. The Europeans led the way; they were the first people, after the Indians, to settle in America.

As early as almost a thousand years ago, Europeans voyaged to America. There were no lasting settlements, however, and for hundreds of years after these first explorers, there was no contact between Europe and America. Then, at the end of the fifteenth century, Europe rediscovered America. First a trickle, then a flood, of adventurers, fortune-seekers, and settlers came to America and stayed.

The Spanish and the French were among the most important of these early explorers and colonists. They mapped thousands of miles of coast and interior, named rivers, lakes, and whole regions, traded with the Indians, and established forts, trading posts, and cities. Only the English, who later took over all of France and Spain's claims in North America, played a bigger role in the history of the United States.

THE AMERICAS

CHAPTER 4

EUROPEANS COME TO AMERICA

For many thousands of years, Europe and America were separate worlds. Europeans and Native Americans lived on their own continents. Neither knew that the other existed. Then, in 1492, Christopher Columbus made the voyage that changed history. The world would never be the same for Native Americans, for Europeans, for Africans, and even for Asians.

BEFORE YOU READ

Sections in This Chapter

1. Visitors to America Before Columbus
2. A Changing Europe
3. A Changing Africa
4. Christopher Columbus

Reading a Map

The world map on the opposite page shows what Europeans before 1492 thought the world was like. Use it to answer the questions below.

1. What dangers did Europeans believe were in the Atlantic Ocean? Do you think these were real or imaginary?

2. Did the Europeans believe it was possible to sail directly from Europe to the Indies?

3. What danger did Europeans believe was in the ocean at the Equator?

4. Compare the map to a modern world map. What are some of the differences between the two maps?

Understanding a Key Concept: TECHNOLOGY

Technology means all the things made by people and all the ways people do things to help them get what they need and want. Technology helps people control nature. It changes with new inventions and ideas. New technology sometimes changes a culture.

Examples of technology are:

using a pointed stick to plant seeds
using sailing ships to travel from place to place
writing books by hand
printing books on a printing press

1. Which of these are examples of technology?

   forests   wagons   deserts   computers

2. List three examples of technology you use today that the Iroquois and Zuni didn't have. Tell how they make life easier or more fun.

3. How did agricultural technology (farming) change life for people who were hunter-gatherers?

Using What You Already Know

Since ancient times, people have traded. Sometimes people trade directly with each other. For example, a farmer might trade his wheat to a weaver in exchange for cloth. Other times, a professional trader called a merchant buys goods in one place and sells them somewhere else. A wheat merchant might buy wheat from farmers and then sell it to flour mills in a city.

Write a sentence or two to answer these questions.

1. Two groups of hunters and gatherers meet. One group has just collected lots of wild fruit. The other group has just killed several large wild animals. What might they do so both groups can have fruit and meat? Do you think merchants will be involved?

2. When the French came to America, they saw that the Indians had many beautiful furs. Furs were very expensive in Europe. The Indians wanted the metal and tools the French had. How did the two groups get what they wanted? Which groups used merchants?

1. VISITORS TO AMERICA BEFORE COLUMBUS

Main Ideas

Think about the following Main Idea questions as you read this section.

1. Why do some people believe visitors from Africa, Asia, and Europe may have come to America before the Vikings?

2. Why did historians decide that the Vikings really did come to America?

POSSIBLE EARLY VISITORS TO AMERICA

Possible Visitors from Africa

Columbus was not the first visitor to America. The earliest visitors may have come from Africa. Huge stone heads carved in Mexico before the time of the Mayas have faces that look African. The pyramids of the Mayas and the mounds of the Mound Builders are similar in some ways to the famous Pyramids of Egypt. But no one knows for sure whether Native Americans developed these things by themselves, or if African visitors arrived in America and showed them how.

Possible Visitors from Asia

It is possible that people from Asia may have crossed the Pacific Ocean before the time of Columbus. Some archaeologists point to similarities between Chinese and Mayan art. Other archaeologists have discovered ancient pots in Peru that are just like ancient pots in Japan. Were there Chinese and Japanese here before Europeans? Once again, no one knows.

Possible Visitors from Europe

Who were the first Europeans to visit America? People still argue over the answer. For more than a thousand years, Europeans have told stories about boats that sailed from Europe to unknown lands in the West. But no one knows if any of these stories is true.

One of the best-known stories is about St. Brendan, an Irish holy man. The story says that he sailed west from Ireland around 550 A.D. in a boat made of leather. He landed on many magical islands, where food would appear out of nowhere or where birds could talk. One of these marvelous islands might have been North America, but no one is sure. Nothing has ever been found to prove that St. Brendan actually arrived here.

LEIF ERIKSSON AND THE NORSEMEN

Leif Eriksson Finds a New Land

Other stories say the first Europeans to sail to America were people from Norway. They were called **Norsemen** (Northmen) or **Vikings**. The Vikings were great sailors. Some of them settled on the islands of **Iceland** and **Greenland**, which are not far from North America.

In the year 1001 A.D., a Greenland settler named Leif (LAFE) Eriksson sailed south. He wanted to find out if a story he had heard about a tree-filled land was true. Stories say he landed in a green, warm land where wild grapes grew. Leif named this place Vinland, or "Wine-land," and stayed there for the winter. In spring he returned to Greenland to tell what he had found.

The Norsemen Try to Settle in America

Several years later, in 1009, another Viking, Thorfinn Karlsefni (TOR-fin karl-SEF-nee), came to Vinland. He started a small village there. But the Indians were not friendly, and they drove the Norsemen away.

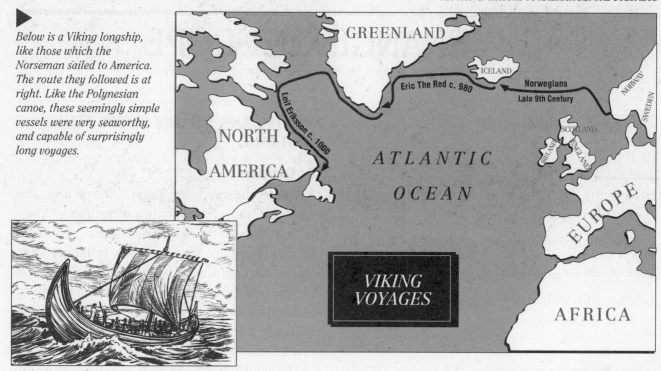

Below is a Viking longship, like those which the Norseman sailed to America. The route they followed is at right. Like the Polynesian canoe, these seemingly simple vessels were very seaworthy, and capable of surprisingly long voyages.

The Norsemen did not try to live in North America again, although they may have returned to fish or cut wood.

In Iceland, the people told stories about the adventures of "Leif the Lucky" and Thorfinn Karlsefni. Three hundred years later, these stories were written down. But nobody could prove they were true.

Then, in 1960, a Norwegian archaeologist found the remains of a Norse settlement on the island of **Newfoundland** in Canada. He found the ruins of Norse houses, fireplaces, and even a metal pin. These discoveries prove that the Vikings did come to America, and that the old Norse stories are based on real events.

Why Didn't the Norse Settlements Succeed?

The Norsemen who came to America had no real effect on history. Most people in Europe never heard about their voyages. Only a few Norsemen ever came here, and a few Native Americans were enough to throw them out.

Europeans didn't yet have the technology to explore, conquer, or settle a land on the other side of the ocean. They had no big ships. Guns hadn't been invented. European countries were not strong enough to conquer lands on the other side of the ocean. The European voyage to America that changed history did not take place until Europe itself had changed, almost 500 years after Leif the Lucky.

SECTION REVIEW

Can you answer these Main Idea questions?

1. Why do some people believe visitors from Africa, Asia, and Europe may have come to America before the Vikings?

2. Why did historians decide that the Vikings really did come to America?

Can you identify and locate these places?

Newfoundland, Iceland, Greenland

Can you identify these people?

Norsemen, Vikings, Leif Eriksson, Thorfinn Karlsefni

2. A CHANGING EUROPE

Main Ideas

Think about the following Main Idea questions as you read this section.

1. How did the Crusades help change Europeans' ideas and trade?

2. How did Europeans get goods from the Indies?

3. How did technology change European life?

4. Why did technological changes in sailing make Portugal an important trading country?

EUROPE IN THE MIDDLE AGES

Historians call Europe's history from about 500 to 1500 A.D. the **Middle Ages.** In Leif Ericsson's time, about halfway through the Middle Ages, Western Europe was a poor place. Most people were farmers who lived in small villages. They knew almost nothing about the rest of the world. There were no large cities, no great stone buildings, no castles, and no powerful kings with large armies. All these came later. The great civilizations of the time were in other parts of the world—in China, Japan, Southeast Asia, India, the Arab countries, North Africa, Peru, Mexico, and in Eastern Europe. Compared to these places, Western Europe was a backward place.

Then, slowly, starting about the year 1000, Western Europe began to change. New ideas, new inventions, and new trading patterns changed it. Old books and old learning were rediscovered. Western European traders and sailors went on long journeys. By the late 1400s, Europeans felt that they were living in a new and exciting age of discovery. Columbus was one example of that age.

EUROPEANS LEARN FROM THE MUSLIMS

The Crusades

One of the first changes in Europe after the year 1000 happened because of religion. When they could, both the rich and the poor traveled to places special to the Christian religion. Most went to see and pray at holy places in Europe. A few went on longer journeys to the Holy Land in the Middle East. The Holy Land was where Christ had lived, taught, and died. It was where Christianity started.

At that time, the Holy Land was ruled by Turks and Arabs. These people were not Christians. They were **Muslims**, or **Moslems**. Muslims follow the religion of **Islam**, which was started by the Prophet Muhammad. The Muslims were more advanced than the Europeans in many ways. They had kept and studied much old information that the Christians had destroyed or forgotten.

Europeans wanted the Holy Land to be Christian, not Muslim. Starting around 1100, they fought wars against the Muslims for control of the Holy Land. These wars are called the **Crusades**. They continued on and off for nearly 200 years.

The Crusaders from Europe failed to take and keep the Holy Land. But the Crusades made Europeans realize that life in other parts of the world was very different from life in Europe.

Europeans who went on a Crusade saw things that they had never seen before. They brought back new foods, like sugar, and new cloth, like silk. These things and the stories they told helped create an interest in the world outside Europe.

Learning from the Muslims in Spain

The Holy Land was not the only place where Christians met Muslims. Muslims from Northern Africa controlled nearly all of Spain. The Spanish fought for almost 800 years to take it back.

As the Spanish recaptured Muslim cities, they found unusual buildings, interesting books, and new foods, like rice. Many of these things became part of Spanish life.

TRADE WITH THE INDIES

Trade Goods from the Indies Come to Europe

In the late Middle Ages, Italian merchants (people who trade goods) began trading with the Muslims. They traded Italian goods like wool, tin, and silver for silk cloth, perfumes, and new spices like pepper. Europeans smoked meat to store it for the winter. It tasted much better when cooked with spices. New perfumes helped cover the smell of people who didn't bathe very often.

Italian merchants got these goods from Muslim traders, but these traders got them from lands far to the east. Europeans called these lands the **Indies**. The Indies were actually China, Japan, India, Indonesia, and other countries in Asia. But Europeans didn't know anything about these places. No European had ever traveled there.

European Land Routes to the Indies

Naturally, European merchants wanted to trade directly with the Indies. They didn't like paying high prices to Muslim traders, but they had no choice. The Turks, who were Muslims, controlled the trade routes to the Indies. They would not allow Europeans to travel on these routes.

Then, in the early 1200s, the Mongols, a warlike people who lived north of China, took control of the routes. They allowed European merchants to travel to Asia. A few Europeans made the long journey to the Indies.

Below are the trade routes followed by Italian traders to China. Because travel by boat was generally faster and safer than land travel, the "land routes" actually went by water as far as they could, almost to the border of Europe and Asia. ▼

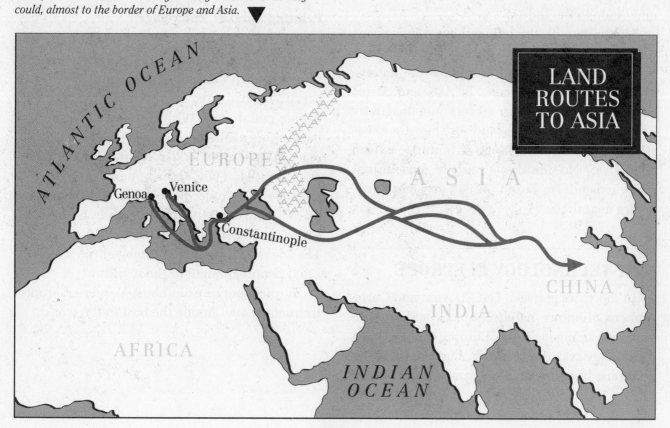

LAND ROUTES TO ASIA

One famous trade route was known as the Silk Road. It went from Turkey to China. Traders traveled by camel and were gone for several years. The goods they brought back were expensive. But they were still cheaper than goods bought from Muslim merchants. Even so, only the rich could afford them.

One Italian trader, named Marco Polo, lived in China for many years. When he returned to Italy, he wrote a book about his adventures. Although every copy of the book had to be copied by hand, thousands of people read it.

The Traders Lose Their Land Routes

For about a hundred years, European traders traveled to Asia. Then the Mongols lost their power, and the new Turkish rulers closed the routes to the East. Once again, Europeans could trade only with Muslim countries like Egypt and Syria. The Italians had a monopoly—that is, they were the only European merchants allowed to trade with the Muslims. But Muslim prices were still high, and other Europeans wanted to trade, too. Merchants all over Europe wanted to find a new route to the Indies.

The trade with the Indies showed Europeans that there was more to the world than they thought. But they still didn't know the details. Their maps had the shapes of Asia and Africa completely wrong. Map makers put imaginary Christian countries in the Indies. They drew seas filled with monsters and islands called "Paradise." No one knew if any of these things really existed. No European had ever been anywhere near them.

NEW TECHNOLOGY IN EUROPE

In the years between Leif Ericsson and Christopher Columbus, new technology and new inventions changed life in Europe. Some of this technology was developed in Europe. Other inventions, like the compass, came from China or from Muslim countries. Still others were improvements of older inventions.

New Machines

With new machines, people could do things that they couldn't do before. Improved simple machines like pulleys made it possible to raise heavy weights. Soon builders were raising great stone buildings all over Europe. Other craftsmen made better looms so they could weave cloth faster. Pumps were developed to get rid of water inside mines and ships. People found ways to use gears and wheels in machines. By the time of Columbus, the inventor Leonardo da Vinci (VIN-chee) was designing machines that amaze us even today.

Gunpowder Comes to Europe

Technology also changed the way wars were fought. Gunpowder came from China to Europe in the 1300s. Soon Europeans were making guns and cannons. Within a hundred years, wars were no longer fought by knights in armor on horseback.

Printing Spreads Knowledge

One very important new technology was printing. Europeans invented new methods of printing when Columbus was a boy. Before this, every book had to be handwritten, and not many people could read. With printing, thousands of books were available, so more people learned to read. How-to-do-it books were among the first ones printed. They spread new technology to anyone who could read. Many ancient books were found in Muslim and church libraries. These were printed and read all over Europe. The ideas in these books changed the way educated people thought of the world.

By the time of Columbus, Western Europe's technology was among the best in the world.

THE PORTUGUESE EXPLORE THE WEST AFRICAN COAST

Prince Henry of Portugal Raids Africa

In 1415, Prince Henry of **Portugal**—the country west of Spain—helped capture a rich Muslim city in North Africa. This gave him an idea. He would use North Africa's wealth to make Portugal rich. Over the next 40 years, he sent out hundreds of raiding and trading expeditions. They sailed down the Atlantic coast of Africa. Henry himself never went on any of these voyages. Nevertheless, he is called "Prince Henry the Navigator."

At first, the Portuguese didn't go very far. And they always sailed close to the African coast. They were afraid of going too far south or of sailing too far out to sea. They thought that monsters or whirlpools would wreck their ships. They were also afraid that winds and ocean currents would keep them from ever getting back home. But the farther they went, the more they learned.

They learned about the African coast, currents, and winds. After many years, they learned how to **navigate**. That is, they learned how to find their way at sea even when land was out of sight. They learned how to use the stars and a compass as guides. These skills helped them find out where they were going, where they were, and how to get home. By the middle 1400s, Portuguese captains were sailing far out in the Atlantic Ocean. They discovered islands nearly a thousand miles from Portugal. They designed and built special ships for ocean voyages.

The Portuguese Reach the Southern Tip of Africa

Portuguese ships brought back pepper and gold dust from Africa. They also brought back slaves—captured African men, women, and children. Many of these Africans were taken to the Atlantic islands that Portugal had discovered.

There they were made to work on huge sugar farms. Portugal became a very rich country.

In the 1480s, King John II of Portugal decided to try sending explorers all the way to the Indies by sailing around Africa. Once in the Indies, the Portuguese could trade for the goods they wanted and then return. They would not have to deal with either Muslim or Italian merchants. They could charge the rest of Europe cheaper prices but still make a lot of money.

In 1488, Portuguese explorers rounded the southern tip of Africa and returned. The way to the Indies was open.

SECTION REVIEW

Can you answer these Main Idea questions?

1. How did the Crusades help change Europeans' ideas and trade?

2. How did Europeans get goods from the Indies?

3. How did technology change European life?

4. Why did technological changes in sailing make Portugal an important trading country?

Can you identify these places?

Holy Land, the Indies, Portugal

Can you identify these people?

Marco Polo, Muslims, Prince Henry of Portugal

Can you define these words?

the Crusades, navigate

3. A CHANGING AFRICA

Main Ideas

Think about the following Main Idea questions as you read this section.

1. What complex cultures and civilizations developed in Africa?

2. How did the Sahara Desert and the Muslim religion affect European contact with most Africans?

3. How did the African slave trade change after Europeans and Americans began using African slaves?

ANCIENT CIVILIZATIONS OF THE NILE RIVER

Ancient Egypt

Until the Portuguese voyages, all that Europe knew of Africa was its northern edge. Yet Africa had civilizations and empires more than a thousand years before Europe did. Five thousand years ago—about 3100 B.C.—one of the oldest and greatest of all civilizations grew up in North Africa. Along the Nile River, the people of **Egypt** created huge cities, temples, and pyramids. Their buildings and art still amaze us even today. Other empires rose and fell. But the ancient Egyptian civilization remained strong for more than 2,000 years.

Nubia

Egypt was not the only civilization along the Nile. South of Egypt, a kingdom of black Africans called **Nubia** or **Kush** grew up at about the same time as Egypt. About 2000 B.C., the Egyptians conquered the Nubians and ruled them. Nubian mines provided most of the gold of Egypt. But Egyptian power became weak, and the Nubians broke away. Led by a king named Piye,

Nubian armies swept north and conquered Egypt. For more than 60 years, black Nubian kings ruled over the land of Egypt. Even after they were driven out, they continued to rule over their own empire on the Nile.

As for Egypt, it never again got its power back. It was conquered by other peoples—among them Persians, Greeks, and Romans. In the year 642 A.D., an army of Muslim Arabs swept into the country. Since then, Egypt has been part of the Arab world of North Africa.

WEST AFRICAN KINGDOMS AND EMPIRES

Ghana

Other parts of black Africa developed complex cultures and kingdoms, too. In the tenth century A.D., at about the time of the Vikings, a rich and powerful kingdom called **Ghana** ruled over much of the grasslands of West Africa. Ghana controlled gold mines. One Arab traveler said that the king of Ghana was "the wealthiest of all kings on the face of the earth."

Mali

Around 1235, Ghana was swallowed up by a neighboring kingdom, **Mali**. Mali became even wealthier and more powerful than Ghana. It became the second largest empire in the world. Only the Mongol empire in Asia was larger.

The people of Mali were Muslims, and their kings made religious journeys to the Muslim holy city of Mecca. On one famous trip to Mecca, the Mali emperor Mansa Musa traveled with 60,000 men and more than a ton of gold. During the trip he spent the gold or gave it away.

The people of Mali were famous for their honesty and sense of justice. In a world where robbers were common, a traveler was completely safe in Mali. One Arab traveler to Mali said, "Of all peoples, the blacks are those who most hate injustice."

Songhai

To the east of Mali another kingdom grew up. This was the kingdom of **Songhai**. Songhai was famous for learning as well as for wealth. Under its great King Askia Muhammad, its university at Timbuktu drew scholars from all over the Muslim world.

The Forest Kingdoms

In the rain forests south and east of Mali and Songhai, in what is today Nigeria, there were smaller kingdoms. The Muslim religion did not come this far south, and the forest kingdoms had little contact with the great Muslim civilizations. They are most famous today for their sculptures in clay and bronze, which are prized possessions in museums around the world.

WHY DIDN'T EUROPEANS KNOW MORE ABOUT AFRICA?

People in Europe knew about ancient Egypt. Why didn't they know more about the other great civilizations of Africa? There are two main reasons: the **Sahara Desert** and Islam.

How the Sahara Kept Europeans out of Africa

When civilization was starting in Egypt, most of North Africa was grassland. Then the rains stopped and the land became dry. By 1500 B.C., the largest desert in the world stretched across the African continent. It is known as the Sahara. The Sahara was almost impossible to cross. Only a few warlike people lived in it. So, although Europeans in the Middle Ages knew about the Arab peoples who lived along the northern edge of the Sahara, they knew almost nothing about the black African kingdoms and empires south of it.

Civilization in Africa is older than civilization in Europe. As the map indicates, many large kingdoms and empires rose, flourished, and fell over the centuries, often to be replaced by another kingdom in the same area.

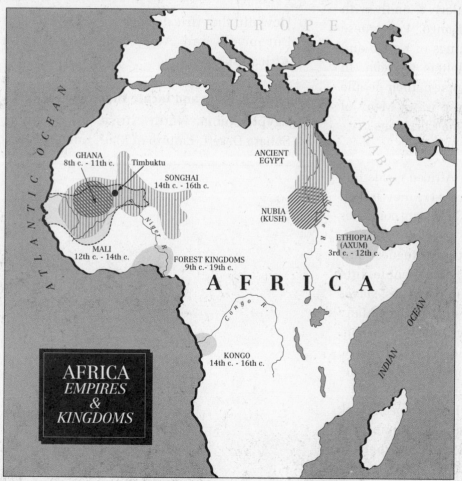

GHANA
8th c. - 11th c.   Timbuktu

SONGHAI
14th c. - 16th c.

ANCIENT
EGYPT

NUBIA
(KUSH)

MALI
12th c. - 14th c.

FOREST KINGDOMS
9th c.- 19th c.

ETHIOPIA
(AXUM)
3rd c. - 12th c.

AFRICA

KONGO
14th c. - 16th c.

AFRICA
*EMPIRES
&
KINGDOMS*

How Islam Kept Europeans out of Africa

The Arabs who lived on the northern edge of the Sahara were Muslims. The desert people of the Sahara and the people in West Africa were Muslims, too. This meant that the people of Ghana, Mali, and Songhai traded and traveled in the Muslim world. They had nothing to do with the Christians of Europe. Muslims believed that Christians were the enemies of Islam and did not allow them to travel or trade inside Muslim lands.

THE PORTUGUESE AND THE BEGINNING OF THE SLAVE TRADE

Portuguese Trade with the Kingdom of Kongo

The Portuguese were the first Europeans to send ships down the coast of West Africa. They met and traded with many different African peoples. They became particularly friendly with people in the kingdom of **Kongo**. Portuguese kings gave rich gifts to the kings of Kongo and wrote polite and admiring letters to them. In return, the Kongo kings sent some of their people to Portugal to learn Portuguese ways. Many of the people in the Kongo became Christians.

The Early Slave Trade

The Portuguese traded for African goods like pepper and gold. Starting in 1441, they traded for slaves, too. Soon other European countries were also trading for slaves.

Neither the Africans nor the Portuguese saw anything wrong in making free people into slaves. In African and Muslim countries, slaves were widely used as servants and soldiers. Many rich African families had slaves. They were considered part of the family. Slaves could marry, raise families, and own property. They sometimes were given important and powerful jobs.

The slave trade changed when Europeans took slaves from Africa. After 1500, huge numbers of Africans were kidnapped and shipped to America. They worked on plantations and in mines. The harder they worked, the richer the slave owners became. So the slave owners made the slaves work as hard as possible.

The African kingdoms that captured people and sold them as slaves became rich. So did the European and American slave traders and the plantation owners. Before slave trading finally came to an end almost 400 years later, between 11 and 15 million Africans had been taken as slaves from Africa to America.

SECTION REVIEW

Can you answer these Main Idea questions?

1. What complex cultures and civilizations developed in Africa?

2. How did the Sahara Desert and the Muslim religion affect European contact with most Africans?

3. How did the African slave trade change after Europeans and Americans began using African slaves?

Can you identify and locate these places?

Egypt, Nubia, North Africa, West Africa, Sahara Desert, Empire of Mali, Kongo

4. CHRISTOPHER COLUMBUS

Main Ideas

Think about the following Main Idea questions as you read this section.

1. What information and experiences helped Columbus form his plan?

2. Who finally helped Columbus and why?

3. What did Columbus find, and was it what he expected to find?

COLUMBUS DEVELOPS A PLAN TO SAIL TO THE INDIES

Young Columbus

Christopher Columbus grew up in the seaport trading town of Genoa, Italy. As a boy, he heard many stories about places outside his country. He left his home to become a sailor when he was a young man.

Columbus worked on several ships, doing many different jobs. During these trips he went as far north as Iceland. He learned about navigating and running a sailing ship. He learned about the wind and currents in the northern Atlantic Ocean. And he heard sailors' stories about islands to the west.

When he was 25, Columbus became a chartmaker with his brother in Lisbon, Portugal. The two brothers met with captains who had sailed along the African coast. They listened to what the captains said about the coastline, currents, and winds. Each new fact was added to their charts and maps.

Columbus Plans to Sail to the Indies

All through his life, Columbus studied sailing and the world. Every educated person knew the world was round, but no one knew exactly how big it was. Columbus studied old writers and new sailing charts. Then he did the math that he thought would tell him the earth's size. Columbus was sure that China and the Indies were not very far away. They should be directly across the ocean from Europe. If he sailed west he would reach them.

Now, he just had to convince someone to give him the ships and sailors for the voyage.

Columbus Looks for Support for His Plan

In 1484, Columbus asked the king of Portugal to give him the ships and sailors he needed. Since Portugal wanted to trade with the Indies, the king had his experts study Columbus's plan.

The experts thought that Columbus's distances were wrong. They said the earth was much bigger than Columbus believed. They warned the king that Columbus could never make it to China by sea. So the Portuguese king said no to Columbus.

Columbus still believed he was right. While his brother tried England, he tried Spain. King Ferdinand and Queen Isabella asked their experts to study Columbus's ideas.

While the Spanish experts studied his plans, Columbus returned to Portugal. In 1488, the Portuguese king was about to say yes, when Captain Bartolomeu Dias returned from Africa. Dias had just sailed around Africa's southern tip. Portugal could soon reach the Indies by going around Africa and sailing east. The Portuguese didn't need Columbus's unknown western route anymore.

Queen Isabella of Spain Supports the Plan

Disappointed, Columbus went back to Spain. The Spanish experts didn't agree with Columbus, but he convinced Queen Isabella to support him anyway. She liked his deep religious feelings and his confidence in his plan. She thought he should be given a chance.

Spain needed wealth. It didn't have many goods to trade with other countries. The voyage wouldn't cost very much, and if Columbus was right, Spain would have the riches of the Indies to trade. It would also be able to convert thousands of non-Christians to the Christian religion.

For all these reasons, King Ferdinand and Queen Isabella agreed to help Columbus.

COLUMBUS' VOYAGES TO AMERICA

The Trip Across the Atlantic Ocean

Columbus was given three small ships—the *Niña*, the *Pinta*, and the *Santa María*—and 90 good sailors. The sailors were glad to come, for they believed in Columbus. They thought the voyage would be safe. Maps showed islands along the way, although no one had actually seen them. They planned to stop at these islands for food and water. Columbus' math said that the distance across the ocean was short, so the sailors didn't plan to be gone very long. No one knew that two continents lay between Europe and China.

Columbus was an excellent navigator. He knew which winds, currents, and stars to follow. He knew that it would be hard to sail directly west from Spain, because the currents and the winds went the wrong way. So he sailed south to where the winds blew to the west. Then he headed across the unknown ocean.

For three weeks the voyagers saw no land, not even an island. The sailors became frightened. They thought they would never see land again. Columbus convinced them to go on.

Finally, the frightened sailors tried to take over the ship and force Columbus to return to Spain. Columbus promised that if they found no land in three days, they would turn back. No one believed they would see land, but they trusted Columbus to keep his word.

The next day, land birds flew by. Branches with flowers and leaves floated in the water. Everyone knew that land was near.

Columbus Lands in the Bahamas

At last they saw a small island in the distance. Everyone believed it was an island near China. When they landed, they said prayers of thanks for bringing them to the Indies. Columbus named the island San Salvador, "Holy Savior." Experts disagree on exactly where they landed, but they do agree that it was somewhere in the Bahamas, off the coast of Florida.

Columbus called the people living on the islands "Indians," because he was sure that he had landed in the Indies. He and his men searched for things to take back to Spain. They traveled to other nearby islands. They found a little gold, but no silk and no spices.

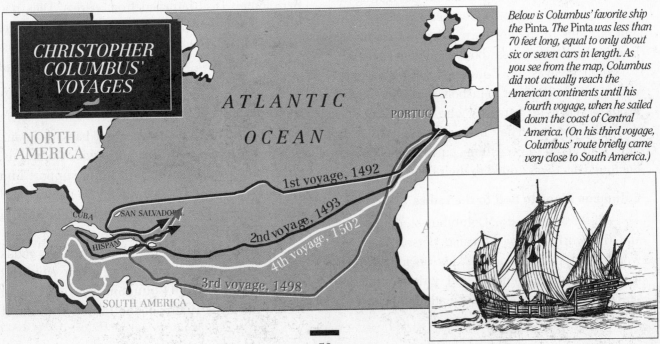

CHRISTOPHER COLUMBUS' VOYAGES

NORTH AMERICA

ATLANTIC OCEAN

PORTUG

CUBA   SAN SALVADOR

HISPAN

1st voyage, 1492

2nd voyage, 1493

4th voyage, 1502

3rd voyage, 1498

SOUTH AMERICA

Below is Columbus' favorite ship the Pinta. The Pinta *was less than 70 feet long, equal to only about six or seven cars in length. As you see from the map, Columbus did not actually reach the American continents until his fourth voyage, when he sailed down the coast of Central America. (On his third voyage, Columbus' route briefly came very close to South America.)*

The Return to Spain

When Columbus and his men returned to Spain, they brought back some Indians and some gold dust. They were heroes. King Ferdinand and Queen Isabella rewarded Columbus in many ways. Everyone thought Columbus had found a route to the Indies. No one in Spain had ever actually been to the Indies. They didn't realize that the lands and people that Columbus had found were very different from the real Indies in Asia.

Columbus Goes on Three More Voyages

Columbus made three more voyages. He visited all the main islands that we now call the "West Indies." He also sailed a short way along the coast of South America. He realized that it was a continent, not just a large island. But he never stopped believing that he had reached the continent of Asia.

Columbus was the greatest navigator of his time. He learned all he could before he developed his plan. Then he believed in it without question. He bravely sailed into the unknown, and never realized what he had found.

The experts were right. It is much farther from Europe to China than Columbus figured. Yet the route that Columbus had opened between Europe and the Americas soon changed everyone's world.

A NEW NAME FOR A NEW WORLD

The Voyages of Amerigo Vespucci

Not long after Columbus returned, other Spanish ships headed west across the Atlantic. An Italian businessman named Amerigo Vespucci (ves-POO-chee) was on one of the ships. He sailed along the coast of South America, and he may have sailed along the coast of North America, too. He realized that Columbus had discovered a place that was completely new to Europeans.

Vespucci's exciting, but not quite truthful, letters were published and read throughout Europe. They contained the first widely read description of what Vespucci called the "New World."

America Gets a Name

In 1507, a German map maker published a large map of the world. He needed a name for the new land. He had read Vespucci's letters, and he decided to name the "New World" after the man he thought had discovered it.

In those days, all educated Europeans spoke and read the Latin language. The map maker took Vespucci's first name in Latin (Americus). He changed its ending to match the ending of the names of the continents of Asia and Africa.

The name he came up with was America.

The arrival of Europeans in America took place because a stubborn man insisted on following his own wrong figures about the size of the earth. It was one of the strangest accidents in history. But it also happened because Europeans had become the best sailors in the world. The 500 years between Leif Ericsson and Christopher Columbus made a big difference both in the way America was discovered and in what happened after that discovery.

SECTION REVIEW

Can you answer these Main Idea questions?

1. What information and experiences helped Columbus form his plan?

2. Who finally helped Columbus and why?

3. What did Columbus find, and was it what he expected to find?

Can you identify and locate these places?

Spain, the Bahamas

Can you identify these people?

Christopher Columbus, King Ferdinand and Queen Isabella, Amerigo Vespucci

AFTER YOU READ

Discussion Questions

1. After the year 1000 A.D., Europeans changed many of their ideas about the world. What happened to make them change their ideas?

2. How were Moslems involved in trade in Europe, Asia, and Africa?

3. How did technology, religion, and trade lead to Columbus's voyage to America?

4. Which trip discussed in this chapter would you have liked to be on and why?

Comprehension Questions

I. Cause-Effect

Almost everything we do has a **cause** and an **effect**. If we are hungry (the cause), we eat (the effect). Many different things can be causes, but new technology often has a big effect on daily life. You have read about many causes and effects. Here is a list of causes. Some are new technology for Europeans. Write at least one effect for each cause. One is done for you.

1. Vikings visit Vinland *stories told about land to west*

2. Crusades
3. new machines, like looms
4. gunpowder
5. printing press
6. improved navigation and ships
7. Portuguese trade along African coast
8. Columbus's trip to America

II. Answer the following questions.

9. Before the time of Columbus, Europeans had many ideas about the world. List two of their ideas that were correct and two that were wrong.

10. Choose one idea from Question 9. Tell why we still believe it or why we don't believe it.

11. How was life for many Africans changed by the European slave trade?

12. Columbus had several purposes in making his first voyage. What were they?

Writing Activity

Pretend you live in Europe or Africa during the time of Columbus. You keep a journal in which you tell what is happening. Choose one of the causes and effects from the cause and effect activity above. Think about how life changed because of it. Write three journal entries. In one, describe life before the change. In the second, tell what is happening while life is changing. The last entry can tell about life after it has changed. Predict what changes you think might happen next.

CHAPTER 5

SPANISH EXPLORERS AND SETTLERS

The Spanish were the first Europeans to explore and settle permanently in America. They created a huge empire—as large or larger than anything claimed by the French (Chapter 6) or English (Chapters 7, 8, and 9)—that stretched from the tip of South America to northern California and Florida. They were the first Europeans to reach the Pacific Ocean and the west coast of North America.

Over a period of 200 years, they established what would become many of the Southwest's most important cities. Their influence on Southwestern architecture and culture is still strong today. Spanish words, like *mustang* or *canyon*, have become part of our language. The story of the Spanish explorers and settlers is an important part of the story of America.

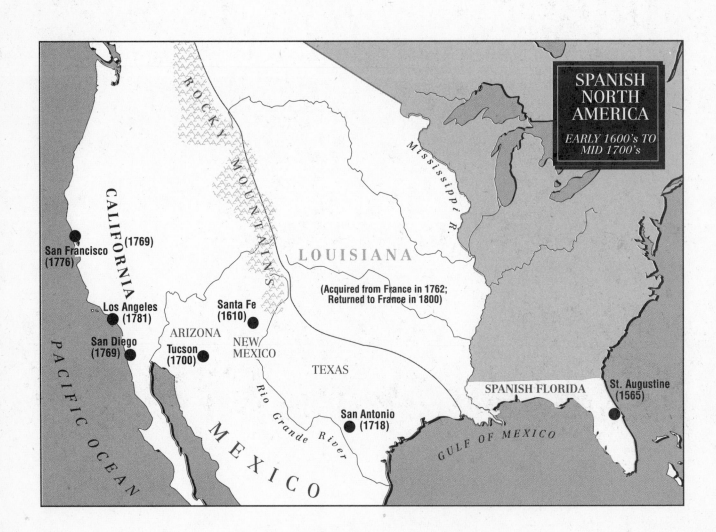

SPANISH NORTH AMERICA

EARLY 1600's TO MID 1700's

ROCKY MOUNTAINS

Mississippi R.

CALIFORNIA

San Francisco (1776)

(1769)

LOUISIANA

(Acquired from France in 1762; Returned to France in 1800)

Los Angeles (1781)

Santa Fe (1610)

ARIZONA

San Diego (1769)

Tucson (1700)

NEW MEXICO

TEXAS

Rio Grande River

San Antonio (1718)

SPANISH FLORIDA

St. Augustine (1565)

MEXICO

PACIFIC OCEAN

GULF OF MEXICO

BEFORE YOU READ

Sections in This Chapter:

1. Voyagers and Conquistadors
2. Exploring and Settling North of Mexico
3. Life in the Spanish Colonies

Reading a Map

Study the map on the opposite page. Then answer these questions about it.

1. What European country claimed control of the unshaded area?

2. Compare this map with a map of North America today. What three countries today cover the unshaded area?

3. Do you think the Spanish settlements were able to keep a tight control on all the land that Spain claimed? What makes you think this?

Understanding a Key Concept: COLONY

Before the twentieth century, countries often sent out groups of people to settle in distant places.

- The country that sent out the settlers was called the **mother country**.

- The places under a mother country's control were called **colonies**.

- The people from the mother country living in the colony were called **colonists**.

- The mother country controlled the colony even if other people already lived there.

- The mother country made laws and sent soldiers, government leaders, and settlers to protect and control each colony.

- The colonists sent natural resources and trade goods back to the mother country.

Mexico was one of Spain's colonies in America.

Use the information about a colony to answer the following questions.

1. Which was the mother country?

2. The Aztecs lived in Mexico before the Spanish came. Were the Aztecs colonists?

3. What do you think happened to the riches that Spanish colonists found in Mexico?

4. Who do you think got rich, the colony (Mexico) or the mother country (Spain)?

5. How do you think the people already living in America felt about Spain's taking control of their land?

Using What You Already Know

Use your own knowledge and what you learned in earlier chapters to answer these questions.

1. Name three civilizations that developed in America before the Europeans came.

2. What are some of the reasons that European countries were exploring the world?

3. What kinds of technology did Europeans have that Native Americans did not have? Choose two from the following list and add two of your own:

   guns   roads   large buildings   riding horses   agriculture   steel swords

4. Think about your answers to the last question. What do you think happened when Europeans first came to America and found people already here? Use your answers to Question 3 to support your prediction. Does your prediction fit with what you learned in Chapter 3?

1. VOYAGERS AND CONQUISTADORS

 Main Ideas

Think about the following Main Idea questions as you read this section:

1. How did Spanish voyagers and explorers add to our knowledge of the world?

2. How did the Spanish treat the Indians?

3. Why were the Spanish able to conquer the Aztecs and the Incas so easily?

4. Why did the Spanish bring Africans to America?

VOYAGERS

Dividing the World

The Spanish were delighted with Columbus's first voyage. The Portuguese were not. They quickly made a treaty with the Spanish that divided up the whole world between them.

The two countries drew a line in the middle of the Atlantic Ocean, dividing the world in half. The treaty said that Spain would control all lands west of the line. Portugal would get all lands east of it. This line is the **Line of Demarcation**.

The treaty simply ignored the rights of any people who already lived in these lands. It also ignored the claims of all other European countries. So these countries paid no attention to the treaty and explored wherever they wanted.

When the Spanish signed the treaty, they thought that all of America was west of the Line of Demarcation. Later, explorers discovered that part of South America was east of it. The Portuguese claimed this area. It became the country of Brazil. This is why Brazilians speak Portuguese, while most other South Americans speak Spanish.

Balboa Discovers the Pacific Ocean

Spanish explorers soon realized that America was not part of Asia. They started looking for ways to sail around it or through it. In 1513, a Spanish explorer named Vasco Núñez de Balboa (VAS-ko NOON-yez de bal-BO-uh) made an important discovery. Looking for gold, he marched through the jungles of Panama, where the American continent is only about 50 miles wide. There, from the top of a mountain, he saw an ocean that nobody in Europe knew about.

Magellan Sails Around the World

In 1519, an explorer named Ferdinand Magellan (Ma-JELL-un) started searching for a water route into the ocean that Balboa had seen. He was Portuguese, but he was working for the Spanish. Magellan's ships sailed thousands of miles down the South American coast. At the tip of the continent, Magellan finally found the route he was looking for. It was a narrow, stormy, and dangerous passage. Today it is called the Straits of Magellan. Once the ships were through it, they entered the ocean that Balboa had seen.

Magellan named this ocean the Pacific Ocean, or "Peaceful Ocean." He continued sailing across it. Many men died on the voyage. Some died from starvation. Others were killed by people who lived on islands where the ships stopped. Magellan himself was killed. Most of his ships were lost at sea. In 1522 the last ship with only 18 men made it back to Spain. They were the first people in history to travel around the world!

Magellan's voyage proved that people could sail around the world. It showed that America was not part of Asia, and that the Pacific Ocean was the biggest ocean in the world. Sailors and explorers finally understood how big the world really is.

Voyages Along the Coasts of North America

Besides making long ocean voyages, the Spanish made many other shorter voyages along the coasts of North and South America. From 1524 to 1530, they explored the Atlantic coast as far north as Canada. In 1542 and 1543, Juan Cabrillo (kah BREE yoh) sailed up the Pacific coast as far north as Oregon.

Wherever the explorers stopped, they claimed the land for Spain. They said it was part of the Spanish Empire, and that the King of Spain governed and owned it. The Native Americans who already lived there didn't count at all.

CONQUISTADORS

Columbus and the West Indies

On his second voyage, Columbus brought the first Spanish settlers to America. They settled on Hispaniola, the large island between Cuba and Puerto Rico.

The settlers only wanted to search for gold. They did not expect hot jungles, strange plants and animals, and hard work. When Columbus wanted them to build houses and grow crops, they rebelled. So Columbus let them capture Indians and use them as slaves to do the hard work.

Columbus' men found a little gold in the streams of Hispaniola. Their discovery set off a rush for gold. Spanish soldiers and adventurers rushed to America, looking for wealth and fame. They are known as **conquistadors** (kon-KEES-ta-dorz). This is the Spanish word for someone who conquers, or takes over a place by force.

The conquistadors came to America for three reasons: God, gold, and glory. Glory would make them famous. Gold would make them rich. And God, they believed, wanted them to convert the Indians to the Christian religion.

The Arrival of Africans

The enslaved Indians were not used to the hard life that the Spanish forced on them. Their bodies did not have natural protection against deadly European illnesses. Millions of them died in a few years. To replace them, the Spanish raided Africa for workers. In 1518, the first boatload of captured Africans came to America. They came as slaves. The Spanish worked them and treated them as cruelly as they treated the Indians. When they died, the Spanish simply brought over more Africans to replace them.

There wasn't much gold in the islands. Later, the Spanish found they could become rich by growing sugar. They started huge sugar farms and forced their African slaves to do the farm work.

A few of these African slaves became explorers themselves. They went on Spanish exploring trips. One of them, an African whom the Spanish called Estevánico (es-tay-VAHN-ee-ko), became an important early explorer of the American Southwest.

Ponce De León Explores Florida

The Spanish soon realized that there was not much gold or glory in the islands of the West Indies. They began to search the mainland. In 1513, the same year that Balboa discovered the Pacific Ocean, a Spanish expedition landed in Florida. It was led by Juan Ponce de León (PAWN-say day lay-AWN), the governor of Puerto Rico. This was the first time the Spanish explored what is now the United States.

Ponce de León marched along the Florida coast, looking for gold and for the "Fountain of Youth." Indian tales said that drinking from the fountain would keep a man young forever. But the Florida Indians drove Ponce de Léon away. When he returned to continue his search, he was killed.

Cortés Conquers the Aztecs of Mexico

In 1519, a conquistador named Hernando Cortés (kor-TEZ) landed in Mexico with a few hundred soldiers. Mexico was the home of the rich and powerful Aztecs. There the Spanish finally found the gold they were looking for.

The Mexican Indians who met Cortés and his men didn't know what to think of them. They had never seen horses, steel swords, or guns. At first, they thought that the horses and their riders in metal armor were a single, huge, terrifying animal. They thought that the Spanish might be gods. The Aztec ruler, Moctezuma (mok-ta-ZOO-ma) (sometimes called Montezuma), sent the Spanish wonderful gold gifts. He hoped these gifts would satisfy the Spanish, and that they would go away. Exactly the opposite happened. The gifts made the Spanish even more eager to take the Aztec riches for themselves.

With luck, skill, and technology, Cortés quickly conquered the powerful Aztecs. He joined with other tribes who were enemies of the Aztecs. The Aztecs fought bravely, but their weapons were no match for the Spanish guns and steel swords. Their bodies had no protection from European diseases. Thousands of Aztecs were killed or died of disease. Cortés took control of the Aztec empire.

The Spanish were very surprised when they saw the huge and beautiful Aztec capital. They found it hard to believe that these non-Christians could build such a beautiful place. Cortés found large amounts of gold and silver. He sent most of it to the Spanish king. He destroyed the Aztec city and built a Spanish-style city in its place. This city, Mexico City, became the capital of Spain's American colony.

Pizarro Conquers the Incas of Peru

In 1532, the Spanish discovered an even richer Indian empire in South America. This was the empire of the Inca Indians of Peru. A conquistador named Francisco Pizarro (pee-ZAR-oh) sailed down the Pacific coast of South America to Peru. With a small band of soldiers, he marched into the Andes Mountains. There, in the heart of the Inca empire, he had a meeting with the Inca ruler, Atahualpa (ah-tah-WAL-puh). At the meeting, Pizarro suddenly took Atahualpa prisoner.

Atahualpa promised to fill a room full of gold for the Spanish if they would let him go. Pizarro agreed. The gold was brought from all parts of the Inca Empire. But the Spanish did not keep their word. They killed Atahualpa. Without their leader, most of the Incas gave up. Spain took over the Inca Empire. Peru became another Spanish colony.

The Aztec and Inca gold and silver made Spain the richest nation in Europe. It also made the Spanish eager to find even more riches.

SECTION REVIEW

Can you answer these Main Idea questions?

1. How did Spanish voyages and exploration change European ideas about the world?

2. How did the Spanish treat the Indians in America?

3. Why were the Spanish able to conquer the Aztecs and Incas so easily?

Can you identify and locate these places?

Mexico, Peru, Florida, California

Can you identify these people?

Ferdinand Magellan, Juan Ponce de León, Hernando Cortés, Francisco Pizarro

Can you define this word?

conquistador

2. EXPLORING AND SETTLING NORTH OF MEXICO

Main Ideas

Think about the following Main Idea questions as you read this section.

1. Why did the Spanish explore the region north of Mexico? What did they find?

2. Why did the Spanish settle Florida, New Mexico, and California?

3. How did the Spanish treat the Indians of New Mexico? And how did the Indians react to this treatment?

EXPLORING NORTH OF MEXICO

Cabeza de Vaca and Estevánico Journey Through the Southwest

The first long Spanish journey into what is now the United States took place by accident. In 1528, a group of Spanish explorers landed in Florida. Within a few months, sickness, swamps, unfriendly Indians, and starvation had killed most of them. The rest escaped, but a storm destroyed their boats. A few lucky men landed on the east Texas coast. They were captured by local Indians, who kept them as slaves for six years. Finally four of the Spaniards escaped, and their real journey began.

A Spanish nobleman named Cabeza de Vaca (ka-BAY-za day VAK-a) led them. He turned out to be a bold and intelligent leader. A black man from North Africa named Estevánico was also in the group. He was tall and fearless, and he learned Indian languages easily. For two years the little group wandered west toward the Gulf of California; then they turned south. Finally

they reached Mexico City. They had traveled almost 6,000 miles since they left Florida.

The Search for the Seven Cities of Cíbola

In Mexico City, Cabeza de Vaca and Estevánico repeated stories that the Indians had told them. The stories told of rich Indian towns to the north. The Spanish thought of the Inca and Aztec gold. They also remembered a Spanish tale of seven golden cities. They decided to search for these cities.

In 1539, Estevánico was sent to search for these cities. The search was led by a priest named Fray Marcos, or "Brother Marcos." Estevánico went ahead and sent back wonderful reports. One of his reports said he had found a land called **Cíbola**, with seven rich Indian cities. But then the reports stopped coming. Fray Marcos learned that Estevánico had been killed by angry Indians.

Fray Marcos returned to Mexico. There he told the governor about the Seven Cities of Cíbola. He added that he had actually seen one of them in the distance—a rich Indian city, with jewels in its walls.

Coronado's Expedition in the Southwest

Fray Marcos's report was all the governor needed. In 1540, he sent out a large expedition led by a soldier named Francisco Vásques de Coronado (kor-o-NAH-doh). Dressed in golden armor, Coronado set out at the head of more than a thousand soldiers and Indians. They crossed the harsh deserts of northern Mexico into what is now Arizona. There, Coronado sent out some small exploring parties. One of them discovered the Grand Canyon.

Coronado went north, then east. Finally he found the "Seven Cities." But they were not golden cities at all. They turned out to be the

Pueblo villages of the Zuni Indians. None of Fray Marcos's stories were true.

But Coronado did not turn back. An Indian guide told him of still another golden land farther east. He led his men around the southern tip of the Rocky Mountains and north onto the Great Plains. He went as far as what is now central Kansas, but he never found any gold. In 1542, the disappointed expedition returned to Mexico. It was the longest land exploration trip in Spanish history.

De Soto's Expedition in the Southeast

At the same time that Coronado was exploring the Southwest, another Spaniard was exploring the Southeast. Hernando de Soto had been a soldier with Pizarro in Peru. Now he wanted to find gold for himself. First he searched from Florida north to the Carolinas. Then he turned west and traveled almost as far as Oklahoma. On the way he met the last of the Mound Builder tribes and discovered the Mississippi River. But he became sick and died before he could return to Mexico. And, like Coronado, he never discovered any gold.

THE SPANISH COME TO STAY

Reasons for Spanish Settlement

Neither Coronado nor De Soto found any cities of gold north of Mexico. But the Spanish had other reasons for settling the area. They wanted to keep other countries from exploring or settling the lands that they claimed. The huge Spanish treasure ships needed safe places along the coast to stop for food and water. Spanish missionary priests wanted to convert the Indians to the Catholic religion. And there was always the hope that some gold, or at least silver, might be found.

The Spanish explored extensively throughout the southern and western portions of what is now the United States. Among the things they discovered are the Rio Grande, which Coronado found, the Grand Canyon, which men from Coronado's expedition found, and the Mississippi River, which De Soto discovered.

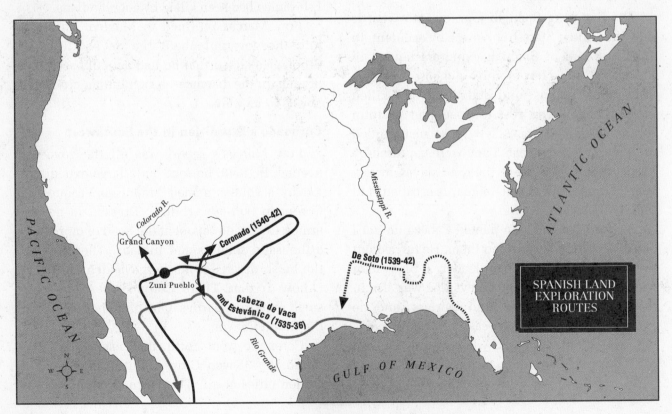

The Founding of St. Augustine in Florida

The first successful Spanish settlement in what is now the United States was started because a group of French settlers built a fort in Florida. The Spanish, who said they controlled Florida, found out about it. They killed all the settlers and destroyed the French fort. In 1565 they founded the town of St. Augustine nearby. It is the oldest successful European settlement in the United States.

St. Augustine kept other countries from starting settlements in Florida. Since it was on the coast, Spanish treasure ships stopped there. But not many Spaniards settled in St. Augustine. The town was never very large.

Settling New Mexico

The most successful Spanish settlements in what is now the United States were in the Southwest. In the mid-1500s, silver mines were discovered in the mountains of Mexico. A Mexican named Juan de Oñate (o-NYA-tay) thought that more mines might be found in the southern Rocky Mountains. In 1598 he led some soldier-settlers and Catholic priests up the Rio Grande river into what is now northern New Mexico.

Oñate didn't find any silver. But gradually, settlers built ranches along the Rio Grande or lived in small villages near Pueblo Indian towns. In 1610, Santa Fe was founded as the capital of New Mexico. It is the oldest state capital in the United States.

The Spanish treated the Indians of New Mexico cruelly. They made the Indians pay high taxes, forced them to work like slaves, killed any that objected, and almost destroyed their religion and way of life. The Indians revolted in 1680. Led by a religious leader named Popé (po-PAY), several Pueblo tribes attacked the Spanish and drove them out of New Mexico.

But Indian control did not last. The pueblos started quarreling with each other. In 1692, after 12 years, the Spanish returned. They quickly defeated the few pueblos that resisted. New Spanish settlers came to the area. Once again, New Mexico was under Spanish control.

Later Spanish Settlements in Arizona, Texas, and California

Other Spanish settlements in the Southwest began much later than in Florida and New Mexico. Tucson, Arizona, was founded in 1700, almost a hundred years after Santa Fe. San Antonio, Texas, was founded in 1718.

In California, there were no Spanish settlers at all until 1769. At that time, the government in Mexico sent a few missionaries, soldiers, and settlers to California. They wanted to stop the Russians, who were coming down the Pacific coast in search of furs. The Spanish forts in California were never very strong, but they showed that Spain controlled the area.

SECTION REVIEW

Can you answer these Main Idea questions?

1. Why did the Spanish explore the region north of Mexico? What did they find?

2. Why did the Spanish settle Florida, New Mexico, and California?

3. How did the Spanish treat the Indians of New Mexico? And how did the Indians react to this treatment?

Can you identify and locate these places?

St. Augustine, Santa Fe

Can you identify these people?

Cabeza de Vaca, Estevánico, Francisco de Coronado, Hernando de Soto, Popé

3. LIFE IN THE SPANISH COLONIES

Main Ideas

Think about the following Main Idea questions as you read this section.

1. What were the purposes of the Spanish missions and presidios?

2. Why and how did the Spanish settle in California?

3. In what ways have the Spanish contributed to modern American life?

MISSIONS AND PRESIDIOS IN THE SOUTHWEST

Spanish settlements in North America were not large. The harsh land, the hostile Indians, and a lack of settlers kept most settlements small. In the Southwest, the land was mostly desert or semi-desert. The Southeast was mostly swamps. Almost everywhere food was scarce and hard to grow.

Missions

At the heart of each settlement was the **mission**. A mission was a combination of a church, a farm, and a workshop. Missions were run by Catholic missionary priests. Their purpose was to turn local Indians into good Christians and good workers. They tried to replace the Indians' culture and way of life with Spanish Catholic culture.

Presidios

Away from the missions, the Indians were often hostile. In Texas and New Mexico, Comanche, Apache, and Navajo Indians raided Spanish settlements. They took horses, cattle, and sheep. In some areas, soldiers protected the missions—and also kept unhappy settlers from returning to Mexico. The soldiers often lived in a **presidio** (prih SEED ee oh), or fort, near the mission or the town.

 A California mission. Self-contained religious communities, the missions were villages in themselves, with living quarters, storerooms, and workshops (left), a church (center—the main building), and even a cemetery (the small courtyard at right). Surrounding farms, worked by Indian labor, provided food and animals.

Ranches and Villages

All these settlements were far from the center of Spanish power in Mexico City. The settlers had no voice in their government. All land was owned by the king or the Catholic Church. The king sometimes gave land to individuals, and they became rich ranchers. But usually land belonged to a whole village, not to the farmers in it.

Some of the settlers used captured Indian children as slaves in their homes and on their ranches. The government in Spain wanted to protect the Indians. But the Spanish king was an ocean away, and his wishes were often ignored.

Spanish law said that the settlers could trade only with Mexico, which was weeks away by sea or by donkey train. Settlers had a long wait for the things they wanted. Sometimes these things never came at all. Not many people wanted to live such a hard life, so few settlers came.

LIFE IN CALIFORNIA

The California Missions

The California missions were more successful than those in Texas and New Mexico. Many were started by one missionary, Father Junípero Serra. Father Serra founded the mission of San Diego in 1769. He started eight others in later years. By the early 1800's, there was a chain of 21 Spanish missions along the California coast. They went from San Diego to slightly north of San Francisco. They were given large amounts of land, and they became very rich.

Almost all of California's Indians were peaceful, and almost all who lived near the missions were converted to the Catholic religion. For these Indians, the mission was church, school, home, and farm. California missions raised farm crops and cattle and made wine. Some had enough hides to trade with other missions and with passing ships.

A Spanish rancher, or "ranchero," surveying his holdings. Spanish cowboys, called "vaqueros," worked the ranches for the rancheros. ▶

Mission life was strict. Indians who tried to leave were forced to come back. Indians had to work long hours, and their Indian customs and religion were taken away. Spanish speech, customs, even food and dress replaced their own ways. Three quarters of the Mission Indians died from Spanish illnesses.

Ranches in California

In 1821, Mexico became independent. All the Spanish lands from Texas to California became part of Mexico. The new Mexican government broke up the California missions. Their lands and cattle were sold to a small number of California settlers who had started ranches. Most of these ranchers became very rich and successful. Because of California's mild climate, California ranchers could raise huge herds of cattle. They lived very well, with plenty of feasting, parties, and celebrations. California was so far from Mexico that the ranchers ignored many Mexican laws and did what they pleased. Sometimes they made trouble for the Mexican governors because they were used to governing themselves.

The Spanish Contribution

There were never more than a few thousand Spanish settlers in what is now the United States. But the Spanish have greatly influenced American life, especially in the West.

The Spanish brought horses, cows, and sheep to this continent. The Indians who rode horses on the Western plains got them from the Spanish. Western-style clothing, from hat to boots, was developed by the Spanish. American cowboys use equipment invented by the Spanish: Western saddles, lassos to rope cattle, and chaps to protect the legs when riding through brush. Western horses have Spanish names, like *bronco* and *mustang*. Even the idea of a ranch—and the word itself—comes from those early Spanish settlers.

Words to describe the Western landscape are often Spanish: *mesa* for a flat-topped hill, and *canyon* for a deep valley with narrow sides. Spanish-style houses are found throughout the Southwest. Western slang has many mispronounced Spanish words, like *savvy* for "know" and *calaboose* for "jail."

Seven Western states have Spanish names or names that the Spanish took from the Indians (Arizona, California, Colorado, Montana, Nevada, New Mexico, and Texas).

Finally, there is the Spanish gift to American music, the guitar, which originally came from Spain.

The Spanish were the first Europeans to see the promise of the New World. They came looking for gold. They found none in what is now the United States, but in looking for it, they explored the Southeast and Southwest. Their small settlements were spread over a huge area. Their missions converted, protected, and caused the death of many Indians. The Spanish changed what they found and were changed by it, too.

SECTION REVIEW

Can you answer these Main Idea questions?

1. What were the purposes of the Spanish missions and presidios?

2. Why and how did the Spanish settle in California?

3. In what ways have the Spanish contributed to modern American life?

Can you identify this person?

Father Junípero Serra

Can you define these terms?

mission, presidio, canyon

AFTER YOU READ

Discussion Questions

1. How did the Spanish act in America? You may wish to discuss such topics as how the Spanish got land, how they treated the Native Americans, and how they got the gold they wanted. Give facts that support each of your answers.

2. Were the Spanish successful in America? List facts that support your answer. What do you mean by success?

3. In what ways was religion an important part of life in the Spanish colonies?

Comprehension Questions

1. Each of the following explorers or conquistadors did something that was very important because it changed the way people thought or lived. Write a sentence which explains what each one did and why it was important.

   a. Ferdinand Magellan

   b. Hernando Cortés

   c. Francisco Pizarro

2. List five places in America that Spain claimed. Choose two and tell what their natural environment was like. Use information from Chapter 1.

3. What goods did the Spanish conquistadors and colonists send back to their mother country?

4. Look at the list below. Which two things were powerful forces back in Spain that controlled what happened in the Spanish colonies?

   Indians, explorers, farmers, the King, Muslims, the Catholic Church, traders

5. The Spanish wanted to change the culture of the people who already lived in America. Explain what they wanted to do. Give two examples of how they tried to do it.

6. Which two of the following statements are supported by facts in the chapter? Write *supported* or *unsupported* for each one.

   a. Colonies quickly become more powerful than their mother country.

   b. Colonies change life for the people who live in a place before the colonists arrive.

   c. Colonies are in beautiful places and quickly fill with colonists.

   d. The mother country took anything from the colonies that would make it rich.

7. Look back at your answers to Question 6. For each statement that you chose, list two facts from the chapter that support it.

Writing Activity

Choose a place in one of the Spanish colonies. Pretend you live there. List everything you know about its natural environment (use Chapter 1 to help you). Then list everything you know about life in that place. Include what people do, government rules, travel, and trade. Finally, use your lists to write a paragraph that tells what you like and don't like about living in this colony.

CHAPTER 6

FRENCH EXPLORERS AND SETTLERS

The French did not settle in America until many years after the Spanish. First they were explorers, looking for a sea route through America to China. Later, French fur traders and farmers came to America. Their early settlements were in the north, along the St. Lawrence River and around the Great Lakes. They later settled along the Mississippi River and founded the city of New Orleans.

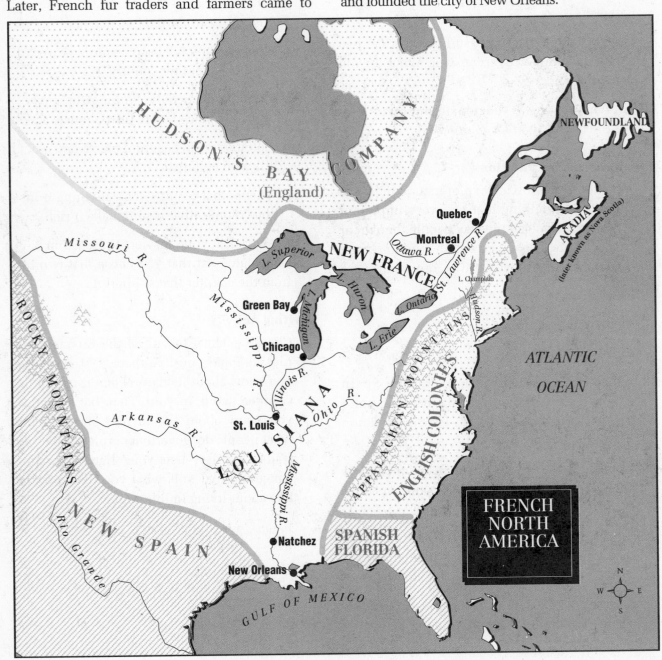

FRENCH NORTH AMERICA

BEFORE YOU READ

Sections in This Chapter

1. Early French Explorers and Settlers
2. The Growth of New France

Reading a Map

Study the map on the opposite page. Then answer these questions about it.

1. What two present-day countries cover the area shown on the map?

2. The French used mostly water routes to explore the area from Nova Scotia to New Orleans. Sometimes they sailed on the Atlantic Ocean, but mostly they used inland water routes. What inland water routes might they have taken?

3. Why do you think the French built their towns along waterways?

4. Compare this map to the one at the beginning of Chapter 5. Did Spain and France claim any of the same area?

Understanding a Key Concept: ALLY

An **ally** is someone who joins with you for a purpose. Usually it is a friend who helps and protects you. You do the same for him or her. The Algonquin Indians were allies with the Huron Indians. They supported and protected each other against their enemies, the Iroquois Indians.

Read each of the situations at the top of the next column. Write a sentence which tells whether or not the people are allies. The first is done for you.

1. Best friends standing up to a bully together

These best friends are allies.

2. The Spanish conquistador Pizarro and the Inca Indians

3. A group of students working together to get better food in the lunchroom

4. The Spanish and Russian colonists in California

5. The European countries that fought the Crusades

6. The Portuguese and the African people of the Congo

Using What You Already Know

The French traded with the Indians. They traded French goods for furs. Think about what you know about the Woodland Indians. List 3 items from the list below that the Indians didn't have but might get from trade with the French.

metal knives   houses   guns   glass beads
food   bullets   animal skins   cotton cloth

Now pick one item from your list. Describe what the Indians used before they had this item. An example is done for you:

The Indians used knives with stone blades before they got metal knives.

1. EARLY FRENCH EXPLORERS AND SETTLERS

Main Ideas

Think about the following Main Idea questions as you read this section.

1. Why did the early French explorers and colonists come to America?

2. Why was the French trade important to the Algonquin and Huron Indians?

THE FRENCH EXPLORE THE COAST OF NORTH AMERICA

Verrazano Discovers New York Harbor

The first explorer to sail from France to America was an Italian, Giovanni da Verrazano, (jo-VAH-nee da vair-uh-ZAH-no). In 1524, he explored the coast from northern Florida to Newfoundland, looking for a water route to China. He was the first European to visit what is now New York Harbor. More than 400 years later a huge bridge was built across that harbor and named for him.

Cartier Explores the St. Lawrence River

A few years after Verrazano, a French explorer named Jacques Cartier (ZHAK kar-TYAY) sailed to America. Like the Spanish explorers, he was searching for gold and a route to the Indies. During his three voyages, Cartier explored the Newfoundland coast and sailed up the St. Lawrence River. He hoped the river was the way to the Pacific Ocean, but it wasn't. Each time he came to America, he traded with the Indians—their furs for French goods, like metal knives.

After Cartier, French explorers lost interest in America. During the next 60 years, only fishermen came here. They also brought back furs that they got from the Indians.

CHAMPLAIN AND THE ST. LAWRENCE RIVER SETTLEMENTS

Champlain Founds New France

In 1604, a company in France decided to build up the fur trade. They sent Samuel de Champlain (sham-PLANE) to America. This was the first of Champlain's 11 voyages to America.

Champlain started the French colony called New France. He built the first French settlement in what is now Nova Scotia, Canada (it was called Acadia at the time). In 1608, he founded the city of Quebec as a trading center on the St. Lawrence River. He explored most of the St. Lawrence Valley, the Great Lakes, and the lake that is named for him, Lake Champlain.

In 1642, the town of Montreal was built where the Ottawa and St. Lawrence rivers join. These rivers were the safest, easiest routes for Indian and French trappers and traders.

Fur Trading with the Huron Indians

A strong friendship grew up between Champlain and the Algonquin and Huron Indians. They became **allies**—people who helped each other in peace and in war. The Hurons were traders as well as trappers. They traveled west to trade with far-away Indians. Then they brought the furs to Montreal.

The furs, especially beaver and otter, were sent to France. There they were made into felt cloth, which was then made into hats. Fur was also used to make coats and to decorate clothes.

Soon Montreal became the center of the French fur trade. The Indians traded their furs for European goods, such as metal tools, kettles, knives, and cloth. The Indians did not have the technology to make metal, glass, or cotton cloth. They had to get these things from the French.

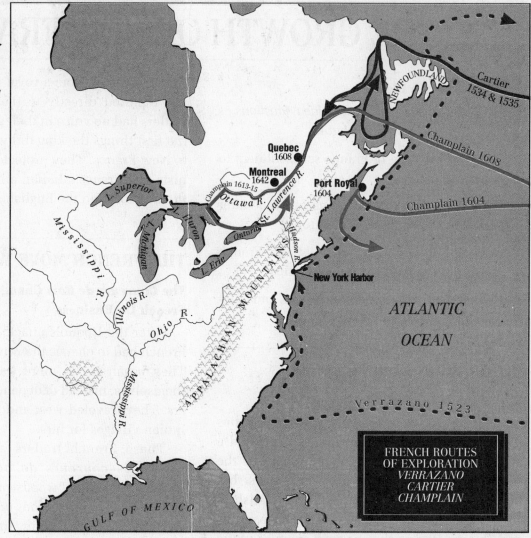

The routes of exploration of three famous French explorers. Verrazano sailed up the coast of North America but never went inland. Cartier explored the area around Newfoundland and partway down the St. Lawrence River. Champlain, the most important of the French explorers, explored extensively along the St. Lawrence, reaching the Great Lakes.

FRENCH ROUTES
OF EXPLORATION
*VERRAZANO
CARTIER
CHAMPLAIN*

Settlers and Farmers in New France

The French government wanted farms as well as trading posts in America, so the fur company promised to bring farmers to New France. The farms that they started were just like those in France. Rich men were given the land, and they sent farmers to work on it. Each farmer paid rent to the landowner. All the settlers wanted to live along the St. Lawrence River. The result was a string of farms, each touching the river.

Not many French colonists came to New France. Most of the ones who did come were men. There were few women or children. And since a fur trader could make more money than a farmer, many farmers left their farms and became traders.

SECTION REVIEW

Can you answer these Main Idea questions?

1. Why did the early French explorers and colonists come to America?

2. Why was the French trade important to the Algonquins and the Huron Indians?

Can you identify and locate these places?

Nova Scotia, Quebec City, Montreal

Can you identify these people?

Giovanni da Verrazano, Jacques Cartier, Samuel de Champlain

2. THE GROWTH OF NEW FRANCE

Main Ideas

Answer these Main Idea questions as you read this section.

1. Why did the king of France send soldiers to America?

2. What happened to the French fur trade after the Iroquois destroyed the Hurons?

3. How did the *coureurs de bois* and French missionaries adapt to life in America?

4. How and why did French explorers and colonists move west and south?

CHANGES IN NEW FRANCE

The Iroquois Destroy the Hurons

The French traded mostly with their allies the Algonquin and Huron Indians. They had a common enemy—the Iroquois Indians to the south. The Iroquois were also fur traders, but they took their furs to the Dutch and English in New York. They were enemies of the Algonquins and Hurons, and so they became enemies of the French as well.

Like other American Indians, many Hurons died from European illnesses. Their tribe grew smaller. And to the south, their enemies the Iroquois were running out of beavers to trap. The Iroquois needed to extend their fur-trapping and trading power. The English encouraged them, for the English and the French were old enemies. In 1649 Iroquois warriors attacked the Huron tribe and forced them off their land. But the Iroquois did not succeed in completely taking over the Huron fur trade. Instead, an Algonquin tribe, the Ottawas, took it over.

The French Government Takes Control

In 1663, the French government took control of New France away from the French company.

New France became a royal colony. The governor reported directly to the French king. The settlers had no voice in their government. One of the first things the king did was to send soldiers to New France. They protected the French colonists and France's Indian allies from attacks by the Iroquois and the English.

THE FRENCH MOVE WEST

The *Coureurs de Bois* Change the Way the French Do Business

After the Iroquois attack on the Hurons, the French had to change the way they did business. They began to do more trapping and trading themselves, instead of depending on Indian traders. They traveled west and traded with distant Indian villages for furs.

These French traders and trappers were known as **coureurs de bois** (koo-RER duh BWAH), meaning "woods rangers." They lived and traveled as the Indians did, but they changed some Indian ways of doing things to fit their own needs. They used waterways and canoes, but they built bigger canoes than the Indians did. They wore skins like the Indians, but made them into European pants, shirts, and jackets. Often they lived among the Indians for several years before they brought their furs back to a trading post.

When beaver and otter became scarce in the East, the traders moved further west or north to where there were still many animals. Soon, small trading posts and forts were built along the Great Lakes. *Coureurs de bois* and local Indians brought their furs to these places instead of to larger, far-away towns like Montreal.

Missionaries in New France

Traders were not the only Frenchmen who went west. Most of the French, like the Spanish,

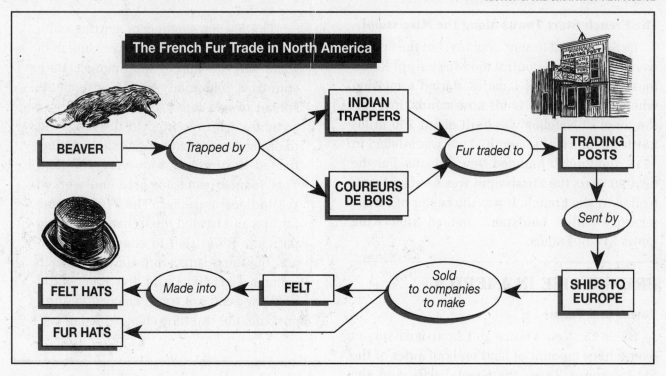

The French Fur Trade in North America

BEAVER → Trapped by → INDIAN TRAPPERS / COUREURS DE BOIS → Fur traded to → TRADING POSTS → Sent by → SHIPS TO EUROPE → Sold to companies to make → FELT → Made into → FELT HATS / FUR HATS

were Catholic. Many French priests came to America to convert the Indians. When a trading post was built, the missionaries moved nearby. They built small missions or lived with an Indian tribe.

The French missionary priests realized that the Indian way of life was very different from their own. They tried to learn about it before working to convert the Indians. They did not try to make the Indians do everything the French way. And, unlike the Spanish, they did not force the Indians to work for them. However, despite the fact that the French missionaries did not treat the Indians badly, very few became Christians. Most kept their own religion and culture.

THE FRENCH EXPLORE THE MISSISSIPPI RIVER

Marquette and Joliet's Expedition

From the western forts and missions, Frenchmen left to explore more of America. In 1673, Father Jacques Marquette (mar-KET), a missionary, and Louis Joliet (zhohl-YAY), a fur trader, left the mission at Green Bay on Lake Michigan.

They traveled by canoe down small rivers until they reached the Mississippi River. Then they paddled down the Mississippi almost to what is now the state of Louisiana.

Marquette and Joliet hoped that the great river might be a route to the Pacific Ocean. It wasn't, and, disappointed, they returned. They traveled up the Illinois River to the tip of Lake Michigan, where Chicago now stands. Marquette and Joliet were the first Europeans to travel down the Mississippi.

La Salle Explores the Whole Mississippi

Eight years later, another French explorer, the Sieur (Lord) de La Salle, followed the same river. He followed it south all the way to the Gulf of Mexico. Along the way he built forts to protect France's claim that the Mississippi Valley belonged to France. France was afraid that English colonies to the east or Spanish colonies to the south and west might take over the area.

A few years later, La Salle brought colonists from France to settle at the mouth of the Mississippi. Unfortunately, he missed the river and began his colony on the Texas coast. His colony failed, and many colonists died. La Salle was killed by angry colonists.

The French Start Towns Along the Mississippi

La Salle failed to start a colony, but the French were still eager to control the Mississippi River. In 1700, French missionaries started a mission where the city of St. Louis now stands. In 1716, the town of Natchez was built about 250 miles north of the river's mouth. Two years later, in 1718, the French founded New Orleans. For the next 50 years the Mississippi was used and controlled by the French. It was the center of a huge territory called **Louisiana**, named after King Louis XIV of France.

FRENCH LIFE IN AMERICA

Towns and Farms

By 1725, New France and Louisiana spread over a huge amount of land on both sides of the St. Lawrence River, the Great Lakes, and the Mississippi River. However, the actual French settlements were small. There were never very many of them, and there were many miles between each one. All of the settlements were built near a waterway, and most were fur trading posts.

In their few villages and farms, the French settlers built log cabins, with the logs placed up and down. They built wide porches on their houses and grew beautiful gardens. In the South, slaves worked on their farms.

French colonists were not allowed to make many of the goods they needed. French law said that they could not spin or weave their own cloth. Cloth had to be brought from France. Furniture, dishes, and other household goods had to be shipped in, too. This trade helped businesses in France, but it cost the colonists a lot of money.

The French, the Indians, and the Wilderness

Unlike the Spanish, the French didn't force the Indians to work for them. They wanted furs from the Indians, and furs were found only in the forests. So they traded with the Indians and did nothing that would destroy the natural environment.

The French method of starting colonies and governing them was similar in some ways to that of the Spanish. Both countries had many small settlements spread over a large area, governed by a governor who reported to the king. But their reasons for settling and the way they treated the Indians were very different. The Spanish came for gold and worked the Indians as slaves. The French came for furs and treated the Indians as trading partners. Both tried to convert the Indians, but the Spanish forced the Indians to become Christians and the French did not. They did not try to change the Indians' life, nor did they change the land.

SECTION REVIEW

Can you answer these MainIdea questions?

1. Why did the king of France send soldiers to America?

2. What happened to the French fur trade after the Iroquois destroyed the Hurons?

3. How did the *coureurs de bois* and French missionaries adapt to life in America?

4. How and why did French explorers and colonists move west and south?

Can you identify and locate these places?

Lake Michigan, New Orleans, Louisiana

Can you identify these people?

coureurs de bois, Father Jacques Marquette, Louis Joliet, La Salle

AFTER YOU READ

Discussion Questions

1. How did the French affect the environment of their American colony?

2. Compare the way the Spanish acted toward the Indians to the way the French acted.

3. Do you think trade or religion was more important in the French colony? What facts support your idea?

4. Which European colonists, the French or the Spanish, do you think were changed the most by America and its people? Support your opinion with facts.

Comprehension Questions

I. Read the following paragraph. Fill in the blanks with ideas from the chapter. For each blank, choose a word or phrase from the list below that correctly finishes the sentence. Read each sentence carefully before you make your choice.

When the French first came to North America, they found the Indians had something they wanted, **1** _____. The French **2** _____ with the Indians for their furs. The French gave them **3** _____, **4** _____, and **5** _____. These were important to the Indians because they did not have the **6** _____ to make these things themselves. The Indians began to **7** _____ the French for these things.

1. gold   furs   canoes   metal tools
2. ate   sang   fished   traded
3. animals   metal pots   furs   gold
4. metal knives   canoes   homes   ships
5. silk cloth   guns   wild animals   slaves
6. money   technology   clothes   wood
7. steal furs from   depend on   attack   feed

II. On a separate sheet of paper, make up a chart that looks like this. Use facts from Chapters 5 and 6 to complete the chart.

	Early Spanish colonies in America	Early French colonies in America
Main things taken from America		
Ways they treated the Indians		
Religion and the Indians		
Environment of colonies		
How colonists made a living		
Where laws made		

Writing Activity

Write a short paragraph that compares the French and Spanish colonies in America. Use your chart. Follow these steps:

- Choose one topic area from the chart. Write a sentence or two that describes either how the Spanish and French colonies were the same or how they were different for that topic.

- Do the same for two other topics.

- Write a topic sentence that is supported by all three of the three sentences you wrote.

- Rewrite your sentences so that they form a single paragraph.

THE ENGLISH

At the same time that the French and Spanish were planting colonies in the New World, so were the English. However, while the Spanish came for gold and the French came for furs, the English came to settle. They did so for many reasons. Some, like the French and Spanish, came mostly in hopes of making a fortune; others came in order to be free to practice their religion, or because they had been poor in England and wanted a second chance. But whatever their reason, they came to make their homes in America.

As a result, it was England, and not France or Spain, that had the largest influence on what would become the United States. This influence can be seen in our society, in our government, and most especially in our shared language, English.

Despite their common roots, the English colonies were not all the same. The colonies in the north (called the New England Colonies) and in the south were very different from each other and from the colonies in the middle. There were differences in how the people in each area earned their livings, in what religion they practiced and how important religion was to them, in how tolerant they were of others—the list goes on and on. These differences, many of which are still with us today, play important roles in American history.

COLONIES

CHAPTER 7

THE SOUTHERN COLONIES

Like the French, the English began settling in America long after the Spanish. Their first North American colonies were along the Atlantic coast. At first, they came hoping to find gold, just like Spain had hoped to find in Mexico and South America. Instead, they found other riches: fish and furs, fertile soil, and tall timber.

The English did something that the Spanish and French did not do. They started many successful farming colonies. These colonies grew rapidly, as thousands of colonists moved to America. The English colonists made America their home and worked hard to change it to meet their needs.

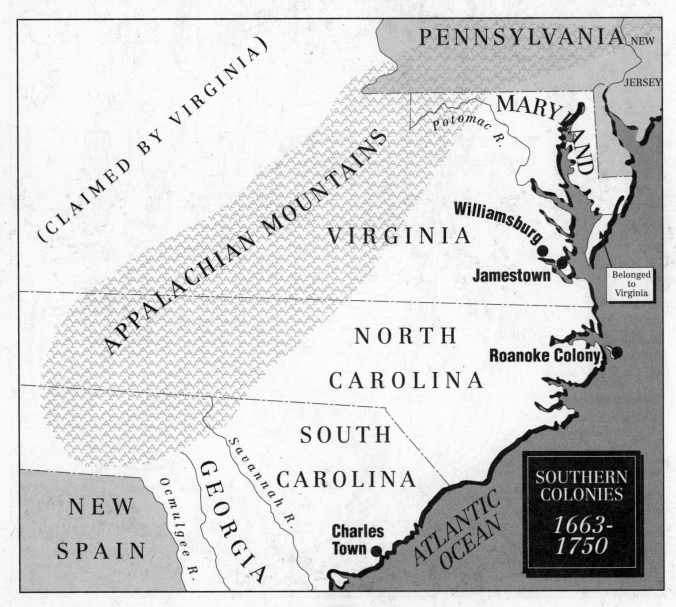

PENNSYLVANIA
NEW JERSEY
(CLAIMED BY VIRGINIA)
Potomac R.
MARYLAND
APPALACHIAN MOUNTAINS
VIRGINIA
Williamsburg
Jamestown
Belonged to Virginia
NORTH CAROLINA
Roanoke Colony
SOUTH CAROLINA
Savannah R.
GEORGIA
Ocmulgee R.
NEW SPAIN
Charles Town
ATLANTIC OCEAN

SOUTHERN COLONIES
1663-1750

BEFORE YOU READ

Sections in This Chapter

1. The English Come to America
2. Virginia—The First Permanent English Colony
3. Other Southern Colonies
4. Life in the Southern Colonies

Reading a Map

Use the map on the opposite page to answer each of these questions.

1. What English colonies are shown on this map?

2. What feature shown on the map might make travel difficult? What might make travel easy? (Remember, you can travel either by land or by boat.)

Understanding a Key Concept: GOVERNMENT

A **government** is an organization made up of people who decide the laws and enforce them. For example, Spain's government was the king and the people he chose to help him. They decided the laws for Spain and for the Spanish colonies, like Mexico. They sent a Spanish governor and soldiers to each colony to enforce these laws.

A **representative government** is one in which the people choose *representatives* to govern them. These representatives decide the laws and enforce them. The English colonies had a governor appointed by the English king. But the colonists also elected representatives to an assembly. The assembly helped the governor write and enforce laws.

Use what you know about government to answer the following questions.

1. Does the United States have a representative government today? Support your answer with a fact about our government.

2. Did the Spanish colony of New Mexico have a representative government?

3. Did the Iroquois had a representative government? Support your answer with facts.

4. Why do you think people like representative governments?

Using What You Already Know

In the American colonies, labor was scarce. There were not enough people to do all the jobs.

1. How did the first Spanish colonists in the West Indies solve the problem of scarce labor for their farms?

2. How did the Spanish in the Southwest and California solve the problem of scarce labor on their missions?

3. Many of the first English colonists were gentlemen. They did not want to do jobs like building houses and growing food. What are some ways they could have solved their labor shortage?

4. Many English colonists had large families. How might this help the problem of scarce labor on their farms?

5. Some colonists paid for poor English people to come to America. These *indentured servants* then had to work for several years for the people who had paid their way. Then they could go off on their own. What kinds of jobs might a colonial farmer give an indentured servant to do?

1. THE ENGLISH COME TO AMERICA

Main Ideas

Think about the following Main Idea questions as you read this section:

1. Why did so many years pass between the time that the English claimed land in America and the time that the first English colonists arrived?

2. The English and the Spanish were rivals. How did this affect their American colonies?

3. Why did the two Roanoke colonies fail?

EXPLORATION AND NEGLECT

John Cabot's Voyage to America

The English first explored America shortly after Columbus's voyages. In 1496, only four years after Columbus's first voyage, King Henry VII of England sent John Cabot to find a northern route to the Indies. Like Columbus, Cabot was an Italian sea captain in the employ of a foreign country.

Cabot started from Ireland and sailed across the northern Atlantic. Although his route was shorter than Columbus's, his trip took just as long. This was because Cabot's ship had to fight winds and currents that were pushing it back toward Europe.

Cabot's men were the first Europeans since the Norsemen to visit North America. They explored the coast and claimed it for England. They landed only one time and didn't find anything that interested them. Their return trip took only half as long as their trip west. This time, the winds and currents were helping them.

Cabot left on a second trip west in 1498. He was never heard from again. His ship may have sunk in an Atlantic storm. These storms often caused problems for ships. During bad weather, a ship might take months to go from Europe to America. Some ships, like Cabot's, just disappeared.

England Loses Interest in America

For almost a hundred years after Cabot, England left North America alone. The English had to solve many problems inside their own country. Few English explorers went out, and no colonies were started. Spain and Portugal were the important European powers in the Western Hemisphere.

THE ROANOKE COLONY

English Adventurers Raid the Spanish

By the time Elizabeth I became queen of England in the late 1500's, England was becoming a strong power again. In trade, religion, and politics, England and Spain were rivals. King Philip of Spain tried to solve these problems. He held talks with the English. He tried to marry Queen Elizabeth. Nothing worked. Spain and England went to war.

Queen Elizabeth wanted Spain's riches for England. She encouraged English adventurers to raid Spanish ships and Spanish colonies. In fact, she helped pay for these private pirate raids. English adventurers, like Sir Francis Drake, attacked Spanish ships and ports. They captured gold, silks, and jewels and brought them back to England.

Sir Walter Raleigh Founds the Roanoke Colony

Sir Walter Raleigh (RAH lee) was another English adventurer. Besides raiding, he planned England's first colony in America in 1585. It was located on **Roanoke Island** (ROH uhn oke), off the coast of what is now North Carolina.

The Roanoke colonists were gentlemen in search of riches. They were not willing to work. The local Indians had never seen people act the way these men did. They didn't plan for winter, and they didn't listen when Indians tried to help. Instead of farming, they raided Indian towns for food and waited for ships to bring them supplies. After a year, an English ship took them back to England. The Indians were not sorry to see them leave.

The Colony Fails

Raleigh tried again. In 1587, he sent more colonists to Roanoke. They didn't have enough supplies, so they sent their leader, John White, back to England to get help.

Help was a long time in coming. In 1588, King Philip of Spain had had enough of English raids. He sent the **Spanish Armada** (ahr MAH duh) to attack England. An armada is a large fleet of ships. The Spanish Armada was the largest naval force Europe had seen up to that time. The Spanish attack turned into a disaster, though. Many Spanish ships were destroyed by the smaller, faster English ships. Even more were destroyed by terrible storms. The Spanish lost so many ships, they were no longer the strongest sea power in the world.

During this time, no English ships went to America, because they were all needed to protect England. The supplies for Roanoke weren't sent until the Armada was destroyed. When Governor White finally returned in 1590, the settlement was empty, and the only clue was a few letters scratched on a pole. What happened to those first English colonists still remains a mystery to this day.

SECTION REVIEW

Can you answer these Main Idea questions?

1. Why did so many years pass between the time that the English claimed land in America and the time that the first English colonists arrived?

2. The English and the Spanish were rivals. How did this affect their American colonies?

3. Why did the two Roanoke colonies fail?

Can you identify these people?

John Cabot, Sir Walter Raleigh, King Philip, Queen Elizabeth

Can you explain these terms?

Spanish Armada, Roanoke colonies

▼ *The Jamestown colony (see next page). The colony was built for defense against Indian attacks: the triangular section was a fort, a wooden wall surrounded the entire colony, and the James River protected the colony's back.*

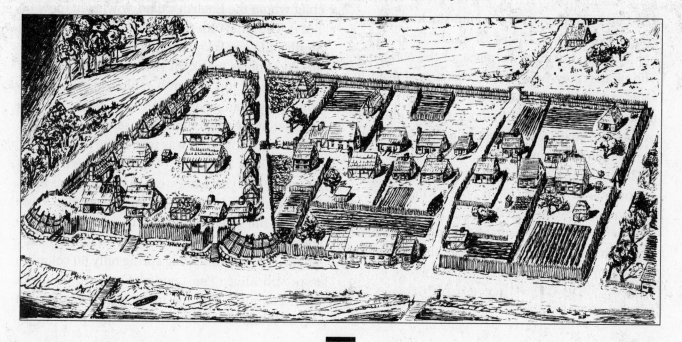

2. VIRGINIA—THE FIRST PERMANENT ENGLISH COLONY

Main Ideas

Think about the following Main Idea questions as you read this section:

1. What problems did the early Jamestown colonists have? How did they solve them?

2. How did tobacco and slavery change life in Virginia for colonists, Africans, and Indians?

3. How did the Virginia colonists solve their problem of scarce labor?

4. What made the House of Burgesses a representative assembly?

THE FOUNDING OF VIRGINIA

The London Company Gets Permission to Start a Colony

About 15 years after the disaster at Roanoke, the English decided to try again. The London Company was formed to start a new colony in Virginia. The London Company was a **joint-stock** company. People would buy shares of stock. Each stockholder owned a share, or piece, of the company. The money they paid for the shares was used to start and run the colony. If the company made money, it would be split among the people who owned the stock. Many people bought shares in the London Company.

The London Company got its charter, or written permission to start a colony, from King James I. The company owned all the land. The company's directors in England made all the important decisions. The colonists just worked for the company.

The London Company Founds Jamestown

The first London Company colonists arrived in Virginia in 1607. They named their town "Jamestown" for King James I, the new king. They built their town (a picture of Jamestown is on the previous page) at what seemed like a good place. Nobody knew that a nearby swamp was filled with mosquitoes which carried disease. Over the years, thousands of colonists would die from disease.

The first colonists, like the colonists at Roanoke, wanted to look for gold, not build houses or plant corn. Over half of them died the first winter. They weren't trained to survive in the woods, to farm, or even to build a house. In addition, the colonists didn't get along well with the Indians who lived nearby.

Captain John Smith Leads the Colony

One leader, Captain John Smith, saved the colony. Smith took control and forced the colonists to work. He also kept an uneasy peace with the Indians. According to legend, he was captured by the Indians, who took him to the important chief whom the English called Powhatan (pow uh TAN). The chief ordered his men to kill Smith, but Smith's life was saved by the chief's young daughter, Pocahontas (pohk uh HAHN tus). She put her own head on top of Smith's, blocking the execution. Powhatan gave in, and even made Smith a member of the tribe. Smith himself told this story, but no one knows if it was really true or not.

Smith was the leader of the Jamestown colony for nearly two years and worked the colonists hard. When he left in 1609, the colonists were glad to see him go. But after he left, no one forced the 500 colonists to work for the good of all, so they stopped. By the following spring only 60 colonists were still alive. The London Company sent out more colonists, but for many years, Jamestown stayed small.

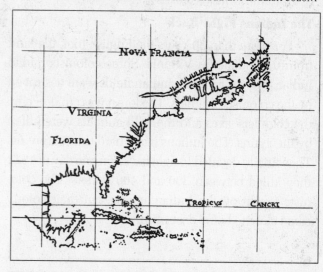

This is how the London Company pictured the east coast of North America in the early 1600's. While there are many mistakes, the general outline can be clearly identified.

Problems in the Colony

The first colonists tried to live as they had in England. They wanted food to be brought to them, rather than hunting or growing it themselves. They would wait for supplies to come from England, or steal food from the Indian villages.

Later colonists learned to do things for themselves. They learned how to use tools they weren't familiar with, like guns and axes. They cut down trees to make fields for planting. They built homes, made cloth, and hunted. They used many skills most people in England had not needed for 100 years or more.

The London Company Gives Land Away

The London Company was not happy with its colony. The Indians were mistreated, no gold had been found, and the colonists kept dying. So the company made some changes.

Instead of owning all the land, the company offered to give land away. For each person who came to Jamestown, 50 acres of land would be given to the person who had paid for their transportation. That way a person who paid for ten people to come over got more land than a person who just paid for himself. From then on, many people came to Virginia to start their own farms. The richest brought many people so they could get lots of land.

The company directors, however, continued to control trade. They demanded that the farmers grow what people in England wanted. They told the farmers to grow silk, sugar, and hemp. Unfortunately, none of these grew well in Virginia. The farmers ignored what the company wanted. They grew the crops that did well in Virginia's climate. The company soon found out that it couldn't enforce its rules from across the ocean.

TOBACCO BECOMES THE MOST IMPORTANT CROP

John Rolfe Brings Tobacco to Virginia

In 1612, a Virginia colonist named John Rolfe made a discovery that changed the Virginia colony forever. He found that West Indian tobacco grew well in Virginia. Tobacco sold for high prices in England. Soon everyone in Virginia was growing it. Rolfe later married Pocahontas, and members of their family still live in Virginia.

Tobacco Causes Problems

People could make so much money growing and selling tobacco that some people grew it instead of food. Rich farmers grew it on large farms called **plantations**. The tobacco farmers ran into an unexpected problem, however. Tobacco quickly uses up the soil. The tobacco farmers needed fresh land every few years.

That didn't bother the colonists. There was plenty of rich land. The colonists believed that the land belonged to the English king, not to the Indians. Besides, the colonists thought, Indians move around a lot. Let them move somewhere else. So the tobacco farmers took over the land. They cut down the forests where the animals lived that the Indians hunted. The animals left, and there was less food for both the Indians and the colonists.

The Indians Fight Back

For more than 30 years the English took the land from the Indians in Virginia. Some colonists raided Indian villages for food. Indian fields were destroyed by the colonists' animals. The forest was cut down by the colonists' axes and the wild animals were killed by their guns. The Indians had a hard time surviving. They finally decided to fight back. On one day in 1622 they killed between 300 and 400 settlers. The colonists fought off the Indian attacks, but their colony came close to being destroyed.

WHO WILL DO THE WORK?

Farmers Do Things for Themselves

Growing tobacco was hard work, but each farmer wanted to grow as much tobacco as possible. There was plenty of land, but not enough workers.

The colonists solved the problem of scarce labor in several ways. First, they learned to do many things for themselves. Back in England, people could hire someone to help with the work. They could buy products that had been made by trained craftspeople. In Virginia, however, there were few craftspeople or people trained for special jobs, like doctors. The colonists had to learn how to do many different tasks themselves. They had to be their own farmers, doctors, teachers, blacksmiths, weavers, and candle makers.

Another way to get work done was to raise a large family. At first there were few women in Jamestown, but soon many women and even families came to Virginia. Colonists had large families, and the whole family worked long hours on the farm.

Indentured Servants

Richer colonists solved their scarce labor problem in still another way. They paid for workers to come from England. These workers were called indentured servants. **Indentured servants** were people who wanted to come to America, but who were too poor to pay their own way. A colonist paid their transportation and then housed and fed them for about five years. In return, the servants worked without pay until their time was up. They were then given some tools, clothes, and maybe a small piece of land. After that they were on their own. Some indentured servants would continue to work for the same people, but for pay. Most, however, wanted to start their own farms. Many had to move west to find empty land.

Slaves from Africa

After 1619 there was another kind of worker. That year, a Dutch ship brought some Africans to Jamestown. No one is sure if these people were sold as slaves or as indentured servants. A few of these first African-Americans became free farmers. But in later years, the Africans that were brought to the colonies were sold as slaves. They didn't have much chance to become free. Before long, all the large tobacco farms used slave labor.

THE FIRST REPRESENTATIVE GOVERNMENT IN AMERICA

The House of Burgesses

In England, many people had a say in their government. The Virginia colonists wanted some say in their government, too. About the time Rolfe brought tobacco to Virginia, the colonial government was changed. The London Company set up the **House of Burgesses**. The London Company still appointed a governor, but now a group of important Virginians helped him make decisions.

The House of Burgesses was the first representative assembly in America. (*Burgess* is an old word that means a representative in a town governmnent.) Virginians elected representatives to the House of Burgesses. These representatives helped make decisions and write laws for the colony. However, all their laws had to be approved by the Company directors in London.

At first, most white men could vote for representatives. Later, only those who owned a certain amount of property could vote. No women or blacks were allowed to vote.

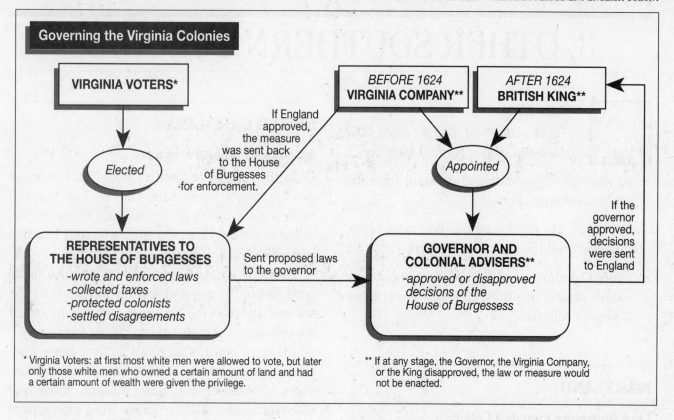

Governing the Virginia Colonies

VIRGINIA VOTERS*

BEFORE 1624 **VIRGINIA COMPANY****   *AFTER 1624* **BRITISH KING****

Elected

If England approved, the measure was sent back to the House of Burgesses for enforcement.

Appointed

If the governor approved, decisions were sent to England

REPRESENTATIVES TO THE HOUSE OF BURGESSES
-wrote and enforced laws
-collected taxes
-protected colonists
-settled disagreements

Sent proposed laws to the governor

GOVERNOR AND COLONIAL ADVISERS**
-approved or disapproved decisions of the House of Burgessess

* Virginia Voters: at first most white men were allowed to vote, but later only those white men who owned a certain amount of land and had a certain amount of wealth were given the privilege.

** If at any stage, the Governor, the Virginia Company, or the King disapproved, the law or measure would not be enacted.

Virginia Becomes a Royal Colony

In 1624 the colonial government changed again. King James I took control of the colony away from the quarreling directors of the London Company. Virginia became a royal colony, and the governor was chosen by the king.

The House of Burgesses continued to help run the government. It wrote laws and collected taxes. Most of these laws were different from English laws, because the colonists were dealing with different problems. No one in England had to protect farms from Indians, build roads through the wilderness, or decide borders. The colonists did.

SECTION REVIEW

Can you answer these Main Idea questions?

1. What problems did the early Jamestown colonists have? How did they solve them?

2. How did tobacco and slavery change life in Virginia for colonists, Africans, and Indians?

3. How did the Virginia colonists solve their problem of scarce labor?

4. What made the House of Burgesses a representative assembly?

Can you identify this place?

Jamestown

Can you identify these people?

Captain John Smith, John Rolfe, Powhatan, Pocahontas

Can you define these terms?

London Company, tobacco, plantation, indentured servants, slaves

91

3. OTHER SOUTHERN COLONIES

Main Ideas

Think about the following Main Idea questions as you read this section:

1. In what way was Maryland different from the other Southern colonies?

2. How was life in Charleston, South Carolina, different from life in North Carolina?

3. James Oglethorpe had certain ideas about how people should live. How did these ideas affect Georgia's colonists?

MARYLAND

Lord Baltimore Founds a Colony

In 1632, King Charles I gave a piece of northern Virginia to his friend Cecil Calvert, Lord Baltimore. Calvert was a Roman Catholic. He wanted to start a colony where Catholics could settle, because Catholics were not welcome in the other English colonies. In 1634 he founded Maryland. Some Catholics came, but most Maryland colonists were Protestants. So that all Christian colonists would be treated the same, Maryland's assembly passed the **Tolerance Act**. It gave religious freedom to all Christians in the colony, but not to people of other religions.

Lord Baltimore did not give Maryland's assembly much freedom. He made the laws. The assembly only approved or disapproved them. When he died, his secretary, Margaret Brent, ran the colony until new leaders arrived from England. She even stopped a revolt of Maryland's **militia** (colonial army).

NORTH CAROLINA

A Colony of Small Farmers

In the mid-1600s, settlers from Virginia began moving south. Soon, King Charles I of England made the area south of Virginia into a new colony, called Carolina. Later, Carolina was split into two parts, North Carolina and South Carolina.

North Carolina had many rivers but not a single good harbor. Pirates and Indians hid along its rivers and attacked the colonists. No one protected the colonists, for there was no city or fort nearby.

Many of North Carolina's settlers came from other colonies. Some had been indentured servants. Most began small farms that grew tobacco or that sent lumber and tar (made from pine sap) to England. Eventually, North Carolina had more people than its neighbor, South Carolina.

SOUTH CAROLINA

Growing Rice and Indigo

At first, South Carolina sent furs, tar, and lumber to England. Then a rice ship was wrecked off the coast. The colonists found that the freshwater swamps were perfect for raising rice. Rice quickly became an important crop.

Several years later, Eliza Lucas introduced **indigo** (IN duh go) to South Carolina. This plant was used to dye cloth blue. Rice and indigo have different growing and harvesting seasons, so large plantations could grow both. Workers, usually slaves, were kept busy all year.

South Carolina also had the largest town in the South, Charles Town. Today it is called Charleston. Most of the year Charles Town was quiet, almost empty. During the hot summer, however, the richer colonists moved from their farms into town. The owners partied in town while slaves or other workers kept the farms going in the broiling heat. When summer ended, the rich farmers returned to their big farms.

Charles Town was a busy port. The products of the Carolinas were shipped from it to England. Entering the port were slaves from Africa, along with a great variety of fancy products from England and the other colonies for use by the rich plantation owners.

GEORGIA

A Colony for Poor People

The last colony that the English started in North America was Georgia. It was the idea of an Englishman named James Oglethorpe. In England, people who owed money were sent to prison if they couldn't pay back what they owed. Oglethorpe wanted to give these people a chance in America to work their way out of being poor.

King George II gave Oglethorpe a charter to settle Georgia. Georgia's first colonists arrived in 1773. Most of them had lived in a city all their lives. Oglethorpe gave each family a farm, but he did not teach them how to be farmers. The colonists did not have a say in running the colony. Because the colony had strict rules, like "no slaves," "no rum," and "you can't sell your land," many

colonists decided to leave. Other colonists just ignored the rules. Only after the rules were changed did Georgia grow.

SECTION REVIEW

Can you answer these Main Idea questions?

1. In what way was Maryland different from the other Southern colonies?

2. How was life in Charles Town, South Carolina, different from life in North Carolina?

3. James Oglethorpe had certain ideas about how people should live. How did these ideas affect Georgia's colonists?

Can you identify and locate these places?

Maryland, North and South Carolina, Georgia

Can you identify these people?

Lord Baltimore, James Oglethorpe

Can you define these terms?

indigo, Tolerance Act

The Major Exports of the Southern Colonies (Almost all exports were sent to England)	
MARYLAND	Tobacco
VIRGINIA	Tobacco
NORTH CAROLINA	Tobacco, Lumber, Tar
SOUTH CAROLINA	Before 1696: Tobacco, Lumber, Tar After 1696: Rice After 1740: Rice, Indigo
GEORGIA	Rice, Indigo

4. LIFE IN THE SOUTHERN COLONIES

Main Ideas

Think about the following Main Idea questions as you read this section.

1. What was life like on a small family farm?

2. What was life like on a large plantation?

3. What problems did frontier farmers have that Eastern farmers did not ?

FARM AND PLANTATION LIFE

Small Farms

Most Southern colonists were from England, but they lived a very different life from the people in their mother country. Almost everyone in the Southern colonies lived on a farm. They might only come to town to trade or when the assembly met.

Most farms were small or medium-sized. Farm families worked alone or alongside one or two indentured servants or slaves. They did everything themselves. They built their own house and cleared their own land. They made their own cloth and clothes, candles, and eating bowls. They grew their own food. Most belonged to the Church of England, but were not very strict about their religion.

Plantations

The large farms were called **plantations**. Typically a plantation grew mostly a single crop, like tobacco or rice. Plantation owners would have 20 or more slaves to do the field work. Because plantations had more workers, they could grow and sell more crops than small farms. Plantation owners became rich and were able to buy more things for themselves from Europe. Food and clothing for the slaves, however, were produced on the plantations.

A large plantation was like a small village built around the owner's house. It often had its own church,

store, and areas for making horseshoes, barrels, cloth, and other goods. It also had slaves' houses—small shacks with dirt floors and no windows.

The owner of a large plantation usually hired an overseer to direct and control his slaves. This gave the owner the time to be a representative in the assembly, to run another plantation, or to travel. Unlike other colonists, a plantation owner made money even when he wasn't working himself. The work of his slaves would continue to make him rich.

White Southern farm families, whether rich or poor, were free, and white indentured servants knew that they would be free in a certain number of years. In early colonial times, some slaves were allowed to buy their freedom with money that they had earned. But later, the slaves lost this chance for freedom. And even free blacks had few rights.

Small Farms vs. Large Plantations	
FAMILY FARMS	**LARGE PLANTATIONS**
small to medium-sized farms	large farms covering a lot of land
worked by family	rich owner owned many slaves to do most of the hahd work
on larger farms, 1 or 2 slaves or indentuued servants might work alongside the owner's family	an overseer was hired to control slaves
grew own food and some crops to trade	grew mostly one crop (such as tobacco) to trade
made own clothes, candles, and furniture	purchased owner's family's clothes and fine furniture; slaves made made such items as candles and slaves' clothes
owner couldn't leave farm for very long	owners traveled, ran other plantations, and served in government (plantation owners were often powerful in government)

Southern Cities Stay Small

Since there were no deep harbors in the South, no large city grew up around a seaport. Cities like Jamestown and Charles Town remained small.

In 1691, Virginians finally moved their capital away from Jamestown's unhealthy swamps. The new capital was the town of Williamsburg, a few miles away. But it too stayed small.

Rivers Are Used as Highways

Rivers were the South's highways. If they were deep enough, ships could come directly to the plantations. At each plantation, they delivered goods ordered from England and loaded tobacco, indigo, or rice for the trip back.

People who lived away from the rivers had to travel on paths or narrow, muddy roads. Travel was so hard, people didn't travel much.

THE SOUTHERN FRONTIER

The Frontier Moves West

The best land along the deep rivers was quickly taken. Colonists who came later, and also freed indentured servants, had to move inland. They built their farms in **wilderness** areas that had not yet been settled by Europeans. The area that they moved into was known as the **frontier**.

On the frontier, the colonists cut down trees and turned the wilderness into farms. More people came, and the line between the frontier and the wilderness moved westward. By 1700, the frontier line had reached the Appalachian Mountains in some places.

Bacon's Rebellion Against Eastern Virginians

In Virginia, differences grew up between the frontier farmers and the farmers of the coast. The frontier farmers had little representation in the House of Burgesses. This assembly, which was controlled by the Eastern farmers, did little to solve frontier problems, such as protecting against Indian attacks or building better roads.

In 1675 the House of Burgesses voted to build forts to protect the plantations in the East against Indian attacks. The Western frontier farmers be-

came very angry. They had more problems with Indians than did the Eastern farmers, but they were not getting the protection. Led by Nathaniel Bacon, a young cousin of the Virginia governor, they twice marched to Jamestown. The second time, they captured and burned it. They also destroyed the villages of peaceful Indian tribes as well as the villages of Indian tribes who were at war with the colonists.

When Bacon became ill and died, the rebellion died with him. Many of the leaders of "Bacon's Rebellion" were captured and hanged. The owners of the large Eastern plantations remained in control of Virginia's government.

The Southern English colonies grew slowly. Colonists had to deal with many problems that didn't exist in England: scarce labor, new crops, fighting with Indians, and a government that was across the ocean.

In all the Southern colonies, the powerful owners of large plantations came to control the government. Small farmers, especially those living on the frontier, didn't like this, but they had neither the time nor the power to change it.

SECTION REVIEW

Can you answer these Main Idea questions?

1. What was life like on a small family farm?

2. What was life like on a large plantation?

3. What problems did frontier farmers have that Eastern farmers did not?

Can you define these terms?

plantation, frontier, Bacon's Rebellion, wilderness

# AFTER YOU READ

Discussion Questions

1. Describe how the government of Virginia changed from Captain John Smith's time until the time it became a royal colony.

2. Why did the Southern colonists need so much labor and use so much land?

3. Contrast (show the differences between) life on a large Southern plantation and life on a small frontier farm.

4. Examine the similarities and differences between life in a Southern English colony and life in a Spanish colony.

Comprehension Questions: Cause and Effect

I. Complete each of the following sentences by giving the most important reason the development happened. Here is an example:

John Cabot explored America for the English because the English wanted a route to the Indies.

1. Sir Walter Raleigh's first colony failed because—

2. Under Captain John Smith, Jamestown was successful because—

3. Tobacco changed life in Virginia because—

4. Virginians began the House of Burgesses because—

5. Cecil Calvert, Lord Baltimore, founded the colony of Maryland because—

6. Farmers in the Southern colonies wanted to live close to deep rivers because—

7. The frontier line moved Westward because—

8. The frontier farmers rebelled against the Eastern farmers because—

9. People bought stock in the London Company because—

10. Labor was scarce in the Southern colonies because English colonists—

Writing Activity

Pretend you are one of the following people living in colonial Virginia:

a Roanoke colonist

a slave on a large plantation

an indentured servant living on a farm

a member of a rich plantation family in South Carolina

a member of a family living on a small frontier farm

Brainstorm all you know about the life of that kind of person. Add the feelings that you might have about the past, present, or future if you were that person.

Now pretend you are that person and write a paragraph about one day in your life.

First, explain who you are. Then, write several sentences using details from your brainstorming. Include both facts and feelings. Finally, write a concluding sentence which tells some of the plans you might have for the future.

BIOGRAPHY

▲ *Portraits of John Smith and Pocahontas. The one of Pocahontas—who is pictured wearing the clothing of an upper class English woman—was painted when she visited England after marrying John Rolfe, one of the Virginia colonists. Descendents of John Rolfe and Pocahontas still live in Virginia today.*

John Smith led a very exciting life. Born on an English farm, he left at age 17 to become a soldier and fought and traveled throughout Europe. While fighting against the Turks, he was wounded and captured. Made a slave, he later escaped through Russia.

Still later, as one of the founders and original colonists at Jamestown, he tried to make the colony a success. However, because he forced the other colonists to work if they wanted to eat, many of them came to dislike him. After only two-and-a-half years, the colonists' resentment and his own health problems forced him to return to England.

While in Virginia, Smith had explored and mapped the area around Jamestown, falling in love with its natural beauty and variety. He also dealt with—and earned the respect of—the local Indians, who thought him very brave; once he had tried to escape from 200 Indians rather than give up his gun. But the Indian King Powhatan became angry at Smith and ordered him killed. Powhatan's daughter, Pocahontas, saved Smith's life, and later warned him of Indian plans against the colony.

After a time, Smith's health improved and he returned to explore and map another part of America, which he called "New England." His map was so good that people used it for 100 years.

Smith was also America's first writer. He wrote several important books about America. Some described events there, while others told of the country's great beauty, and of how the Indians lived.

CHAPTER 8

THE NEW ENGLAND COLONIES

Thirteen years after the first English settlement in Virginia, a second English colony was started. It was founded in what is now New England. Soon, more colonies were started in that area. The New England colonists had different ideas from the colonists who settled Jamestown. Many of them came to America for religious and not for economic reasons. They had to adjust to a different environment, and so they developed a different way of life than the Southern colonies.

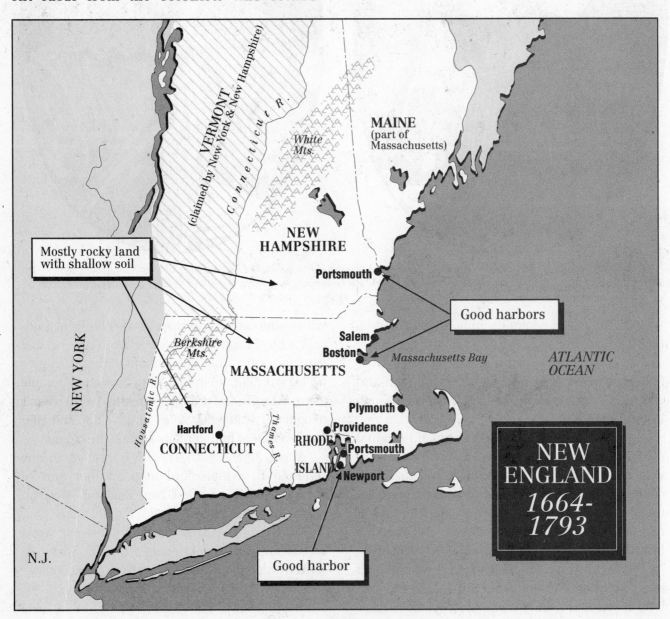

Mostly rocky land with shallow soil

VERMONT (claimed by New York & New Hampshire)

Connecticut R.

MAINE (part of Massachusetts)

White Mts.

NEW HAMPSHIRE

Portsmouth

Good harbors

NEW YORK

Berkshire Mts.

Housatonic R.

Salem

Boston

MASSACHUSETTS

Massachusetts Bay

ATLANTIC OCEAN

Plymouth

Providence

Thames R.

Hartford

CONNECTICUT

RHODE ISLAND

Portsmouth

Newport

Good harbor

N.J.

NEW ENGLAND 1664-1793

BEFORE YOU READ

Sections in This Chapter

1. Massachusetts
2. Other New England Colonies
3. Life in New England

Reading a Map

Answer the following questions using the map on the opposite page.

1. List the New England colonies.

2. Where are most of the towns and cities in New England located? What effect do you think this might have had on what the colonists there would do for a living?

Understanding a Key Concept:
THE PURITAN RELIGION

Religion is a very important part of most cultures. Every religion has a set of rules and beliefs about how people should live and what their relationship with God should be.

The Puritans and Pilgrims had very strict religious beliefs. Their beliefs included:

Hard work pleases God.

Puritan beliefs are the only right ones.

Only Puritan leaders know what is best for the colony.

Everyone should be able to read the Bible.

Bright colors and decorations are wrong.

Each statement at the top of the next column describes something about Puritan life in the Massachusetts Colony. Choose the Puritan belief that best explains why people did each thing. One is done for you.

1. When bad weather stopped Puritans from farming, they did not relax, but instead made goods to trade.

   <u>Hard work pleases God.</u>

2. Puritans did not wear fancy clothes.

3. Only the Puritan church was allowed.

4. Schools were free to all children.

5. Only important church members could vote.

Using What You Already Know

European countries believed that colonies should help their mother country become rich and powerful. A system to control colonial trade, called **mercantilism** or the mercantile system, was developed. In this system,

- All goods in a colony had to come from or go to its mother country.

- More money had to go into the mother country than went out.

Use the information above and what you learned in earlier chapters to answer these questions.

1. What did Cortés and Pizarro send back to Spain that made it rich—silk, gold, or slaves?

2. Who got richest from the French fur trade in America—fur companies in France, the French trappers, or the Huron Indians?

3. Where did the Southern English colonies go to sell crops and buy goods—England, Spain, or the Indies?

4. Under mercantilism, who becomes richer—the colony or the mother country?

5. Under mercantilism, who controls the trade—the colony or the mother country?

1. MASSACHUSETTS

Main Ideas

Think about the following Main Idea questions as you read this section:

1. Why did the Separatists, or "Pilgrims," agree to move to America?

2. What did the Pilgrims do once they arrived in America?

3. How did the Puritans blend religion, government, and daily life?

RELIGION IN ENGLAND

The Church of England

In England, there is an official religion supported by the government. At one time this official religion was the Catholic religion. At that time, it was also the official religion of France and Spain.

Then King Henry VIII started a new church, the Church of England. The new church kept many of the old Catholic customs and practices. However, many people in England wanted to change these practices.

Puritans and Separatists

As the years went by, different groups formed within the Church of England. Some people wanted to make the Church "pure" by getting rid of the things that made it like the Catholic Church. They were called **Puritans**.

Other people thought that so many changes were needed that the Church of England would never be the way they wanted it. They wanted to separate from the Church, so they were called **Separatists**.

The Church of England disliked the Puritans and Separatists. The English government passed laws against them. Some Puritans and Separatists decided to leave the country.

PLYMOUTH COLONY AND THE PILGRIMS

The Pilgrims Start the First Colony in Massachusetts

One group of Separatists left England and moved to Holland. They still thought of themselves as English, however. They became upset when they realized that their children were forgetting the English language and losing their English ways.

An English joint-stock company called the Plymouth Company solved the Separatists' problem. It got a charter at the same time that the London Company got one. Its colony was to be in the northern part of Virginia.

The Plymouth Company needed colonists. It offered the Separatists in Holland the chance to move to America. The company would pay their way, if they would work for the company.

The Separatists agreed. They left England on the ship *Mayflower* in 1620. After many storms, they finally landed hundreds of miles north of Virginia, near Cape Cod, Massachusetts. They decided this was a good place to settle, so they stayed. They named their settlement "Plymouth."

Today, we call these Plymouth Separatists the **Pilgrims**.

The Mayflower Compact—the First Written Constitution in America

Since they were not in Virginia as originally planned, some Pilgrims felt that the Plymouth Company was not responsible for them. This meant that they wouldn't live and work according to the company's rules. They wrote an agreement, or "compact." In this **Mayflower Compact** they agreed to help each other. They would govern themselves and work together for the good of their community. The Mayflower Compact was the first written agreement of this kind in what is now the United States.

The First Year and the First Thanksgiving

The Pilgrims landed in December. They were not ready for the harsh winds, deep snow, and biting cold of a New England winter. Nearly half of them died.

When spring came, the local Wampanoag Indians helped those that were left. They taught the Pilgrims how to grow American crops, such as corn and squash, and how to hunt wild animals and birds, such as the turkey. With the Wampanoags' help, the Pilgrims took in many crops that fall.

To thank God for the harvest, the Pilgrims held a feast. It lasted three days. It was the first Thanksgiving in America. The Indians probably wondered why the Pilgrims were using up food they would need in order to survive the winter. That winter the Pilgrims learned that they needed more food than they had. They would have to be more careful with their food in the future.

MASSACHUSETTS BAY COLONY AND THE PURITANS

A Colony Settled by Its Shareholders.

In 1629, the Massachusetts Bay Company was founded by a group of English Puritans. This joint-stock company sold its shares only to other Puritans. The shareholders were also the colonists. When the Puritan colonists left for Massachusetts, they took the company's charter with them. Unlike other company colonies, their directors lived in the colony and knew the colony's problems. These colonists governed themselves.

The Puritans set up their colony at Salem in Massachusetts. Soon after, they founded the city of Boston. They wanted to create what they felt was an ideal or perfect place. They would create it using English laws, hard work, and their Puritan religion. They wanted their example to change the way people in England thought about life and religion.

The colony at Plymouth. Like Jamestown, Plymouth was built along a river, and was built for defense—note the blockhouse with guns at right, and the high wooden walls.

The Puritans were both religious and practical. They knew that they themselves did not have all the skills needed to survive. Therefore they brought farmers, blacksmiths, and other craftspeople with them. These 900-1,000 people were the largest group of colonists to leave England together.

A Government Based on the Puritan Church

The Puritans felt religion and government should be combined, so their laws did just that. By law, everyone had to attend a Puritan church. Only certain Puritans, called church members, could vote. The church members elected the assembly and a governor. The Puritans believed people should spend their time working hard or worshiping God. "Fun" activities like dancing and holiday parties were outlawed. (For more information about the Puritans, see the end of Chapter 10.)

SECTION REVIEW

Can you answer these Main Idea questions?

1. Why did the Separatists, or "Pilgrims," agree to move to America?

2. What did the Pilgrims do once they arrived in America?

3. How did the Puritans blend religion, government, and daily life?

Can you identify and locate this place?

Massachusetts

Can you identify these people?

Puritans, Separatists, Pilgrims

Can you define these terms?

Mayflower Compact, Plymouth Colony, Massachusetts Bay Company

2. OTHER NEW ENGLAND COLONIES

Main Ideas

Think about the following Main Idea questions as you read this section:

1. Why were the Rhode Island and New Hampshire colonies started?

2. How was each New England colony similar to the Massachusetts Bay Colony? How was it different?

Many religious leaders in Massachusetts disagreed with the strict Puritan views on religion or laws. Those leaders either left the colony or were made to leave. Some began new colonies in other parts of New England. The colonies of Rhode Island, New Hampshire, and Connecticut all started this way. Each New England colony was a little different from the others, but they all had strong governments based on strong religious beliefs.

Two of today's New England states were not separate colonies. Maine was part of Massachusetts, and both New York and New Hampshire claimed what is now the state of Vermont.

RHODE ISLAND

Roger Williams Founds Providence

Roger Williams was a Puritan minister in both Salem and Plymouth. He had some very strong beliefs that differed from those of other Puritan leaders. He wanted to separate the church from the government, and he wanted to allow people who weren't church members to vote. He felt that all people should be allowed to choose their

By the time New England was settled, the Church of England had split off from the Catholic Church. The Puritans and Pilgrims who settled New England had in turn split off from the Church of England. In the 17th century, groups of Puritans moved out of Massachusetts into Connecticut, Rhode Island, and New Hampshire. Some of their leaders are shown on the far right.
The Puritans were not unanimous in their views on religion. Many of these leaders had their own ideas about how religion should affect people's lives.

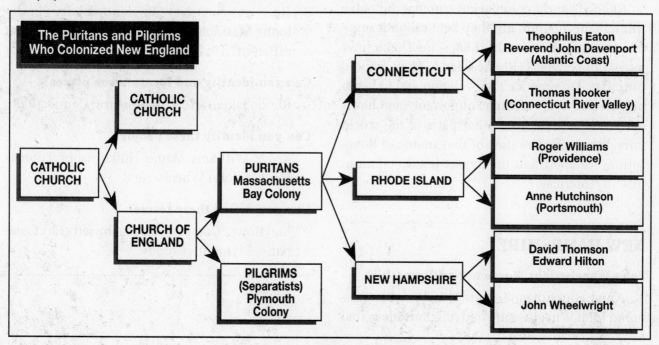

own religion and not be forced to attend Puritan services. He also believed that the King did not own all the land, but that the Indians did. He felt the colonists should buy the land from the Indians and not get it from the King.

The Puritans tried to convince Williams that he was wrong, but he held onto his beliefs. They decided to send him back to England. Instead, he escaped and fled to what is now Rhode Island. In 1636, he bought land from the Indians and started the city of Providence.

Anne Hutchinson Founds Portsmouth

Anne Hutchinson also had different beliefs from most Puritans. She gave talks on religion in her house. Many people in Massachusetts, including the governor, agreed with her teachings. Angry church leaders finally forced her to leave the colony. With a group of followers, she went south and founded the town of Portsmouth. It later joined with Williams' Providence to form the colony of Rhode Island. Unlike the Puritans' Massachusetts Bay Colony, all religious opinions were allowed in Rhode Island. Hutchinson later moved to a farm near New York, where she was killed in an Indian attack.

The Jewish Community in Rhode Island

Rhode Island's colonial government did make rules about religion, but they kept religion separate from government. In 1658, some Dutch Jews moved to Newport, Rhode Island. They wanted the chance to practice their religion and to begin businesses. They became important merchants and traders. Jews from other parts of the world joined them. By the time of the American Revolution, Newport had the largest Jewish community in America.

NEW HAMPSHIRE

John Wheelwright Moves to New Hampshire

Anne Hutchinson's brother-in-law, the Reverend John Wheelwright, had religious ideas that were similar to Hutchinson's. He and his followers left Massachusetts and moved north to towns where they had more freedom.

The Massachusetts Bay Company forced these towns to remain part of its colony. But later, when Massachusetts became a royal colony, these towns formed a new, separate colony. They became the colony of New Hampshire.

CONNECTICUT

Thomas Hooker

In 1636, the Reverend Thomas Hooker left Massachusetts. He and a group of followers built a settlement along the Connecticut River. He based the laws of his colony on those of Massachusetts, but allowed more people to vote. All church members, not just church leaders, made the decisions.

SECTION REVIEW

Can you answer these Main Idea questions?

1. Why were the Rhode Island and New Hampshire colonies started?

2. How was each New England colony similar to the Massachusetts Bay Colony? How was it different?

Can you identify and locate these places?

Rhode Island, New Hampshire, Connecticut

Can you identify these people?

Roger Williams, Anne Hutchinson, Thomas Hooker, John Wheelwright

Can you define these terms?

Mayflower Compact, Massachusetts Bay Company, Plymouth Colony

3. LIFE IN NEW ENGLAND

Main Ideas

Think about the following Main Idea questions as you read this section:

1. What was a New England town like?

2. How did New England's natural environment effect farming and trade?

3. How did the English government try to change America's trade after the English Civil War?

4. What caused King Philip's War?

NEW ENGLAND TOWNS AND FARMERS

New England was a Colony of Towns From the Beginning

The Massachusetts Bay Company gave land to whole towns, not to individual families. The people in each town shared the best farm land and divided up the rest for their homes, a church, a school, and private fields.

Since all colonists had to go to church, they lived in town, near the church. Houses were built around a town square. Storekeepers and craftspeople quickly opened shops. Schools were started, and all children attended. Town meetings decided important matters, such as roads, schools, and timber cutting. These meetings were open to all men who owned land.

Many new settlers came to Massachusetts. If they wanted to move into a town, they had to be accepted by everyone who already lived there. Other new colonists joined together, got a grant from the Company, and built new towns to the west. Soon there were many small towns in the colony. The towns and farms they created looked very much like those in England, so the area was called New England.

A Hard Environment for Farming

The New England environment was very different from the South. There were few rivers for transportation, so roads had to be built. Travel between towns was slow and rough. The thick forests and the many rocks in the soil were hard to clear for farming. Also, the soil was not rich, and the long winters meant a short growing season. Farmers could grow enough food to feed their families, but not grow enough to send crops to other places. They did not use slaves, but a few had indentured servants. Most of the work was done by the family.

NEW ENGLAND SHIPPING AND TRADE

Family Businesses at Home

All over New England, the colonists had to adapt to the harsh winters. Since their religion said they must work hard all the time, they used the long winter days spent in front of the fire to make things, like buttons, brooms, or nails.

When a family made more than they could use, they traded the extra goods with their neighbors. Then, after they had traded with everyone in town, they took their goods to other towns. These family businesses were New England's first industries.

The Start of the Shipping Industry

New England had many good natural harbors. Ships could stop at these deep, protected places, so seaports grew. Many New Englanders became sailors and merchants. They took New England's raw materials, like wood, and manufactured goods, like rum, to England and to other parts of the world. The English used the tall, straight New England trees to build ships. Soon New England colonists began to build ships, too. New England's ships carried fish, furs, farm animals, and homemade products. They took these things to other colonies, to England, to Africa, and to the West Indies.

The Triangle Trade

New England's ships followed many trade routes. Some just went directly to England and then returned. Other ships followed a triangle trade route. They took food and livestock to the West Indies. Then West Indian molasses and sugar was taken to England. Finally, they returned to the colonies with European products.

Another triangle trade route involved Africa. Ships took rum, guns, and other trade goods from New England to Africa. African chiefs traded captured African men and women for these goods. The captives were taken to the West Indies or to the Southern colonies, where they were sold as slaves. In the West Indies, captains bought molasses and sugar and then returned to New England, where these goods were made into rum. In the Southern colonies, the captains loaded tobacco, rice, and indigo and took them to New England or England. Then the triangle traders began their routes again. All this trade made both England's and New England's merchants and shipbuilders rich.

ENGLAND TRIES TO CONTROL TRADE IN THE COLONIES

The Colonies are Ignored During a Period of Civil War in England

From 1642 to 1649 there was a civil war in England. English Puritan landowners fought against the king for control of the government. Things did not get back to normal until 1660.

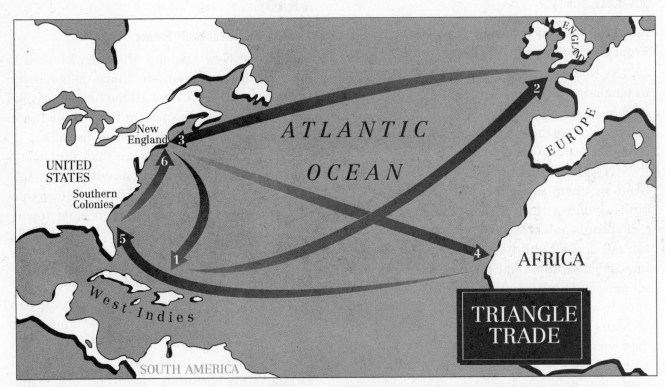

▲ *There were actually two different "triangle trades" at this time. In the first, (1) food and livestock were brought to the West Indies; (2) West Indies molasses and sugar were taken to England; and (3) European manufactured goods were then brought back to the colonies. In the second, (4) rum, guns, and other trade goods were brought to Africa; (5) African slaves were brought back across the Atlantic to the West Indies or the Southern colonies; and (6) finally molasses and sugar from the West Indies, or tobacco, rice and Indigo from the Southern colonies, were brought North.*

During that time, the English government left the colonies alone. Each colony protected itself, wrote its own laws, and developed new trade routes. In addition, the colonies did not send all their goods to England the way they were supposed to.

Mercantilism

After England's political problems calmed down, the English government looked carefully at its colonies. It didn't like the fact that it no longer had tight control of its colonial trade.

Control of trade was important to the English government. In the English view, the way for a country to become rich and powerful was to **export** (sell to other countries) more than it **imported** (bought from other countries). This view of trade was called **mercantilism** (MUHR kuhn teel izm).

Under mercantilism, colonies were not supposed to trade directly with other countries. They were supposed to send raw materials to the mother country. The mother country would use the materials to make manufactured goods. The manufactured goods would then be sold back to the colonies and to other countries for a high price. But the colonies had stopped doing what they were supposed to during England's civil war.

England Passes the Trade and Navigation Acts to Impose Mercantilism on the Colonies

To regain control of the colonies' trade, the English government passed many Trade and Navigation Acts. The purpose of these laws was to make England a strong, rich mercantile country. One law said that only English or American ships could trade with the colonies. Another law said that goods from other countries could not be imported directly into the colonies. Instead, they had to go through England first. That way, English merchants could make money reselling them to the colonies. Still another law listed raw materials that had to be shipped from America directly to England. These could not be exported directly to any other country. Rice, mo-

lasses, and furs were on this list, which got longer and longer as the years went on. Some raw materials that were also produced in England, such as wool, could not be shipped out of the colonies at all. The English wanted to protect their own wool growers and wool trade from competition.

Most of the Trade and Navigation Acts were not well enforced. The colonists ignored them and continued to trade in many places. But other mercantile laws followed. The colonists knew that none of these laws were for their benefit. Eventually, English mercantilism split England and its colonies apart.

KING PHILIP'S WAR

Indian Anger at the Colonists

When the New England colonies were first settled, the Wampanoag Indians had welcomed the English colonists. They helped the colonists learn how to live in a new environment.

But as more colonists came, life for the Indians themselves changed for the worse. The colonists settled wherever they wanted. Their animals destroyed the Indians' cornfields. The forests and the animals that the Indians depended on were beginning to disappear. The Indian tribes grew smaller and smaller as European diseases killed many of the Indians. The number of colonists, however, kept growing as thousands came from Europe to the colonies.

Many Indians grew resentful. Some of them traded for guns and then turned the guns against the colonists.

King Philip Goes to War

One chief, Metacomet, whom the colonists called "King Philip," saw his people losing their land and their power. In 1675, King Philip struck back at the colonists. His people and several other tribes destroyed the colonists' cattle, crops, and houses. Many colonists were killed. Others fled East for protection.

All the New England colonies joined together against King Philip. Indians who were still friendly to the colonists helped them. This group of allies defeated King Philip's Indian tribes and destroyed their food supply. King Philip himself was tracked down and shot. His wife and son were sent to the West Indies and sold as slaves. Although the war ended most Indian problems in New England, people remained afraid. Some Western lands were not settled again for many years because the colonists feared to be too far from protection.

Massachusetts Becomes a Royal Colony

Not long after King Philip's War, the Massachusetts Bay Company lost its charter. Massachusetts then became a Royal colony like Virginia. Five years later, Plymouth Colony became part of Massachusetts. The king, not the Puritan company, was now in charge. Some laws were changed, but life in New England remained much the same.

By 1700, New England had developed into a special place. Religion had brought the earliest colonists to New England, and religion shaped their life in their new home. Because communities were centered on the church, towns grew. The hard land and hard weather kept farms small, but good harbors made it possible for many New Englanders to earn a living as sailors and traders. From the beginning, religion, towns, the land, and trade shaped the life of New Englanders to be very different from that of their fellow English colonists in the South.

SECTION REVIEW

Can you answer these MainIdea questions?

1. What was a New England town like?

2. How did New England's natural environment effect farming and trade?

3. How did the English government try to change America's trade after the English Civil War?

4. What caused King Philip's War?

Can you identify this person?

King Philip

Can you define these terms?

triangle trade, Trade and Navigation Acts, mercantilism, import, export

AFTER YOU READ

Discussion Questions

1. How did religion affect life in the New England colonies?

2. How did New England's triangle trade fit or not fit England's ideas on mercantilism?

3. How did the relationship between the colonists and the Indians change from the first Thanksgiving to King Philip's War? Why did these changes happen?

4. What would you have liked about living in a Puritan colony like Massachusetts? What would you have disliked about it?

Comprehension Questions: Problems and Solutions

I. History is full of problems and of the ways people tried to solve them. Read each problem below, and tell how people tried to solve it. The first one is done for you.

1. *Problem:* The Plymouth Company needed colonists.

   Solution: <u>They offered the Separatists a chance to move to America as colonists.</u>

2. *Problem:* The Puritans did not have the skills needed to survive in America.

   Solution:

3. *Problem:* The Puritans wanted the colonial government to fit their religious beliefs.

   Solution:

4. *Problem:* Roger Williams and Ann Hutchinson didn't agree with Puritan leaders.

   Solution:

5. *Problem:* All colonists had to go to church, but travel was hard.

   Solution:

6. *Problem:* The English lost control of colonial trade during the English Civil War.

   Solution:

7. *Problem:* The Indians were angry at what the English colonists did in America.

   Solution:

II. Pretend you just visited relatives on a plantation in Virginia, and then relatives who live in a Massachusetts town. Picture in your mind what you'd see in Virginia. Picture what you'd see in Massachusetts. Make notes on a chart to show what would be the same and what would be different. Include information about the land and the types of farms, towns, crops, industries, and workers you would see.

Your chart might look like this one:

	DIFFERENCES	SIMILARITIES
VIRGINIA	many large plantations	
MASSA-CHUSETTS	many small towns	
BOTH		English spoken

Writing Activity

Write a letter to someone in England about your trips to Virginia and Massachusetts. Describe what you saw and tell which colony you liked best and why. Use your chart to support your opinion with facts about life in that colony.

CHAPTER 9

THE MIDDLE COLONIES

There were four colonies between New England and the Southern colonies. New York, New Jersey, Pennsylvania, and Delaware are called the **Middle Colonies**. Two—New York and Delaware—were not started by the English, but England took them over.

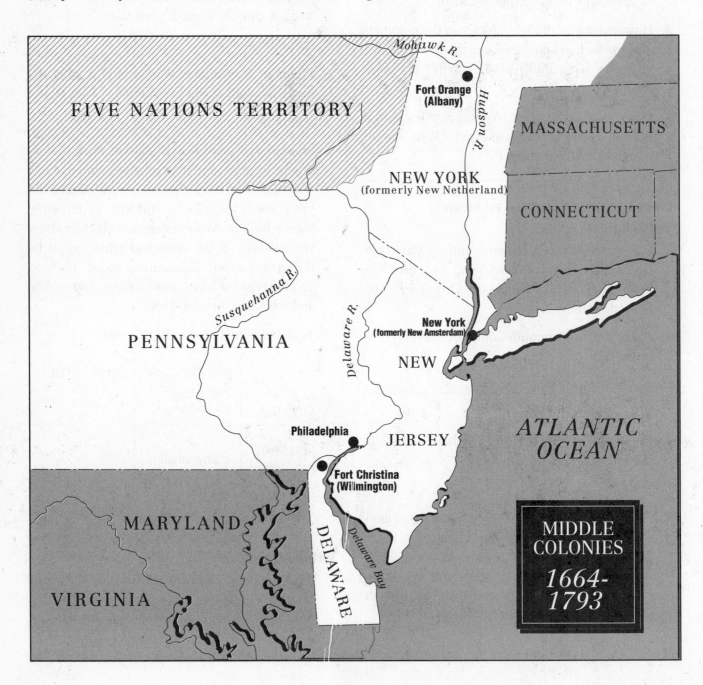

FIVE NATIONS TERRITORY

Mohawk R.

Fort Orange
(Albany)

Hudson R.

MASSACHUSETTS

NEW YORK
(formerly New Netherland)

CONNECTICUT

Susquehanna R.

PENNSYLVANIA

Delaware R.

New York
(formerly New Amsterdam)

NEW

ATLANTIC
OCEAN

Philadelphia

JERSEY

Fort Christina
(Wilmington)

MARYLAND

DELAWARE

Delaware Bay

VIRGINIA

MIDDLE
COLONIES
*1664-
1793*

BEFORE YOU READ

Sections in This Chapter

1. New York
2. The Other Middle Colonies

Reading a Map

Use the map on the opposite page to answer these questions.

1. What are the names of the middle colonies?

2. Locate Fort Orange on the map. How do you think did the first Europeans traveled to the area?

3. What cities are in the middle colonies?

4. What natural features were important to these cities becoming trading centers?

Understanding a Key Concept: FREEDOM

Freedom is being able to do, say, or think as you please. There are different kinds of freedom.

- **Personal freedom** is the right to make your own decisions and live as you please.

- **Religious freedom** is the right to practice your religion without anyone's stopping you.

- **Freedom of speech** is the right to say anything that is not dangerous to others.

Read the following statements about colonial life. Write the type of freedom the people had or didn't have. The first is done for you.

1. Spanish missionaries forced Indians to give up their ceremonies and beliefs and become Catholics. <u>No religious freedom</u>

2. A Massachusetts Bay Colony law said people had to attend the Puritan church.

3. Roger Williams allowed Jews and Quakers to practice their religion in Rhode Island.

4. Slaves had to do everything their owners commanded.

5. Colonists could move from crowded colonies to less crowded colonies.

6. Frontier colonists in Virginia spoke against the Eastern colonists who controlled the government.

7. Ben Franklin became a printer, scientist, writer, and important person in the government.

Using What You Already Know

When Europeans moved to America, they brought many ideas with them. They tried to make their life like it had been in Europe. They also used ideas and materials they learned in America. Often, they combined European ideas with materials from America.

Read the sentences below. For each, write "Europe," "America," or "both" to show where the colonists got their ideas. The first is done for you.

1. *Coureurs de Bois* made European pants and shirts out of animal skins.

    both

2. Colonists learned to grow squash from the Indians.

3. The House of Burgesses helped run Virginia's government.

4. Even in summer, some colonists wore dark, hot clothing like the clothing they wore in Europe.

1. NEW YORK

Main Ideas

Think about the following Main Idea questions as you read this section:

1. How did trade help the colony of New Netherland (later New York) grow and change?

2. What different types of jobs did colonists living in New Netherland have?

3. How did the government of New Netherland change when it became New York? How did its trade change?

HENRY HUDSON'S VOYAGES

Henry Hudson Explores the Hudson River

The first European explorers and settlers in New York were the Dutch, not the English. (The Dutch are the people who live in the Netherlands, also called Holland.) Like the French, the Dutch wanted to find a northern route to the Pacific Ocean for their ships. In 1608 the Dutch asked an English sea captain named Henry Hudson to find a shortcut to Asia and the Indies.

Hudson searched the North American coast from Newfoundland down to Delaware Bay. In what is now New York State, he went far up a long inlet that turned out to be a river. Today it is named after him: the Hudson River. When they returned to the Netherlands, his sailors told about the friendly Indians along the river who had beautiful furs to trade.

The Death of Hudson

A year later, Hudson set sail on another voyage. This time he worked for the English. Again he searched for a passage to the Pacific. He went further north this time and discovered Hudson Bay in Canada. But his crew hated the cold. They rebelled and put Hudson, his son, and seven other crew members into a small open boat. Hudson and his companions were never seen again.

THE DUTCH COME TO STAY

The Dutch West India Company Founds New Netherland

In Holland, Dutch businessmen decided to trade for furs along the river that Hudson had found. In order to do that, they formed the Dutch West India Company. In 1624, they founded a colony in North America. It was called New Netherland, after their homeland. They built a trading post at Fort Orange, where Albany, New York, now stands. At Fort Orange, Iroquois and Algonquin Indians traded their furs for blankets, metal tools, and cloth.

Although the Iroquois and Algonquins were enemies, the Dutch traded with both. But each Indian group wanted all the fur trade. Finally, the Iroquois promised to travel farther to get more furs if the Dutch would trade guns to them.

The Algonquins were angered. The Dutch had already taken much of their land. Now, the Dutch were giving guns to their enemies, the Iroquois. The Algonquins became **allies**, or friends, with the French. Many battles were fought between the Iroquois and Algonquins for trade routes. Other battles were fought between the Indians and the Dutch settlers for the land.

The Founding of New Amsterdam

The Dutch built a second trading post on Manhattan Island, where there was a good harbor. Today, Manhattan Island is part of New York City. The Dutch governor, Peter Minuit, is said to have bought the island from local Indians for $24 worth of beads and cloth. The new trading post was called New Amsterdam, after an important city in the Netherlands. A small town was built nearby.

Because of its good harbor, New Amsterdam became one of the most important trading cities in North America. Ships brought tobacco from Virginia. From there it was shipped to Holland instead of to England.

The Dutch West India Company appointed a governor and a council to control New Netherland. The Dutch colonists did not vote or have a say in the government. The West India Company didn't do much for the colony. It was more concerned about richer colonies in other parts of the world.

The Dutch Settle Along the Hudson River

New Netherland grew slowly. The land was good for farming, but the company gave the best land to rich men called **patroons**. A patroon received a huge amount of land if he could find 50 people to rent farms on it. Most settlers wanted to own their farms, not rent them. Soon there were small farms and towns all along the Hudson River.

Most settlers lived as close to the Hudson as possible. They used the river as their highway. Roads were narrow, muddy, and filled with ruts. It sometimes took several days for farmers to drive a wagon less than ten miles to the river. At the river, a boat picked up their crops and took them to New Amsterdam to sell or export.

Other People Come to New Netherland

Few Dutch people wanted to leave their homeland, so the government allowed people from other countries to settle in New Netherland. This gave some people their first chance to move to the American colonies. People with different religions, like German Lutherans and Spanish Jews, came. Even English colonists from Massachusetts and Connecticut moved into New Netherland. Most people continued to speak their own language and to practice their own religion.

Peter Stuyvesant (STY ves uhnt) was the last governor of New Netherland. He was a harsh and unpopular man. He strictly enforced trade laws, and he tried to make all the colonists worship in the Dutch church. He put anyone who did not agree with him in jail. His hot temper made him many enemies.

NEW AMSTERDAM BECOMES NEW YORK

The English Take Over New Netherland

New Amsterdam's free trade rules angered the English. By English law, goods from English colonies had to go to England on English ships. Instead, some goods from English colonies were being shipped to New Amsterdam. In 1664 the King of England's brother, the Duke of York, sent armed ships to New Amsterdam. Peter Stuyvesant wanted to fight, but his colonists didn't. Finally he surrendered. New Netherland became the English colony of New York.

New York was a **proprietary colony**. This is a colony owned by one person—its proprietor, or owner. New York's proprietor was the Duke of York, who had sent the English fleet. He named both the colony and its largest city New York. He

Peg-legged Peter Stuyvesant, the last governor of New Amsterdam.

113

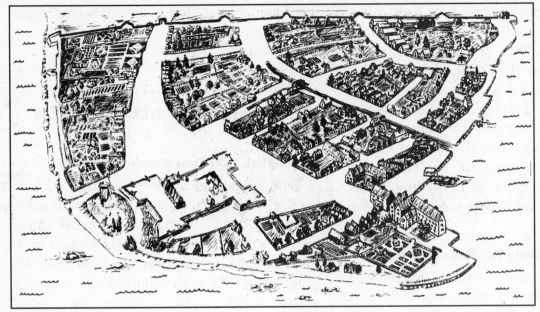

New Amsterdam 1664, just before its capture by the English. Most of the streets shown are still in New York City today. The wide street on the far left is New York's famous Broadway. The street running at a right angle to it, at the very top of the picture, is Wall Street. Wall Street was called that because it was next to the wall which protected the colony from Indian attacks. (The wall is the dark line near the top edge of the picture.)

appointed the governor, granted land, decided on the government, and controlled trade.

Life in New York

The Dutch were allowed to keep their property and their language. However, they were not allowed to vote until many years later. The English took over the Dutch trading posts, and the Iroquois became England's allies.

Many English colonists already lived in New York. They wanted a voice in the government. The Duke of York allowed them to elect an assembly. Rich landlords, New York City merchants, and small farmers were elected. Each group had different ideas about what the colony needed.

Most of the colonists were farmers. The Duke gave huge areas of land to a few rich Englishmen, who divided the land and rented small farms to poor colonists. Other colonists owned their own small farms. Most small farmers grew only enough for their own needs. As everywhere else in the colonies, there was lots of land but few people to work it. If a farmer had enough money, he might buy some slaves to help him. But most farmers did all the work themselves.

The Duke also gave colonists permission to buy large areas of land from the Indians. These lands were on the **frontier**, or edge of the colony.

Attacks by Indians and the French, and the long distance to any English town, made living in frontier areas dangerous. In New York, mostly fur traders lived along the frontier.

New York grew slowly. Its farms did not export as much as other colonies. Trading was its major business. Goods from all over the world came into and went out from New York harbor.

SECTION REVIEW

Can you answer these Main Idea questions?

1. How did trade help the colony of New Netherland (later New York) grow and change?

2. What different types of jobs did colonists living in New Netherland have?

3. How did the government of New Netherland change when it became New York?

Can you identify and locate these places?

Holland, Hudson River, New Amsterdam

Can you identify these people?

Peter Stuyvesant, the Duke of York

Can you define this term?

proprietary colony

2. THE OTHER MIDDLE COLONIES

Main Ideas

Think about the following Main Idea questions as you read this section.

1. Compare how and why the colonies of New Jersey, Pennsylvania, and Delaware were founded.

2. How did William Penn's ideas and actions affect the people who lived in Pennsylvania?

3. Where did the colonists who settled in Pennsylvania and Delaware come from?

NEW JERSEY

Berkeley and Carteret Start a Colony

The Duke of York gave two of his friends, Lord John Berkeley and Sir George Carteret, part of New Netherland. They founded the proprietary colony of New Jersey. Berkeley and Carteret allowed freedom of religion and an elected assembly. They also offered good land at a reasonable price. The colony attracted many hard-working people of different religions.

PENNSYLVANIA

The Quakers in England

A member of the Quaker religion named William Penn started Pennsylvania. The Quakers, or "Friends," believed that every person had God's spirit inside. Because they were guided by the Spirit of God, they felt that they didn't need churches or ceremonies. Instead, they had simple meetings. Sometimes they quaked, or shook, when they felt the Spirit of God. They were a peaceful and religious people, but they did not belong to the Church of England. Many people disliked them, and the English government passed laws against them.

The illustration at left, taken from an old painting, shows William Penn signing a treaty with Native Americans. Even though the King of England had given him the land, William Penn also bought it from the Indians. This helped to earn their goodwill. His colony would remain at peace with the Indians for many years.

William Penn Starts a Colony

William Penn hoped to start a colony where Quakers could live in peace. And since Quakers believed all people possessed the Spirit of God, he wanted his colony to be a place where everyone was equal. In 1681, King Charles II gave Penn land in America instead of paying back money he owed Penn's father. The new colony was named Pennsylvania, or "Penn's woods."

Penn planned the capital city, Philadelphia. He picked a good spot on the Delaware River, and Philadelphia quickly became an important seaport. Wheat and vegetables from Pennsylvania and Maryland farms were shipped from Philadelphia to the West Indies. Tobacco from Southern colonies was shipped to England.

Since Pennsylvania was a proprietary colony, William Penn was responsible for its growth. He sold good land at reasonable prices. He brought doctors, businessmen, and farmers to Pennsylvania. He also brought people who could print books and make things from silver. Many of the people Penn brought to his colony were educated. They liked to read and discuss many topics. Soon, Philadelphia had many bookstores, printers, and the first library in the colonies.

Settlers from Ireland and Germany

In Northern Ireland and Germany, many people were having political and religious problems. Penn invited some of these people to settle in Pennsylvania. There they found religious freedom and a chance to create a new life. The Germans were especially good farmers. Their farms soon produced enough wheat to export. Their methods of farming didn't use up the soil. Most of the Northern Irish, or "Scotch-Irish," moved west to the frontier and built small frontier farms.

DELAWARE

A Swedish, Dutch, and English Colony

In 1638, at the mouth of the Delaware River, some colonists from Sweden built log cabins.

They were led by Peter Minuit—the same man who had bought Manhattan Island for the Dutch. The Swedes called the place Fort Christina after their queen. It is now Wilmington, Delaware.

Few Swedish colonists came to Delaware. The Swedish government allowed people from other countries to come, but the colony remained small and weak.

In 1655, Peter Stuyvesant and a small Dutch army took over the colony. For a short while the Swedish colony was part of New Netherland. When the English took over New Amsterdam, it became a separate English colony named "Delaware."

The Middle Colonies were settled by colonists with many different backgrounds: Dutch, English, Swedish, Irish, and German. Their ideas, plus the fertile land and good seaports, made the Middle Colonies busy and successful centers of farming and trade.

SECTION REVIEW

Can you answer these Main Idea questions?

1. Compare how and why the colonies of New Jersey, Pennsylvania, and Delaware were founded.

2. How did William Penn's ideas and actions affect the people who lived in Pennsylvania?

3. Where did the colonists who settled in Pennsylvania and Delaware come from?

Can you identify and locate these places?

New Jersey, Philadelphia

Can you identify these people?

Lord John Berkeley, Sir George Carteret, William Penn

Can you define this term?

Quakers

AFTER YOU READ

Discussion Questions

1. The Middle Colonies allowed colonists from countries other than England to settle in them. How did this make life there different from life in Massachusetts or Virginia?

2. Compare the government of a proprietary colony, like Pennsylvania, with that of a chartered colony, like Massachusetts.

3. What freedoms and ideas were different in the Middle Colonies than in the Massachusetts Bay Colony or the Virginia Colony?

Comprehension Questions

I. One word is incorrect in each of the following sentences about the Middle Colonies. Copy the sentence and replace the incorrect word with one that makes the sentence correct. The first one is corrected for you.

1. The first Europeans to live in New York were Swedish.

   The first Europeans to live in New York were Dutch.

2. Fort Orange was founded as a trading post for trading fish.

3. The main transportation route in New York was the Mississippi River.

4. Pennsylvania was founded by Catholics who wanted religious freedom.

5. Penn brought many different types of people to Maryland.

6. New York and Boston became important trading cities in the Middle Colonies.

7. The Middle Colonies only had settlers from England.

II. Each English Colony was different from the others in some ways. Based on what you have learned about these colonies, answer questions one through five. Choose the best answer from the three choices listed below.

   a. *New England Colonies*

   b. *Middle Colonies*

   c. *Southern Colonies*

1. Which colonies had a natural environment containing rich soil and deep harbors?

2. Which colonies had small family farms on poor, rocky soil?

3. In which colonies were the colonial governments run by religious groups?

4. Which colonies had large plantations and small farms so far apart that people seldom went to church?

5. Which colonies had the fewest large cities?

Writing Activity

Pretend you live in colonial Philadelphia. Brainstorm all the things you might see in the city. Now pretend you have visitors from England. Use your details to describe what you'd show them on a walk through the city. Be sure to point out what makes Philadelphia different from other cities.

CHAPTER 10

THE CHANGING COLONIES

By the middle of the 1700s, the English had been settling in America for 150 years. Each colony did things its own way, and most colonists thought of themselves as Virginians or as New Yorkers, not as "Americans." Yet in spite of their differences, the colonists had many things in common, and, as colonial life changed, they found that the number of things that they had in common was growing.

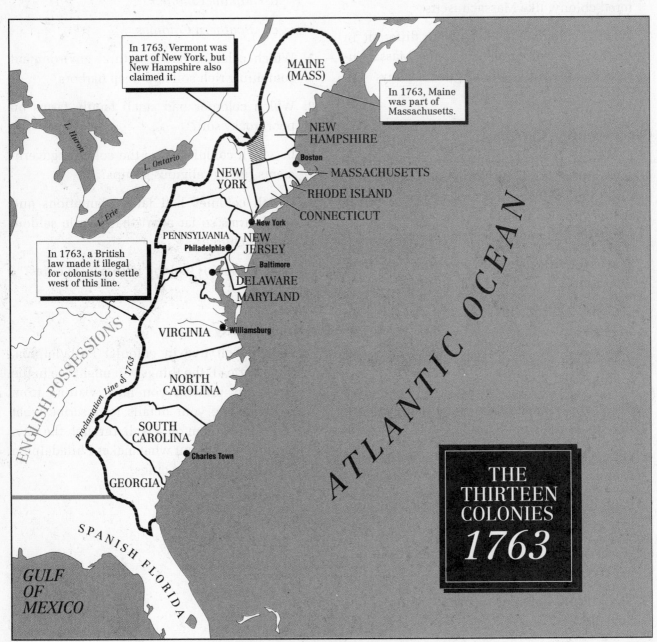

In 1763, Vermont was part of New York, but New Hampshire also claimed it.

In 1763, Maine was part of Massachusetts.

In 1763, a British law made it illegal for colonists to settle west of this line.

MAINE (MASS)

NEW HAMPSHIRE

Boston

NEW YORK

MASSACHUSETTS

RHODE ISLAND

CONNECTICUT

New York

PENNSYLVANIA

Philadelphia

NEW JERSEY

Baltimore

DELAWARE

MARYLAND

VIRGINIA

Williamsburg

NORTH CAROLINA

SOUTH CAROLINA

Charles Town

GEORGIA

ENGLISH POSSESSIONS

Proclamation Line of 1763

L. Huron

L. Ontario

L. Erie

ATLANTIC OCEAN

SPANISH FLORIDA

GULF OF MEXICO

THE THIRTEEN COLONIES 1763

BEFORE YOU READ

Sections in This Chapter

1. Colonial Similarities
2. Colonial Differences

Reading a Map

Use the map on the opposite page to answer each of these questions.

1. List the English colonies in each of these sections:

   Northern

   Middle

   Southern

2. Which colonies had frontier areas?

3. Refer to the map on page 84. What geographic feature slowed the movement of the frontier in the Middle Colonies and in the South?

Understanding a Key Concept: MIDDLE CLASS

Population is the number of people in a place. During the 1700's the population of the American colonies kept growing.

- Most American colonists belonged to the **middle class**. They weren't rich, but they weren't poor, either. Most middle-class colonists owned their own farms or shops. They worked for themselves, not for a boss. They worked hard, but did not have a lot of power or money.

- In most colonies the rich were the most powerful people. They had the time and the money to take part in the government.

- The poor had little power. They couldn't vote and they had to work for someone else. Some poor people also had little personal freedom.

Write three headings: *middle class, rich,* and *poor*. Think about each person listed below. Write each one under the heading which best describes that person's position.

plantation owner	*small farmer*
skilled worker	*indentured servant*
large merchant	*shop owner*
slave	*blacksmith*

Choose one person from each list and write a sentence which tells why you think that person belongs to that group. For example, you might write:

<u>A blacksmith belongs to the middle class because he owns his own business.</u>

Using What You Already Know

Below are the beginnings of five sentences about transportation in the English colonies. Finish each one so that it tells about colonial transportation.

1. In many colonies, like Virginia and New York, rivers _____.

2. Because of the bad roads in the colonies, the easiest way to travel from Boston, Massachusetts to Charles Town, South Carolina, was by _____.

3. Because travel was slow, news and letters _____ .

4. Most frontier farmers didn't get to seaports because _____ .

1. COLONIAL SIMILARITIES

Main Ideas

Think about the following Main Idea questions as you read this section:

1. How had the populations of the colonies changed by 1750? How was the make-up of the population different?

2. What was family life like for colonial farmers?

3. How were both free and enslaved African Americans treated in the colonies?

4. How did news or people travel in the colonies?

5. How did religion change from Puritan times to the 1740s?

GOVERNMENT

England and Scotland Become "Great Britain"

In 1707, the governments of England and Scotland joined together to form one nation. This united country was called either "Great Britain" or just "Britain." Its colonies were called the **British colonies**.

The Government of the Royal Colonies

By 1750, all but four British colonies in America were **royal colonies**. In a royal colony, the king and his advisors were in charge, not a company or a proprietor. Each colony still had a governor, but the king chose him.

Each colony had an assembly that made laws and collected taxes. Only white men—not women, servants, Native Americans, or African Americans—who owned a certain amount of property could vote. They had to own even more property to run for office. In some colonies, like

New York and South Carolina, government was controlled by the very rich.

The Population Grows by Almost Five Times

All the colonies were growing. In 1700, about 250,000 colonists lived in America. By 1750, the number had grown to almost 1,200,000. Colonists had large families, new colonists arrived almost every day, and captive Africans were continually being brought in as slaves.

During the 1700s America became a place filled with people from many different cultures and religions. Most colonists were still English Protestants, but more and more were coming from other countries such as Ireland, France, and even Brazil.

Soon every colony contained people of several religions. Some, like the French Huguenots (HEW guh notz), who were Protestants, and Brazilian Jews, came to find religious freedom. There were Jewish merchants and peddlers, German Catholic plantation owners and barrel-makers, and Quaker farmers, printers, and shopkeepers. In most colonies, these people couldn't vote or hold office, but they still helped make the colony a success.

African Americans were also a growing part of the colonial population. Large numbers of slaves had been brought in during the 1700's. Slaves had children who were slaves, too. Every colony had both slaves and free African Americans. Their work also helped make colonies successful.

FARM LIFE

Family Life in a Country of Farmers

The family was the center of colonial life, just as it had been in Europe. In most families, the husband or father made the important decisions.

For women, life in the colonies was different from life in England. Few English women had ever had the chance to work outside the home. But in America, women helped in the fields and in other businesses. Some even ran newspapers or shops on their own.

Large families of five to eight children were common. By the time children were eight or nine, they were working beside their parents in the home and fields. If one parent died, the other often remarried quickly. There was too much work for one adult.

Most colonists lived on farms that they owned. Farming made only a few people rich: the plantation owners and others who had large farms with many workers. Some merchants also became rich, by exporting farm products and importing goods to sell to the farmers. However, most people were neither rich nor poor, but were middle class—small farmers who owned their own farms, shopkeepers in small towns, or skilled workers and craftspeople.

On small frontier farms the family did all the work. On medium-sized farms a few indentured servants or slaves helped. On the great southern plantations, however, nearly all of the work was done by slaves.

ENSLAVED AND FREE BLACKS

The Voyage from Africa to America

To feed the demand for labor, thousands of men, women, and children were captured in Africa and packed into ships. Crowded conditions, sickness, and bad food killed many of them on the voyage to America. When they arrived, everything, including even the food and trees, was different from what they were used to. They were separated from their families and forced to do hard, tiring work. They were treated as property, not as people.

Slaves and Free Blacks in the South

There were many more slaves in the Southern Colonies than in the North because plantations depended on slave labor. Plantation owners who could afford many slaves became very rich.

Slaves had no freedom and few rights. Free African Americans had few rights, too. Southern assemblies passed many laws to control blacks, both free and slave. In Virginia, a slave had to have written permission to leave the plantation. In South Carolina, blacks were not allowed to work in any kind of trade. In Georgia, slaves could not be taught to read or write. Free blacks could be forced back into slavery if they did not pay their taxes. Whites had to be at any meeting of blacks, free or slave.

Slaves and Free Blacks in New England and the Middle Colonies

In New England and the Middle Colonies, a smaller number of colonists owned slaves. These colonists usually lived in a city or on a small farm and had only a few slaves to help them. They didn't depend completely on their slaves the way people in the South did. Many taught their slaves to read or taught them a skill and treated them well. The Northern Colonies did not have as many laws to control slaves as did the South. Some slaves even earned their freedom, and either began farms or businesses of their own or worked for pay.

But in all the colonies, white people believed that they were better than blacks. Even free African Americans were not given as many chances for education or jobs as whites. They had few rights, and no black person anywhere was allowed to vote.

SKILLED WORKERS

Masters and Apprentices

Each colony contained skilled workers as well as farmers. They never had enough skilled craftsmen, though, such as cobblers (shoemakers), blacksmiths (iron workers), and coopers (barrel makers). To make up for the lack, most craftsmen trained new ones. A father would·bring his son to a skilled master craftsman for training. The boy, called an apprentice, lived and worked with the master, learning how to do all parts of the job. Women did not become apprentices, but many still learned to do skilled jobs from their fathers or husbands.

After the apprentice had worked for the master for several years, he went out on his own. He moved to a small town that needed skilled workers. The town's people would help him set up his own business because they needed someone with his skill.

TRAVEL PROBLEMS

Poor Roads, But Dependable Ships

Few colonists ever traveled, and most farm families never saw a city. Farmers only traveled when they didn't have work to do. Since this only happened during bad weather, they seldom took trips.

People traveled by water when they could. Roads were just muddy paths. Water travel was slow, but it was still faster than the roads. Small boats were used on streams and rivers, and large ships on deeper rivers and along the coast. Ships were often the best way to get from one colony to another. They were also the only way to reach the rest of the world.

Slow Letters and News

Because travel was slow, it took a long time for news and letters to reach people. The only way to contact another person was to write them or to ask someone to tell them something. These messages followed the slow travel routes and letters often took weeks to reach the next colony, and then even longer to reach a person's home.

THE PRINTED WORD

Pamphlets, Broadsides, and Newspapers

In the colonies' early years, books and newspapers had to be brought from England. When printing presses arrived, religious books were the first books printed. Soon the presses were also printing pamphlets and single sheets of paper, called **broadsides**, which told about recent events or new ideas.

Later, newspapers were started. In 1725 there were only five newspapers in the colonies. By 1765 there were twenty-five. Most were four pages long and came out once a week. Newspaper editors wrote about local news. World news stories were copied from English newspapers. This news was often months old before it reached the reader.

Almanacs

Almanacs were booklets written for people who didn't get newspapers. They were collections of useful facts—information about the tides, seasons, boat schedules, farming tips, and even recipes.

The most famous almanac was **Poor Richard's Almanac**. Philadelphia printer and scientist Benjamin Franklin used the name "Richard Saunders" in writing and printing it. Poor Richard's Almanac became famous for Franklin's clever sayings and proverbs, such as "A penny saved is a penny earned." Next to the Bible, it was the most popular book in the colonies.

Freedom of the Press and the Zenger Trial

Colonial governments paid close attention to what was printed. They didn't allow stories which criticized the government. John Peter Zenger was a newspaper editor in New York. He was arrested when his newspaper printed stories that criticized the governor. The governor said that any criticism of a governor was a crime. Zenger was tried, but the jury did not agree with the governor. They decided that the stories were true and that Zenger was not guilty. The Zenger trial was a victory for freedom of the press.

RELIGION

The Puritan Church Loses Political Power

As different types of people poured into the colonies, religious leaders began to lose political power. The change was greatest in those colonies that had been founded on religion, like Massachusetts. When Massachusetts became a royal colony, the Puritan church no longer controlled the government, although the church's leaders remained important.

The Salem Witch Trials

The Puritan church also lost power because of events in the town of Salem, Massachusetts. In May 1692, a group of children and young women claimed that they were being cursed by witches. Church leaders believed them and began a witch hunt. More than 200 people were arrested for being witches. Nineteen were tried, found guilty, and hanged .

After several months, people turned against the witch trials. Several church leaders finally admitted that they had been wrong. But by that time, nineteen innocent people had been killed.

▲ *The Salem Witch Trials. In the scene above, a young girl is pointing at two women whom she has accused of being witches.*

The church leaders never fully got back the respect and trust they had lost.

The Great Awakening

The way people practiced their religion changed, too. By the early 1700's, many people had stopped going to church. Then, beginning in the 1730's and lasting through the 1740's, the **Great Awakening** took place. Traveling ministers gave fiery sermons on the terrors of Hell and the joys of God's forgiveness. They made people think seriously about their religion and feel it in their hearts.

People began to go to church again. They traveled miles to hear well-known ministers, thousands coming to hear the most popular ones. People sang, shouted, and even fainted in church. This was very different from religion in the Puritan church and the Church of England.

SECTION REVIEW

Can you answer these Main Idea questions?

1. How had the populations of the colonies changed by 1750? How was the make-up of the population different?

2. What was family life like for colonial farmers?

3. Describe how both free and enslaved blacks were treated in the colonies.

4. How did news or people travel in the colonies?

5. How did religion change from Puritan times to the 1740's?

Can you identify this person?

John Peter Zenger

Can you define these terms?

Great Britain, royal colonies, apprentices, the Great Awakening, almanacs, Salem Witch Trials

2. COLONIAL DIFFERENCES

 Main Ideas

Think about the following Main Idea questions as you read this section:

1. How did New England, the Middle Colonies, and the Southern Colonies differ from each other?

2. How was the frontier different from areas where Europeans had lived for many years?

FOUR AREAS DEVELOP DIFFERENTLY

New England

There were four New England colonies: Massachusetts, New Hampshire, Connecticut, and Rhode Island. Many felt that this region, with its many small towns, looked like England. Most people owned farms but lived in town. Each town also had skilled workers and stores. New industries started up, making such things as guns and paper. Most people were middle class, and most men could vote. Laws were no longer based on religion. Instead, rich merchants from seaport cities like Boston, Massachusetts, made important decisions. They wrote laws based on trade and business, not religion.

The Middle Colonies

The four Middle Colonies were New York, New Jersey, Pennsylvania, and Delaware. They were sometimes called the "Bread Colonies" because so much wheat and grain was grown in them. Crops were exported from Philadelphia and New York.

Like New England, most of the Middle Colonies had many middle-class farmers, shopkeep-ers, and skilled workers. New York, though, was different. It had fewer colonists than the other colonies. A powerful group of rich families controlled the government, owned most of the land, and ran important businesses.

The Southern Colonies

The five Southern Colonies were Maryland, Virginia, North Carolina, South Carolina, and Georgia. In all these colonies, the rich owned large plantations and were far and away the most powerful people. Both rich plantation owners and small farmers could vote. However, few small farmers could afford to leave their farms to serve in the assembly. The plantation owners kept the power and made the laws.

The South had the fewest skilled workers and the smallest middle class. There were few towns and only one real city, Charles Town in South Carolina.

The large plantations used slaves to work in the fields and homes. Sixty percent of the blacks in all the colonies lived in Maryland and Virginia. In South Carolina, over half the population was black. Southern whites lived in constant fear of slave revolts. Because they were afraid, they wrote more and more laws to control the slaves.

The Frontier

Throughout the colonial era, colonists moved west to find unfarmed land. In many places the Appalachian Mountains stopped them. Some colonists traveled westward into Pennsylvania. Others took an old Indian trail down the Shenandoah Valley in Virginia. This became known as **The Great Wagon Road**.

Frontier colonists owned only their horses or oxen and a few goods. They searched until they found flat, rich land with a good supply of water. Often it was deep in the wilderness, far from any town.

Many of these colonists were Scotch-Irish or German. The Germans built neat, large farms on the northern frontier, particularly in Pennsylvania. The Scotch-Irish built smaller farms further south, in the valleys of the Appalachian Mountains.

Because they were far from towns, frontier families learned to live off the land. Their food, homes (log cabins), and clothes (deerskin) came from what they found nearby. These colonists lived like the earliest English colonists did. They had to supply everything they needed themselves.

By the middle of the 1700's, the British colonies were no longer just a few tiny settlements along the Atlantic coast. New colonists filled the land between the ocean and the Appalachian Mountains. For most people, the farm and family remained the center of life, but trade and towns were becoming more and more important. Colonial life was increasing in variety and vigor.

SECTION REVIEW

Can you answer these Main Idea questions?

1. How did New England, the Middle Colonies, and the Southern Colonies differ from each other?

2. How was the frontier different from areas where Europeans had lived for many years?

Can you define these terms?

Bread Colonies, Great Wagon Road

AFTER YOU READ

Discussion Questions

1. List some of the problems the colonists had. Which of these are no longer a problem?

2. Discuss how skilled workers and farmers depended on each other.

3. What kinds of freedoms did white colonists have that free and enslaved blacks did not ?

4. If you could change one area of colonial life, what would you do? How do you think this would change life in the colonies?

Comprehension Questions

I. Read the following sentences about the life of a colonial family. As you come to a blank, use information from the chapters about the English colonies (Chapters 7, 8, 9, and 10) to write a phrase that completes the sentence correctly. The information in the other sentences can help you, too. The first is done for you.

John and Mary Williams lived on a small farm in the frontier area of North Carolina.

1. Their family was very large.

2. The work on the farm was done by _____.

3. On their farm they grew _____.

4. The Williams did not go to town often, because _____.

5. John Williams voted for a representative to the _____.

6. Mary Williams did not vote because _____.

7. Peter Jones lived near the Williams family. He was a blacksmith. He was teaching blacksmithing skills to his ____.

8. John often talked over the news with Peter. They learned what happened in New York or London when _____.

9. Although there was no church nearby, the two families went to hear _____.

10. There was no school, but Mary Williams _____.

11. Jack Rip owned a huge plantation nearby. On it, most of the work was done by _____.

12. The richest and most powerful person in the area was _____ because _____.

II. Reread the sentences you have written about colonial life. Add three more sentences of your own that tell other details about life for the Williams family, Jack Rip, Peter Jones, or any other person who lives nearby.

Writing Activity

Pick a colony. List details about the first European colonists who settled there. Make another list of details about the colonists who lived there after 1700. Include what they did for a living, the kinds of farms and towns they built, their government, workers, and businesses. Use your lists to write a short essay describing the changes that happened in that colony. You can follow the form below.

Paragraph 1: early colonists.

Paragraph 2: later colonists.

Paragraph 3: compare the two times— tell which time you like best and why.

PROFILE OF A PEOPLE

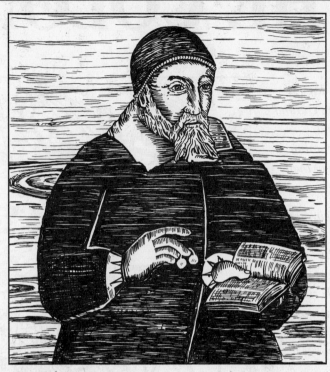

By the mid-1700's, the Puritan Church—as it had been known by the earliest colonists—no longer existed. What was it that had disappeared? What had the original Puritan lifestyle been like?

In the earliest days, when they had first come over from England, Puritan life had been defined by the Puritan religion. They had come to America to be free to practice it, and also in order to set an example for the rest of the world. In America, they planned to build the life they believed everyone should live. Others, they thought, would then follow their example.

The Puritans believed that everyone had to work together to create this perfect place. Everyone had to watch their family, friends, and neighbors to make sure they were following the rules.

These rules—which came from the way they read the Bible—included attending church and being hard working and thrifty. There were rules about everything: food, drink (people could drink alcohol, but not get drunk), clothes (dark colors), even hobbies (have one, but don't do it too often).

Because the Puritans thought that all of life's answers were in the Bible, they believed that everyone should know how to read, and therefore built schools to make sure that their children learned. They also founded Harvard College for men who wanted to continue their education.

Puritan churches were plain, and had no organ music, religious pictures, statues, or fancy ceremonies. They were very different from the huge, ornate churches in England.

The Puritans could be very intolerant. They believed that they had the only true religion. If someone had an idea that was different from what their church said, other Puritans would try to change that person's mind. If that didn't work, the person had two choices: keep quiet and go to church anyway, or leave Massachusetts.

The Puritan's believed that only a few people were chosen by God, and that these were the only people who could tell if someone else was really "chosen." Being one of the Chosen—who also made the important decisions and ran the government—was like being a member of an exclusive club.

After more than 150 years, the thirteen British colonies were coming into their own. Culturally and economically, they were becoming more than just an extension of their mother country.

They were developing their own identity, separate from that of Britain. An American identity—despite their differences, New England colonists and Southern colonists had more in common with each other than they had with Englishmen.

American raw materials were being traded on both sides of the Atlantic, carried on American ships. Certain high-quality or luxury goods still came to America from Britain, but increasingly, the colonies didn't need Britain anymore, not the way they had in the beginning.

However, the colonies were still politically tied to Britain; they were ruled from an ocean away. And Britain still felt that the colonies were there for Britain's benefit. That was, after all, why most of the colonies had been settled—because doing so was to Britain's advantage.

Growing American national identity struggled against British self-interest. The stage was set for one of the most important events ever—the American Revolution.

CHAPTER 11

COLONIAL UNHAPPINESS

In 1689, England went to war with France. This was the first of four colonial wars fought by England and France (and sometimes Spain). The last of them, called the French and Indian War, ended the French Empire in America. British colonists were proud to be part of the winning British Empire. But within ten years, discontent with British laws, British taxes, and the British army were splitting the colonies from the British government. Within fifteen years, the colonies and Britain were at war.

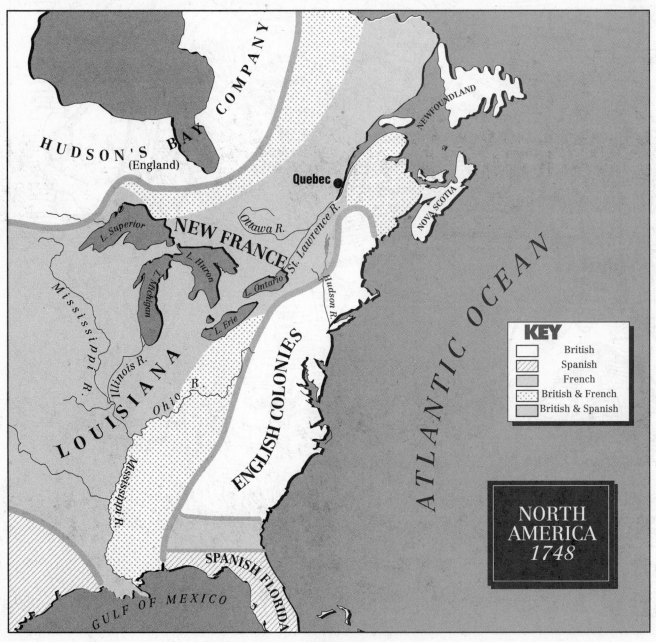

HUDSON'S BAY COMPANY
(England)

Quebec

NEWFOUNDLAND

L. Superior   NEW FRANCE   Ottawa R.   St. Lawrence R.   NOVA SCOTIA

L. Huron

L. Michigan

L. Ontario

L. Erie

Mississippi R.

Illinois R.

LOUISIANA   Ohio R.   Hudson R.

Mississippi R.

ENGLISH COLONIES

ATLANTIC OCEAN

SPANISH FLORIDA

GULF OF MEXICO

KEY
- British
- Spanish
- French
- British & French
- British & Spanish

NORTH AMERICA 1748

130

BEFORE YOU READ

Sections in This Chapter

1. The Colonial Wars
2. Strains Between England and the Colonies
3. A Series of Crises

Reading a Map

Using the map on the previous page, answer the following questions.

1. For each place below, tell which European country claimed it in 1748?

   a. Quebec

   b. northern Mississippi River

   c. Nova Scotia

   d. Florida

2. Did Britain, France, and Spain all agree on which territory each country owned?

3. Which country had the most territory in the eastern half of North America? The least territory?

Understanding a Key Concept: CRISIS

A **crisis** is an event that marks a turning point. Life changes because of what happens during a crisis. All throughout history there have been important crises. For example, the Aztec Empire was at a crisis when Cortés landed in Mexico. The Aztec and the Spanish could have handled the crisis in many ways— talking peacefully, becoming allies, fighting immediately, giving up, or become slaves. Do you remember what actually happened? For each crisis below, list three ways that it might have been solved. Then complete the sentence with the way it actually happened. One is done for you.

1. Columbus' colonists on Hispaniola needed workers.

   To solve the crisis the colonists could have:

   worked harder; brought in Europeans to work; or made the Indians into slaves.

   <u>Columbus' colonists on Hispaniola needed workers, so they made the Indians into slaves.</u>

2. Pizarro and his Spaniards killed the Inca king.

   To solve the crisis the Inca could have:

3. The Pueblo Indians didn't like how the Spanish treated them.

   To solve the crisis the Indians could have:

4. The Jamestown settlers weren't working hard enough to survive.

   To solve the crisis the settlers could have:

5. The first winter the Pilgrims didn't have enough food.

   To solve the crisis they could have:

Making Use of What You Already Know

Use what you already know about the British government and the colonial governments to answer to the following questions.

1. King George III was king of Great Britain. What power did he have over the British colonies?

2. Another part of the British government was its legislature, or Parliament. People in Britain elected representatives to Parliament. The British colonies also had legislatures. What were they called?

3. Who elected the representatives to the colonial legislatures?

4. What did the colonial legislatures do?

1. THE COLONIAL WARS

Main Ideas

Think about the following Main Idea questions as you read this section:

1. How were wars in Europe different from wars in America?

2. Why did important people like Benjamin Franklin believe that the colonies had to work together?

3. Why were the British able to win the French and Indian War?

4. How did the colonists help or hurt the British chances to win?

THE FIRST THREE WARS BETWEEN BRITAIN AND FRANCE

Three times between 1689 and 1748 British and French colonists fought. They fought over the fur trade, over borders, and because the two mother countries were fighting in Europe. Most of the fighting took place in the North, along the New York and New England frontiers and in Canada.

A Different Kind of Fighting Than in Europe

The fighting in America was different from the fighting in Europe. There, armies fought battles and their fighting followed certain rules. They stood in long lines and fired at each other in open fields. Only professional soldiers fought.

In America, these rules didn't apply. Along the frontier, the French and their Indian allies burned farms, villages, and towns. The colonists and the Indians on the British side did the same. Both sides killed men, women, and children.

The colonists fought without help from Britain and without professional soldiers. They had to form volunteer armies, or *militias.* Each colony had its own militia and protected itself.

Britain Gains Some French Lands in Canada

At the end of the third war, called King George's War, Britain gained land in North America. The French colony of Acadia in Canada became the British colony of Nova Scotia. Years later, the French who lived there were forced to move. Many moved to the area around New Orleans, which was still a French colony. Their French-speaking descendants still live there now. Their name has been shortened from "Acadians" to "Cajuns."

Both Spain and France wanted to make sure that British settlers did not move onto their land. They sent soldiers to protect their colonies and started more settlements. The French, for example, started settlements in southern Illinois and built forts in the Ohio Valley.

THE ALBANY CONGRESS

A Failed Plan for Union

Benjamin Franklin and other important men in the British colonies realized that the colonies needed to work together. The British government also realized this. In 1754 it asked the colonies to meet together and come up with a plan for dealing with hostile Indians and protecting themselves.

The meeting, or **congress**, was held in Albany, New York. Seven colonies sent representatives. Many of the representatives knew about the successful League of the Iroquois. They kept the League in mind when they put together their own plan for uniting the colonies. This plan— called the Albany Plan— said that the colonies would work together and would pay taxes to a united government.

The Albany Plan was sent to each colonial assembly, but not one agreed to it. In addition, the British government feared that the plan would make the colonies too independent. The work of the Albany Congress was not wasted, though. During the American Revolution, the Albany Plan was used to help plan the first United States government.

Talks with the Iroquois

During the Albany Congress, the colonists met with several Iroquois chiefs to ask them to remain allies with the British. However, the Iroquois knew that the French were building forts and that the British weren't. They also thought that the British colonists couldn't work together. The Iroquois made no promises.

Other Indians supported the French, who were trying to stop the British from settling more land. British settlers were cutting down forests, planting fields, driving away the animals, and forcing the Indians to leave. The French, on the other hand, traded with the Indians and left the wilderness alone. For that reason, many Indians liked the French colonists better.

THE FRENCH AND INDIAN WAR

George Washington Starts a War

The last of four colonial wars between Britain and France began in 1754. A 22-year-old commander of the Virginia militia named George Washington led several hundred militiamen to the Ohio Valley to build a fort to keep the French out of land claimed by the British. However, near where Pittsburgh is today, he found a French fort, Fort Duquesne.

The Virginians attacked a small group of French soldiers, but the French chased them away. George Washington had started a war.

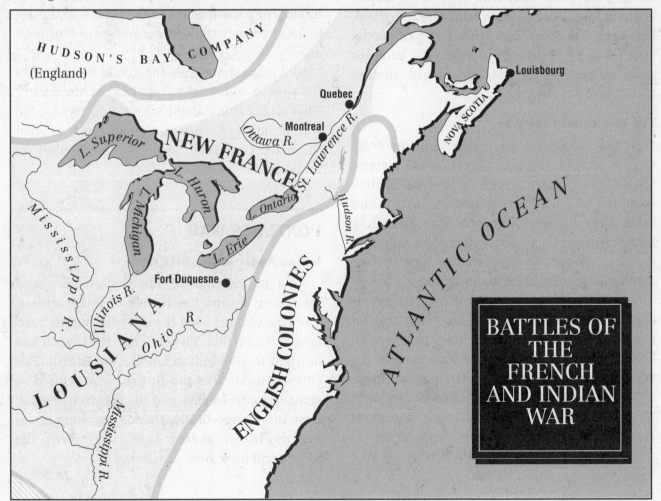

BATTLES OF THE FRENCH AND INDIAN WAR

General Braddock's Defeat by the French

The British sent an army to America to protect their valuable colonies. The British general, Edward Braddock, was brave but stubborn, and had no experience fighting the way the colonists did.

With Washington at his side, General Braddock set off to capture Fort Duquesne. In their bright red coats, the British marched close together along a narrow wilderness road, making themselves perfect targets. French soldiers and their Indian allies hid in the woods and shot the British down. General Braddock and almost a thousand of his men were killed.

The War Spreads to Europe

War soon broke out in Europe. The British fought both the French and the Spanish. At first the British lost battles in Europe, the Pacific, and in America. Then, in 1756, a new, strong leader, William Pitt, became prime minister of England. He changed the way the British were fighting the war. He appointed new generals, paid Britain's allies to fight in Europe, and moved another British army to America.

The British Win the War

When the British army arrived in the colonies, it faced many problems. Colonial assemblies did not want to pay or feed the British soldiers. Few colonists joined the army, and those who did were unhappy with army life. Many returned home before they were supposed to. The colonists only wanted to protect their families, not to fight in distant places.

Another problem was that the British generals did not understand the American way of fighting. They didn't understand why the colonists dressed to blend in, hid behind trees, or ran through the forest instead of marching in lines.

Nevertheless, the British planned carefully. They won many battles and took important French forts in New York, New England, Pennsylvania, and Canada. When the British army took the key French forts of Louisbourg, Montreal, and Quebec, everyone knew that the French had lost their power in America. A peace treaty was signed in 1763. Britain had won the war.

France Loses Its American Colonies

The French and Indian War changed who controlled America. France lost all her land and colonies there, except for a few tiny islands.

The British took over all the French land east of the Mississippi River, including Canada and the Ohio River valley. The British also took Florida from the Spanish, although 20 years later the Spanish got it back. Spain received New Orleans plus Louisiana—France's lands west of the Mississippi River.

Winning the war made the colonists proud to be British. They were also glad that they didn't have to worry about the French or Spanish anymore. They thought that the Indians would remain at peace without their powerful European allies.

Colonists started moving into Indian lands on the western side of the Appalachian Mountains. They didn't think about who would pay for the war, or how to govern all the new land, or what the Indians might do about the new settlers on their lands.

PONTIAC'S WAR

Indian Anger at the British

In 1763 the Ottawa Indians started a war of their own against the British and the settlers. The Ottawas had been the main fur trading partners of the French. They felt that the French had no right to give Indian land to the British. The Ottawas didn't like the British, who refused to give them gifts each year as the French had done. Even more importantly, the Indians were afraid that the British settlers would cut down the forests and turn them into farms.

A Two-Year Frontier War

The Ottawa Indians struck first at the British fort near Detroit, Michigan. They were led by Pontiac, a chief who lived nearby. Before the war was over, eighteen tribes had joined the Ottawas to fight the colonists. From the Great Lakes to Virginia, people were killed and farms and forts burned.

After two years of fighting, British soldiers and colonial militias crushed the Indian attacks. Most of the Indians soon accepted peace. The British had won again. The colonists were pleased because another threat to settlement was gone.

SECTION REVIEW

Can you answer these Main Idea questions?

1. How were wars in Europe different from wars in America?

2. Why did important people like Benjamin Franklin believe the colonies had to work together?

3. Why were the British able to win the French and Indian War?

4. How did the colonists help or hurt the British chances to win?

Can you identify and locate these places?

Albany, Ohio River Valley, Louisiana, Detroit

Can you identify these people?

George Washington, General Braddock, Pontiac, William Pitt, Ottawa Indians,

Can you define these terms?

militia, congress

2. STRAINS BETWEEN BRITAIN AND THE COLONIES

Main Ideas

Think about the following Main Idea questions as you read this section:

1. What plans did the British government have for the new lands it controlled? Did these plans differ from the plans the colonists had or from what the Indians wanted?

2. What ideas did many English people have about the British colonists?

3. Why were many colonists upset with the British government?

4. Why did the colonists believe that they were victims of taxation without representation?

PROBLEMS WITH BRITISH PLANS FOR THE NEW LANDS

A Law Limits Settlement West of the Appalachians

The colonists weren't pleased with the results of the French and Indian War for long. The British government realized that the huge, new, unsettled lands that they had won would be hard to govern. In addition, the British didn't want any more trouble with the Indians. So, even before Pontiac's War broke out, Parliament passed the **Proclamation of 1763**. This law said that no settlements could be started west of the Appalachian Mountains. No colonists would be allowed to move into the land that Britain had just won from France and Spain.

The colonists were very upset. The population along the coast was growing, and many people wanted to move west and build farms on the new, rich lands. Besides, said several colonial assemblies, that land was already given to us in our charters.

Angry colonists complained, but no one in Britain listened. Many colonists ignored the Proclamation and moved into the new areas anyway.

The British Take Over Canada

When the British took over Canada from the French, they made important changes. Canada became an British colony and the center of the English fur trade was moved from New York to Montreal. This upset the New York merchants.

Then, 11 years later, the British made new decisions about Canada. They said that the

▲ *King George III. He was only 22 when he became king, and about 30 when this portrait was painted. King George was a complex figure. Very moral and dignified in his private life, he was also subject to bouts of insanity.*

French colonists there could keep their language, religion, and land. But the new colonial government of Canada would not have an elected assembly. This worried the other British colonies, who were afraid that the British government might take away their own assemblies. They also feared that France might try to take Canada back.

Problems with a New King and His Advisors

George III became the British king during the French and Indian War. Many men advised him about what to do in the colonies. Each had a different opinion, but none had ever visited America.

Some advisors believed that the colonists had a right to take part in the British government. Others felt the colonists should have a separate government in America. Still others felt that because Parliament represented everyone in the British Empire, no changes were necessary. Finally, some advisors believed that the king alone could decide important matters about the colonies. The new king believed this, too.

The British Look Down on the Colonists

An important Philadelphia columnist, Benjamin Franklin, went to England in 1757. He was surprised at how little the English people knew about their colonies. While there, he met many of the king's advisors, some of whom thought that the colonists could not take care of themselves, even though they had been doing so for 150 years. Others thought that the colonists were not equal to the English. They didn't understand that most of the colonists were from England, thought of themselves as English, and wanted the same rights that people in England had.

DISAGREEMENTS OVER TAXATION

The British Tax the Colonists to Pay for the War

The British had won the French and Indian War, but it had been expensive. They had borrowed heavily and had to repay the money after the war. Parliament felt the American colonies, who had benefited from the war, should help with the repayment. They began to tax the colonists, placing taxes on sugar, indigo, coffee, and molasses.

Before, the colonists had often ignored taxes because no one had forced them to pay. Now, though, a British army was staying in America. British soldiers could force the colonists to pay the new taxes.

The colonists were worried. There were no enemies to fight, but the British army stayed in America anyway. Some colonists felt as if they were the enemy now. Others worried because the British were taxing their trade without asking them. They were afraid Parliament would add other taxes without asking. Colonists began to worry about the future.

Taxation without Representation

Before the French and Indian War, the British government didn't help the colonists build roads or fight Indians. Each colonial assembly did those things for its own colony, taxing the colonists and using the money for what was needed. The

▲ *Stamps used in the Stamp Act. (See Section 3.) These were not stamps like postage stamps, but were more like the inked stamps used with stamp pads.*

assemblies did the same job for their colonies that Parliament did for Britain.

After the war, though, Parliament added more taxes for the colonists to pay. The colonists had no say in the matter, for no one represented them in Parliament. They weren't allowed to elect members to Parliament, and the men in Parliament represented only the people in Britain who had elected them.

The colonists wanted their own assemblies to write all their laws and taxes, or else they wanted to be able to elect members to Parliament. Either way, they wanted to have a say in the taxes they paid. They didn't want **taxation without representation**, but instead wanted a chance to consent, or agree, to the laws and taxes that controlled their lives.

For the next thirteen years the colonists and the British disagreed about taxes and rights. The colonists felt that the British government was taking away their basic rights, while the British government felt that the things the colonies wanted were not their rights at all.

SECTION REVIEW

Can you answer these Main Idea questions?

1. What plans did the British government have for the new lands it controlled? Did these plans differ from the plans the colonists had or from what the Indians wanted?

2. What ideas did many English people have about the British colonists?

3. Why were many colonists upset with the British government?

4. Why did the colonists believe that they were victims of taxation without representation?

Can you identify this person?

King George III

Can you define these terms?

Proclamation of 1763, taxation without representation

A cartoon showing the burial of the Stamp Act (the small coffin held by the fourth man from the front) in a grave holding other violations of freedom, such as general warrants. The original cartoon, of which this is a copy, is said to have been published within minutes of the Stamp Act being repealed. A discussion of the Stamp Act can be found in Section 3 (next page).

3. A SERIES OF CRISES

Main Ideas

Think about the following Main Idea questions as you read this section:

1. Why did the colonists feel the Stamp Act was taxation without representation?

2. How did Parliament try to raise money from the colonists?

3. Compare the reactions of the colonists and of the British to the Boston Massacre and the Boston Tea Party. How were they similar? How were they different?

4. How did the colonists react to the new laws that the king and Parliament passed?

THE STAMP ACT

A Tax on Printed Items

The first big crisis between the colonists and the British government was over the **Stamp Act**. Parliament passed this law in 1765. Newspapers, legal papers, even ads and playing cards had to have a special stamp. The British government sold these stamps to raise money and promised to use the money in the colonies. But this was the first time Parliament had tried to tax the colonists directly, instead of just taxing their trade. Every colonist was affected by the new tax, and they didn't like it at all.

Negative Reaction to the Stamp Act

Many people in Parliament knew that the colonists wouldn't like the Stamp Act, but no one had guessed just how strongly they would react. In the colonial assemblies, great speakers, such as Patrick Henry of Virginia, spoke about whether or not Parliament had the right to tax the colonists. In Boston, Samuel Adams formed a group called the Sons of Liberty to fight the Stamp Act. Similer groups formed throughout the colonies. Mobs attacked the men who sold the stamps. Many stamp sellers quit. Others asked the British army for protection.

For the first time, the colonists joined together as Americans to solve a problem. Nine colonies sent representatives to New York for a **Stamp Act Congress**. The congress wrote to Parliament. Their letter stated that each colonial assembly could tax its own colony, but no one else could. They sent copies of the letter to every colony, because they wanted every American to understand their ideas.

For a time, the colonists **boycotted** English goods—that is, they stopped doing business with England. No goods were sent to or bought from England. Then, slowly, business began again, but without the stamps. No one used or bought them. Everyone just ignored the Stamp Act.

Parliament Repeals the Stamp Act

Parliament saw that it could not enforce the Stamp Act. They could not make the colonists buy and use the stamps. English merchants, who had been hurt during the boycott, wanted it to end. The year after it was passed, Parliament **repealed**, or did away with, the Stamp Act. The colonists celebrated when the news reached them.

This was the first time the colonies had worked together for something they believed in. But few people in England realized how important this was.

THE BOSTON MASSACRE

New Laws and New Taxes

Even after the Stamp Act was repealed, neither Parliament nor the king tried to find ways to work with the colonies. The king's advisors changed, but the new ones simply wrote new laws and new taxes. The **Townshend Acts**, named for the king's advisor, Charles Townshend, taxed many goods shipped to the colonies. Another law forced colonists to house and feed British soldiers. Still another allowed soldiers to search a colonist's home at any time, without any reason. When colonial assemblies tried to fight these laws, Parliament passed laws against them, too.

Soldiers Are Sent to America to Enforce the Laws

To enforce the laws, more British soldiers were sent to American cities like Boston and New York. Colonists were forced to let the soldiers live in their homes. Many soldiers openly showed their dislike of the colonists, who called them "redcoats" because of their uniforms. Colonial newspapers printed letters opposed to the soldiers, the new laws, and the new taxes. Pamphlets said that Parliament had gone too far, and could not take over colonial governments.

The Boston Massacre

Boston colonists hated having British soldiers in their city. For months, crowds there listened to people like Sam Adams speak against the soldiers and the British government. The colonists got angrier and angrier.

Then, on March 5, 1770, a crowd of colonists threatened a small group of redcoats. They threw snowballs at them and called them names. The crowd grew and the eight soldiers became frightened. Suddenly a gun went off, and the crowd began to move. The soldiers fired into the crowd.

Five men died, ordinary men just like many others who lived in Boston. Crispus Attucks was an African-American sailor. James Caldwell was learning to sail a ship. Samuel Maverick was a 17-year old apprentice, and Sam Gray was a rope maker. Patrick Carr was a worker from Ireland. Because of how they died, they became heroes to the colonists.

The next day thousands of angry colonists met to discuss the events some were already calling the **Boston Massacre**. Everyone who had been there told a different story. These stories

The Boston Massacre. The illustration at right is based on Paul Revere's famous engraving. Revere's picture exaggerated the situation, making the rioters appear very peaceful and non-threatening, and the British more cold-blooded than they were. Revere's engraving was a powerful piece of anti-British propaganda.

were repeated in pamphlets, letters, newspapers, and political cartoons. Often they were written in order to make people angry. Both in England and in the colonies, the stories about the Boston Massacre grew and grew.

The Trial of the Soldiers

All British soldiers were moved out of Boston. The eight soldiers who had been at the massacre were put on trial. John Adams, an important Boston lawyer, defended them. They were found not guilty, which surprised many colonists.

After the trial, the colonies became quiet. The anger seemed gone and the colonists began to think that better times had come. They thought Parliament had learned its lesson. In Massachusetts, Samuel Adams, the head of the Sons of Liberty, still tried to get people to fight Parliament, but few colonists paid much attention. The colonial assemblies went back to fighting between themselves. New York and New Hampshire almost went to war over where their border was. For a while, it looked as if the troubles with Britain were over.

THE BOSTON TEA PARTY

An English Company gets a Monopoly on Tea

In 1773 the colonies exploded again. This time the crisis was over tea. Parliament gave one company in England the right to sell *all* the tea in the colonies. No one could import or sell tea except that company. The colonists were furious. Once again, English merchants were being given more rights than American merchants.

Americans boycotted the company and refused to buy tea. In some colonies tea was never taken off the ships. In others, it sat on the docks unsold.

Samuel Adams Organizes a Tea Party

In Boston, the reaction was more violent. In December 1773, Samuel Adams and his Sons of Liberty dressed up as Mohawk Indians and dumped three shiploads of tea into Boston Harbor. This became known as the **Boston Tea Party.**

The colonists also set up groups called **Committees of Correspondence** in different towns. The committees wrote to each other to trade ideas about resisting the British. Special riders, like Paul Revere, carried the letters and other news quickly from town to town.

In Britain, the king and Parliament were furious. In 1774, they passed special laws to punish the colonies. Very few Englishmen tried to understand why the colonists felt and acted as they did.

THE INTOLERABLE ACTS AND THE FIRST CONTINENTAL CONGRESS

The Intolerable Acts Punish Massachusetts

Something that is so bad that people can barely stand it is said to be intolerable. The colonists called the laws that Parliament passed after the Boston Tea Party **The Intolerable Acts**.

The Intolerable Acts were aimed at Massachusetts. The king believed Massachusetts was acting alone. After all, he thought, the colonies couldn't work together to fight the Indians—how could they work together over some tea? The king thought that when the other colonies saw how he punished Massachusetts, they would never try anything against the British government again.

The Intolerable Acts changed Massachusetts' government. The assembly and town meetings were stopped, and General Gage, the commander of the British army in America, was made governor. Boston's harbor was closed. No ships could come in or leave until someone paid for the tea that had been dumped during the Boston Tea Party. Everyone in the city and the colony was being punished for what a few had done.

In every colony people suddenly changed their opinion of the British government. They knew that the Intolerable Acts could never have happened to a town in Britain.

A few men in the British government, like former prime minister William Pitt and even General Gage, tried to make Parliament understand why the colonists were upset. They warned that the colonies would join together to fight these acts and that Britain could lose her colonies because of them. But not enough people listened.

A Congress Meets in Philadelphia

In September and October, 1774, the **First Continental Congress** met in Philadelphia. Fifty-six men came from every colony except Georgia. Only a few of the men wanted independence. All wanted freedom, though, the same freedom that people in Britain had.

The First Continental Congress had no real power. It was not a true legislative body, but was simply a meeting of a group of men sent by their colonial assemblies. These men represented many different places, ideas, and ways of life. Some were plantation owners, some small farmers, some lawyers. Some wanted to fight, and some just wanted to talk. All wanted to find an answer to their problems with Parliament.

The Continental Congress Acts

First, the Congress agreed to help Massachusetts. Since Boston harbor was closed, food could not be sent to Boston by ship. So the Congress secretly sent it to Boston by land.

The Congress also said that the Intolerable Acts were against the basic laws of Britain, and that the colonists should not obey them. Congress asked people to form militias to resist the Acts. They also asked all colonists to stop trading with Britain.

Finally, the Congress wrote a **Declaration of Rights and Grievances**. It sent this to the king, not to Parliament. The Declaration listed the rights the colonists thought they had and their problems with Parliament. It asked for the same kind of government they had before the French and Indian War.

The wars with the French made the colonists feel closer to Britain and to each other. But after the wars, Britain and the colonies did not want the same things. Britain wanted to control the colonies' trade and to tax them without their permission. It also wanted to prevent trouble with the Indians by stopping the colonies from expanding. The colonists resisted, rioted, and disobeyed British laws. The actions of the First Continental Congress to deal with the crisis mark the end of the colonial period. War had not yet started, but a revolution had begun.

SECTION REVIEW

Can you answer these Main Idea questions?

1. Why did the colonists feel the Stamp Act was taxation without representation?

2. How did Parliament try to raise money from the colonists?

3. Compare the reactions of the colonists and of the British to the Boston Massacre and the Boston Tea Party. How were they similar? How were they different?

4. How did the colonists react to the new laws that the king and Parliament passed?

Can you identify these people?

Sam Adams, Sons of Liberty, Paul Revere

Can you define these terms?

Stamp Act Congress, boycott, repealed, Townshend Acts, Committees of Correspondence, Intolerable Acts, First Continental Congress, Declaration of Rights and Grievances

Can you describe these crises?

Boston Massacre, Boston Tea Party

AFTER YOU READ

Discussion Questions

1. How did the French and Indian War lead to the colonists' unhappiness with the British government?

2. What crises caused problems between the British government and the colonists? What might have been done to create better relations between them?

3. What stand would you have taken at the First Continental Congress, and why?

Comprehension Questions

I. One way to organize events is on a **timeline.** On a timeline, events are listed in the order in which they happened. Copy the dates below and then write each event under the year it took place. When more than one event took place in the same year, list them in the order in which they happened.

1754   1763   1765   1770   1773   1774
French and Indian War   Intolerable Acts
First Continental Congress   Stamp Act
Boston Massacre   Boston Tea Party

II. Another way to organize events is to identify *causes and effects*. Causes tell why something happened. Effects tell what happened.

The two lists at the top of the next column consist of parts of cause-and-effect sentences. When matched correctly, each sentence will tell why something happened and what happened. Match the parts to create the correct cause-and-effect sentences about several colonial crises. Rewrite the correct sentences.

CAUSES

1. Because wars were fought differently in Europe and in America, _____

2. Many people in the British government didn't think that the colonists were equal to people living in Britain, _____

3. When the colonists boycotted English goods, _____

4. Because of the Intolerable Acts, _____

5. Because of all the crises between the colonies and the British government, _____

EFFECTS

A. Parliament repealed the Stamp Act.

B. many colonists became angry at the British soldiers and the British government.

C. General Braddock's army was defeated.

D. so they agreed to taxation without representation and other harsh laws for the colonies.

E. the First Continental Congress sent the Declaration of Rights and Grievances to the king.

Writing Activity

Choose a crisis from Chapter 11. Brainstorm everything you know about it. Now pretend you are a colonial newspaper editor. Decide what your opinion would be about the crisis. Decide how you think the crisis should be resolved. Choose facts that support your opinion. Write an editorial for your newspaper which tells your opinion and gives facts that support it.

CHAPTER 12 THE AMERICAN REVOLUTION

The letter that the First Continental Congress sent to King George in 1774 did no good. Fighting soon broke out between Britain and the colonies. In 1776, the Second Continental Congress declared that the United States was independent of Britain. But the Declaration of Independence alone could not make the country free. Americans would have to fight a long war, called the American Revolution, before Britain would accept the loss of its colonies.

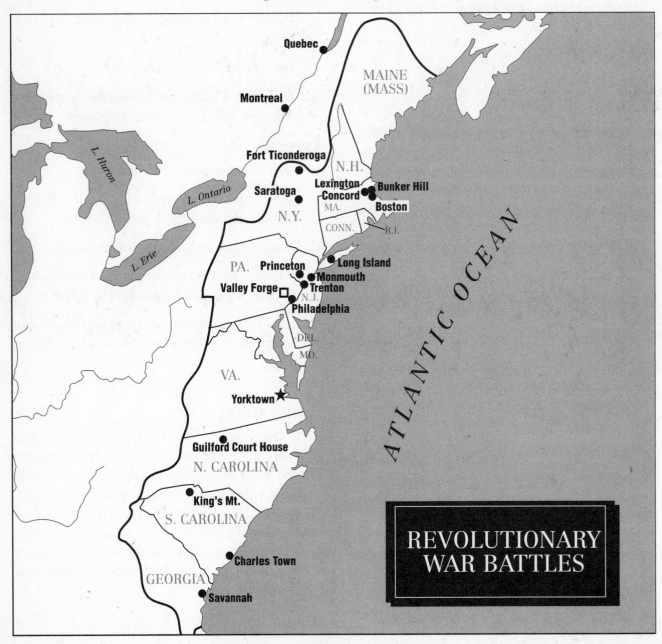

REVOLUTIONARY WAR BATTLES

BEFORE YOU READ

Sections in This Chapter

1. The War for Independence Begins
2. Independence and its Problems
3. The War in the North
4. War in the West and South

Reading a Map

The map on the opposite page shows where battles happened during the Revolution. Use it to answer the questions below.

1. In which states did battles take place?

2. Where outside the thirteen colonies did battles take place? What modern country is this?

3. Using the map, predict ways the British Navy might help the British Army win the war.

Understanding a Key Concept: INDEPENDENT COUNTRY

An **independent country** has its own government and makes its own decisions and laws. A colony is not independent because it depends on its mother country to run its government and make its laws. Some British colonists wanted to remain a colony, but with more freedom. Other colonists wanted to become an independent country.

Write these three headings on a piece of paper: COLONY BEING CONTROLLED, COLONY WITH SOME FREEDOM, INDEPENDENT COUNTRY. Write each of the following sentences under the heading that best describes it.

1. The Spanish king appointed everyone in Mexico's government.

2. Virginia's governor was appointed by the king, but its colonial assembly collected taxes.

3. The U.S. government writes laws that all people in the United States must follow.

4. American colonists protected themselves until the French and Indian War.

5. The British government said English colonists could not trade with France or Spain.

6. The United States controls its own trade with foreign countries.

Making Use of What You Already Know

War began between the 13 colonies and the British government. Those colonists who disagreed with the British government were called **Patriots**. Those who supported the British were called **Loyalists** or **Tories**. Read each sentence below. Write whether it describes the actions of a Patriot, a Tory, or the British. The first is done for you.

1. Paul Revere carried messages for the Committees of Correspondence. **Patriot**

2. Farmers joined the militia to stop the British soldiers.

3. They warned their neighbors to support the British or their farms would be destroyed.

4. They helped the British army wherever they could.

1. THE WAR FOR INDEPENDENCE BEGINS

Main Ideas

Think about the following Main Idea questions as you read this section:

1. Was the British army's trip to Lexington and Concord a success or a failure? What facts support your answer?

2. How did George Washington finally drive the British Army out of Boston?

FIGHTING AT LEXINGTON AND CONCORD

Preparations for Fighting

In early 1775, events in Massachusetts moved rapidly. Several towns formed special militia groups called **Minute Men**, who were ready to fight with only a minute's warning. The Minute Men started storing guns and supplies in their towns.

In April, General Gage, the British commander in Boston, received a message from England telling him to use his soldiers against the colonists. He decided to capture the cannons and other supplies that the colonists had hidden in the town of Concord, about 20 miles west of Boston.

Gage tried to keep his plans secret, but the colonists found out about them. The Minute Men hid the guns and supplies. The night before the British marched, two well-known Boston patriots, Paul Revere and Will Dawes, rode out from Boston to warn the Minute Men that the British were coming. This was Paul Revere's famous ride, in which he has often been pictured galloping madly down the road shouting "To arms, to arms. The British are coming! The British are coming!"

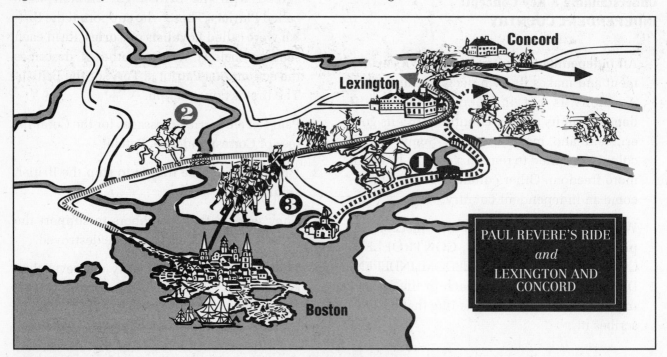

PAUL REVERE'S RIDE
and
LEXINGTON AND CONCORD

▲ ① *This was the route Paul Revere followed, when he rode out to warn the Minute Men that the British were on the march.* ② *William Dawes' route.* ③ *The route the British troops took, from Boston to Lexington and Concord.*

146

The Fighting Begins at Lexington and Concord

To get to Concord, the British had to march through the town of Lexington. At Lexington, they found Minute Men blocking their way.

Suddenly a shot was fired. No one knows who fired it. It may even have been an accident. Whoever fired it, and whether it had been an accident or not, this shot became one of the most famous shots ever fired. It was *the shot heard 'round the world,* and in a very real sense it represented the start of the American Revolution. British soldiers, reacting to it, fired at the Minute Men, killing eight. The rest of the Americans fled. The British marched on to Concord.

News of the shooting spread quickly. Soon Minute Men and thousands of other armed colonists took up hiding places along the road from Boston to Concord.

The British entered Concord and searched it. They found very little. As they marched back to Boston, the colonists hidden along the road fired on them. The British soldiers' bright red coats made them easy targets. More than 250 British soldiers were killed or wounded that day.

THE BRITISH IN BOSTON

The British Are Trapped Inside Boston

Once the British were back inside Boston, the militia surrounded the city. They were joined by militia from other colonies. Suddenly, the British were facing more than just a few farmers fighting for their land.

Whether anyone had wanted it or not, war had begun. At Lexington, a British army had fired on British colonists. At Boston, the British now faced an American army willing to fight for its rights.

The Battle of Bunker Hill

The British Army was never able to break out of Boston. They tried only once, at a battle called "The Battle of Bunker Hill," even though it was actually fought on nearby Breed's Hill. Many

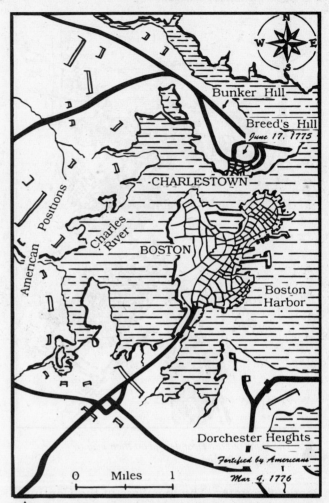

▲ *The Siege of Boston. The thick dark lines are roads; the American postions surrounding Boston are represented by the symbols that look like benches or sawhorses. Dorchester Heights was an important hill fortified with cannons from Fort Ticonderoga.*

British soldiers died attacking the hill. Finally, though, the Americans ran out of bullets and gunpowder and had to *retreat,* or move back.

The British took the hill, but nothing important had changed. The militia still surrounded Boston, and the British Army was still trapped.

The Second Continental Congress Raises an American Army

In May 1775, the **Second Continental Congress** met in Philadelphia. The men at this Congress wanted their rights, but still were not sure whether they wanted war. Most would have agreed to stop fighting if their rights were given back to them. Only a few, like Samuel Adams and his cousin John Adams, talked of an inde-

▲ *The Guns of Fort Ticonderoga on their way to the siege of Boston.*

The Guns of Ticonderoga Force the British out of Boston

Men came from all over New England, Virginia, Pennsylvania, and Maryland to join Washington's army. Each man brought his own gun, because the new army had few supplies. But no real fighting took place. The British knew that they could not break out of Boston, and Washington knew that he could not force them out. But he had a plan.

A Vermont patriot named Ethan Allen and his "Green Mountain Boys" had captured a British fort, Fort Ticonderoga on Lake Champlain in New York. The fort was falling apart, but it contained cannons and guns that the Continental Army needed.

Washington sent his artillery expert, Henry Knox, to Fort Ticonderoga. Knox's men dragged the fort's heavy cannons over snow-covered mountains to Boston. Once the guns were pointed at the city, the British sailed away, never to return.

pendent country. The members of the Continental Congress sent a new message to the king, once again asking for the colonists' rights.

The Congress also sent George Washington to Boston to take charge of the colonial militia. The militia surrounding the city became the **Continental Army**. It was the first American army, and Washington was its first commander-in-chief.

The Continental Army was very different from European armies at that time. There were no professional soldiers. Instead, the Continental Army was made up of farmers and skilled craftsmen, workers, and merchants. It was an army of the people. The Continental Army had less equipment and training than the British soldiers it was facing, but it did have some advantages. Many American soldiers were experienced hunters. They were good shots and knew the land well. And the American soldiers were highly motivated because they were fighting for their homes and their rights

SECTION REVIEW

Can you answer these Main Idea questions?

1. Was the British Army's trip to Lexington and Concord a success or a failure? What facts support your answer?

2. How did George Washington finally drive the British Army out of Boston?

Can you identify and locate these places?

Lexington, Concord

Can you identify these people?

General Gage, Paul Revere, John Adams, George Washington

Can you define these terms?

Minute Men, Continental Army, Second Continental Congress

2. INDEPENDENCE AND ITS PROBLEMS

Main Ideas

Think about the following Main Idea questions as you read this section:

1. Why did the Second Continental Congress write the Declaration of Independence? Why did they send it to so many places?

2. How were Tories different from Patriots?

3. What problems did the new country and its government have?

AN INDEPENDENT UNITED STATES

Americans were fighting British soldiers. Yet most colonists still were not sure that they should become independent. They wanted their rights, not their freedom. But little more than a year after the fighting had started, most had changed their minds: now they wanted independence.

King George Hires Hessian Soldiers

One thing that changed colonists' minds was that King George hired soldiers from other countries to fight them. Many of these soldiers were from the German state of Hesse, so they were called **Hessians**.

The Hessians were hired because the British Army was very small. Also, few Englishmen wanted to fight the colonists. Many were starting to think that the colonists might be right.

Hiring the Hessians enraged many colonists. They felt that the king was paying foreign soldiers to kill his own people.

Thomas Paine and Common Sense

Early in 1776, a pamphlet changed the minds of even more of the colonists. It was called **Common Sense**, and its author, Thomas Paine, was an Englishman who had been in America for only a year.

In strong, clear, exciting words Paine called for Americans to break all ties to Britain. King George III, he wrote, was a cruel and unjust king. Paine called him "The Royal Brute of Britain."

Everyone understood Paine's ideas. More than a hundred thousand people read **Common Sense** in its first three months. It helped convince colonists that they should be independent of Britain.

The pamphlet also helped pay for the war. Half a million copies were sold, and Paine gave Congress all the money he made from its sale.

The Declaration of Independence

By June 1776, the Continental Congress was ready to act. It formed a committee to write a **Declaration of Independence**. Thomas Jefferson from Virginia did most of the writing. Benjamin Franklin from Pennsylvania and John Adams from Massachusetts helped him.

The Declaration of Independence said that everyone has God-given rights to life, liberty, and the pursuit of happiness, and that people have a right to a say in their own government. Because King George had tried to take these rights away from the colonists, the colonists had the right and even the duty to break away from Britain. The Declaration listed all the things that the king had done wrong and said that now a new government would be formed to make sure that the people kept their rights. America would be independent.

Jefferson presented the Declaration he had written to the Continental Congress, whose members talked it over. Some parts, like a section against slavery, were dropped, but most of Jefferson's ideas stayed the same.

The official date of accepting the Declaration was July 4, 1776. Today, we celebrate July 4 as **Independence Day**.

The Declaration of Independence.
▶

The Declaration of Independence

*In Congress, July 4, 1776, the unanimous Declaration of the
thirteen united States of America*

When in the Course of human events, it becomes necessary for one people to dissolve the political bands which have connected them with another, and to assume among the Powers of the earth, the separate and equal station to which the Laws of Nature and of Nature's God entitle them, a decent respect to the opinions of mankind requires that they should declare the causes which impel them to the separation.

We hold these truths to be self-evident, that all men are created equal, that they are endowed by their Creator with certain unalienable Rights, that among these are Life, Liberty and the pursuit of Happiness. That to secure these rights, Governments are instituted among Men, deriving their just powers from the consent of the governed. That whenever any Form of Government becomes destructive of these ends, it is the Right of the People to alter or to abolish it, and to institute new Government, laying its foundation on such principles and organizing its powers in such form, as to them shall seem most likely to effect their Safety and Happiness. Prudence, indeed, will dictate that Governments long established should not be changed for light and transient causes; and accordingly all experience hath shown, that mankind are more disposed to suffer, while evils are sufferable, than to right themselves by abolishing the forms to which they are accustomed. But when a long train of abuses and usurpations, pursing invariably the same Object evinces a design to reduce them under absolute Despotism, it is their right, it is their duty, to throw off such Government, and to provide new Guards for their future security.—Such has been the patient sufferance of these Colonies; and such is now the necessity which constrains them to alter their former Systems of Government. The history of the present King of Great Britain is a history of repeated injuries and usurpations, all having in direct object the establishment of an absolute Tyranny over these States. To prove this, let Facts be submitted to a candid world.

*[A list of wrongs done to the colonies by the King of England and the
British Government follows.]*

We, therefore, the Representatives of the united States of America, in General Congress, Assembled, appealing to the Supreme Judge of the world for the rectitude of our intentions, do, in the Name, and by Authority of the good People of these Colonies, solemnly publish and declare, That these United Colonies are, and of Right ought to be Free and Independent States; that they are Absolved from all Allegiance to the British Crown, and that all political connection between them and the State of Great Britain, is and ought to be totally dissolved; and that as Free and Independent States, they have full Power to levy War, conclude Peace, contract Alliances, establish Commerce, and to do all other Acts and Things which Independent States may of right do. And for the support of this Declaration, with a firm reliance on the Protection of Divine Providence, we mutually pledge to each other our Lives, our Fortunes and our sacred Honor.

Each member of the Continental Congress signed the Declaration. John Hancock, the president of the Continental Congress, was the first to sign. It is said that he signed his name very large so that King George would have no trouble reading it.

Copies of the Declaration of Independence were sent to every colony, to Britain, and to other countries. It explained to the world why the American colonies were breaking away from Britain.

LOYALISTS AND PATRIOTS

A Divided America

The war that America fought to become independent of Britain is called the American Revolution or the Revolutionary War.

The American Revolution split the country. Men and women, blacks and whites, farmers and Indians—all were on both sides. Even some families, like Benjamin Franklin's, were divided. Franklin was a leader in the fight for independence. His son, William, was the Royal Governor of New Jersey. The war divided Americans as well as uniting them.

Loyalists, or Tories, Support the British

Not every American wanted independence. Many felt the country should stay loyal to the king. These people were called **Loyalists** or **Tories**.

People were Loyalists for many different reasons. Some, like William Franklin, worked for the British government. Others were merchants who didn't want to lose their trade with Britain. Some feared the kind of government an independent America might have. Rich Tory landowners were afraid they would lose their land and power to small farmers. In North Carolina, however, many small western farmers became Tories when they heard that the big plantation owners were against the king. They didn't really agree with the British government, but they were against the powerful plantation owners.

Some Tories helped the British Army. Others left the country. But most stayed and kept quiet about what they believed.

Some slaves joined the British Army because they were promised their freedom. But many free blacks fought on the American side.

Some states asked people to swear that they were loyal to the new country. Many Loyalists refused. Some were put into jail, and everything they owned was taken away.

Patriots Support the Cause of Independence

Many Americans supported the fight for independence. They were called **Patriots**. Most wanted a bigger say in the government, like merchants who wanted fewer trade rules. Others supported the Continental Army because they didn't like the actions of the British army, and not because they cared who controlled the government.

The Declaration of Independence said that "all men are created equal." Under British rule, though, many—like Catholics, Jews, and free blacks—did not have full rights. They hoped that a new government would treat them as equal to any other American.

Most Americans didn't actually take part in the Revolution, but many did. Some joined the Continental Army, while others helped form new state and national governments, or acted as spies.

When men left to join the army or to work for the government, women kept the farms and businesses going. They kept their husbands informed by writing letters. These letters encouraged the men and talked about the British, the new government, and the crops or business.

A few women, like Deborah Sampson, dressed as men and joined the army. In some places, women even fought openly alongside the men. Women also nursed and hid and fed as many soldiers as they could. Thousands of Americans, men and women, young and old, helped win the war by their many small, brave acts.

PROBLEMS OF THE NEW GOVERNMENT

A New Government is Born

The Continental Congress had to form a whole new **federal** (national) government while the war was going on. This new government would be for the whole country, not just for one colony.

Many ideas from this new government are still found in our government today. However, it was not a strong government like the one we have now. It could not tax people, for example, or make them join the army. It had to ask each state for money, men, and supplies.

The Government has Problems with the States

Often, the states did not send enough of anything to the new federal government. Each state assembly wanted to keep everything inside its own state. No state wanted to lose power, or even share power with other states The federal government had a hard time because the states didn't always cooperate.

To get money to pay for the war, the states taxed their people. But they didn't want to give the money to the federal government. Since the states wouldn't pay, the federal government had to borrow money from individuals and from other countries. Both the federal government and the states printed money.

Help Comes from Other Countries

The Continental Congress sent men to France, Spain, and other countries to ask for help against the British. Money, and also guns, gunpowder, and even clothes were needed, because America had only a few workshops that could make these supplies. France gave the most help. At first, the French secretly sent supplies to America. Later, France sent an army and a navy to help the Americans.

Spain, too, finally agreed to fight Britain, although the Spanish disliked the idea of American independence. They were afraid that their own American colonies would also want to become free.

America especially needed help at sea, because it didn't really have a navy. During the war, British warships blocked sea routes to America. Some American captains, like John Paul Jones, raided British ships. But only a large navy, like France's, could fight the powerful British fleet.

SECTION REVIEW

Can you answer these Main Idea questions?

1. Why did the Second Continental Congress write the Declaration of Independence? Why did they send it to so many places?

2. How were Tories different from Patriots?

3. What problems did the new country and its government have?

Can you identify these people?

Hessians, Thomas Paine, Thomas Jefferson, Loyalists, Tories, Patriots

Can you define these terms?

Common Sense, Declaration of Independence, federal government

3. THE WAR IN THE NORTH

Main Ideas

Think about the following Main Idea questions as you read this section:

1. What was General Burgoyne's plan, and why didn't it work?

2. How did people help the Continental Army?

3. What were some of the important turning points of the war? What changed after each?

EARLY DEFEATS FOR THE AMERICAN ARMY

The Americans Fail to Win Canada

In May 1775, the Second Continental Congress sent George Washington to Boston. At the same time, it sent American soldiers to Canada. The Congress thought that Canadians wanted the same things American colonists did, and would join them against the British. But events did not turn out as Congress hoped. The Americans attacked and captured Montreal. Then, led by the brilliant Benedict Arnold, they tried to capture the city of Quebec. But the Canadians did not help the Americans at all, and the American attack failed.

The next spring, British ships loaded with soldiers began arriving in Canada, forcing the Americans to return home. By the time the Declaration of Independence was signed, the American soldiers had already left Canada.

Washington Loses the Battle of Long Island

The first real battle of the American Revolution was fought in August 1776, a month after the Declaration of Independence was signed. It would be the biggest battle of the war, and it took place on Long Island, in what is now Brooklyn, New York. The Americans lost the battle. George Washington was not trained in planning battles

and had no real plan for fighting this one. In addition, many officers and soldiers didn't follow orders. They had never been in an army before, and didn't know how to work together. Finally, the British outnumbered the Americans by almost 3 to 1. The Americans discovered that they needed more than courage and rifles to win the war.

But after the battle, luck helped the Americans. A bad storm kept the British Navy away while the American army was secretly moved from Long Island to safety on Manhattan Island. All night long, New England fishermen rowed small boats back and forth, in rain and fog. The entire army and its supplies silently disappeared across the water. The British didn't even know the Americans were gone until morning!

Washington's Army Retreats to Pennsylvania

For the next few months, Washington tried to keep control of New York City and the nearby countryside. But, after a series of small battles, he was forced to leave. More than half his army had been killed or captured. In late autumn he led what was left of his army through New Jersey and across the Delaware River into Pennsylvania.

New York City became the headquarters for the British army. Many of the people there were Tories who welcomed the British. For much of the war, there were three times as many British soldiers as Americans in the city.

Washington Crosses the Delaware and Wins a Victory

By December 1776, George Washington knew he had serious problems. His small army in Pennsylvania kept getting smaller. Many men were leaving for home. Soon those who had agreed to stay until January 1777, would leave.

On Christmas night, Washington led a bold attack. He and his men crossed the frozen and dangerous Delaware River from Pennsylvania into

New Jersey. Down icy roads they marched, into the town of Trenton. There they surprised and captured 900 Hessians, many of whom were still tired from their Christmas parties. A week later, Washington defeated British soldiers who had come to chase the Americans from Trenton.

Suddenly, Washington's men felt better about the war. Many decided to stay in the army. As news of the American victories spread, the new country became proud of its army.

VICTORY AT SARATOGA

British General Burgoyne Plans to Split the Colonies

In the spring of 1777, British General John Burgoyne put together a plan to separate New England from the rest of the states. Three British armies would march through New York. Burgoyne would lead the first army south from Montreal. The second would move north from New York City. The third would march east from Fort Niagara on Lake Ontario. All three would meet in Albany, splitting the new country.

In July 1777, Burgoyne's army left Montreal, bringing with it supplies, cannons, and twenty wagons of Burgoyne's personal goods. They marched into the forest, where they had to build log roads as they went. In places, Burgoyne could have taken an easier water route but didn't, giving the Americans time to get ready.

Burgoyne's Army is Defeated at Saratoga

An army engineer from Poland, Tadeusz Kosciuszko (ko-SHUSH-ko), helped the American army get ready. They built defenses near the town of Saratoga, just north of Albany. When Burgoyne's army arrived, the American Army and militia, under General Gates and Benedict Arnold, were waiting for them. There was no sign at all of the other two British armies.

The British weren't sure how to fight men in fur hats with long rifles, who sent orders to each other by gobbling like turkeys. During the fight-ing, Benedict Arnold was wounded as he led a raid on the British. On October 17, 1777, after two battles, General Burgoyne surrendered. It was the first defeat of a large British army, an important victory for America, and the turning point of the war.

The Army That Never Arrived

What had happened to the other two British armies? In New York City, General Howe didn't follow Burgoyne's plan. He captured Philadelphia instead. Washington lost two battles trying to stop him, but the fighting kept Howe's army so busy that it couldn't march to Albany. Another general, General Clinton, did lead his men up the Hudson. They chased New York's new state government as far as the town of Kingston. The British burned the town, but then returned to New York City instead of continuing north to join Burgoyne.

Fighting in Western New York

In western New York, the third British army joined with New York Tories and with Iroquois led by the Mohawk chief Joseph Brant. Many local people joined together to stop this force. Neighbor fought neighbor as Mohawks and rich Tory landlords fought against Patriot farmers and Iroquois from the Oneida and Tuscarora tribes.

The third British army finally returned to Fort Niagara. But the Indians and Tories kept attacking New York and Pennsylvania settlers until 1782, when a large American army was sent to crush them. Afterwards, many New York Tories moved to Canada. The Iroquois Confederacy split. Most Mohawks and Cayugas moved to Canada. The Oneidas moved west to Wisconsin, while other Iroquois groups remained in New York.

THE END OF THE WAR IN THE NORTH

A Harsh Winter at Valley Forge

At the start of the winter of 1777-1778, Washington's army moved to Valley Forge, Pennsylvania, a little town about 20 miles north of Philadelphia. The men were in terrible shape. Their shoes were falling apart and their clothes were in rags. They had hardly any soap. Their feet and hands became infected. They had to build wood and mud huts to protect themselves from snow and freezing temperatures. It was a hard winter, but the men still believed in George Washington and in what they were fighting for.

Things began to get better. Army officers from Europe, like Kosciuszco, came to help. Baron von Steuben, a German officer, trained small groups of men at Valley Forge. The men he trained then taught other soldiers how to work together as an army. A teenaged French nobleman, the Marquis de Lafayette, brought money and supplies. He became an important general in the war and a favorite with the American troops.

Nature helped, too. In the spring, supplies arrived, and so did a huge run of fish in the streams. Friendly Iroquois Indians of the Oneida tribe sent 800 bushels of corn. Martha Washington came and set up a hospital. Soon, Valley Forge was a happier, healthier camp.

Good news helped as well. After the American victory at Saratoga, France decided that America had a chance to win. Benjamin Franklin talked the French into joining the war as America's ally. The French sent supplies and soldiers. Most importantly, they sent the French navy.

General Clinton Returns to New York

The American victory at Saratoga made the British government rethink how they would fight the war. First, General Clinton replaced General Howe as commander. Second, the British also offered Congress a deal—if the Americans would give up the idea of independence, their rights would be granted.

Congress might have agreed, but they heard from France first. They knew that with France's help, America had a good chance to win the war.

The British knew it, too. Fearing an attack by the French Navy, General Clinton moved the British out of Philadelphia. There was one last battle in the North. It was at Monmouth, New Jersey, in June 1778. Neither side won, and Clinton's men returned to New York City. There were no more major battles in the North during the rest of the war.

Benedict Arnold Becomes a Traitor

In 1780, however, the British almost captured an important American fort without a fight. The fort was West Point, and it guarded the Hudson River.

The commander at West Point was Major General Benedict Arnold, the hero of Canada and Saratoga. But Arnold was angry at Congress, and he also needed money, so he secretly agreed to let the British take over the fort.

Fortunately, Arnold's British contact, Major John André, was captured. The men who captured him found that he was carrying secret papers from Arnold. When Arnold realized what had happened, he escaped to a British ship. André was hanged as a spy, and Benedict Arnold became America's most famous traitor.

SECTION REVIEW

Can you answer these Main Idea questions?

1. What was General Burgoyne's plan, and why didn't it work?

2. How did people help the Continental Army?

3. What were some of the important turning points of the war? What changed after each?

Can you identify and locate these places?

Montreal, Long Island, Valley Forge, West Point

Can you identify these people?

General Burgoyne, Tadeusz Kosciuszko, Benedict Arnold, General Howe, Joseph Brant, Baron von Steuben, Martha Washington

4. WAR IN THE WEST AND SOUTH

Main Ideas

Think about the following Main Idea questions as you read this section:

1. Why were the frontier battles of George Rogers Clark so important to the new country?

2. How did the British anger people in the South?

3. How did Greene's army fight the British?

4. What events led to the surrender of Lord Cornwallis at Yorktown?

THE FRONTIER WAR

Indian Trouble in Kentucky

During the Revolution, the famous frontiersman Daniel Boone brought many frontier families west across the Appalachians. They traveled through the **Cumberland Gap** in the mountains into Kentucky. However, settlers all along the new frontier were being attacked by Indians. The Indians' guns and supplies came from the British fort at Detroit.

George Rogers Clark Wins the West

A young frontier surveyor named George Rogers Clark thought of attacking the British forts west of the Appalachians. He asked Virginia for troops and supplies, but all he got was about 175 men.

With this small force, Clark set out for the Illinois frontier in June 1778. He quickly surprised and captured settlements that had once been French but were now British. He never had to fight a real battle. When British soldiers arrived from Detroit, Clark captured them, too, by fooling them into believing that he had more men than he really had.

Because of Clark's victories, the United States got all of the land west of the Appalachian Mountains, as far as the Mississippi River, when the war finally ended.

WAR IN THE SOUTH

The British Armies Move South

In 1778, the British government again changed its plans for the American war. They ordered the fighting moved to the South because they thought that the many Tories in the Carolinas would help them.

Under General Lord Cornwallis, the British Army sailed south. Early in 1779 they took control of Savannah, Georgia. By April 1880, Charles Town in South Carolina had been captured and so had much of the American Southern army. It looked as if the British plan was working.

The British Run into Trouble and Lose Support

The British sent a Tory army inland. The Tory commander warned frontier settlers that they would be killed if they didn't support the British. That was a bad mistake. Angry settlers joined together and wiped out the Tory army at the Battle of King's Mountain.

The British had trouble along the coast, too. Crafty American leaders like Francis Marion, nicknamed "the Swamp Fox," formed small groups of fighters who attacked the British soldiers and then disappeared into the swampy land they knew so well. The British couldn't follow them into the unfamiliar, dangerous swamps.

But worst of all for them, the British angered many people in the South. They burned the homes and farms of their own supporters, the Tories. They tried to get slaves to rebel and join them, but they also seized slaves and resold them in the West Indies instead of freeing them. They took food and horses from Americans because it took so long for supplies to come from Britain. Many people ended up helping the Continental Army because they were angry about the way the British army treated them.

Nathanael Greene Fights a Hit-and-Run War

In December 1780, Washington sent Nathanael Greene to command the Southern army. Greene was from Rhode Island, and at first the Southerners didn't like the idea of a New England commander. But Greene proved to them that he was a good leader and became a Southern hero.

Greene did not want to fight large battles. Too many Americans would die. Instead, he divided his men into small groups that took little bites out of the big British army. The British were forced to return to the coast. The Americans soon controlled most of Georgia and the Carolinas.

THE END OF THE WAR

General Cornwallis is Trapped at Yorktown

Cornwallis decided to take his army north into Virginia. After several small battles, his army moved onto the peninsula of Yorktown. There Cornwallis planned to meet with British soldiers who were being sent by sea from New York. But the soldiers never arrived. The French Navy arrived instead cutting off Cornwallis's army from its supplies.

In the north, a French army landed. The French general, Rochambeau, generously divided his money with Washington. They bought supplies, and then the two armies marched south. Arriving at Yorktown, they surrounded the British. Their cannons pounded the British army. Cornwallis was trapped.

The British Surrender

The army that surrounded Cornwallis was very different from the one that had surrounded Boston six years earlier. They knew how to fight together and how to obey commands. Soldiers from one state were proud of officers from another, and they were all proud of their commander-in-chief, George Washington.

On October 17, 1781, the huge French and American cannons stopped firing in order to move to better positions. In the quiet, a British drummer boy stepped onto Yorktown's wall and began tapping his drum. Someone else waved a white flag. General Cornwallis was surrendering.

Two days later every British soldier in Yorktown laid down his gun. British soldiers were still in New York City, Charles Town, and Savannah, but most of the fighting was over. America had won.

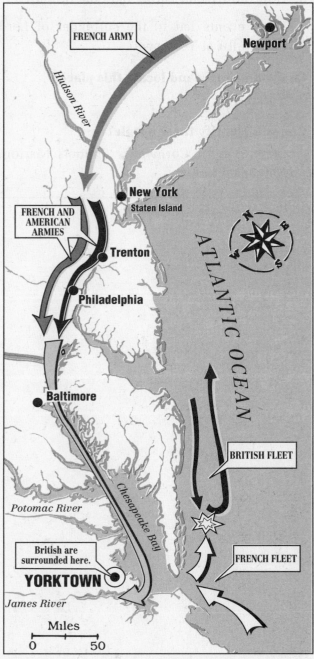

The Battle of Yorktown. A British fleet carrying reinforcements was turned away by the French Navy, while a joint American-French army marched south to trap Cornwallis.

King George Signs a Peace Treaty with America

Even after Yorktown, King George didn't want peace, but his advisors forced him to agree to it. In Paris, Benjamin Franklin, John Adams, and John Jay met with the British. They wrote and signed the **Treaty of Paris**, which ended the American Revolution.

The treaty gave America everything it wanted. America became an independent country. It reached from Canada to just above Florida, and from the Atlantic Ocean to the Mississippi River. Congress approved the treaty in April 1783. The war was over, even though the British army did not leave New York City until December.

It had been a long, hard fight. Hunger, sickness, cold, and poor training slowed the Americans. The state governments did not always give everything they could, but men from every state fought alongside each other until the end. People who had stayed at home fed soldiers from distant states. Soldiers saw parts of the country that were new to them and became friends with people who lived far away. The experiences of the American Revolution helped tie thirteen separate states together into a new nation, the United States of America.

SECTION REVIEW

Can you answer these Main Idea questions?

1. Why were the frontier battles of George Rogers Clark so important to the new country?

2. How did the British anger people in the South?

3. How did Greene's army fight the British?

4. What events led to the surrender of Lord Cornwallis at Yorktown?

Can you identify and locate this place?

Yorktown

Can you identify these people?

General Lord Cornwallis, Francis Marion, Nathanael Greene

AFTER YOU READ

Discussion Questions

1. Why do you think the first shot fired at Lexington was called *the shot heard 'round the world*?

2. What was the importance of the Declaration of Independence?

3. Describe how people who were not soldiers took part in the Revolution and in running the country.

4. Compare and contrast the British and Continental armies, their leaders, soldiers, plans, and problems.

5. How and why did the Continental Army change during the war? How did this affect the war's outcome?

Comprehension Questions

I. Read the general statements below. Then fill in the blanks with the statement that summarizes each set of details. The first one is done for you.

General Statements:

The British Army was prepared for war.

Americans held different opinions.

Indian tribes took part in the Revolution, too.

The war changed the lives of many Americans.

The British made mistakes during the war.

1. _The British Army was prepared for war._

   The British army had many cannons and guns.

   The British soldiers had strong shoes and new uniforms.

   The British soldiers were trained before they came to America.

2. _____

   Many men left home to fight in the army.

   Many women took over the farming.

   Many Tories moved to Britain or Canada.

3. _____

   General Clinton didn't follow General Burgoyne's plan.

   Lord Cornwallis' army angered Southern Americans with their actions.

4. _____

   Some Americans wanted the British to win.

   Some Americans hoped to take power away from richer Americans.

5. _____

   Joseph Brant's Iroquois fought with the British.

   The Oneida helped the New York militia.

   The British sold guns to Indian tribes.

Writing Activity

Pretend you are one of the following people:

- A representative to the Second Continental Congress

- A soldier at Valley Forge

- A farmer, after British soldiers have taken your crops and horses

As that person, write a letter to your family. Describe your problems and opinions. Tell what you are doing to help the Americans win or lose the war.

CHAPTER 13

AFTER THE REVOLUTION

During the Revolution, Americans worried about winning the war. Once it was over, they faced a new challenge—governing themselves as a single nation. It was something that they had never done before. In the years after the war, the fledgling nation faced a number of problems. Unfortunately, the new government was unable to handle many of them.

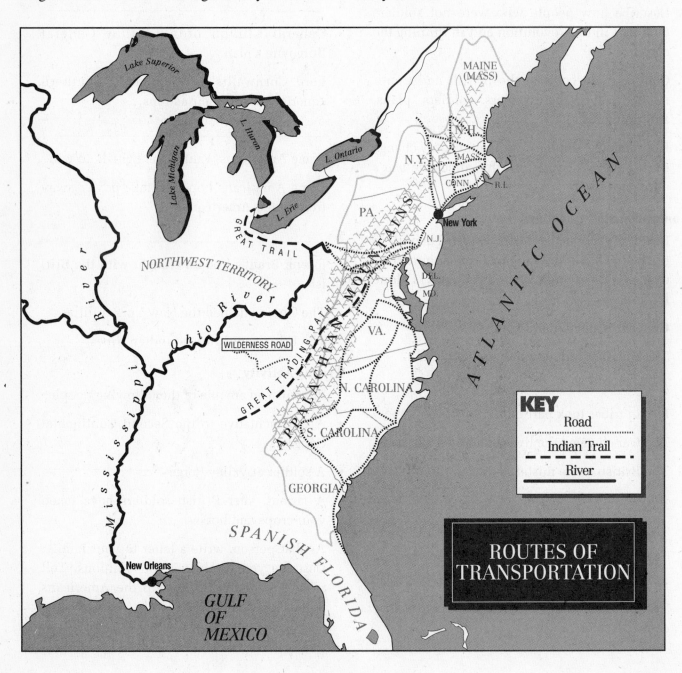

ROUTES OF TRANSPORTATION

KEY
Road
Indian Trail
River

BEFORE YOU READ

Sections in this Chapter

1. The United States After the War
2. Forming New Governments
3. The New Government at Work

Reading a Map

The map on the opposite page shows transportation routes used around the time of the Revolution. Use it to answer the questions below.

1. What land and water routes might people take from the Atlantic Coast to the Northwest Territory?

2. What rivers helped settlers move around the western lands?

3. Where else could people go by using water routes from the Northwest Territory?

4. Why do you think it was easier for western farmers to take their crops by water to New Orleans than by wagon to New York?

Understanding a Key Concept: CONSTITUTION

A **constitution** lists the rules of a government. It tells how the government will work and what it can and cannot do. The first Constitution of the United States was called the Articles of Confederation. In addition, after independence each colony became a state and wrote its own constitution.

Choose the word which best describes each sentence and write it after the sentence.

*constitution   governor   legislature
Congress   taxes   Articles of Confederation*

1. This person is the head of a colony or state.

2. This can be any group of elected representatives who have the power to make laws and decisions for a country or state.

3. This is the name given to the national legislature of the United States.

4. This is the list of written rules that tell what a government can do.

5. The money people pay to the government and which is used to run the government.

6. These were the first rules for the government of the United States.

Making Use of What You Already Know

To **import** goods means to bring goods into your country to sell. To **export** goods means to sell goods from your country in other countries. Use what you know about trade in the thirteen British colonies (before independence) to complete the following: after each item, write where Americans sent the goods (exported) or where they brought the goods from (imported). The first is done for you.

1. sugar—imported from the West Indies

2. rum

3. slaves

4. factory goods

5. tobacco

6. tea

Now answer the following two questions:

7. Which country was the colonies' most important trading partner?

8. How do you think that might have changed after the Revolution?

1. THE UNITED STATES AFTER THE WAR

Main Ideas

Think about the following Main Idea questions as you read this section:

1. What were some of the changes in the United States after the Revolutionary War?

2. What did other countries think about the new country's chances for success?

OTHER COUNTRIES THINK THAT THE UNITED STATES WON'T LAST

The British Hope to Return

The United States had won its war. But other countries weren't sure if the new country would last. Some people in Britain believed that they would soon be able to return and take over America again. The British kept many soldiers in Canada and the Northwestern forts—just in case.

The French Refuse to Loan More Money

The French also were not sure that the United States would last. They had helped the new country during the war. Now they stopped doing so. France would not loan the new government any more money. In fact, the French wanted the Americans to pay back everything they borrowed.

Congress sent Thomas Jefferson to France to get their help again. John Adams was sent to Great Britain, but Britain sent no one in return to the United States. Britain felt that the new country wasn't important enough.

CHANGES INSIDE THE COUNTRY

The Revolution caused many changes inside the United States. A new flag waved over buildings. New roads, built by the army, made travel between towns easier. Charles Town, South Carolina, changed its name to Charleston because it didn't want to sound like a city named for a British king.

The Army Goes Home

The government decided not to have a **standing army**—that is, the United States wouldn't have an army unless it needed one. Washington said farewell to his officers, and Congress sent the rest of the army home. It couldn't pay the soldiers money, so it gave them papers that they could use to buy land. Some soldiers kept the papers or traded them for land. Others needed money and had to sell their papers, often for less than the land would have been worth.

Tories Leave, and Speculators Get Their Land

During and after the war, large numbers of Tories left the United States. A few, like Benedict Arnold, moved to England, but most moved to Canada. They helped create the close ties between Great Britain and Canada that remain strong today.

Many of these Tories had been rich. The land they had owned was taken by the states, which then sold it. Much Tory land, especially in New York, was bought by people called **speculators**. These were men who bought land cheaply, often with borrowed money. They would divide the land into many small farms which they would sell for high prices. Some speculators made a great deal of money in this way.

Merchants and Planters Lose Money

During the war, many small American farmers made money by selling their crops to both armies. Other people weren't so lucky. Merchants couldn't trade with Britain anymore. First the war, and later new British laws, stopped the trade. Southern planters were having problems, too. Britain no longer bought all their tobacco and rice.

Americans Begin to Think of Themselves as One Nation

One of the most important results of the Revolution was that Americans began to think of themselves as one country. They were Americans as well as Virginians or New Yorkers.

Soon, the arts reflected this national feeling. American artists painted pictures of important American war heroes and Revolutionary battles. Books about America became very popular. **Noah Webster** wrote new school books that were different from those used in England. When he wrote his famous dictionary, *Webster's Dictionary*, he even gave some words special American spellings. We still use many of these spellings today. For example, we write color, not "colour," and tire, not "tyre."

SECTION REVIEW

Can you answer these Main Idea questions?

1. What were some of the changes in the United States after the Revolutionary War?

2. What did other countries think about the new country's chances for success?

Can you identify these places?

Charles Town, Charleston

Can you identify this person?

Noah Webster

Can you define these terms?

standing army, speculators

2. FORMING NEW GOVERNMENTS

Main Ideas

Think about the following Main Idea questions as you read this section:

1. What did state governments do about slavery?

2. In choosing state representatives, who was allowed to vote? Who wasn't?

3. What powers did the federal government have under the Articles of Confederation?

4. What powers did the federal government lack under the Articles of Confederation?

STATE GOVERNMENTS

State Constitutions

A **constitution** tells how a government works. Most states had a written constitution by the end of 1777. These constitutions were based on the states' colonial charters. They kept the same basic government as they had had before independence, but made sure it was **democratic**. That is, the people of the state elected and controlled the government.

Each state organized its government a little differently. In most states, the colonial assembly became a **legislature** made up of two parts, called **houses**. Pennsylvania's legislature was the one exception. It had only one house.

In every state the legislature was elected by the voters. Every state also had a governor and judges, but the legislature was the strongest part of the state government.

Who Can Vote?

To vote, a man had to own property, but he needed less property to do so than during colonial times. The amount of property that a voter needed was different in each state. Where small

farmers helped write the state constitution, less property was needed and more men could vote.

In some states free blacks could vote. However, women, slaves, or Indians could not. Many smaller farmers were elected to the state legislatures. This meant that not just the rich were making laws.

State Constitutions Guarantee Basic Rights and Freedoms

Most state constitutions promised every person certain rights. These rights were those that the British had ignored before the Revolution, like freedom of the press and freedom of speech. Slaves, however, did not enjoy these rights.

State Constitutions and Slavery

In some states, mostly in the North, slaves born after a certain date were freed. Most states stopped importing slaves. In some Southern states, like Virginia, many slaves were freed, but many more remained as slaves.

THE FEDERAL GOVERNMENT AND THE ARTICLES OF CONFEDERATION

Planning a New Government

No country had ever needed to begin a whole new government. To do so was an enormous job. Congress had in fact begun planning the new government even before the Declaration of Independence had been signed.

Because Congress had to run the war as well as to form a government, they didn't have time to invent new ideas. They based the new government on what they already knew, like the Albany Plan and the Iroquois Confederation. At the same time, they had to settle differences between the states, so everyone could agree on the new government.

Many Americans were afraid that the new government would give itself too much power. They remembered how the British government had wanted more and more power over the colonies. They wanted a federal government that would not have much power over the states. They also wanted those powers written down so that everyone could be sure what they were.

It was several years before Congress came up with a plan of government. Then every state had to agree to what Congress had decided. For a while, the new government couldn't start because Maryland refused to agree. It wanted the states that claimed land in the West, especially Virginia, to give that land to the federal government. Virginia agreed, but first made sure that the land would not all be sold to speculators.

The Articles of Confederation—Our First Constitution

Finally, in 1781, our first national constitution, called the **Articles of Confederation**, became law. The new government was to be a **federal** government. This means it was a government in which the states joined together as equals.

The new country was also to be a **republic.** This meant that the people would elect representatives to make decisions and run the country.

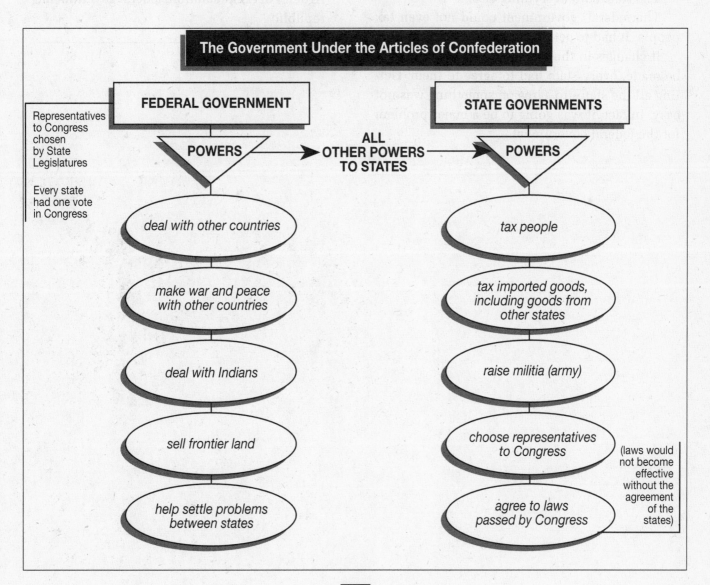

The Government Under the Articles of Confederation

Representatives to Congress chosen by State Legislatures

Every state had one vote in Congress

FEDERAL GOVERNMENT

POWERS

ALL OTHER POWERS TO STATES

STATE GOVERNMENTS

POWERS

deal with other countries

make war and peace with other countries

deal with Indians

sell frontier land

help settle problems between states

tax people

tax imported goods, including goods from other states

raise militia (army)

choose representatives to Congress

agree to laws passed by Congress

(laws would not become effective without the agreement of the states)

But the new government was different from the one we have today. The government had only one branch, Congress, which kept most of the powers it already had. Each state had one vote in Congress. There was no president and no Supreme Court or federal court system.

A Weak Federal Government

Under the Articles of Confederation, the federal government had much less power than it does today. It could only

—deal with other countries and with the Indians;

—make war and peace;

—settle problems between states.

The states did everything else.

The federal government could not even tax people. It had to get its money in other ways.

If changes in the federal government were to be made, every state had to agree to them. Getting all the states to agree on something was not easy. In fact, it was going to be a major problem for the federal government.

SECTION REVIEW

Can you answer these Main Idea questions?

1. What did state governments do about slavery?

2. In choosing state representatives, who was allowed to vote? Who wasn't?

3. What powers did the federal government have under the Articles of Confederation?

4. What powers did the federal government lack under the Articles of Confederation?

Can you define these words?

constitution, democratic government, the Articles of Confederation, federal government, republic

3. ACCOMPLISHMENTS AND PROBLEMS OF THE NEW GOVERNMENT

Main Ideas

Think about the following Main Idea questions as you read this section:

1. What were the main accomplishments of the new federal government?

2. What did the Northwest Ordinance do?

3. What two countries caused trouble for the United States in the West?

4. What were the main problems that the new federal government couldn't solve?

THE NORTHWEST TERRITORY

Settlers Cross the Appalachian Mountains

The federal government needed money but could not tax people. Only the states could do that. The federal government depended on the states for money, and they were not giving it enough. The government could borrow money, but it already owed a lot. So Congress decided to sell a huge area of western land to speculators. This area, north and west of the Ohio River, was known as the **Northwest Territory**. Today, the states of Ohio, Indiana, Michigan, and Illinois are there.

By the time the Revolution ended, settlers were pouring over the Appalachian Mountains into the lands on the other side. The Land Ordinance of 1785 divided this land into large pieces. But most settlers could not afford to buy them because they were so big.

The Northwest Ordinance

In 1787 Congress wrote a law to protect the people who bought land in the Northwest Territory. It was called the **Northwest Ordinance**. (An *ordinance* is a kind of law.)

The Northwest Ordinance set up a **territorial government**. This was a government with a governor and judges appointed by Congress. When the Northwest Territory had enough people, a legislature would be elected. The legislature could send one person to Congress, but he could not vote. No slavery was allowed, and people's rights were protected. When enough voters lived in an area, it could become a state.

The British Remain a Problem

The British, however, were still a problem from Lake Champlain to Michigan. They had never left their forts, and they still traded with the Indians: guns for furs. The British didn't listen to the United States when it asked them to leave, and the United States had no army to make them get out. A new, weak country like the United States didn't have the power to make a strong country, like Britain, do what it wanted.

THE SOUTHWEST AND A QUARREL WITH SPAIN

Farmers Use the Mississippi River to Ship Their Crops

During the Revolution settlers had also moved into the Southwest—the lands south of the Ohio River. After the war, many more people came. Because the roads over the Appalachian Mountains were terrible, farmers in Kentucky and Tennessee couldn't send their crops back east. Instead, they sent them by water to the Spanish-owned city of New Orleans.

Crops were put on rafts and floated down the Ohio or the Tennessee rivers into the

▲ *Farmers taking their crops down the Mississippi on a flatboat. The flatboats were basically big rafts. They floated downstream with the river, but couldn't go against the current. Generally, they were sold for their wood in New Orleans, and their crews returned home by land.*

Mississippi, which took the farmers and their crops to New Orleans. Ships from New Orleans then took the crops to New York or Europe.

Spain Threatens to Close the Mississippi to Americans

Spain, however, threatened to close New Orleans to the Americans. The Spanish tried to make a deal with New England merchants—through their representatives in Congress—who wanted to trade in Spain's Caribbean and South American ports. The merchants almost agreed to the closing of the Mississippi. The Southwestern farmers were furious. Many of them thought about leaving the United States and becoming a Spanish colony.

But on the whole, the new country did a good job in dealing with its Western lands. It was not, however, so successful with its other problems.

MONEY PROBLEMS

Debt, but No Way to Pay It

Money problems affected both the government and the people. The United States had borrowed heavily to pay for the Revolution. The country owed money both to individuals and to governments such as France and Holland.

The federal government depended on the states for money. But the war had cost the states a lot of money, too. They didn't have much to give. The federal government could not tax to get money for itself. The money it got from selling western land wasn't enough. The federal government wanted to tax imported goods, but one state always said no. And since every state had to agree, the import tax never became law.

Inflation after the Revolution

Prices rose, too. Something that cost one dollar before the war cost ten dollars and then fifty dollars after the war. Money did not buy as much as before. A money problem like this is called **inflation**. Inflation is common, but it is rarely as bad in this country as it was after the Revolution. Because of inflation, many farmers could not pay what they owed or buy what they needed. They also couldn't pay the high state taxes.

SHAYS' REBELLION

Rebellion in Massachusetts

In 1786, a western Massachusetts farmer named Daniel Shays did what many people had done before the Revolution. He led a rebellion, **Shays' Rebellion**. He and his followers wanted state judges to stop sending people to jail because they couldn't pay what they owed. They couldn't get the laws changed by voting, because they didn't own enough property to vote. Finally, mobs of angry farmers forced the courts in western Massachusetts to shut down.

Massachusetts rapidly raised a special army, called a militia. Shays and his men tried to steal guns from the state militia in Springfield, but the militia drove them off. The rebellion fell apart. Later, though, the Massachusetts legislature passed laws that helped the farmers pay what they owed.

Newspapers all over the country told the story of Shays' Rebellion. Americans became worried. They didn't want anyone's life or property threatened, but they knew that many people couldn't pay what they owed. Something had to be done.

THE STATES QUARREL

The States Quarrel Over Taxes and Borders

Sometimes the states acted against each other. Some states taxed goods coming in from other states. They did this to raise money, but it also hurt trade and caused bad feelings.

States also fought about their borders. Vermont did not become a state until 1791 because no one wanted to anger either New York or New Hampshire, who were fighting over it. The British even tried to talk the people of Vermont into becoming part of Canada!

Why the Federal Government Couldn't Settle State Quarrels

The federal government didn't do much about these problems. The states were much more powerful than the federal government. It was the state legislatures, not the voters, who elected the members of Congress. They chose people who would put protecting their state's power ahead of solving the federal government's problems.

There was another problem with having the state legislatures pick the members of Congress. Because the voters didn't elect Congress, its members didn't listen to common Americans with problems, like Daniel Shays. Congress did not really represent these people. People like Daniel Shays didn't have much more say in the national government than they had had before the Revolution, under the British.

In addition, each state legislature had to agree to every law Congress passed. If any state didn't agree with what Congress was doing, it could stop a law or not send money.

Problems with Trade and Shipping

After the Revolution, trade was very slow. The British were willing to sell goods to America, but they would not buy American goods. Nor would they would let American ships trade in Canada or the West Indies. The triangle trade of New England's food and rum, West Indian sugar and slaves, and the South's tobacco was hurt. (See Chapter 8, Section 3.) American merchants tried trading in new places, like China. They had to be careful, though. The United States had no navy to protect American ships.

The new nation had its independence, but it also had a lot of problems. The federal government was deeply in debt from the Revolution, but couldn't tax in order to raise money. Some of the states were arguing with each other, or taxing each other's goods and hurting commerce, but the federal government couldn't force them to cooperate. The United States had to find new places to trade, but didn't have a navy to protect its ships. The Articles of Confederation weren't working: something had to be done.

SECTION REVIEW

Can you answer these Main Idea questions?

1. What were the main accomplishments of the new federal government?

2. What did the Northwest Ordinance do?

3. What two countries caused trouble for the United States in the West?

4. What were the main problems that the new federal government couldn't solve?

Can you identify this place?

Northwest Territory

Can you define these terms?

Northwest Ordinance, territorial government, inflation, Shay's Rebellion

AFTER YOU READ

Discussion Questions

1. Compare the powers of the national government and state governments under the Articles of Confederation.

2. How did the French, the British, and the Spanish affect life in the new country?

3. What problems did Americans and the new federal government have? Which problems was the government unable to solve?

4. How has the Constitution changed since it was ratified?

Comprehension Questions

Think about the following different types of people and their likely attitudes toward the new country, the United States of America. From the list below, choose the person who might have said each of the following quotes. The first is done for you.

slave
farmer from Massachusetts
Frech government official
State Representative to Congress
Western farmer
land specultator
British general

1. "We'll get out of these forts near the Great Lakes when we're good and ready!"
   British general

2. "If the United States government agrees to let Spain close New Orleans to our trade, we will become part of Spain's colonies. Why should we stay under a government that is hurting our freedom to trade?"

3. "I'll buy thousands of acres of land at $1 an acre. Then I will divide it up and sell small pieces for $2 or $3 an acre. Even if I don't sell it all, I will become rich."

4. "My state votes against this federal tax on imported goods."

5. "My state wrote a constitution that protects the rights of everyone but people like me. I have no rights. I have no freedom. I am treated like the cattle and the pigs."

6. "Mr. Jefferson, he United States must pay back what they owe us immediately. Being a new country is no excuse."

7. "Shays is right. Poor people shouldn't go to jail because they owe money. Also, they should be able to vote. Just because they are poor doesn't mean they shouldn't have a say in the government.

Writing Activity

The people in the Comprehension Questions at left had different ideas about what the new country should be like. Choose one of these people and another person who would have had very different ideas from him or her. The second person you choose doesn't have to be from the list at left, but could be any other person who would have lived during this time. Make a list for each person of the ideas and opinions they might have had. Then use your lists to write a conversation between these two people. They can ask each other questions and share their opinions on topics that are of interest to them.

BUILDIN

Looking backwards, gaining independence was, if not easy, at least straightforward. What needed doing had been obvious—equipping and training an army, winning battles, and forming an alliance with the French.

Now, though, the former colonists had to build a nation and how to do that was far from obvious. The problems the new nation faced were enormous: paying off the cost of the Revolution, establishing a national government, holding onto and extending the country's territory, dealing with other nations . . . the list goes on and on. Things which the British used to do for them, such as protecting their trade, they now had to do for themselves. The odds against success were enormous.

And yet, despite all odds, Americans succeeded. In less than fifty years, they would extend their country's borders thousands of miles, all the way to the Pacific; they would earn the respect of European nations; and they would create a government that has lasted more than 200 years.

There were false starts: the United States' first attempt at a national government failed. Nor would all the country's problems be resolved: one such issue, slavery, would nearly tear the country in two not many years later. But overall, the first fifty years of the United States must be considered one of the most exciting and spectacular periods of any nation.

CHAPTER 14

THE CONSTITUTION

By the late 1780's, many Americans had become unhappy with the federal government because it was not dealing with many of the country's problems. Finally, Congress called a convention to change the Articles of Confederation. But instead of changing the Articles, the convention wrote an entirely new plan of government. This new plan was the Constitution of the United States, and it is the government we live under today.

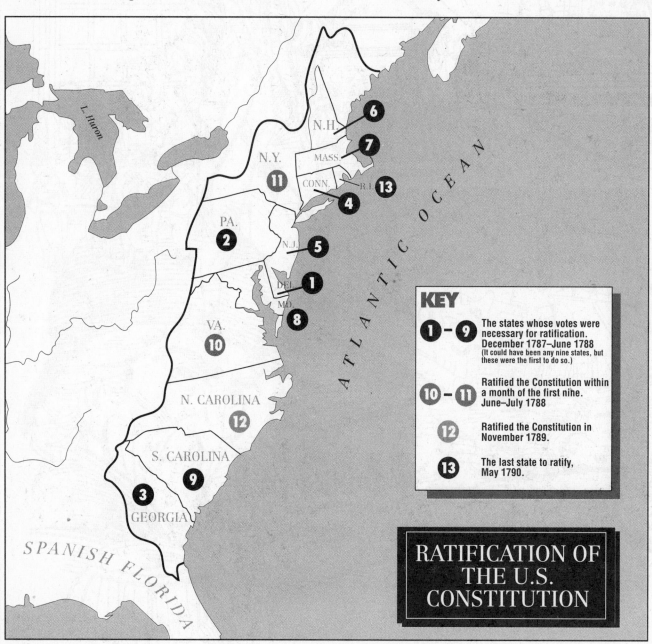

KEY

1 – 9 The states whose votes were necessary for ratification. December 1787–June 1788 (It could have been any nine states, but these were the first to do so.)

10 – 11 Ratified the Constitution within a month of the first nine. June–July 1788

12 Ratified the Constitution in November 1789.

13 The last state to ratify, May 1790.

RATIFICATION OF THE U.S. CONSTITUTION

BEFORE YOU READ

Sections in this Chapter

1. The Constitutional Convention
2. Deciding on the Constitution
3. Ratification

Reading a Map

The map on the opposite page shows the order in which states ratified the Constitution, and whether their vote was necessary or not.

1. Which was the first state to ratify the Constitution? The last?

2. The votes of how many states were necessary for ratification?

3. When did New York and Virginia ratify the Constitution?

4. When did North Carolina ratify the Constitution?

Understanding a Key Concept:
THE BRANCHES OF GOVERNMENT

The first state constitutions described governments that had three parts or **branches**.

The **legislative branch** is the state legislature. The **executive branch** is the governor. The **judicial branch** consists of the courts and judges.

Use what you know about the first United States government and today's government to write the name of the correct branch in each sentence.

1. The United States Congress is most like the states' _____ branch.

2. The federal government under the Articles of Confederation had no _____ branch and no _____ branch.

3. Today the president of the United States is in charge of the _____ branch of the federal government.

4. Today both state governments and the federal government have judges in their _____ branch.

Making Use of What You Already Know

Americans and their government had many problems under the Articles of Confederation. Choose the answer that best describes life under the Articles.

1. Who did the frontier settlers expect to protect them from the Indians?
   a. the state government
   b. the federal government

2. Why did the government need to collect taxes?
   a. to pay the money it owed
   b. to have power over trade

3. Why were large states unhappy with their representation in Congress under the Articles of Confederation?
   a. they had no votes in Congress
   b. they had the same vote and power in Congress as the small states

4. What did Shays' rebellion show about the federal government?
   a. it needed an army to protect people from the British
   b. it needed more power to help people and the states

1. THE CONSTITUTIONAL CONVENTION

Main Ideas

Think about the following Main Idea questions as you read this section:

1. How did the Constitutional Convention get started?

2. Where did the men at the convention get their ideas from?

A CONVENTION IS CALLED

The Annapolis Convention

In 1786 Virginia asked the states to send representatives to a meeting, or **convention**, to discuss trade problems. It was called the **Annapolis Convention** because it was held in Annapolis, Maryland.

Only five states sent representatives. They asked Congress to call a second convention to discuss more than trade. They wanted to change the Articles of Confederation. Congress agreed.

A Second Convention in Philadelphia

The next year, 1787, Congress asked each state to send men to a second convention in Philadelphia. They wanted changes made in the Articles of Confederation so that the government could work better.

Each state would have only one vote, but most sent several of their best men. Rhode Island, on the other hand, didn't send anyone.

THE MEN AND IDEAS

The Men at the Convention

Fifty-five of the country's most important men went to the convention in Philadelphia. Many of them knew each other because they were already in government. Some had helped to write the Declaration of Independence, the Articles of Confederation, or their state constitutions. Several were in Congress.

George Washington was in charge. Benjamin Franklin, 81 years old and sick, gave advice.

Two men were very important at the meeting: Alexander Hamilton of New York and James Madison of Virginia. Hamilton had been an assistant to George Washington during the Revolution. He was a brilliant young lawyer and politician, famous as a speaker and writer. He had many ideas for a strong national government.

Madison was a close friend of Thomas Jefferson. He had studied hundreds of books about different governments. He probably knew more about the subject than anyone else in the country. He came to the convention with a plan for a totally new federal government.

The Ideas at the Convention

The ideas of the men at the convention came from several sources. Some ideas came from the British government. Others came from the members' state constitutions and town meetings. Many important ideas came from writers on government who lived in France and Great Britain. Some ideas may have come from the Iroquois Confederacy. And some came from the best parts of the Articles of Confederation.

Most members wanted to keep a democracy, that is, a government in which the people and their representatives make the laws and decisions. They had studied what democracy was like in ancient Greece and Rome. But they had to put their ideas into a form that would work in America.

▲ The Constitutional Convention—one of the greatest gatherings of political thinkers and statesmen ever. George Washington, the president of the Convention, is standing behind the desk (at center).

THE CONVENTION BEGINS ITS WORK

The convention to change the Articles of Confederation began on May 25, 1787. It ended on September 17, after doing something very different. During those four months, a totally new plan of government, the U.S. Constitution, was put together. This is the plan of government that Americans live under today.

No one had ever planned a government this way before. At the Constitutional Convention, every man and every state was interested in different things. Some were interested in trade, some in slavery, and some in banks. To form a government that they could agree on, they had to **compromise**. That is, everyone had to give up something to help the whole country. Even so, some members couldn't agree and left the convention.

The members voted to keep all their talks secret. They wanted the freedom to say what they thought and to change their minds without everyone finding out. But James Madison kept a careful diary, which was published many years later. That's how we know what happened.

SECTION REVIEW

Can you answer these Main Idea questions?

1. How did the Constitutional Convention get started?

2. Where did the men at the convention get their ideas from?

Can you identify this place?

Philadelphia

Can you identify these people?

Alexander Hamilton, James Madison

Can you define these terms?

Annapolis Convention, the Constitution, compromise

2. DECIDING ON THE CONSTITUTION

Main Ideas

Think about the following Main Idea questions as you read this section:

1. What was the Virginia Plan?

2. What was the Great Compromise?

3. How did the Constitution deal with the problem of slavery and the slave trade?

4. What is meant by the terms "checks and balances" and "separation of powers"?

THE VIRGINIA PLAN

A Proposal for a New Government with Three Branches

When the convention started, no one knew what would happen. Some men just wanted to fix the Articles of Confederation. Others thought the Articles of Confederation could never keep the country together. More and more representatives began to realize how hard it would be to fix the country's problems just by patching up the Articles of Confederation.

Then Governor Edmund Randolph of Virginia read the **Virginia Plan**. This was the plan that Madison had drawn up. It outlined a whole new government made up of three branches:

- An **Executive Branch**, with a President at its head.
- A **Legislative Branch**, Congress, made up of two "houses"—the House of Representatives and the Senate—instead of just one. Together the two houses of Congress would make the laws.
- A **Judicial Branch**, made up of a Supreme Court and lower courts.

The convention was now starting to create a new government instead of just fixing the old one.

Objections to the Virginia Plan

The Virginia Plan became the basis for the Constitution. But the smaller states didn't like it at first. They were afraid that it gave the large states too much power.

They especially disliked Madison's ideas about Congress. Under his plan, the people would elect the House of Representatives. The states with the most people would have the most representatives. Then the representatives would elect the senators. But this meant that the largest states, which had the most representatives, would control the choice of senators. The smaller states would not have much say in choosing senators, even their own.

The New Jersey Plan and Alexander Hamilton's Plan

The smaller states suggested another plan, called the **New Jersey Plan**. It kept Congress the way it was under the Articles of Confederation: one house where each state had one vote, no matter what its size was. The New Jersey plan was not passed.

Alexander Hamilton came up with a plan of his own. It called for a very strong federal government. The states would have almost no power. No one liked it. The convention was getting nowhere.

THE GREAT COMPROMISE

The People Elect the Representatives and the State Legislatures Select the Senators

The Constitutional Convention debated for more than a month on how representatives and senators should be chosen. Finally the members came to an agreement. Both small and large states agreed to a plan suggested by the group from

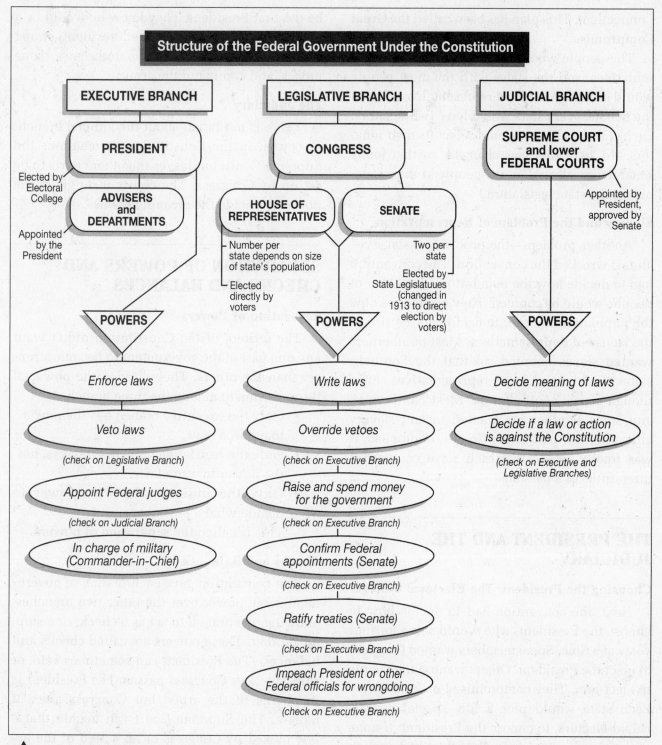

Structure of the Federal Government Under the Constitution

EXECUTIVE BRANCH

PRESIDENT

Elected by Electoral College

Appointed by the President

ADVISERS and DEPARTMENTS

POWERS

Enforce laws

Veto laws

(check on Legislative Branch)

Appoint Federal judges

(check on Judicial Branch)

In charge of military (Commander-in-Chief)

LEGISLATIVE BRANCH

CONGRESS

HOUSE OF REPRESENTATIVES

- Number per state depends on size of state's population
- Elected directly by voters

SENATE

Two per state

Elected by State Legislatuues (changed in 1913 to direct election by voters)

POWERS

Write laws

Override vetoes

(check on Executive Branch)

Raise and spend money for the government

(check on Executive Branch)

Confirm Federal appointments (Senate)

(check on Executive Branch)

Ratify treaties (Senate)

(check on Executive Branch)

Impeach President or other Federal officials for wrongdoing

(check on Executive Branch)

JUDICIAL BRANCH

SUPREME COURT and lower FEDERAL COURTS

Appointed by President, approved by Senate

POWERS

Decide meaning of laws

Decide if a law or action is against the Constitution

(check on Executive and Legislative Branches)

▲ *Our federal government, as established by the U.S. Constitution. Many people complain that the government sometimes has trouble getting things done, but that is in part deliberate: as you can see in the diagram above, each branch has the ability to check, or interfere with, the other two. (The legislature can check the Judicial branch by rewriting a law so that it is more clearly written—this leaves less room for interpretation by the courts.) By making it harder to get things done, the men who wrote the Constitution made it harder for any one branch of government to seize too much power.*

Connecticut. This plan has been called **the Great Compromise**.

The people would elect the House of Representatives, and the states with the most people would still have the most representatives. But in the Senate, every state would have two senators. Each state legislature would select its own senators. (In 1913 this was changed, so that today senators are elected by the people of their state, not by the state legislature.)

Slavery and the Problem of Representation

Another problem—the problem of slavery—almost wrecked the convention. The convention had to decide how the population, or number of people, would be counted. They needed to know the population in order to decide on the size of the House of Representatives. Most Southerners wanted slaves counted, so that the Southern states could have more representatives, even though slaves couldn't vote. Most Northerners and some Southerners wanted to end slavery altogether. As part of the Great Compromise, it was finally agreed that each slave counted as three-fifths of a person.

THE PRESIDENT AND THE JUDICIARY

Choosing the President: The Electoral College

Next, the convention had to decide how to choose the President, who would serve for four years at a time. Some members wanted Congress to elect the President. Others wanted the people to elect him. They compromised on a new way. Each state would pick a few special people, called **electors**, to choose the President. If none of the people running for President had enough **electoral votes** to win, the House of Representatives would decide the winner.

The Powers of the President

When people at the convention talked about the President's powers, they were all thinking of George Washington. Everyone knew he would be the first President. They knew he would be a good one, so they gave the President strong powers. The President was to enforce laws, name judges, and command the army.

The Judiciary

There is not much about the judicial branch, or courts, in the Constitution. It mentions the Supreme Court, but leaves the other courts to be set up by Congress. The courts were given the power to decide the meaning of laws.

SEPARATION OF POWERS AND CHECKS AND BALANCES

Separation of Powers

The writers of the Constitution didn't want any one part of the government to become stronger than the others. They divided the power of the government among the three branches.
- Only the executive branch has the power to enforce laws.
- Only the legislative branch, Congress, has the power to write laws.
- Only the judiciary has the power to decide what a law means.

This is called the **separation of powers**.

Checks and Balances

The convention gave each branch of government some power over the other two branches, allowing one branch to act as a **check**, or a stop, on another. These powers are called **checks and balances**. The President can sometimes **veto**, or stop, the laws Congress passes. The President is in charge of the army, but Congress gives it money. The Supreme Court can decide that a law passed by Congress or an action of the executive branch is against the Constitution.

OTHER DECISIONS

Trade and Slavery

Some of the angriest talks of the convention were about trade. Northern states fought with

Southern states. The North wanted the government to protect its shipping and trade. The South didn't want the government to tax the crops they exported or the goods they imported. Northern states said they wouldn't agree to the Constitution unless their trade was protected.

In addition, some Southerners were afraid Congress would stop the slave trade, which brought slaves into America. Men from the North, and even a few from the South, spoke against it. South Carolina threatened to leave and become a separate country if slavery wasn't protected.

No one really wanted to stop the new government before it began. So the convention found more compromises. Congress could not tax goods sent out of the country. Two thirds of the Senate had to agree to treaties, including trade treaties. Finally, Congress could not stop the slave trade until 1808. However, it could charge a tax on slaves coming into the country.

New Territories and States

The convention knew that the country would continue to grow, so it gave the federal government control over the territories. Congress was to admit new states when they were ready. They would be equal to the other, older states.

Amending the Constitution

The men who wrote the Constitution knew it wasn't perfect. They knew that the country would change and that the Constitution would have to change with it. However, they didn't want it to be easy to change the Constitution. They agreed that changes, or **amendments**, could be added to the Constitution. But two-thirds of Congress and three-fourths of the states had to agree to any changes. They also added one other way to change the Constitution: if two-thirds of the states asked for a new convention, that meeting could suggest amendments.

The Final Constitution

When everything had been agreed on, Gouverneur Morris of Pennsylvania wrote the final draft of the Constitution. Morris added the **Preamble** at the beginning to tell what the Constitution is about. It says "We the people of the United States . . ." are forming a government to bring justice, peace, security, and liberty for ourselves and those who come after us.

Changes were made until the very last day. When it was all over, most members felt it was the best government they could get. Only three men refused to sign it. No one got everything he wanted, but most thought their state would agree to it. Soon, the Constitution was being read all over the country.

The Constitution created a government that was something completely new. No other government in history was like it. It was a **representative democracy**, where the people and those they elect make the laws. In some areas the federal, or national, government had final power. In other areas, the state governments made and controlled the laws.

The Constitution is the highest law of the land. Neither the federal government nor the state governments may do anything against it.

SECTION REVIEW

Can you answer these Main Idea questions?

1. What was the Virginia Plan?

2. What was the Great Compromise?

3. How did the Constitution deal with the problem of slavery and the slave trade?

4. What is meant by the terms "checks and balances" and "separation of powers"?

Can you identify this person?

Gouverneur Morris

Can you define these terms?

executive branch, legislative branch, judicial branch, separation of powers, checks and balances, amendment, Preamble, representative democracy

3. RATIFICATION

Main Ideas

Think about the following Main Idea questions as you read this section:

1. How was the Constitution ratified?

2. What are some of the important rights in the Bill of Rights?

3. How has the U.S. government changed since the Constitution was ratified?

THE FIGHT FOR RATIFICATION

The Ratification Process

The government set up by the Constitution didn't begin automatically. First, the Constitution had to be accepted by the states. The voters of each state had to elect representatives to a special state convention. Each convention would decide if its state agreed to, or **ratified**, the new government. When nine of the thirteen states agreed, the government could begin.

Federalists—Supporters of the Constitution

People everywhere talked about the Constitution. Those who agreed with the Constitution were called **Federalists**. Their leaders were the writers of the Constitution. One New York City newspaper printed articles written by John Jay, Alexander Hamilton, and James Madison. They explained the Constitution and helped people understand it. These articles were printed together as *The Federalist Papers*.

Anti-Federalists—Against the New Constitution

Those against the Constitution, for any reason, were called **Anti-Federalists**. Many Anti-Federalists just didn't like the idea of a stronger federal government. Some people in important states, like New York and Virginia, didn't want their states to lose power. Other Anti-Federalists wanted the Constitution to list the people's rights, so the government could never take them away.

The States Decide

Some states, like Delaware and Georgia, quickly ratified the Constitution. Other states also agreed to it but asked for a **Bill of Rights**. A Bill of Rights is a list of those basic rights that all people have. Many states already had a Bill of Rights in their own constitutions. A federal Bill of Rights would list rights that the federal government could not take away and things that the federal government could not do.

In some states, the talks went on for a long time. In Massachusetts and Virginia, the Federalists had a hard fight. They won by only a few votes. Nine states had already ratified the Constitution before Virginia voted. When people in Virginia realized that the government could start without them, some of them changed their minds. They voted for the new government.

Soon, New York was the only large state that hadn't ratified the Constitution. Hamilton warned the state that New York City might leave and become its own state under the Constitution if the state didn't ratify it soon. Finally, New York agreed, but only by three votes.

Rhode Island didn't sign until 1890. By that time, George Washington was already President.

The Writers of the Constitution in the New Government

Many of the writers of the Constitution worked in the new government. Two of them, George Washington and James Madison, became President. Others ran for President but were not elected. Some became Vice President. Many served in Congress or on the Supreme Court.

THE BILL OF RIGHTS

The Bill of Rights Becomes Part of the Constitution

Shortly after Washington became President, James Madison wrote a Bill of Rights. He wrote it as a set of amendments to the Constitution. Congress passed twelve of them, and the states agreed to ten. They became the first ten amendments of the Constitution.

These ten amendments are still called the **Bill of Rights**. They list rights that the government cannot take away. These rights are often called **constitutional rights**.

Constitutional Rights

Here are some of the most important constitutional rights that the Bill of Rights gives to every citizen:

- Freedom to practice whatever religion you wish
- Freedom of speech
- Freedom of the press
- Freedom to get together with others and ask the government to change something that is wrong
- Freedom to keep and bear arms
- Freedom from unreasonable searches by the police
- The right to a fair trial
- The right not to have life, freedom, or property taken away unless the government has followed all the rules, such as giving an accused a fair and public trial—this is called the right to "due process of law"

James Madison, who is often called the Father of Our Constitution. His Virginia Plan was the basis for the structure of our government. He also wrote the most important amendments to our Constitution, the Bill of Rights, and went on to serve as our fourth President.

OUR CHANGING CONSTITUTION

Amendments Since Ratification

The Constitution was a framework, or outline, for a government. It allowed change, and over the years it has in fact changed. For example, it begins "We the People . . ." What is meant by "the People"—that is, the voters—has changed. When the Constitution was written, the only voters were white men who owned some property. The Fifteenth Amendment added blacks, although their right to vote wasn't always enforced. The Nineteenth Amendment gave women the vote. Finally, the Twenty-sixth Amendment added people between the ages of eighteen and twenty-one.

Other important amendments have changed the way the President and senators are elected. The Thirteenth Amendment freed the slaves. The Fourteenth Amendment says that a state may not take away a person's Constitutional rights.

Other Changes in Government

Congress, the President, and the courts have changed our government, too. Here, for example, is a list of some important things in our government that are not mentioned in the Constitution:

- Political parties
- Presidential elections in which the people vote

- The ability of the Supreme Court to declare a law unconstitutional
- The President's cabinet
- The committees that Congress sets up to help it do its work

New laws and new ideas have frequently changed the way the government works. Several times, the courts have decided on a new meaning for a law or part of the Constitution. The Constitution is great because it allows change while still protecting the people.

> The Constitutional Convention gave this country a new Constitution. That Constitution set up a democratic framework for our government that has lasted for more than 200 years. As soon as the new government began, changes began, too. The writers of the Constitution knew nothing about these changes, but had planned for change to happen. The Constitution has allowed the government to grow and change for over 200 years.

SECTION REVIEW

Can you answer these Main Idea questions?

1. How was the Constitution ratified?

2. What are some of the important rights in the Bill of Rights?

3. How has the U.S. government changed since the Constitution was ratified?

Can you identify these people?

Federalists, Anti-Federalists

Can you define these terms?

ratify, *The Federalist Papers*, Bill of Rights

AFTER YOU READ

Discussion Questions

1. What were the major disagreements at the Constitutional Convention and how were they resolved?

2. Why was ratification of the Constitution a difficult fight in some states?

3. Describe the framework set up by the Constitution.

4. How has the Constitution changed since it was ratified?

Comprehension Questions

I. Write a heading for each of the different branches of the United States Government:

LEGISLATIVE   EXECUTIVE   JUDICIAL
BRANCH   BRANCH   BRANCH

Below is a list of governmental powers from the United States Constitution. Write each one under the branch that has that power.

pay army
write laws
raise taxes
veto Congress' bills
in charge of the army
enforce laws
decide the meaning of laws
declare laws unconstitutional

Now use your lists to answer the following questions:

1. If you wanted to write the President to ask him to veto a bill before it became a law, to which branch would you write?

2. If you wanted to find out about a Supreme Court decision, to which branch would you write?

3. If you wanted a new law passed, to which branch would you write?

4. If you wanted to complain about a new tax, to which branch would you write?

Writing Activity

Pretend that you are a newspaper reporter during the time that the Constitution was being ratified. Decide whether you are a Federalist or an Anti-Federalist. Make a list of facts about the Articles of Confederation, America's problems under it, and how the Constitution would solve or not solve these problems. Then use these facts to write a newspaper article describing your position and why you've chosen it.

CHAPTER 15

POLITICS AND THE NEW GOVERNMENT

After the Constitution was written and signed, Americans had to start their new government. A President and a new Congress had to be elected. Taxes had to be agreed on, and a way to collect them set up. Federal courts had to be created. The government grew, but so did the differences between its leaders. Something happened that the writers of the Constitution hadn't thought of: political parties formed. In addition, Americans had to choose sides on events taking place in Europe. Sometimes these events widened the split between the nation's leaders, such as Jefferson and Adams. Some events even made the new country bigger.

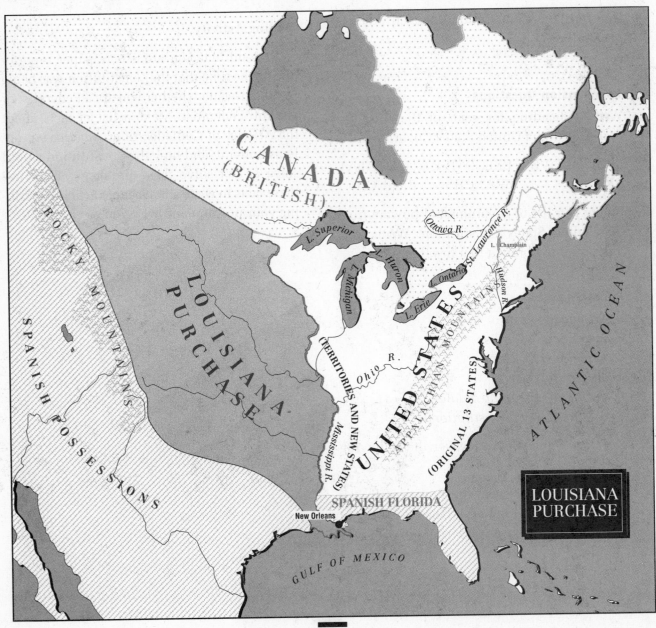

BEFORE YOU READ

Sections in this Chapter

1. The New Government
2. Trouble with France, England, and Spain
3. When John Adams was President
4. When Thomas Jefferson was President

Reading a Map

The map on the opposite page shows North America in 1801. Use it to answer the following questions.

1. What European countries had colonies in North America in 1801?

2. In what French colonial city did Northwestern farmers trade?

3. Why might the United States be worried about European countries having colonies so close to its borders?

Understanding a Key Concept:
FOREIGN RELATIONS

Foreign relations are the events and happenings that occur between two countries, and how well they get along. Before the Declaration of Independence, Great Britain controlled the foreign relations of the thirteen colonies. After the United States became an independent country, it controlled its own foreign relations. Each sentence below describes an event which occured between two countries. Write a sentence about two different ways the two countries might resolve their problem.

1. Americans became angry when French officials wouldn't talk to their representatives unless the French were paid money.

2. The British navy captured American ships. The British army wouldn't leave forts in the Northwest.

3. The rulers of Tripoli demanded money or else they would send pirates to attack American ships.

4. The Spanish tried to close New Orleans to Northwestern farmers.

Making Use of What You Already Know

Thomas Jefferson began the political party called the Republican-Democrats, usually called the Republican Party. Jefferson and the Republicans agreed with the ideas of James Madison.

Alexander Hamilton began the political party called the Federalists.

Use what you know about these people to answer the following questions.

1. Which person helped write the Declaration of Independence: Thomas Jefferson or Alexander Hamilton?

2. Which person wanted the Constitution to create a strong central government run by the rich: Thomas Jefferson or Alexander Hamilton?

3. Use your answer to decide which political party supported more federal power and less state power: the Republican Party or the Federalist Party?

4. Which party supported more power for every voter: the Republican Party or the Federalist Party?

5. What are the names of the two major parties in the United States today?

1. THE NEW GOVERNMENT

Main Ideas

Think about the following Main Idea questions as you read this section:

1. How did Hamilton's and Jefferson's ideas differ?

2. How did the first political parties form?

3. What incident showed that the federal government intended to enforce its laws?

CONGRESS

The New Congress

The new government began with American citizens. They took part in their political system. They voted, ran for office, and told their representatives what they thought about important topics. Elections were held, and the government began to take shape within the framework of the new Constitution.

The first Congress wrote some very important laws. James Madison and other members of the House of Representatives drew up the Bill of Rights, the first ten amendments to the Constitution. Congress also passed a tax on goods and ships from other countries. Tax collectors were hired. The taxes they collected gave the government money to pay its workers and to rent places to meet.

Sometimes small groups of congressmen joined together to fight certain laws, but usually they all worked together. There were no political parties yet.

Congress Sets Up the New Judiciary System

The Constitution did not set up the federal courts or list all their duties, so in 1789 Congress passed the **Judiciary Act**. It gave the Supreme Court a Chief Justice and five associate justices.

(Today there are nine justices on the Supreme Court.) The Judiciary Act also set up lower courts throughout the country.

PRESIDENT WASHINGTON AND HIS CABINET

George Washington—The First President

In 1789, George Washington was elected the first President of the United States. He was already being called "The Father of Our Country," and no one voted against him. Once in office, he refused to be called "Your Majesty." His only title was "President of the United States."

Washington set up his branch of the government, the executive branch, but he left Congress alone. He asked several men to advise him and to run different departments of the government. They were called the **Cabinet**. Two members of the cabinet were very important. Thomas Jefferson was Secretary of State, in charge of foreign affairs. Alexander Hamilton was Secretary of the Treasury, in charge of collecting taxes and paying the government's bills.

A Split Between Hamilton and Jefferson

Alexander Hamilton wanted a strong federal government, one that would make the United States an important country in business and trade. He felt that the country wouldn't last unless rich people and business leaders believed in it. He believed in the British way of government, where the rich were in charge.

Thomas Jefferson, though, thought that all people should be part of the government, not just the rich. He believed in the idea that everyone was equal. He didn't want a strong federal government. Instead, he wanted the states to have most of the power. He didn't like cities or the big businesses. He wanted the United States to stay a country of farmers.

Each man disliked the other. Each thought that the other's ideas would hurt the country. Neither man believed in political parties, but their differences led to the first ones.

The First Political Parties Form

Over the years, many members of Congress took sides with either Hamilton or Jefferson. Some voted for the laws that Hamilton wanted. Others voted for the laws that Jefferson wanted. The group that Hamilton led was called the **Federalists**. The other group, led by Jefferson and James Madison, became the **Republican-Democrats**, or **Republicans** for short. Gradually, the Federalists and the Republicans grew into political parties.

In many towns, people got together to talk about politics. Small farmers, skilled workers, and teachers supported the Republican party. The Federalist party was strongest among New England merchants, traders, and ministers. Some Southern planters joined the Federalists, but not many small farmers. The Federalists had a national newspaper which often attacked the Republicans. Soon, the Republicans began their own newspaper.

In Congress, members of the same political party began voting together. They helped others from their party get elected. Local political groups began working to win state and local elections. Political parties became part of most elections.

George Washington tried to stay apart from the new political parties. He believed that the President should represent the whole country, not just one political point of view. He did support Hamilton more often than Jefferson, though. He was angry and hurt when Republican newspapers attacked him for his pro-Federalist actions.

Competing Ideas of Government: Hamilton vs. Jefferson	
HAMILTON	**JEFFERSON**
favored government run by wealthy people	had faith that the common people could govern themselves
favored a strong federal government and weaker state governments	favored strong state governments along with a strong federal government
believed the key to the economy was business and trade	believed that farmers and farming were vital to the country
wanted the government to pay money to the people who held its notes	wanted the government to pay money to people who had first been given the notes
proposed the creation of a Bank of the United States	against a Bank of the United States
favored a tax on some farm products, such as whiskey	against a whiskey tax
believed in strong trade with the British; distrusted the French	admired the French; distrusted the British

MONEY PROBLEMS AND A TAX REBELLION

Who Gets Paid?

The old government still owed a lot of money. Both the federal government and the states owed money to Americans and to other countries. Hamilton believed that if it all was paid back, everyone would feel that the new government was strong enough to last a long time.

Jefferson agreed the money should be paid, but he disagreed with Hamilton on who should be paid. Many soldiers and farmers had been given **notes** by the government. These notes were not real money; they were promises for money later. Many people had to sell their notes because they needed money immediately. They sold them for less than they were worth. Jefferson wanted some government money to go to the people who had been forced to sell their notes. Hamilton wanted to pay only the people who owned the notes—mostly merchants. In the end, Hamilton's plan was passed.

The federal government also agreed to pay what the states owed. Northern states were the

Alexander Hamilton. Revolutionary (he served with Washington during the Revolutionary War), politician, and statesman, Hamilton was wholly or partly responsible for a number of important American institutions, such as the national bank and political parties.

ones that owed the most money. Therefore, the South would not get as much money from the federal government. The South didn't like that, so everyone agreed on a compromise. The government would pay what the states owed, and a new capital city would be built in the South. Washington, D.C., was soon started between Maryland and Virginia.

When Hamilton wanted to form the **Bank of the United States**, Jefferson objected. The Constitution said nothing about a bank. He felt that a government bank would make the federal government too strong. Again, Hamilton won. The Bank was started. It was run by rich businessmen, not by the government.

The Whiskey Rebellion in Pennsylvania

Congress passed many taxes to get the money it needed. One tax was on whiskey. This tax hurt small farmers in the West who grew grain. Roads in the west were so bad that it was hard to get the grain to Eastern cities. It was much easier for farmers to make whiskey with some of it and sell the whiskey close to home. The farmers did not make much money on the whiskey, and didn't want to pay tax on it.

Finally, in 1794, farmers in western Pennsylvania fought back. They scared tax collectors and burned their homes. George Washington and Alexander Hamilton marched west with a large army. When they arrived, the farmers had disappeared. There was no fighting and no trouble. The whole country learned that the federal government would enforce its laws. It would even use the army, if necessary.

SECTION REVIEW

Can you answer these Main Idea questions?

1. How did Hamilton's and Jefferson's ideas differ?

2. How did the first political parties form?

3. What incident showed that the federal government intended to enforce its laws?

Can you identify these people?

George Washington, Alexander Hamilton, Thomas Jefferson

Can you define these terms?

Judiciary Act, cabinet, political parties, Federalists, Republicans, notes, Bank of the United States, Whiskey Rebellion

2. TROUBLE WITH FRANCE, BRITAIN, AND SPAIN

Main Ideas

Think about the following Main Idea questions as you read this section:

1. How was the French Revolution different from the American Revolution?

2. What did Citizen Genêt try to do in the United States?

3. What were the results of Jay's Treaty and Pinckney's Treaty?

TROUBLE WITH FRANCE

The French Revolution Makes France a Republic

The new country had to build new relationships with other countries such as Britain, France, and Spain. These foreign affairs gave Washington and later Presidents many problems.

France had helped the United States during the American Revolution. Americans thought of the French as their friends. Then in 1789, the first year George Washington was President, the French people began their own Revolution. They revolted against their king and his government. At first, they only wanted what Americans had: freedom and a bigger say in their government. But the leaders of the French Revolution changed quickly, and so did the Revolution itself. It turned bloody. By 1793 so many thousands of people were being killed that this period of French history is called **The Reign of Terror.** The king's head was cut off. So were the heads of many nobles and people in the government. All across France, people were killed because someone thought they were against the Revolutionary

government. People in England, Spain, and even the United States feared that the killing would spread to their country.

France and Britain went to war. Both Hamilton and Jefferson wanted the United States to stay out of this war. Jefferson didn't want the President to say anything, but President Washington took Hamilton's advice. He told the world that the United States would not help either side. It would remain neutral.

Citizen Genêt Meddles in American Politics

In 1793 the French Revolutionary government sent a diplomat named Citizen Genêt to the United States. His job was to talk President Washington into helping France. Genêt saw that the United States wouldn't change its neutral stand. He made plans on his own. He started to get ships ready to fight the British. He planned to send an army of frontiersmen into Spanish territory. Some Republicans supported him, and he even began to stir up American citizens against President Washington. All of Washington's cabinet, including Jefferson, voted to send Citizen Genêt back to France. However, the French government changed again. Genêt was afraid he would be killed. He decided to stay in the United States and eventually became an American citizen.

TROUBLE WITH BRITAIN

John Jay's Unpopular Treaty with Britain

France was not the only country causing trouble for Americans. As part of the war against France, the British navy seized more than 250 American ships that were carrying goods to French ports in the West Indies. In addition, the

British governor of Canada tried to get the Indians in the Northwest Territory to attack American settlers.

The Republicans in Congress were ready to go to war with Britain again. To prevent this, George Washington sent Chief Justice John Jay to England in 1794. Jay got the British to pay for the goods that their navy had taken from American ships. He also got the British to leave their forts in the Northwest Territory. They did not agree to stop capturing American ships, though.

The Republicans were furious with Jay's Treaty. They felt that Jay had given in to the British. The Senate finally agreed to the treaty, but only by one vote.

A TREATY WITH SPAIN

Pinckney's Treaty with Spain Gives Americans What They Want

Spain had never agreed to the southern and western borders of the United States. In addition, it had not agreed to let Americans use the Mississippi River. But Spain was at war with France. It didn't want a quarrel with the United States as well.

In 1795, Spain gave in to all the American demands. It signed a treaty with Thomas Pinckney of the United States. A southern boundary was agreed on, and Americans were free to use the Mississippi.

SECTION REVIEW

Can you answer these Main Idea questions?

1. How was the French Revolution different from the American Revolution?

2. What did Citizen Gênet try to do in the United States?

3. What were the results of Jay's Treaty and Pinckney's Treaty?

Can you identify this person?

Citizen Gênet

Can you define these terms?

the French Revolution, the Reign of Terror

3. WHEN JOHN ADAMS WAS PRESIDENT

Main Ideas

Think about the following Main Idea questions as you read this section:

1. What was unexpected about the results of the election of 1776?

2. What was the XYZ affair?

3. What were the Alien and Sedition Acts?

4. What was unexpected about the election of 1800, and what was done about it?

ELECTION PROBLEMS

Washington Decides Not To Run

By 1796 George Washington had decided not to run for President again. He felt that two terms were enough. His example became an unwritten rule. For almost 150 years, no President served more than two terms.

The First Election with Political Parties

The election of 1796 was the first election for President in which political parties were important. The Federalists nominated Washington's Vice President, John Adams, for President. The Republicans nominated Thomas Jefferson.

During the campaign, Federalists warned that a Republican victory might lead to terrible things. They said that the Republicans agreed with French revolutionary ideas, and pointed out that French revolutionaries had killed many people during their Revolution. The same thing could happen here, the Federalists said, if the Republicans won.

Adams Becomes President and Jefferson Vice-President

Many people believed the warnings, and John Adams was elected President. But something else happened that no one expected. Thomas Jefferson, the Republican candidate for President, was elected Vice President.

How did this happen? When the Constitution was written, there were no political parties. The Constitution said that the person with the majority of votes would become President, and the person in second place would become Vice President. No one had thought that the President and Vice President might be political enemies.

FRENCH OFFICIALS DEMAND BRIBES IN THE XYZ AFFAIR

The French Seize American Ships

While John Adams was President, relations with France got worse. The French were angry at the Jay Treaty. They felt that the United States was supporting the British. And so they began capturing American ships, just as the British were doing.

In 1797 President Adams sent men to France to settle the problem. Three Frenchmen met with the Americans. These men said that the French foreign minister would not even talk to the Americans unless he was paid a bribe of $250,000.

"Millions for Defense, but Not One Cent for Tribute!"

Furious, the Americans refused to pay the bribe. President Adams had the story printed in the newspapers, using the letters XYZ instead of the names of the three Frenchmen. Almost overnight, Americans changed what they thought of France. Everyone was upset about the way France was treating the United States. The slogan "Millions for defense, but not one cent for tribute!" swept the nation. People were willing to pay for a war ("defense") but not for a bribe ("tribute"). But President Adams didn't want a war. He kept the country at peace. In 1800, France backed down and signed an agreement with the United States.

THE ALIEN AND SEDITION ACTS PUNISH OPPONENTS OF THE GOVERNMENT

Federalists Pass the Alien and Sedition Acts

In 1798, the Federalists took advantage of the nation's anger at France. They passed four laws that they hoped would silence their political enemies, the Republicans. These laws are called the **Alien and Sedition Acts**.

Three Laws Against Foreigners

Three of these laws were supposed to stop foreigners (mostly from France) from causing problems in the United States. The **Naturalization Act** said that people coming into the United States would have to wait 14 years to become naturalized—that is, to become citizens. The two **Alien Acts** allowed the President to send aliens, or foreigners, back to their countries if he considered them dangerous.

A Law Against Criticizing the Government

The fourth law, the **Sedition Act**, was aimed at American citizens. It said that talking **sedition**—that is, stirring up people against the President or the government—was against the law.

The Sedition Act was used by Federalists against the Republicans, not against foreign troublemakers. During the elections in 1800, Republican newspapers were closed down for sedition. Editors, and even a congressman, were arrested and jailed because they spoke against the President.

Today, federal courts would say that the Alien and Sedition acts were **unconstitutional**, or against the Constitution. The Sedition Act in particular violates one of our most important rights, freedom of speech. But in President Adams' time the federal courts did not say this. So the laws remained until Jefferson became President.

ELECTION PROBLEMS AGAIN

Adams Against Jefferson Again

The election of 1800 was as angry as the one in 1796. Once again, John Adams and Thomas Jefferson ran against each other. Once again, the Federalists said that terrible things would happen to the country if the Republicans won. But this time, Adams lost the election.

Jefferson did not win, though. He and Aaron Burr, a New York Republican, got the same number of votes. The election was a tie between Jefferson and Burr. The House of Representatives would have to decide which one would be President.

Hamilton turns Against Burr, and Jefferson is Elected

The House voted 35 times. The Federalists voted for Burr. The vote was always a tie. Finally Alexander Hamilton stepped in. He knew Burr well, and he disliked and distrusted him. Hamilton persuaded a few Federalist congressmen to stop voting for Burr. That gave Jefferson the most votes, and he became President.

A New Amendment and a Peaceful Change of Presidents

As a result of the election of 1800, the 12th Amendment to the Constitution was passed in 1804. It changed the way the President and Vice President were elected. Electors now vote for both the President and Vice President together. The type of tie that happened in 1800 cannot happen again.

The most important result of the election of 1800 was that the Federalists' warnings did not come true. The job of President and all its power passed peacefully from the Federalist Party to the Republican Party. Jefferson changed some things, like the members of his cabinet. Other things, like the Whiskey Tax and the Alien and Sedition Acts, he ended. Still other things, even some that he disagreed with, like the Bank of the United States, he left alone. Americans saw that political power could change without destroying the government.

Burr Kills Hamilton

In 1804, Aaron Burr got his revenge. He challenged Alexander Hamilton to a duel in which Hamilton was killed. Burr later took part in many plans and plots. At one point, he was even put on trial for treason because he tried to take over the West and start a new country there. He was found not guilty, but his political career was ended.

For more about the duel between Alexander Hamilton and Aaron Burr, turn to the end of this chapter.

SECTION REVIEW

Can you answer these Main Idea questions?

1. What was unexpected about the results of the election of 1776?

2. What was the XYZ affair?

3. What were the Alien and Sedition Acts?

4. What was unexpected about the election of 1800, and what was done about it?

Can you identify these people?

X, Y, and Z; Aaron Burr

Can you define these terms?

XYZ affair, Alien and Sedition Acts

4. WHEN THOMAS JEFFERSON WAS PRESIDENT

 Main Ideas

Think about the following Main Idea questions as you read this section:

1. Why did France want to sell Louisiana?

2. Why did Jefferson want to buy it?

3. How did John Marshall make the Supreme Court more powerful?

4. What was the result of the Barbary Coast war?

THE LOUISIANA PURCHASE DOUBLES THE SIZE OF THE UNITED STATES

France Offers to Sell its Lands in North America

In 1762, at the end of the French and Indian War, France had been forced to give Spain its land west of the Mississippi River. Then, in 1800, Spain agreed to return this land to France. The whole area was known as Louisiana. It extended from the Mississippi to the Rocky Mountains.

After the XYZ affair, Americans were afraid that the French might start new colonies in Louisiana. They were also worried that France might lose its war with Britain and the British take over Louisiana, just as they had taken over Canada at the end of the French and Indian War. British colonies would then border much of the United States. Either way, the United States would have a strong western neighbor who might close the city of New Orleans to American trade.

President Jefferson sent men to France to buy New Orleans. To their surprise, the French offered to sell them all of Louisiana. The Emperor Napoleon, the new ruler of France, was planning to fight Britain again. He wanted money instead of faraway lands.

Jefferson Buys the Louisiana Territory

When Jefferson heard about Napoleon's offer to sell Louisiana, he was not sure whether he should agree to it. He wanted the land, but he didn't know if he had the power to buy it. The Constitution said nothing about a President buying land. Finally, Jefferson followed the Federalists' idea of a more open Constitution instead of his own idea of a strict one. He knew most Americans wanted the land, so he bought it for 15 million dollars.

The Louisiana Purchase was Jefferson's most important act as President. Suddenly, the United States doubled its size. The only problem was that no one knew where the country's new western borders were. Jefferson had to send out several groups of explorers to find out where they were.

JOHN MARSHALL MAKES THE SUPREME COURT IMPORTANT

John Marshall is Appointed Chief Justice

Just before leaving office, President John Adams made his Secretary of State, John Marshall, the third Chief Justice of the Supreme Court. Although he was Jefferson's cousin, Marshall was a Federalist. He believed in a strong federal government and a flexible Constitution. He was an excellent speaker and gave careful thought to each case. Even the Republican justices agreed with much of what he said. Although he had never been a judge before, he became our greatest Chief Justice.

Marshall Says Some Laws Are Unconstitutional

Marshall made the Supreme Court a key part of our government. Since the Constitution said little about the Court's powers, the Court itself had to decide what they were. In one important case, Marshall decided that the Court had the power to review ANY state or federal law. If the Court decided that a law went against the Constitution, then that law was said to be **unconstitutional**. This meant that the law was no longer a law, for no law can go against the Constitution— the Constitution is the highest law of our land. But the Court could not enforce what it decided: that was the President's job.

Later, a case about the Bank of the United States came before the Supreme Court. The Court followed what Marshall believed. The Constitution said nothing about allowing Congress to create a Bank, but Marshall said it didn't have to. As long as the law that created the bank wasn't against anything in the Constitution, it was all right.

Everyone agreed with Marshall that the Supreme Court's job was to protect Americans by deciding whether or not laws followed the Constitution. Under John Marshall, the Court had made a place for itself—a place with strong powers.

THE UNITED STATES WINS A WAR AGAINST NORTH AFRICAN PIRATES

A Naval War on the Barbary Coast

Trade and shipping were important American businesses. Yet the ships of other nations were stopping American trading ships. America had only a small navy, and it couldn't do much to protect the ships.

Protecting our ships became a real problem right after Jefferson became President. The rulers of several Arab countries along the "Barbary Coast" of North Africa demanded money to let any foreign ship pass peacefully. Most countries paid these pirate rulers to leave their ships alone.

But when the ruler of Tripoli (called Libya today) wanted more money from the United States, President Jefferson refused. Tripoli began attacking American ships. President Jefferson sent warships to Tripoli, and these ships were attacked, too.

The war with Tripoli lasted four years. In 1805, Tripoli's ruler was forced to make peace. He had to stop attacking American ships and demanding money. Ten years later the American navy forced the other Barbary States to stop, too. Finally the threat to American ships in that area was ended.

America was developing a new government. It grew in ways that surprised even the writers of the Constitution. The rise of political parties and a strong Supreme Court showed that many changes could be made within the framework of the Constitution. The rest of the world noticed the United States, too. But America still had to fight to prove that it was an independent country. European countries didn't quite accept that . . . yet.

SECTION REVIEW

Can you answer these Main Idea questions?

1. Why did France want to sell Louisiana?

2. Why did Jefferson want to buy it?

3. How did John Marshall make the Supreme Court more powerful?

4. What was the result of the Barbary Coast war?

Can you identify and locate these places?

Barbary Coast, Tripoli

Can you identify this person?

John Marshall

Can you define this term?

Louisiana Purchase

AFTER YOU READ

Discussion Questions

1. What issues divided Americans into two political parties?

2. How did the growth of political parties affect elections for President?

3. Describe how foreign relations between the United States and France, Britain, Spain, and Tripoli changed from the time of the American Revolution to the end of the Barbary War.

Comprehension Questions

I. Read each unfinished sentence carefully. Each one gives a cause. You must complete each sentence with the correct effect to tell what happened.

1. Americans wanted to be sure that their rights were in the Constitution, so Congress _____.

2. Alexander Hamilton and Thomas Jefferson disagreed, so their followers _____.

3. Western farmers fought against paying the whiskey tax, so President George Washington and Alexander Hamilton _____.

4. Because of the elections of 1796 and 1800, Congress changed _____.

5. The French Emperor, Napoleon, needed money, so he _____.

6. Because of John Marshall's Supreme Court decisions, that court _____.

II. Now answer the following questions by listing one or more causes of each event.

1. What caused the Barbary War?

2. During the American Revolution, the United States had very good relations with France. What caused this to change?

3. What caused Congress to change the way Presidents and Vice Presidents were elected?

Writing Activity

Pretend you are one of the people below. Each has a problem. Write a letter to your representative in Congress about your problem. Tell him or her what is wrong, what you want done, and why.

1. You were a soldier in the Revolution. The army paid you with notes, but you had to sell them for less than they were worth in order to buy food and farm supplies.

2. You are a western farmer who makes his corn into whiskey. You don't like the new whiskey tax.

3. You are arrested for sedition because you wrote a newspaper article criticizing the Federalists.

4. You are a merchant who exports goods to Europe. Your ship and goods were taken by the Barbary pirates.

BIOGRAPHY

Alexander Hamilton, whose face appears on the ten dollar bill, was many things in his time: Revolutionary soldier, congressman, one of the fathers of the Constitution, and Secretary of the Treasury. His many contributions to our country include creating the First Bank of the United States and, as Secretary of the Treasury, paying off the national debt at full value. This helped give people confidence in the new government.

Hamilton believed in a strong national government and in the importance of business and trade to the nation's future. Jefferson and Madison, with whom he disagreed, made some of their greatest contributions in working to protect the average American from the government with the Bill of Rights. Hamilton's greatest contribution, however, was to help make the government strong enough to survive and to do its job. Hamilton and Jefferson are often seen as representing two competing sets of beliefs and values in American politics.

Hamilton's rivalry with Burr, however, which led to his death, resulted much more from personal dislike than from a clash of ideas. Hamilton did not trust Burr. He helped Jefferson defeat Burr in the presidential election of 1800. Later, he stopped Burr from becoming the governor of New York. Burr then challenged Hamilton to a duel.

Both men fired one shot, Hamilton fell dying, and his own bullet hit only air. Public upset over Hamilton's death led to the end of dueling.

CHAPTER 16

THE WAR OF 1812 AND BEYOND

America continued to have trouble with France and Britain during Thomas Jefferson's second term. Problems with Britain became worse when Jefferson's friend James Madison followed him as President. In 1812 the United States went to war against Britain. It was the second time that Americans fought the British, but the first major war for the new nation. Neither side really won. Fortunately, the problems disappeared after the war. For a short time, the United States enjoyed an "Era of Good Feelings."

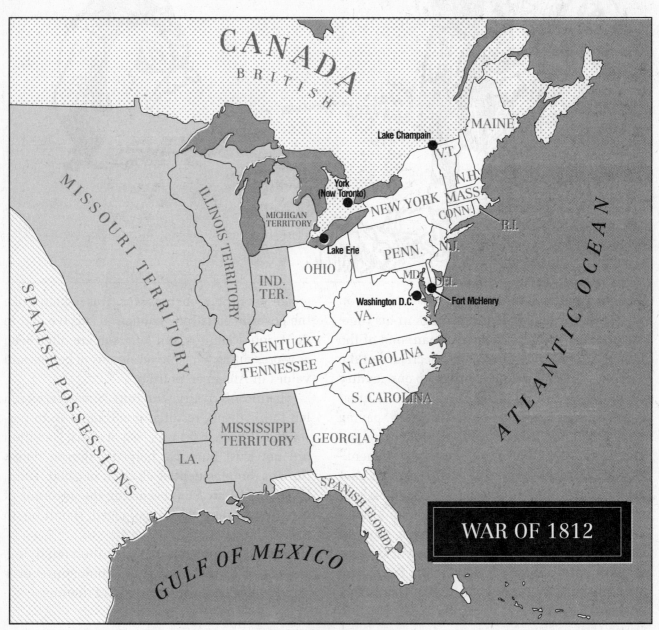

WAR OF 1812

BEFORE YOU READ

Sections in this Chapter

1. Problems with the British and the Indians
2. The War of 1812
3. After the War

Reading a Map

The map on the opposite page shows the major battles fought during the War of 1812. Use it to answer the following questions.

1. Where outside of the United States was a battle fought?

2. On which lakes were battles fought? Why do you think battles were fought there?

Understanding a Key Concept: ECONOMY

A country's **economy** is all the ways people earn a living and produce goods. A strong economy is one where most people are earning a good living and many goods are being made, traded, and sold. In the early 1800's, the economy of the United States was strong. But because different parts of the country depended upon each other, events in one section would affect the economy in another. Read each of the following sentences and use what you know about the American economy to predict what could happen. The first is done for you.

1. Southern plantation owners sent their cotton to Britain on New England ships. How would a southern drought which killed the cotton crop affect New England ship owners?

   New England ship owners wouldn't have cotton to carry in their ships, and so would have less business and make less money.

2. Northwestern farmers shipped grain from New Orleans to New York, where it was made into bread. What would happen to bakers in New York if New Orleans was closed to American ships?

3. Northeastern bankers loaned money to Northwestern farmers so that they could buy more land to grow more grain. What would happen to the bankers if heavy rains destroyed the crops?

4. New England factories made goods to sell in the Northwest Territory. If those farmers had no money to buy these goods, what would happen to New England factory workers?

5. A **depression** is when the economy slows down. Both business and trade are reduced. Predict what would happen to the rest of the country if New York and New England went into a bad depression.

Making Use of What You Already Know

The relationship between the United States and Great Britain began long before the United States became a country. Think about the following events and write them in the correct order.

British colonists take land from the Indians.

The British lose the American Revolution.

The Thirteen Colonies object to British trade laws and taxation without representation.

Americans fight for independence from Britain.

The British navy seizes American ships.

The British ignored the colonists, so the colonists took care of themselves.

1. PROBLEMS WITH THE BRITISH AND THE INDIANS

Main Ideas

Think about the following Main Idea questions as you read this section:

1. What were the problems with Britain that led to the War of 1812?

2. What were the results of Jefferson's embargo?

3. Why did Tecumseh try to unite the tribes against the Americans?

PROBLEMS WITH BRITAIN AND FRANCE AT SEA

The British Stop American Ships at Sea

The United States wanted to trade with both France and Britain. But Britain was at war with France again, and did not want the United States to trade with the French. The United States said that it was a neutral country and had the right to trade with anyone. Neither Britain nor France listened. The British navy stopped American ships headed for France and took their goods. France stopped American ships, too. A thousand American ships were stopped in just three years.

The British navy also stopped American ships to look for **deserters**—sailors who had run away from the British navy because life there was so terrible. But the British badly needed sailors. When they stopped American ships, they were not very careful about whom they took. Nor did they ask permission. They just took any sailors that they thought were British, even if they were American. They also took food and goods. One British warship even seized an American navy ship in American waters and took off four sailors. Americans were furious at this treatment. Many of them were ready to go to war against Britain.

Jefferson's Embargo Halts Trade with England and France

President Jefferson did not want war. He thought that if Americans stopped trading with both France and Britain, both countries would be hurt. They would then have to leave American ships alone and allow Americans to trade with everyone. So Jefferson began an **embargo**. This meant that Americans were not allowed to trade with Britain or France.

The embargo was a disaster. People all over the country hated it. They couldn't sell their goods. They couldn't sell their crops, and they couldn't buy the goods they wanted. Finally, just before Jefferson left office in 1809, Congress ended the embargo. It hadn't hurt France or England. It had just hurt the United States.

Madison Tries a New Plan

James Madison became President three days after Jefferson ended his embargo. The new President tried something different. He permitted trade with Britain and France. At the same time, he gave both countries a year to agree to let American shipping alone.

Madison's plan did not work any better than Jefferson's did. The French pretended to agree, then kept American ships in French ports anyway. The British kept on seizing American ships and taking sailors off them.

TECUMSEH AND INDIAN PROBLEMS IN THE NORTHWEST

The Destruction of Northwest Indian Life

At the same time, settlers in the Northwest Territories were again having troubles with the Indians. The Territories had been peaceful for a while. The British had finally left the area after Jay's Treaty of 1794. That same year, Indians in Ohio were defeated in the Battle of Fallen Timbers. They were forced to move west to Indiana, Illinois, and even across the Mississippi River.

Over the next 15 years, treaties took more and more land from the Indians, who often received little or no payment for it. Settlers came, and the Northwest settlements grew quickly. Ohio became a state in 1803. But the Native Americans who lived there were being destroyed by drink, disease, and hopelessness.

Tecumseh and the Prophet Bring the Tribes Together

Two brothers from the Shawnee tribe saw what was happening to their people. Tecumseh and Tenskwatawa (called "The Prophet") tried to do what no other Indians had done before: they tried to bring together Indians from many tribes to resist the whites. Tecumseh traveled all over the country, from Wisconsin to Florida, trying to put together a Native American confederation. He and his brother told their people to give up liquor and to return to the life they led before the white men came.

William Henry Harrison Gains a Victory at Tippecanoe

In 1811, a group of Indians in Illinois attacked some white settlers because they wanted their land back. General William Henry Harrison, the governor of the Indiana Territory, claimed that they were followers of the Prophet. He destroyed Tecumseh's main village at Tippecanoe. Harrison became a hero to the country, but he had started another Indian war. Tecumseh joined with the British in Canada. Once again, the British helped Indians attack American settlers.

SECTION REVIEW

Can you answer these Main Idea questions?

1. What were the problems with Britain that led to the War of 1812?

2. What were the results of Jefferson's embargo?

3. Why did Tecumseh try to unite the tribes against the Americans?

Can you identify this place?

Tippecanoe

Can you identify these people?

Tecumseh, The Prophet, William Henry Harrison

Can you define these terms?

embargo, deserters

2. THE WAR OF 1812

Main Ideas

Think about the following Main Idea questions as you read this section:

1. What were the principal American successes in the War of 1812?

2. What were the principal British successes in the War of 1812?

3. What were some important results of the War of 1812?

THE WAR THAT SHOULD NOT HAVE HAPPENED

The United States Declares War

On June 16, 1812, the United States finally declared war on Britain. This **War of 1812** was a war that should never have happened. Only one day before, the British had decided to stop capturing American ships. But because news traveled slowly, President Madison didn't know about the British decision.

Many Americans opposed the war. In New England, merchants and shipping companies wanted to trade, not fight. Although their ships were being stopped, they were still making money.

Others, mostly from the West, were eager for war. Some Congressmen, like Henry Clay of Kentucky and John C. Calhoun of South Carolina, were called **War Hawks** because they wanted war so much. They wanted to take over Canada and end the Northwest's Indian problems, which they believed were caused by the British. Some Southern War Hawks thought that a war would give them a good chance to take over Florida.

In reality, the United States wasn't ready for a war. Americans couldn't make enough war goods, so they never had enough guns, clothes, or ships. The United States had only a small army and a tiny navy. Most men did not want to fight, so few joined the army. At the same time, however, they wanted more land. They also wanted the British to leave American ships alone.

A WAR WITH NOBODY WINNING

American Battles at Sea

At first, several American warships destroyed large British warships. One American ship, the *Constitution*, became a legend. She was nicknamed "Old Ironsides" because British cannonballs seemed to bounce off her. The British were shocked by the American victories. The Americans were proud. However, there were only twelve ships in the U.S. Navy. That wasn't enough to stop the whole British Navy.

The War on Lake Erie and in Canada

At the start of the war, British soldiers moved down from Canada and into the Northwest forts again. They took control of the Great Lakes. The Americans quickly built a few boats on Lake Erie. Commander Oliver Hazard Perry couldn't get enough guns or sailors for his new boats, so each had only a small, untrained crew. Twenty-five percent of these brave crews were black. What Perry didn't know was that the British ships didn't have enough sailors, either.

In the first battle, Perry's ship was destroyed and most of his crew killed. Instead of surrendering, though, he jumped into a boat and rowed over to another ship, the *Niagara*. Then he attacked instead of running. The surprised British gave up quickly. They had lost many sailors and their ships were badly damaged. Perry sent General William Henry Harrison a famous message: "We have met the enemy and they are ours."

Perry's victory on Lake Erie allowed the American army under Harrison to take back the Northwest forts. Tecumseh, who had become a British ally, was killed during one of the battles. After his death many Indians quit fighting and returned to their homes. The American army continued into Canada. They burned Canada's new capital, York (now called Toronto), but could go no further.

The British Burn Washington, D.C.

In 1814 the British captured the French ruler, Napoleon. The fighting in Europe stopped. Britain turned its attention to the war against the United States. More British soldiers and ships were sent to America. A British army marched south from Montreal, but returned to Canada after the Americans won a battle on Lake Champlain.

But along the Atlantic coast, the war did not go well for the Americans. British ships burned several American towns. In Washington, D.C., President Madison watched the American army run from British soldiers. His wife, Dolley Madison, took the silver and a painting of George Washington from the White House just before the British arrived. In revenge for the American burning of the Canadian capital, the British burned the White House and most of the government buildings. Then they marched toward Baltimore, but were stopped by an angry militia.

The Writing of "The Star-Spangled Banner."

In Baltimore harbor, British ships fired on Fort McHenry as a young American lawyer watched. Despite the best efforts of the British navy, the American fort never surrendered. In the morning, after firing on Fort McHenry "all through the night," the British gave up and sailed away. The lawyer, Francis Scott Key, was inspired to write a poem titled "Defence of Fort M'Henry." The poem was immediately popular

▼ *The* Constitution *defeating the British ship* Guerriere. *The* Constitution, *one of the United States Navy's most celebrated warships ever, went on to defeat another British ship. A sister ship of the* Constitution, *the* United States, *captured a British frigate. The performance of the American Navy in this war helped to establish a strong naval tradition for the new nation.*

and later, after being set to music, became our national anthem, "The Star-Spangled Banner."

THE WAR ENDS

Andrew Jackson Wins the Battle of New Orleans

Another part of the British war plan was to take New Orleans. The American general, Andrew Jackson, was a frontier hero and Indian fighter from Tennessee. Many of his soldiers were members of the Tennessee militia. Others were from New Orleans. Some soldiers were free blacks and some were Indians. There was even a group of pirates fighting on the American side.

The British army was sure it could win a battle against these untrained Americans. But Jackson planned carefully, and his men followed his orders. In the **Battle of New Orleans**, over 550 British soldiers and their Indian allies died. Only 13 died on the American side.

The British lost, but the battle did not change the war. It had been fought two weeks after a peace treaty had been signed. The war was already over, although no one in New Orleans knew it.

Andrew Jackson became a national hero. People saw him as a symbol of the brave and tough American frontiersman. In the years after the war, he rose to become the most important political figure in the country.

Making Peace

On Christmas Eve, 1814, the British and the Americans signed a peace treaty ending the War of 1812. Neither side won. Both sides agreed to the same borders as before the war. Other problems were resolved later at meetings between the two countries.

The most important results of the war weren't in the treaty. Other countries began to treat the United States as an independent country. They realized it was separate from Europe and its wars. The British never actually said they would stop taking American ships, but they stopped any-way. Since the European wars were over, the British didn't care whom America traded with. They didn't need the deserting sailors anymore, either.

After the War of 1812, Americans stopped thinking that they could take over Canada. The treaty prohibited armies or warships on the Great Lakes. Ever since then, there have never been any military forces along the Canada–United States border. American pride grew. They had fought the most powerful nation in the world, and they hadn't lost.

SECTION REVIEW

Can you answer these Main Idea questions?

1. What were the principal American successes in the War of 1812?

2. What were the principal British successes in the War of 1812?

3. What were some important results of the War of 1812?

Can you identify and locate this place?

Lake Erie, New Orleans

Can you identify these people?

James Madison, the War Hawks, Oliver Hazard Perry, Andrew Jackson

Can you define these terms?

the Battle of Lake Erie, the Battle of New Orleans

3. AFTER THE WAR

Main Ideas

Think about the following Main Idea questions as you read this section:

1. Why was President Monroe's first term called the "Era of Good Feelings"?

2. What was the Monroe Doctrine, and what events led up to it?

3. What was Henry Clay's "American System," and what became of it?

4. What was the Missouri Compromise, and why was it necessary?

THE ERA OF GOOD FEELINGS

James Monroe and the Era of Good Feelings

James Monroe, also a Virginia Republican, followed Madison as President in 1817. All the political problems of the country's early years seemed solved.

The Federalist Party, which had opposed the War of 1812, faded away. The United States was no longer in the middle of quarrels between Britain and France. And the American economy was growing. People were producing more goods and making more money.

The **economy** is all the ways that people earn a living and produce goods. In 1815, the American economy was still mostly agricultural, or farming. That was changing, though. After the War of 1812, trade and industry grew. More factories were being built, and new industries (such as the textile industry) were turning raw materials, like cotton, into manufactured goods for sale and trade, like cloth.

America had a strong, growing economy. Business was good. Americans seemed to be do-

ing well. There were no big problems in politics. For all these reasons, the first years of Monroe's presidency are often called **The Era** (or Age) **of Good Feelings**.

The United States Gains Florida

South of the United States, a big change was taking place. Spain's huge American empire was falling apart. One of the weakest Spanish colonies was Florida. It had become the home of Indians who had been pushed out of Georgia and Alabama by white settlers. These Indians, called **Seminoles**, raided American settlers in Georgia and then slipped back into Florida. The Spanish government had no control over the Seminoles. So President Monroe ordered Andrew Jackson to stop them.

In 1818 Jackson led 2,000 soldiers into Florida. He captured several Spanish forts. This was not legal, but Jackson once again became a hero to many people.

The Spanish were angry. But they knew they couldn't hold onto Florida, so they sold it to the United States. In 1821, Andrew Jackson became Florida's first American governor.

As part of the same treaty, the Spanish agreed on the borders between the Louisiana Territory and Spanish lands in the West. Texas was to be part of Mexico, and American fur trappers were allowed to trap in the Rocky Mountains.

The Monroe Doctrine Warns Europe to Stay out of America

People in the Spanish colonies had been watching the United States. They had seen it revolt, become independent, and grow stronger. They wanted the same chance to be free, so they too revolted.

Between about 1810 and 1820, the Spanish colonies fought wars for independence against

Spain, just as the United States had fought against Britain. When the colonies became independent countries, the United States was the first country to recognize them. Soon many American merchants were trading with them.

In 1823, President James Monroe sent a message to Congress. Years later it was called the **Monroe Doctrine**. It warned European countries that they could not start new colonies in either North or South America, or interfere with any government in the Western Hemisphere. If a European country attacked a country in the Western Hemisphere, it would be like attacking the United States. The United States would fight back.

The United States couldn't really enforce these rules, and the Monroe Doctrine didn't become important until years later. This speech, however, told the whole world that America would help its neighbors.

Panic and Depression in 1819

During the Era of Good Feelings after the War of 1812, times were good in America. Crops sold for high prices. The West was growing. Steamboats began running. Then, in 1819, the good times suddenly disappeared. One reason was that the Bank of the United States had not controlled the flow of money well.

The results were terrible. Banks failed and stopped paying out money. A sudden failure of the banking system like this frightens everyone. It is known as a **panic**, and it damages the economy badly. During the Panic of 1819, the price of crops dropped. Northwestern farmers couldn't pay their debts to the Northeastern bankers. Bankers couldn't lend money to factory owners. Southern planters couldn't sell their cotton to Britain at high prices, and so they couldn't afford to buy food from Northwestern farmers. Soon it was a bad year for everyone. The country was in a **depression**—a huge bust after an economic boom.

A new National Bank president, Nicholas Biddle, controlled the money better. Neverthe-

less, many people believed the depression was caused by the Bank. They thought that Biddle's new controls were just making life worse. Their dislike of Biddle and of the Bank became an important issue in national politics.

Henry Clay's "American System"

The Panic of 1819 scared a lot of people in Congress. Henry Clay of Kentucky, who had been a War Hawk in 1812, wanted to make changes in American business and trade. Clay called his plan the **American System**. Its purpose was to change the economy so that fewer raw materials would go to Europe. Instead, American factories would use them. Part of the plan was for the government to build transportation improvements, like canals, inside the country. These improvements would help American goods—both raw goods and factory goods—reach all parts of the country. The plan would make America much more independent. It wouldn't have to depend on foreign trade.

Some of Clay's American System became law. But his idea that the government should build transportation improvements did not. Many people were afraid it would give the federal government too much power in state and local affairs. Instead, transportation improvements were built by local governments or private persons.

THE MISSOURI COMPROMISE: TROUBLE BETWEEN FREE AND SLAVE STATES

The Balance Of Power Between Free and Slave States

In 1818, the country had 22 states. The 11 northern and northwestern states had made slavery illegal (against the law). They were called free states, because all African-American people in these states were free. The 11 southern and southwestern states still allowed slavery. The slave owners in these states were afraid that if the Northern states had more power, they would force the South to free all its slaves. This would force the slave owners to change their way of life, something which they didn't want to do.

There was a **balance of power** between free states and slave states in the Senate, because there were equal numbers of free and slave states and each state had two senators. In the House of Representatives, however, the free states had more votes because they had more people. As a result, the House often passed bills which the North wanted but the South didn't. These bills were then stopped by Southern votes in the Senate, where each side had the same number of senators. But the South often had trouble passing any bills it wanted.

Missouri Asks to Become a State, and the Balance of Power is Destroyed

Then Missouri asked to become a state. Most of Missouri's settlers came from slave states. Naturally, Southern Congressmen and these settlers wanted Missouri to be another slave state. But Northern Congressmen wanted it to be a free state. In debates, some Northern Congressmen called slavery "evil." This was the first angry attack on slavery in Congress.

There were other reasons besides slavery for disagreement. The South wanted to have more seats in the House and the most members in the Senate. The North, however, wanted to limit the South's power. Southern Congressmen said it was the right of a new state, not of Congress, to decide if slavery should be allowed. Neither side would change its stand.

Congress Decides on the Missouri Compromise

A **compromise** is an agreement in which each side gives up part of what it wants and keeps something that it wants. In 1820 Congress, led by Henry Clay, agreed on the **Missouri Compromise.** Missouri became a slave state. At the same time though, Maine entered the Union as a free state. The balance in the Senate stayed the same. In addition, the Missouri Compromise said that slavery would never be allowed in the northern part of the Louisiana Territory.

Many people saw the quarrel in Congress as a warning. They knew the trouble between the North and South would not go away.

In the War of 1812, Americans fought to be free of British control. Although no one won, the United States would never again have to go to war to defend its independence. In the "Era of Good Feelings" it began expanding to the west and south. But the good times didn't last. A depression hit America's businesses and slowed American growth. And a quarrel over slavery showed the deep differences between the North and the South.

SECTION REVIEW

Can you answer these Main Idea questions?

1. Why was President Monroe's first term called the "Era of Good Feelings"?

2. What was the Monroe Doctrine, and what events led up to it?

3. What was Henry Clay's "American System," and what became of it?

4. What was the Missouri Compromise, and why was it necessary?

Can you identify and locate these places?

Missouri, Maine

Can you identify these people?

James Monroe, the Seminoles, Henry Clay

Can you define these terms?

economy, the Era of Good Feelings, panic, depression, Monroe Doctrine, balance of power, compromise, Missouri Compromise

AFTER YOU READ

Discussion Questions

1. What events led up to the War of 1812, and why was it called "the war that shouldn't have been"?

2. How did the American economy change in 1819, and how did this affect Americans?

3. What was the Missouri Compromise, and why was it so important?

Comprehension Questions

I. Read the beginning of each sentence below. Decide which choice will complete the sentence correctly, and copy the completed sentence.

1. One result of the War of 1812 was that American industries—

   a. grew quickly to make war supplies.
   b. disappeared because the men became soldiers.
   c. wanted to stop trading with Great Britain.
   d. used up all of America's raw materials.

2. If communications between Britain and the United States had been faster, the War of 1812 and the Battle of New Orleans—

   a. would have been won by the Americans.
   b. wouldn't have been fought.
   c. would have been won by the British.
   d. would have killed many more men.

3. The Era of Good Feelings was created at least in part by—

   a. a good economy and no war.
   b. a war with Spain.
   c. a depression and the War of 1812.
   d. the French and the Missouri Compromise.

4. The Missouri Compromise settled the problem of—

   a. the slave state vs. free state balance in the Senate.
   b. the border between Missouri and Canada.
   c. the price of corn to western farmers.
   d. the slave trade.

Writing Activity

Americans had to solve several important problems after President Jefferson left office. Americans disagreed on how they shold be solved. Choose one of the disagreements listed below. Tell what each side thought about the issue. Make a list of the facts and feelings for each side. Then use your list to write two paragraphs which describe the disagreement and how it was finally resolved.

The British stopped American ships and took sailors off the ships.

The Indians attacked settlers in the Northwest.

The South wanted Missouri to be a slave state.

The Star-Spangled Banner

Oh—say! Can you see, by the dawn's ear-ly light, What so proudly we hailed at the twi-light's last gleam-ing? Whose broad stripes and bright stars through the per-i-lous fight, O'er the ram-parts we watch'd were so gal-lant-ly stream-ing? And the rock-ets' red glare, the bombs burst-ing in air Gave proof through the night that our flag was still there. Oh say does that Star-span-gled Ban-ner yet wave O'er the land of the free and the home of the brave!

The song commemorates the successful defense of Fort McHenry. The "Star- Spangled Banner" is the American flag, which has a star for each state. Traditionally, a nation's flag is lowered to indicate that a unit of that country's armed forces—whether it be a ship, an army, or a fort—has surrendered. The fact that the American flag still flew over Fort McHenry showed that the fort had not surrendered.

"The rockets' red glare, the bombs bursting in air" refers to the flashes of light that accompany a battle at night. These flashes, which showed that the fight was still going on, "gave proof through the night" that the fort was still fighting back.

Now and again, some people have suggested that *The Star-Spangled Banner* should be replaced as our national anthem. They feel that because *The Star-Spangled Banner* is about a military victory, it focuses on the wrong thing, war. Instead, they suggest that a song that has nothing to do with fighting or bloodshed, like *America The Beautiful*, should be our national anthem.

But what *The Star-Spangled Banner* is really celebrating is not the fight itself, but the courage and determination that the American soldiers who defended Fort McHenry showed. That was the same sort of courage and determination which the colonists showed during the Revolution, and which led to independence. It is also the same sort of courage and determination which Americans have shown in our finer moments in peacetime. As such, it is worth singing about.

A PERIOD O
WESTWAR

"*It was the best of times, it was the worst of times," wrote Charles Dickens in* A Tale of Two Cities. *The events in the book occured during the French Revolution, but Dickens could also have been writing about the United States in the years between 1824 and 1850.*

During this period, the United States grew, settlers pushing the frontier westward and leaving cities and towns behind them. But in the process, Native Americans were pushed westward too, forced from their homes against their will. Thousands died, and generations have lived in poverty on the poor land that was all they were left. Our Southwest borders were secured, but at the price of a war with Mexico. The economy industrialized and grew, but the growth was often costly: some of our worst depressions occured during this time. Politics and government were opened up to the common man, but corruption and incompetence were also common.

Even as the nation was growing in pride and power, our greatest shame—slavery—was growing, too.

The best of times, the worst of times. This period of change and westward expansion was certainly both.

F CHANGE AND
D EXPANSION

Staton.

THE AGE OF JACKSON

From 1801 until 1825, all our Presidents were Republican gentlemen-farmers from Virginia. All three were close friends. But beginning in the 1820's, a very different type of person became important in politics—the rough frontier hero.

Andrew Jackson was this kind of man. He served two terms as President. The period from 1829 to 1837 is often called the "Age of Jackson." It was the first time the "common man" instead of the "gentleman" had political power.

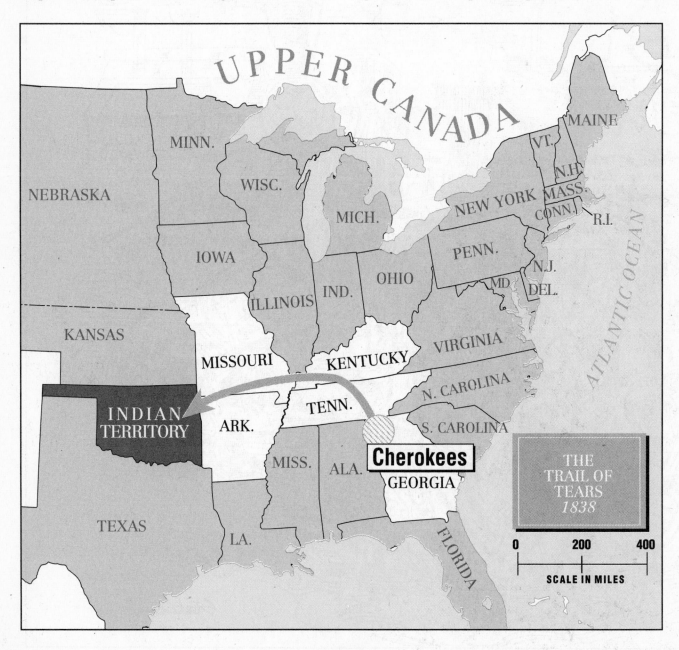

THE
TRAIL OF
TEARS
1838

0   200   400

SCALE IN MILES

BEFORE YOU READ

Sections in This Chapter

  1. A New Kind of President

  2. Indian Removals

  3. After Jackson

Reading a Map

Use the map on the opposite page and what you know about North American geography to answer these questions. You may wish to refer to the maps in Chapter 1.

1. The government forced the Cherokees to move west. What geographic features did their route cross on the way to the Indian Territory?

2. Use the mileage scale to determine how far their old home was from their new home.

3. Was the environment of their new home similar to that of their old home?

Understanding a Key Concept:
COMMON PEOPLE

Americans who were not rich, not well-educated, and not slaves were called the **common people**. The common Americans worked hard at their small businesses, farms, or jobs. Some were city people. Others owned small farms or lived on the frontier.

1. Below are descriptions that could apply to different kinds of people List those that could describe one of the common people.

hard worker   *has a very large house*

has a job   *has a family*

owns no slaves   *wears fancy clothes*

owns a factory   *has little free time*

expects to have a say in government

2. Andrew Jackson was supported by common Americans, but he wasn't really a "common man." Below is a list of facts about Andrew Jackson. Copy those that show that he was not really a common man.

owned a plantation and slaves

was a general in the army

worked hard to get what he had

didn't dress fancy

had rough manners

was a land speculator

Using What You Already Know

Think about the United States Constitution and how rights and powers are divided between the state and the federal governments.

1. Write the two headings below:

STATE GOVERNMENTS CAN

STATE GOVERNMENTS CAN'T

Now write each of the following rights or powers under the appropriate heading.

tax people   *control education*

have courts   *ignore federal laws*

make war on a foreign country

stop freedom of the press

2. Predict what will happen when South Carolina refuses to enforce a federal law.

1. A NEW KIND OF PRESIDENT

Main Ideas

Think about the following Main Idea questions as you read this section:

1. What kinds of voters supported Andrew Jackson?

2. Why did the tariff bill anger the South?

3. What did South Carolina do about the tariff bill, and what happened as a result?

4. Why did Jackson want to destroy the National Bank, and what happened when he did?

TWO BITTER ELECTIONS

The Election of 1824 and the Rise of the "Common Man"

Since the Revolution, many states had changed their election laws. Women, blacks, and Indians still weren't allowed to vote. But now, men who owned little or no property could vote. These **common men**, like small farmers and factory workers, wanted different laws than people with lots of property. They also wanted a different type of person to represent them.

The Election of 1824 showed just how much the country was changing. There were four candidates for President:

General Andrew Jackson was a frontier hero. He had won the Battle of New Orleans in the War of 1812 and had also won two Indian wars.

The Speaker of the House, Henry Clay, was the most powerful man in Congress. He, like Jackson, was from the frontier.

President Monroe's Secretary of State, John Quincy Adams, was the son of the second President, John Adams. He was from the Northeast.

Finally, Secretary of the Treasury William Crawford represented the Southern planters.

However, he became sick and was not important in the campaign.

Jackson got the most votes, but not enough to win. Once again, the House of Representatives had to decide who would be President. Clay knew he didn't have enough votes to win. Instead, he asked his supporters to vote for Adams. Adams, with his own votes plus those of Clay, was elected President. He then appointed Clay Secretary of State.

Jackson was furious. His supporters joined together against Adams and formed what became the **Democratic Party**. This new party said that it was for the common man. Guided by a clever New York politician named Martin Van Buren, it began gathering votes for the 1828 election. In Congress, the Democrats used their power to keep Adams from doing what he wanted to do as President.

Jackson Wins the Election of 1828

The Democrats worked hard to get votes for their party. They signed up factory workers and farmers who had never voted before. Jackson gave newspaper interviews and went to political meetings. He was very careful, though, never to say much about important ideas, like states' rights. No one knew what he really believed. Most people didn't care, either. They liked him because he was a tough frontier hero who never backed down from a fight.

Jackson was not really a "common man." He had made lots of money on land speculation and he owned a plantation and slaves. But he talked directly to the common man in words that common people could understand. He made them feel that he could solve their problems, and they gave him their support, love, and votes.

John Quincy Adams didn't understand the Democrats' new way of getting votes. He was a very serious and dignified man. He did not make speeches or go to meetings, and so he lost the Election of 1828.

PRESIDENT JACKSON AND THE SPOILS SYSTEM

A President for the Common Man

The day Jackson became President, thousands of farmers and workers came to Washington, D.C. A mob of these Jackson supporters crashed the inauguration party for the new President. The White House was almost torn apart. A new age in America had begun.

Jackson took his power seriously. He was the first President elected by a majority of the white men in the country. He defended the people's rights, as he saw them. He didn't always agree with Congress. He vetoed more bills than all of the Presidents before him put together.

To his supporters, he was "Old Hickory," as tough as the toughest American tree. But to his enemies, Jackson became "King Andrew the First." They said he acted more like a King than a President.

The Spoils System

One of the first things Jackson did was to fire many government officials. In their place, he hired Democrats who had worked hard for his election. Other Presidents had hired officials this way. But Jackson's enemies said that he used government jobs as **spoils**. (*Spoils* are goods taken away from enemies in battle.)

The **spoils system** gave government jobs to party workers. It became was an important part of American government during most of the 1800's.

TROUBLE WITH THE SOUTH

A Tariff Bill Angers the South

A **tariff** is a tax on imported goods—that is, goods brought in from a foreign country. Tariffs protect certain industries. A tariff on iron, for example, protects American iron mills, because the tax on foreign iron makes it cost more. Since American iron costs less, more of it is sold. However, the tariff hurts those factories that have been buying cheap iron from outside the country.

High tariffs were part of Henry Clay's "American System" plan to help America grow. The Northwest and some of the Northeast wanted tariffs on textiles, iron, hemp, and wool. Tariffs would help these industries grow. New England, though, was against them. Its factories would have to pay more for the imported raw materials that they needed. The South was against any tariffs at all. Their main crop, cotton, was not imported, so they didn't need protection. However, a tariff would raise the prices of the imported things that Southerners bought.

In 1828 a tariff bill was passed by Congress. People in South Carolina became very angry. They called the tariff a **Tariff of Abominations**— that is, a disgusting and horrible tariff. South Carolina was upset that the federal government had the power to pass such a tariff. It was afraid that a powerful federal government could also free their slaves. South Carolina made the tariff into a fight for **states' rights**. It wanted the states to have more power, or "rights," than the federal government.

Calhoun and the Fight over Nullification

The most important speaker for South Carolina was Jackson's Vice President, John C. Calhoun. Calhoun quit being Vice President so that he could fight the tariff. He wrote, and South Carolina passed, a state law called the **Nullification Act**.

To *nullify* a law means to wipe it out. The Nullification Act tried to wipe out the tariff. It said a state could refuse to obey any federal law that it didn't like. South Carolina used this law to stop the tariff from being collected there. People in South Carolina even talked about becoming a separate country. They said that they didn't have to stay part of the United States, or

"**Union**," if the federal government tried to take away their liberty.

Daniel Webster of Massachusetts was the most powerful speaker in the Senate. In one of his most famous speeches, he answered South Carolina: "Liberty and Union, now and forever, one and inseparable!" He said what many Americans felt: No state could stop being part of the country.

Many people thought Andrew Jackson would support states' rights, but South Carolina went too far for him. Jackson felt that nothing should divide the country. Federal laws must be enforced. At a dinner party, he stared straight at

A cartoon showing Andrew Jackson as "King Andrew the First." The "Common Man" President was often criticized for his high-handed style and insistence on getting his own way.

Calhoun and said: "Our Union: It must be preserved." He sent soldiers into South Carolina after an army had formed there to fight "King Jackson."

The fear of a fight led to another of Henry Clay's compromises. The tariff was lowered over several years. Calhoun and South Carolina accepted this, but never said its ideas about nullification were wrong.

JACKSON'S WAR ON THE NATIONAL BANK

The National Bank

The country and its economy grew while Jackson was President. Southern farmers moved onto the lands that had been taken from the southern Indians, and Western farmers bought more land. Northeastern factories grew. The states built canals and railroads. All this took money. People, states, and companies borrowed money from banks to keep growing.

The federal government kept its money in the Bank of the United States. It was the most powerful bank in the country. When the Bank lent money to other banks, it made them pay it back in gold or silver. That left the smaller banks with less money to loan.

When the Bank of the United States asked Congress to allow it to keep operating, Jackson refused. He was against all banks, but especially this one. He disliked the Bank's head, Nicholas Biddle, and he was not alone. Many people still blamed Biddle and the Bank for the Panic of 1819. Westerners were against the bank because it made loans for land hard to get.

Jackson Destroys the National Bank

But instead of changing the banking system to make it work better, Jackson destroyed it. During the **"Bank War,"** Jackson changed his Secretary of the Treasury three times until he found someone who would do what he wanted.

The government's money was taken out of the Bank of the United States and put into several state "pet banks." This meant these banks had lots of money, but there were few laws to control them. They could use the money anyway they wanted.

The Bank System Runs out of Control

Jackson thought he was protecting the people against the rich. Instead, rich bankers and powerful businessmen gained more control over the country's money. Banks printed their own paper money. They printed more paper money than they had gold and silver. Then they gave large loans for land speculation. Some banks loaned more money than they had.

The American banking system was running out of control. Finally, in his last year as President, Jackson tried to do something. He ordered the federal offices that sold western land not to accept any more of the paper money issued by the banks. The land offices were told to accept only **specie**—gold and silver—as payment for land.

Jackson's cure was too strong. The banks didn't have enough gold and silver to make more loans. Soon everyone was suffering.

SECTION REVIEW

Can you answer these Main Idea questions?

1. What kinds of voters supported Andrew Jackson?

2. Why did the tariff bill anger the South?

3. What did South Carolina do about the tariff bill, and what happened as a result?

4. Why did Jackson want to destroy the National Bank, and what happened when he did?

Can you identify these people?

John Quincy Adams, "Old Hickory," John C. Calhoun, Daniel Webster, Nicholas Biddle

Can you define these terms?

common man, Democratic Party, spoils system, tariff, Tariff of Abominations, states' rights, nullification, Nullification Act, Union, the Bank War, specie

2. INDIAN REMOVALS

Main Ideas

Think about the following Main Idea questions as you read this section:

1. What caused the Black Hawk War, and what happened to the tribe at the end of it?

2. Why did Georgia want the Cherokees' lands?

3. Both the Cherokees and the Seminoles resisted removal. How did the ways they resisted differ?

4. What happened to the tribes after removal?

THE BLACK HAWK WAR IN THE NORTHWEST

The Indian Removal Act

When Jackson became President, there were still many Native Americans living east of the Mississippi. White people wanted to settle on their lands. Jackson, who had led several wars against the Indians, supported the settlers. In 1830, Congress passed his **Indian Removal Act**. It allowed the government to take the Indians' eastern homelands and force them to move west of the Mississippi. This was called "**removal**."

Black Hawk Fights Back

In the Northwest, many Indians had already signed treaties and moved farther west. Two tribes, the Sauk and Fox, were allowed to live on their Illinois land until settlers wanted it. In 1828, a group of these Indians were away hunting when some whites took over their homes. The Indians were forced to move across the Mississippi, where disaster after disaster happened to them. In 1832 they returned, led by a chief named Black Hawk. Black Hawk and his followers fought for a short time, but no other tribes joined them

The Black Hawk War was the last of the Indian wars in the Northwest. It ended when Black Hawk was captured. Once again, the Indians were forced west of the Mississippi.

INDIAN REMOVALS FROM THE SOUTHERN STATES

The Removal of the Civilized Nations

In the South, five Native American tribes—called the **Civilized Nations**—lived on land that the whites wanted. They were the Cherokees, the Creeks, the Chickasaws, the Choctaws, and the Seminoles. They were called "civilized nations" because they had taken up some of the white settlers' ways of life. Beginning in 1831, nearly all of the people of the Civilized Nations were driven out of their homes. They were forced to move to "Indian Territory" in what is now Oklahoma.

The Cherokees Fight in the Courts

One of the "Civilized Tribes," the Cherokees of northern Georgia, tried to fight the removal in the law courts. The Cherokees had been very successful in learning many of the white settlers' ways of life. A few Cherokees owned large plantations with slaves, while others owned small farms. One Cherokee, named Sequoyah, invented a special alphabet for the Cherokee language. Within a few years, most Cherokees were reading. The Cherokees printed newspapers using Sequoyah's alphabet and translated the Bible. In 1828 they wrote a constitution for the tribe based on the U.S. Constitution.

But white settlers wanted the Cherokees' land. They wanted the federal government to take it away from the Cherokees and give it to the state of Georgia. When gold was discovered on Cherokee lands, Georgia stopped waiting: although the

Cherokees had treaties with the U.S. government that were supposed to protect their rights, Georgia passed laws taking these rights away. Gold miners and farmers seized Cherokee property.

The Cherokees did not go to war. They went to court instead, all the way to the Supreme Court. They won their case. Chief Justice John Marshall said that Georgia's actions were unconstitutional. The Cherokees and the federal government had a treaty. Georgia, a state, could not end it.

But even the Supreme Court could not help the Cherokees. President Jackson refused to enforce the Supreme Court's decision. Before he became President, he had fought two wars with the Creek Indians. Now he wanted all the Indians removed.

The Trail of Tears

In 1838, fifteen thousand Cherokees were forced to walk from their homes to the Indian Territory in Oklahoma. The government gave them rotten grain to eat and badly made wagons to travel in. When winter came early, four thousand tired, starving Cherokees died. Their journey is known as the **Trail of Tears**.

A few Cherokees refused to move. They hid in the mountains of North Carolina. Today they are known as the Eastern Band of the Cherokee tribe.

The Seminoles Resist Removal

The Seminoles of Florida tried another way to fight removal. They went to war.

White settlers had a special reason for trying to get rid of the Seminoles. Many escaped black slaves—and free blacks as well—had become part of the Seminole people. Southern slave owners were afraid that more slaves would try to escape and join the tribe.

Between 1835 and 1842, the U.S. Army tried to move the Seminoles to the Indian Territory. Most Seminoles refused and escaped into the Everglades, the swamps of southern Florida. For years, the government sent soldiers into these swamps in a war that cost over 20 million dollars.

Finally, most of the Seminoles were captured and sent to the Indian Territory. But some never surrendered and were never caught. Their descendants still live in the Everglades today.

PROBLEMS IN THE INDIAN TERRITORY

Fighting Between Tribes and Promises Not Kept

The Indian Territory was supposed to be a permanent home for the Indians. But Eastern and Plains Indians were mixed together. Different tribes with different ways of life fought among themselves. Creek Indians even kidnapped some Black Seminoles and sold them into slavery. Many of the remaining Black Seminoles escaped south to Mexico.

The Army built forts to control the Indians. Many whites who worked with the Indians cheated them to get rich. And Congress stopped the payments it promised.

SECTION REVIEW

Can you answer these Main Idea questions?

1. What caused the Black Hawk War, and what happened to the tribe at the end of it?

2. Why did Georgia want the Cherokees' lands?

3. Both the Cherokees and the Seminoles resisted removal. How did the ways they resisted differ?

4. What happened to the tribes after removal?

Can you identify these people?

Sauk and Fox, Black Hawk, Civilized Nations, Cherokees, Seminoles

Can you define these terms?

Black Hawk War, Indian Removal Act, Trail of Tears

3. AFTER JACKSON

Main Ideas

Think about the following Main Idea questions as you read this section:

1. What caused the Panic of 1837, and what happened as a result?

2. Why was the Whig Party started?

3. What happened after the first Whig President was elected?

THE PANIC AND DEPRESSION OF 1837-1843

Van Buren and the Panic of 1837

In 1837, Jackson left office. His Vice President, Martin Van Buren, became the next President. Van Buren had been President only a few weeks when the banking system finally collapsed.

The panic began when Congress ordered the banks to pay the states some of the federal money that had been kept in the banks. However, the

Below is a chart showing how the Panic of 1837 happened. You can see from the chart that the effects of the banks' problem (they didn't have enough money, because they had loaned too much) spread out through the economy. For example, because banks didn't have enough money, many factory workers—most of whom probably didn't even have bank accounts or much to do with banks—ended up losing their jobs.

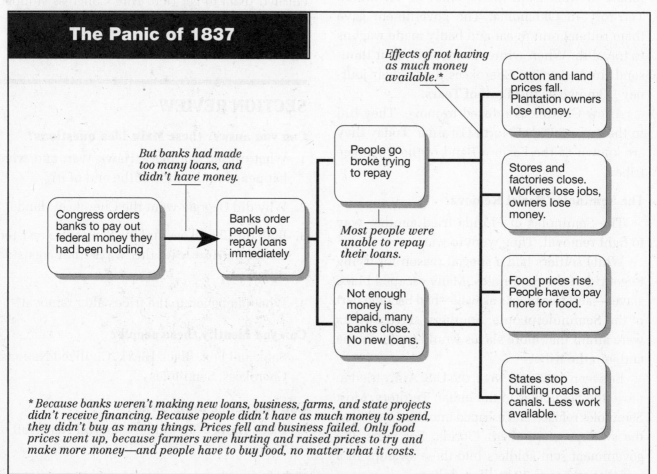

The Panic of 1837

But banks had made too many loans, and didn't have money.

Congress orders banks to pay out federal money they had been holding → Banks order people to repay loans immediately

Most people were unable to repay their loans.

People go broke trying to repay

Not enough money is repaid, many banks close. No new loans.

Effects of not having as much money available.*

Cotton and land prices fall. Plantation owners lose money.

Stores and factories close. Workers lose jobs, owners lose money.

Food prices rise. People have to pay more for food.

States stop building roads and canals. Less work available.

* Because banks weren't making new loans, business, farms, and state projects didn't receive financing. Because people didn't have as much money to spend, they didn't buy as many things. Prices fell and business failed. Only food prices went up, because farmers were hurting and raised prices to try and make more money—and people have to buy food, no matter what it costs.

banks didn't have the money, because they had loaned it all out. To get the money they needed, they demanded that all loans be paid back immediately.

But few people could do so. They had spent the loans on land, factories, and raw materials.

Banks closed, and the American economy fell apart. Cotton prices and land prices dropped because people didn't have the money to buy them. Food prices jumped. Stores and factories went out of business. Many people couldn't find jobs. In New York, people rioted over the high price of flour.

The Panic Becomes a Depression

The Panic of 1837 turned into one of America's worst depressions. It lasted almost six years. States stopped building railroads and canals. They stopped paying back loans. Factories had no customers. Workers had no jobs.

To make things worse, the federal government put all its money into safes instead of banks. Therefore, banks didn't have any money to loan to people and businesses. The depression probably would have happened anyway, but the government's actions had made it worse.

The government did not help the victims of the depression. People needed food, jobs, and loans, but the government did nothing. The economy took a long time to recover.

THE RISE AND DECLINE OF THE WHIGS

Anti-Jackson People Start the Whig Party

When Jackson became President, the new Democratic Party was strong. But many Democrats didn't like what Jackson was doing. The Bank War divided the party. Other Democrats were against the tariff.

Anti-Jackson people, some Democrats and some not, formed the National Republican Party, which soon was called the **Whig Party**. The Whigs had been an English party against King George. The American Whigs wanted everyone to know they were against "King Andrew" Jackson.

The Whigs learned from the Democrats' successes. They nominated frontier heroes, too, like the colorful Davy Crockett. Henry Clay became a Whig. In addition, many anti-Catholics joined the Whigs. This is an old, old game in politics—stirring people up by blaming the country's problems on some group which is seen as "different," the way Catholics were then (the United States was mostly Protestant).

Democratic President Martin Van Buren was not a frontier hero. He was a clever politician, known as the "Little Magician." He was not liked the way Jackson was. It was his bad luck to be President during the Panic of 1837 and the depression that followed.

The Country Elects a Whig President

In 1840, the country was still deep in the depression. The Democrats nominated Van Buren for President again. The Whigs nominated the old frontier general, William Henry Harrison. John Tyler, a Southern planter, was nominated for Vice President.

The Whigs told of Harrison's frontier fighting and his victory against the Indians at the Battle of Tippecanoe. They chanted "**Tippecanoe and Tyler, too**" and "Van, Van is a used-up man." Since many voters blamed the Democrats for the depression, they didn't do very well. Harrison won. But one month after taking office, he died. John Tyler, his Vice President, became President.

Tyler was a Southern planter. His ideas were different from most Whigs. He vetoed banking bills, tariff bills, and improvements that other Whigs wanted. His cabinet quit. He fought with Henry Clay. Very soon he was forced out of the Whig Party and became a Democrat. He then asked Southern Democrats to help him run the country.

By 1844, both the Whig and Democratic parties were splitting up. Party members from different sections of the country were fighting. Northern Whigs didn't agree with Southern Whigs. Northern Democrats didn't get along with Southern Democrats. The Age of Jackson had ended.

The Age of Jackson was an important period in American history. Jackson's election showed the new political power of the common man. Jackson made the Presidency a more powerful office than it had ever been. The country and its economy grew rapidly, but soon that growth was running out of control. The United States truly became one nation, all of its parts interconnected. This interconnectedness meant that what benefitted one section often helped others, like the way the growth of the West helped the Northeast by increasing demand for manufactured goods. But it also meant that problems in one area could hurt the rest of the country, as happened in the Panic of 1837.

SECTION REVIEW

Can you answer these Main Idea questions?

1. What caused the Panic of 1837, and what happened as a result?

2. Why was the Whig Party started?

3. What happened after the first Whig President was elected?

Can you identify these people?

Martin Van Buren, William Henry Harrison, John Tyler

Can you define these terms?

Panic of 1837, Whig Party, "Tippecanoe and Tyler, too"

AFTER YOU READ

Discussion Questions

1. How did Andrew Jackson try to help the "common man" while he was President? Did he always succeed? Give examples to support your answer.

2. Why was the Whig party started, and why did it disappear?

3. What were states' rights, and why did the issue divide the political parties?

4. How did the Indian Removals and the Depression affect American life?

Comprehension Questions

During the Age of Jackson, several events caused problems for thousands of Americans.

1. Copy the following headings.

   Tariffs and States' Rights

   Indian Removals

   Economic Depression

2. Under each heading, write the sentences from the list below that go with it.

   New England agreed to a tax on imports.

   The government took Indian land.

   Banks closed.

   South Carolina nullified the tax.

   No loans were made to people.

   President Jackson didn't enforce the Supreme Court's decision.

   Native Americans traveled The Trail of Tears.

   President Jackson felt nothing should divide the country.

   The Supreme Court and President Jackson disagreed.

   The Seminole War was fought.

   People died because the government didn't supply what it promised.

   Many people all over the country didn't have jobs or food.

   Factories and stores closed.

3. Using your lists, write a sentence about how each problem affected someone living during the Age of Jackson.

Writing Activity

Pretend you are a Cherokee who lived in the East until the government forced you to "remove" to the Indian Territory. Write five journal entries about your journey on the Trail of Tears. Include facts and feelings about the journey.

CHAPTER 18

THE NORTHEAST AND ITS CHANGES

The Northeast is made up of the states north of Maryland and east of Ohio. In the first half of the 1800's, life in the Northeast changed a lot. In 1800, the Northeast was a region of family farms and a few small port cities. Fifty years later, it had factories, large cities, powerful banks, and a large population of immigrants.

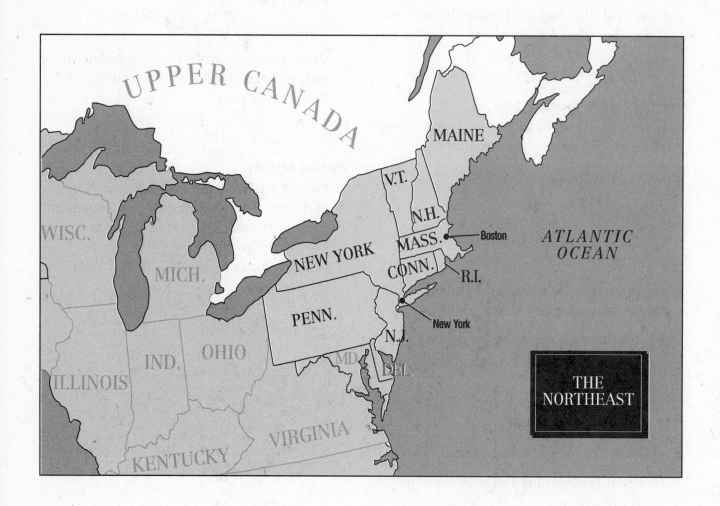

THE NORTHEAST

BEFORE YOU READ

Sections in This Chapter

1. Farming and Shipping
2. The Industrial Revolution and the Factory System
3. Immigrants to the Northeast

Reading a Map

The map on the opposite page shows the eastern half of the United States in the first half of the nineteenth century. Use this map to answer these questions.

1. Which states are in the Northeastern part of the United States?

2. Compare this map to the one at the beginning of Chapter 8. Are exactly the same states in New England and the Northeast?

3. What were the major cities in the the Northeast in 1850?

Understanding a Key Concept:
IMMIGRANTS

Immigrants are people who move from one country and settle in another country. People who move from Mexico to live permanently in the United States are Mexican immigrants. **Immigration** is the movement of people from one country to another.

In the early 1800's, many people from European countries moved to the United States as immigrants. Use information from the graph in section three of this chapter to answer the questions below.

1. The largest number of immigrants left which country to come to the United States?

2. The smallest number of immigrants left which country to come to the United States?

3. Between 1820 and 1829, only 23,000 immigrants came to the United States. But over one million came between 1846 and 1850. What about America might have interested these people?

4. Do you think most immigrants were rich, poor, slaves, or in the middle class?

Making Use of What You Already Know

The **technology** Europeans brought to America helped them take control of people whose technology wasn't as advanced. But then technology didn't advance much until well after the American Revolution, when the **Industrial Revolution** changed life. New machines were invented, which led to new ways of doing things. These changes affected everyone. Below are pairs of sentences. One of each pair tells about a way of doing things before the Industrial Revolution. The other tells about a way of doing things after the Industrial Revolution began. Write down the sentence from each pair which describes how things were done after the Industrial Revolution.

Ships used the wind to sail across the ocean.
Steamships didn't depend on wind.

Clothes were sewn by hand.
Clothes were made on sewing machines.

Cloth was made at home on a loom.
Huge looms were powered by water.

People traveled by train.
People traveled on horses.

Steam engines ran machines of all sizes.
Small machines were run by people or animals.

1. FARMING AND SHIPPING

Main Ideas

Think about the following Main Idea questions as you read this section:

1. How did life change for Northeastern farmers in the early 1800s?

2. What were the new trade patterns of Northeastern ships in this period?

3. What new kinds of ships were built in the middle 1800s?

4. Why did bankers in New York and Boston become more important in the early 1800s?

CHANGES IN AGRICULTURE

Some New England Farmers Move West

In the early 1800's, most Americans were farmers. But much of the land in the Northeast is not good for farming. Pennsylvania and New York have good soil, but in New England most of the land is rocky and poor. To find better land, many New England farmers moved west. They began new farms in western New York, in Ohio, and even further to the west. These new Northwestern farms grew large crops of grain. Newly built canals brought the grain to eastern cities.

Not many people moved to New England to take the place of those who moved west. The population of New England got smaller. As a result, New England lost seats in the House of Representatives, causing it to lose some of its power in the government.

Northeastern Farmers Change What They Grow

The farmers who stayed in the Northeast had to change what they grew. The grain from the new Northwestern farms was much cheaper than Northeastern grain. So some Northeastern farmers stopped growing grain and began growing fruits and vegetables instead. Others began dairy farms. They sold their farm products in nearby cities. However, even though the crops changed, daily life on small Northeastern farms did not change much. Families still worked their farms without slaves or hired workers.

SHIPPING AND BANKING EXPAND

New Shipping and Trading Patterns

The Northeast continued to control the country's shipping. A new triangle trade developed, taking food and manufactured goods from Northeastern cities to the South. From there, ships took cotton and tobacco to Europe and returned with fancy European factory goods, especially cloth. Most ships returned to New York City, but some went to other cities like Boston and Philadelphia.

Northeastern trade was widespread. Ships carried food, building materials, flour, tar, and coal up and down the Atlantic coast. New England whaling ships searched the Pacific Ocean for whales. They hunted the whales for their oil (used in lamps) and for their springy "whalebone," which is found in a whale's mouth and which was used in ladies' corsets.

New Kinds of Ships

The ships themselves changed, too. Steampower took over from sail. Steamboats were run by engines that burned coal. They didn't have to depend on the wind, as sailing ships did. They moved at a steady speed no matter what the weather, so they could keep a regular schedule. They were faster, too. Steamboats first traveled along rivers, lakes, and the Atlantic coast. By the middle of the 1800's steamships regularly crossed the Atlantic.

For a time, many American shipbuilders continued to build sailing ships. They created the great **clipper ships**, the fastest and most beautiful sailing ships ever built. But the clipper ships needed a lot of sailors, and they couldn't carry a big cargo. As steamships became more important, American shipbuilders lost business to British steamship builders.

Boston and New York Become Important Banking Centers

Besides being important trading ports, Boston and New York City were also important banking centers. Banking and shipping activities gave these cities power over other parts of the country. They loaned money to businesses and farms. They controlled the important transportation systems, like canals and ships. They decided what goods would be shipped and where they would go.

SECTION REVIEW

Can you answer these Main Idea questions?

1. How did life change for Northeastern farmers in the early 1800s?

2. What were the new trade patterns of Northeastern ships in this period?

3. What new kinds of ships were built in the middle 1800s?

4. Why did bankers in New York and Boston become more important in the early 1800s?

Can you define this term?

clipper ship

▼ *In the new triangle trade, Northeastern ships brought food and useful manufactured goods to the South, where they were sold and cotton and tobacco bought for sale in Europe. There, fine European manufactured goods, particularly cloth, were picked up for the return trip to the Northeast.*

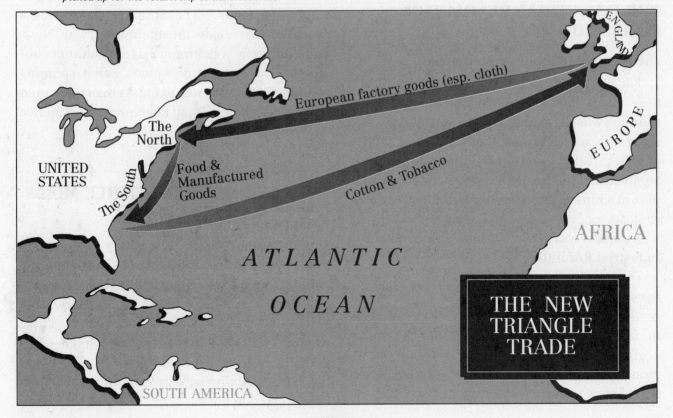

European factory goods (esp. cloth)

Cotton & Tobacco

The North

Food & Manufactured Goods

The South

UNITED STATES

ATLANTIC OCEAN

SOUTH AMERICA

AFRICA

EUROPE

ENGLAND

THE NEW TRIANGLE TRADE

2. THE INDUSTRIAL REVOLUTION AND THE FACTORY SYSTEM

Main Ideas

Think about the following Main Idea questions as you read this section:

1. What was the Industrial Revolution, and how did it change the way things were made?

2. How did the Industrial Revolution start in the United States?

3. How did Samuel Slater, and then Francis Cabot Lowell, change the way cloth was made?

4. How did the Industrial Revolution affect the environment?

5. What changes did steam power bring about?

THE INDUSTRIAL REVOLUTION COMES TO AMERICA

The Industrial Revolution in Europe

For most of human history, people used hand tools and a few simple machines—such as the spinning wheel—to make things. Most things were made at home. Then, starting in the late 1700's, people in Britain and other European countries began making things in factories, using large, complex machines. These machines used water, coal, or steam for power. This change in the way things were made was a revolution. It is called the **Industrial Revolution**.

During the Industrial Revolution, fewer and fewer products were made by hand in homes and small shops. Instead, they were made by machines in factories. New technologies, like the steam engine, were put to use in manufacturing and on farms. New products and new ways of doing things were invented. The way many people—be they farmer, sailor, or craftsman—did their jobs changed.

The Industrial Revolution Comes to America

By 1800, the Industrial Revolution had changed Britain. The British wanted to keep their machines a secret. They hoped to prevent other countries from making and selling factory goods. For this reason, it was against British law to take the factory machines or the plans to make them out of the country. As a result, for several years no one in America knew how to build them.

However, in 1789 a young Englishman named Samuel Slater arrived in Rhode Island. He had been a worker at an British **textile mill**, which used new machines to spin thread and weave textiles, or cloth. Slater knew how textile machines were made. He built America's first "Spinning Jenny." The Spinning Jenny was a machine that made thread from cotton. Now, nine children watching a large machine could do the work of many women using spinning wheels. Each child was paid less than one dollar a week. The Industrial Revolution in America had begun.

IMPROVEMENTS IN TEXTILE MILLS

Early New England Mills

During the War of 1812, many textile factories were built in New England. They spun the South's cotton into thread. But from there on, the work was done by hand. Each factory hired women to weave the thread into cloth. These women worked at home on hand looms. The factory sold some of the cloth. The rest was sewed into clothes or bags by other women who also worked at home.

Lowell Improves the Textile Factory

In 1814, Francis Cabot Lowell changed the way cloth was made. He built America's first power loom. This machine wove thread into cloth. Lowell built the first mill that both spun thread and wove cloth, all by machine, in one factory.

Since men workers were scarce, Lowell hired women and children. He offered young, single, farm women a job with many extras. "Lowell's Girls" got good pay, good housing, and a good education. But other factories paid their workers less money and gave them no extras. Lowell was forced to spend less on his workers in order to make a profit. They no longer got free housing and an education.

Factory Towns Grow Up Along Rivers

To provide power for their machines, early textile mill owners built their factories on the banks of rivers, often near a waterfall. The running or falling water moved giant water wheels that turned gears to run the machines.

The owners also used the river for transportation. Boats brought in raw materials (like cotton) and took away the finished goods (like cloth). Factory towns grew up around the factories.

THE SPREAD OF THE INDUSTRIAL REVOLUTION

The Industrial Revolution Spreads to Other Industries

Textile mills were not the only kind of factory in the Northeast. Iron, steel, shoes, wood products (like furniture), and farm tools were also made in factories.

In Connecticut, the inventor Eli Whitney and his partner Simeon North built guns with interchangeable parts. Whitney's machines, and not skilled gunsmiths, made the parts. Almost anyone could then put the parts together to make a gun. Many factories used Whitney's ideas. Soon unskilled workers were running complex machines. Gunsmiths and other skilled workers began to worry that factories would take away their jobs.

New Inventions

Some new inventions made life easier for everyone. Elias Howe invented the sewing machine and Isaac Singer improved it. Since the sewing machine was so easy to use, many factories began making clothing as well as weaving cloth. Suddenly, ready-made clothes became cheaper and better looking. Other new inventions changed daily life. The pencil, the match, and the soda-water machine were all invented before 1860.

A New Kind of Power: Steam Power

A new kind of power became important. In 1804, Oliver Evans had developed a steam engine that could run machines. Gradually factories began to use it. Steam engines soon ran textile mills, factories, printing presses, railroad engines, and boats.

A factory that used steam for power could be built anywhere, not just near a river. As factories switched from water power to steam power, many factories moved to the big cities, like New York. These cities had more workers and better transportation systems.

THE FACTORY SYSTEM CHANGES AMERICA

Factories Get Raw Materials from All Over America

Factories used raw materials from all over America. In 1860, the Northeast's most important industries were making flour from Western wheat and manufacturing cotton textiles and clothes from Southern cotton. They made wooden goods from American forests. They made boots and shoes from the hides of Northeastern and Western cattle. They made men's clothing from Northeastern wool and iron from Northeastern mines. These raw materials were brought to the factories by ships, canal boats, and soon on trains.

American industries were becoming very important. New York bankers loaned them money to help them grow. Immigrants worked in their factories. Northeastern ships carried their finished products all over the world.

The Industrial Revolution Changes the Environment

In America the Industrial Revolution also changed how the land looked. Mines were dug, and forests were cut down to provide factories with the raw materials they needed. The environment near the factories changed, too. Fields became cities. Rivers were poisoned with factory waste. The sky became dark with factory smoke.

But most people saw this as progress. They believed that America's future depended on factories. They were willing to put up with the problems in order to live a better life with manufactured goods.

SECTION REVIEW

Can you answer these Main Idea questions?

1. What was the Industrial Revolution, and how did it change the way things were made?

2. How did the Industrial Revolution start in the United States?

3. How did Samuel Slater, and then Francis Cabot Lowell, change the way cloth was made?

4. How did the Industrial Revolution affect the environment?

5. What changes did steam power bring about?

Can you identify these people?

Francis Cabot Lowell, "Lowell's Girls," Eli Whitney, Elias Howe

Can you define these terms?

Industrial Revolution, textile, "Spinning Jenny"

3. IMMIGRANTS TO THE NORTHEAST

Main Ideas

Think about the following Main Idea questions as you read this section:

1. What are some of the reasons that immigrants come to America?

2. What kinds of work did immigrants do, and what were working conditions like?

3. Which people in the United States were glad the immigrants came, and which people were not?

4. What was city life like for an immigrant?

5. How did the immigrants react to the political life of America?

WHY IMMIGRANTS CAME TO THE NORTHEAST

Immigration after 1812

By the early 1800's, Europe was very crowded, and much of its land was worn out—not many crops would grow. Many people wanted to leave. Everyone had heard about America, where people were free and crops grew well. Many Europeans dreamed of moving to America. In the hundred years after the War of 1812, 30 million people left Europe and came to America. It was, up until then, the largest movement of people in the history of the world.

People who enter a country to live there are called **immigrants**. The first immigrants to America after the War of 1812 were small farmers and skilled workers from England and Germany. Large numbers of young people also came to America from Ireland. All of the immigrants came searching for a better life.

The Irish Potato Famine

Disaster hit Ireland. Many Irish had small farms and grew potatoes. In the 1840's a disease killed their potatoes and the farm families had nothing to eat. About a million Irish starved. Thousands and thousands of poor Irish crowded into dark, dirty ships and sailed to America. From 1845 to 1860, one-and-a-half million people came to the United States from Ireland.

Immigration from Germany and Great Britain

Ireland was not the only country where people were starving. In the 1830's and 1840's, Germany also had poor crops and political problems. Many skilled German workers and farmers came to the United States with enough money to buy land. Most of these Germans moved to the Northwestern states, like Ohio, where good land was cheap.

Other immigrants came from England, Scotland, and Wales. Many were skilled workers, like the Welsh coal miners. They moved to the places their skills were needed. Other immigrants, like the German Jews, remained in cities and started small businesses and stores.

The Immigrants Were Different

Suddenly, America was home to many people who were very different from those who had come before them. Since before the Revolution, most Americans had been Protestants whose ancestors had come from England. Now, new immigrants brought different ideas, languages, and skills. Many didn't speak English. Many were Catholics, not Protestants.

Without intending to, these new immigrants created new problems. Most other Americans had a hard time understanding and accepting them. They were afraid the immigrants would change America too much.

IMMIGRANTS BECOME LABORERS, FACTORY WORKERS, AND SERVANTS

Factory Owners Hire Immigrants

One important group of Americans welcomed the coming of the immigrants: factory owners, who needed people who would work for low pay.

The first factories had a hard time finding workers. Most American men wanted to own their own farm or business, not work for someone else. In addition, many people were leaving the Northeast to find land in the west. For a while, factory owners tried to get the government to stop selling cheap land and building routes to the west. They wanted to keep people in the Northeast, so that they would have a good supply of workers.

When large numbers of immigrants began coming into the country, factory owners hired them. Immigrants would take the lowest-paying factory jobs because these were often the only jobs they could find. In 1830, most factory workers were paid only about $1.25 a week. By 1860, they worked 16 hours a day and earned only about $6.00 a week. Other immigrants worked at home, sewing clothes or making shoes. They were paid a few cents for each piece they finished.

Irish Workers on Canals and Railroads

Many of the immigrant workers were Irish. Because the Irish had had bad luck on their farms in Ireland, most decided not to be farmers. Instead, they stayed in whichever city their ships arrived. They had no skills, but were willing to work hard for very cheap wages. They took any job they could find, not just factory jobs. Some became servants and waiters. If a man was lucky, he got a well-paying job digging New York's Erie Canal or building railroads in Ohio. His family stayed in the city. Many Irish women and children under 16 worked in factories.

Blacks and Irish workers often wanted the same jobs, which sometimes led to bad feelings between them. Bad feelings were also created when American-born white workers lost jobs to immigrants or blacks.

CHANGES IN THE CITIES

Factories Move to Big Cities

As factories switched from water power to steam power, many moved to big cities, like New York. These cities had more workers and better transportation systems. As a result, Northeastern cities grew rapidly. New York, for example had only 60 thousand people in 1800. By 1860 it had a population of a million.

Immigrants from the same country tended to live close together. Many Irish, for example, lived in New York City's Lower East Side. Because America was strange to them, they felt better living near people who shared their background. Blacks lived in another area of a city. Rich bankers and factory owners built big, new houses away from the city's center.

Big-City Slums

The areas where immigrants and blacks lived turned into **slums**. Slums are crowded, dirty city areas. Because they were so awful, rents were low and they were the only places poor people could afford to live.

Owners divided up old houses and rented each room to as many people as possible. Some people lived in damp, dark cellars, or in small wooden shacks. They had no running water or sewers. Finding fresh food was also a problem. Farmers sold fruits and vegetables in the city, but other foods, like milk, were expensive and hard to find. Many got sick from living in slums.

THE LIFE OF THE WORKER

The Hard Life of a Factory Worker

Factory workers worked long hours in factories or in slum rooms. They were often tired and sick. Their pay was so low they could barely afford food, housing, or clothes for their family.

Families spent little time together. Parents didn't have time to teach their children. Many immigrants spent their free time at their church or at the local saloon (bar). The Catholic Church was very important to the Irish. It reminded them of Ireland and helped them deal with life in this new, very different country.

The dreams of many immigrants died in America. Some began stealing or drinking too much. Cities became filled with criminals and sick, starving people.

Sometimes, the problems in the cities led to violence. Free blacks in the slums of Providence, Rhode Island, rioted in 1831. They wanted better living conditions. In 1837, bread riots broke out in New York City. Many workers believed that the flour merchants were hiding flour to keep the prices high.

Some Cities and States Try to Help

Some cities and states tried to help the workers. Hospitals were built. Immigrants who landed at Castle Garden in New York City could get some help as soon as they landed.

Most immigrants, however, did not ask for help. They came from countries were the government was their enemy. They didn't understand American life.

As more and more people crowded into cities, the problems became worse.

IMMIGRANTS AND POLITICS

Immigrants Gain Power in City Politics

Rich whites, middle-class whites, working-class whites, and free blacks all lived in cities. But for many years, city politics was controlled by rich businessmen and middle-class whites only. Then, as thousands of immigrants arrived, city politics began to change.

At first, the American political system was strange to the immigrants. They came from countries where they had no say in the government. In addition, important issues in America, like states' rights or changing the banking system, weren't important to them. They were more worried about day-to-day problems, like finding work, earning enough money for their families, and improving their living conditions.

Tammany Hall

The powerful Democratic politicians who ran New York City belonged to a political club called Tammany Hall. To stay in power, they helped the immigrant Irish. They found jobs for the newcomers and places for them to live. In return, the Irish voted for Tammany Hall politicians. Some

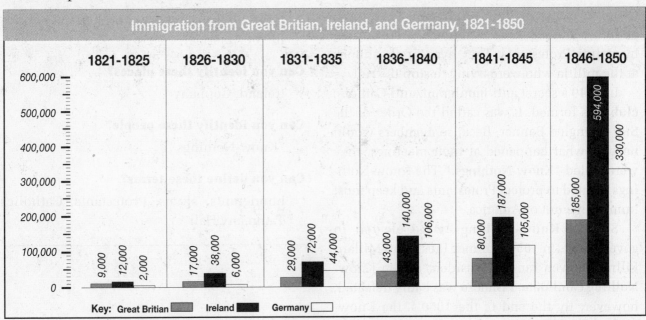

Immigration from Great Britian, Ireland, and Germany, 1821-1850

	1821-1825	1826-1830	1831-1835	1836-1840	1841-1845	1846-1850
Great Britian	9,000	17,000	29,000	43,000	80,000	185,000
Ireland	12,000	38,000	72,000	140,000	187,000	594,000
Germany	2,000	6,000	44,000	106,000	105,000	330,000

Key: Great Britian █ Ireland █ Germany □

In the twenty-nine years between 1821 and 1850, immigration increased drastically. Between 1821 and 1825, 23,000 immigrants came from Great Britain, Ireland, and Germany. But between 1846 and 1850, over a million came—fifty times as many as during the earlier period. The Irish became the biggest group of immigrants: by 1850, more Irish were coming than British and Germans combined.

of the Irish became powerful Democratic politicians themselves.

By the 1860's, Tammany Hall was almost completely Irish, and day-to-day politics had passed into their hands. Immigrant groups gradually gained power in other cities, too.

As cities grew, they elected more representatives to the state legislatures and to Congress. The growing importance of cities upset many Americans who were comfortable with the old way of doing things.

The Anti-Immigrant "Know-Nothing" Party

In the 1830's, many native-born Protestant Americans began to feel that too many immigrants were coming into the country. They felt that the immigrants were arriving too fast, were too different, and were getting too much political power.

In addition, nearly all the Irish immigrants and about half of the German were Catholic, which frightened Protestant Americans. Protestants disliked the Catholic version of the Christian religion and feared the power of the Catholic Church. They were afraid that the Pope would take over the United States government.

In Boston, Irish homes were set on fire. In 1834 a mob burned down a girls' school run by Catholic nuns. In Philadelphia in 1844, Irish churches and blocks of Irish homes were burned by rioting Protestants. They even fired cannons at the militia who were trying to stop the riot.

In 1849 a secret anti-immigrant, anti-Catholic club was formed. It was called the Order of the Star-Spangled Banner. Because members would not tell what happened at their meetings, they were called "**Know-Nothings.**" The Know-Nothings wanted to protect Protestants and keep most immigrants out of America.

Several Know-Nothings were elected to government. In 1856 a former President, Millard Fillmore, even ran for President as the Know-Nothing candidate. Fillmore was badly defeated, however. By the end of the 1850's, the Know-Nothing political party had disappeared. The quarrel over slavery pushed it from the scene.

The Northeast changed in the first half of the Nineteenth Century. It had started out as an agricultural area. But by the 1850's, the Industrial Revolution had made factories more important than farming. Cities grew, because of immigrants and factories. The Northeast became the center of America's business and industry. It was very different from the rest of the country.

SECTION REVIEW

Can you answer these Main Idea questions?

1. What are some reasons that immigrants come to America?

2. What kinds of work did immigrants do, and what were working conditions like?

3. Which people in the United States were glad the immigrants came, and which people were not?

4. What was city life like for an immigrant?

5. How did the immigrants react to the political life of America?

Can you identify these places?

Ireland, Germany

Can you identify these people?

"Know-Nothings"

Can you define these terms?

immigrants, slums, Protestants, Catholics, Tammany Hall

AFTER YOU READ

Discussion Questions

1. What changes did the Industrial Revolution make in American Life?

2. How did the large number of Irish and German immigrants change American city life?

3. How did geography influence the development of farms, factories, and shipping in the Northeast?

Comprehension Questions

I. Read the following paragraphs. Use the words in this list to fill in the blanks so that the sentences below tell about America in the 1850's.

New York City   *Industrial Revolution*
unskilled   *factories*
banking   *raw materials*
shipping

Northeastern cities were important 1_____ and 2_____ centers. From ports like 3_____ steamships took goods to foreign countries.

The 4_____ _____ changed life in the Northeast. In water-powered textile 5_____ huge machines made cloth. In other factories, 6_____ workers used complex machines to make many different kinds of goods. Factories changed 7_____ _____ from all over America, like the South's cotton, into goods to sell to the world.

II. The new immigrants to America had a different life than people already living in America. Use what you know to answer each of the following questions.

1. Where did the immigrants come from?

2. Why did the immigrants leave their country?

3. Why did they come to America?

4. What jobs did the immigrants do in America?

5. Why did the Irish immigrants live in cities?

6. What were slums like?

7. Why did immigrants live in slums?

8. What problems did both immigrants and free African Americans have in common?

9. How did immigrants get political power?

Writing Activity

Pretend you are an Irish immigrant in New York City in the 1850's. Write a letter home about your experiences in America. Make notes about the following topics to help you organize your thoughts. Include your ideas in your letter.

your home

your family's jobs

the city and its problems

differences between life in America and in Ireland

How do you like life in America?

What would you change if you could?

CHAPTER 19

THE OLD NORTHWEST

During the first half of the 1800's, most of the East was settled. The frontier moved west, where there was still wilderness. In the Northwest, from Ohio to Iowa, most settlers became farmers who sold their crops to the rest of the country. They were able to sell their crops in distant places because the Industrial Revolution brought new kinds of transportation—steamboats, canals, and railroads. Gradually, frontier life disappeared and farming became a business like any other. By 1850 the

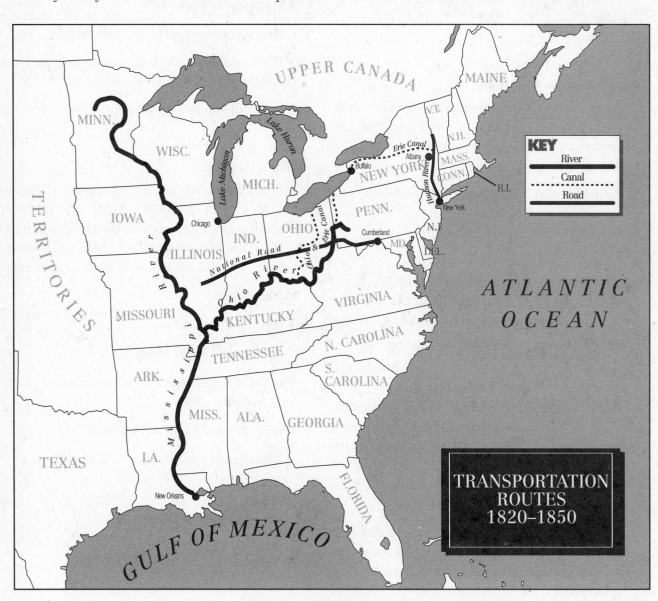

KEY

River
Canal
Road

TRANSPORTATION ROUTES
1820–1850

BEFORE YOU READ

Sections in This Chapter

1. Life on the Frontier
2. Internal Improvements

Reading a Map

The map on the opposite page shows routes of transportation to the Northwest. Use this map to answer these questions.

1. What was the main road in the United States?

2. The Erie Canal was in New York State. At which cities did it begin and end?

3. Locate the water route between New York City and Chicago which used the Erie Canal. List each river and lake on that route.

4. What cities besides Chicago and New York City do you think received goods that traveled on the Erie Canal?

Understanding a Key Concept:
CHANGING CULTURES

Americans moved into the Northeastern and Northwestern wilderness. As more people came, the culture changed three different times.

Frontier people had a hard life. They had to do everything themselves.

People living during the **Age of Homespun** still did most things themselves, but they had neighbors to help them.

Later, **business farmers** grew crops to sell. Instead of doing everything themselves, they hired workers and bought goods in stores.

Read each of the following sets of phrases. Write each set in the order in which they happened. First list what frontier settlers did.

Then write what Age of Homespun farmers did. Finally, write what business farmers did. The first is done for you.

1. built log cabins in the wilderness (frontier)
2. neighbors helped build houses (Age of Homespun)
3. hired skilled workers to build their house (business farmers)

wore clothes made from animal skins
bought factory-made cloth and clothes
made own cloth and sewed own clothes

traded a cow for a table made by a neighbor
bought new factory-made furniture
sat on rough log benches

sold most of their crops in Eastern cities
grew enough to feed family and trade a little
ate what they found in the forest

Making Use of What You Already Know

Write the word or phrase which correctly completes these sentences.

1. Early colonists depended on factory goods from _____ .
   a. England
   b. the Indians

2. People who settled on the frontier did not depend on factory goods from the Northeast because _____ .
   a. goods were hard to transport to the frontier.
   b. factories were everywhere.

3. Before 1800, everyone depended on _____ to provide important goods such as horseshoes and barrels.
   a. skilled workers
   b. patriots

1. LIFE ON THE FRONTIER

Main Ideas

Think about the following Main Idea questions as you read this section:

1. What was life like on a pioneer farm?

2. What was religious life like in the Age of Home-spun?

3. How did the farmers of the Northwest use the Mississippi River and the Erie Canal?

4. How did John Deere's plow and McCormick's reaper change farm life?

THE PIONEERS

On the Edge of the Frontier

The first people to settle in a frontier area are called **pioneers**. At the time of the American Revolution, pioneers were beginning to cross the Appalachian Mountains into Kentucky and Tennessee. As these frontier areas became settled, pioneers pushed further north, south, and west. When an area seemed too full, they continued on, always hoping for something better.

Pioneers moved into Ohio, Indiana, Illinois, Alabama, and Mississippi. They crossed the Mississippi River. Then, at the edge of the prairies, they stopped. They didn't think that those flat lands had good soil, because so few trees grew there. In addition, the soil of the plains was too tough and sticky for their plows.

Getting There

Rivers were the easiest way to travel, for there were no roads. But no rivers cross the Appalachian Mountains. Therefore the early pioneers had to cut their own roads through the forest.

Pioneer families walked alongside a loaded horse or ox. They brought very little: an ax, a rifle, a frying pan, a bed quilt, a bag of corn meal, and their clothes. The first year they ate only what they had brought or could find in the woods.

Starting a Home

The pioneers came with the hope of finding a better life. When they found the land they wanted, some began farming without buying the land. Others bought land from the government. In some places land speculators bought the best land, then sold it at a higher price. Not many settlers could pay for their land all at once; instead, they had to borrow money from a bank to pay for it. Then they would pay back their loan a little at a time.

The 19th-century pioneers cleared the land just as the early colonists had. A family would quickly build a log cabin and plant a small corn and vegetable garden nearby. When a field was clear of trees, they planted more crops. If there were any extra crops, the family traded them for goods.

The first settlers had few neighbors. They welcomed strangers because they brought news about the outside world. But when an area started filling up with people, many pioneers moved further west, opening up new frontiers.

The Southwest and the Northwest Become Different

After the first pioneers, the Old Northwest and the Old Southwest grew in different directions. The Northwest became more like the Northeast, while the Southwest became more like the Southeast.

In the Southwest, settlers from the South built plantations and cotton farms.

In the Northwest, settlers from the Northeast and from Europe started small family farms. They grew corn and wheat and raised hogs.

The Frontier Moves West

People settled in western New York and Pennsylvania shortly after 1800. The population west of the Appalachian Mountains doubled between 1810 and 1820. The Northwest, from the Appalachians to the Mississippi River, grew quickly. Territories became states: Ohio (1803), Indiana (1816), Illinois (1818), Michigan (1837), Iowa (1846), and Wisconsin (1848). Ohio grew so fast during the 1820's that it had the fifth largest population in the country!

THE AGE OF HOMESPUN

Life on the Farm

As the frontier moved west, the area behind it filled up with people. Immigrants and farmers from back east moved into empty log cabins or built their own. They cleared more land. Since there were few towns, farmers did as much as they could for themselves. They grew flax—which is used to make linen—and cotton. The women spun fibers from these plants into thread and wove the thread into cloth, from which they made their clothes. This cloth, called **homespun**, gave this time its name: the **Age of Homespun**.

Women helped with farming. They also cooked and preserved food. Oxen were used to pull the plows, and the whole family planted and harvested. They didn't need much from the store. Their lives were controlled by the farm and by what needed to be done each season.

Traveling Workers and Peddlers

Sometimes a skilled worker, like a weaver or shoemaker, came by the farm. He would use the farmer's materials (like leather) to make what the farmer needed (like shoes). Traveling peddlers, many of them Jewish immigrants, stopped, too. Their mules or wagons were loaded with goods for sale—pots and pans, ribbons, and candies.

Towns Grow Up

Towns grew slowly. First came a store, then a flour mill, a church, and maybe a school. Few schools had full-time teachers, though. Most people were too busy on their farms to teach.

Families Help Each Other

As more people moved into an area, they did more and more things together. At gatherings called **quilting bees**, women visited each other while they sewed quilts. At a **husking bee**, everyone got together to take the outside husks off corn. They would make a party of it. At harvest time whole families helped each other. At a house raising, many neighbors got together to put up most of a house in one day. After the work was done, everyone enjoyed food and games, singing, and sports.

Like the frontier itself, the Age of Homespun happened in different places at different times. It followed the frontier as it moved west, and it ended wherever farming for the purpose of selling crops took its place.

Religion: Circuit Riders and Camp Meetings

Religion was important in frontier and homespun areas. People looked forward to Sunday services. Two Protestant religions grew quickly: the Methodists and the Baptists. Both were spread by preachers who spoke in everyday words and who were not college-trained.

Methodist preachers rode a **circuit**. Each week, a preacher would speak at a different church on his circuit. People looked forward to their church's turn.

Another important religious event was the **camp meeting**. Whole families traveled to a meeting place and camped there. For three or more days people listened to preachers, sang, and prayed. Many preachers warned that the "fire and brimstone" of Hell waited for those who did wrong. Many people believed they were saved from this terrible fate by "getting religion" at these camp meetings. At one famous 1801 Kentucky meeting, between 10,000 and 25,000 people attended.

NORTHWESTERN FARMERS START SELLING THEIR CROPS

The Mississippi River and the Erie Canal Take Farm Produce South and East

As farmers cleared more land and grew more crops, they looked for places to sell their extra. Their roads were rivers. The Illinois, the Wabash, and the Ohio rivers took flatboats filled with corn and hogs to the Mississippi River. The Mississippi carried the flatboats south. The crops were sold to Southwestern planters along the way. Large towns like Cincinnati and St. Louis grew up along these river routes.

After 1825, the Erie Canal connected Northwestern farmers to Eastern cities. The farmers found a huge new market. They shipped their wheat down the Great Lakes to Buffalo, New York. From Buffalo it traveled on the canal to the Hudson River, and then down the Hudson to New York City.

Some of the wheat was sold in the Eastern cities to feed immigrants and factory workers. The rest was shipped to Europe or to the South. America's wheat, grown far from the sea, fed people on both sides of the Atlantic Ocean.

New Inventions Change Farming Methods

Since farmers now had an easy way to send their crops to market, they raised more crops to sell. This gave them more money, but it took more time. This meant they no longer had the time to make the goods and tools they used. Instead, they bought improved, factory-made tools and machines.

In turn, the new tools and machines helped them plant more crops. In the 1850's, new steel plows invented by **John Deere** started breaking into the prairies. The rich prairie soil stuck to ordinary iron plows like glue, but it didn't stick to Deere's steel plow. A mechanical reaper invented by **Cyrus McCormick** cut wheat more quickly.

The use of Deere's plow and the McCormick reaper opened up a huge area of prairie land to the farmers. The use of machines also meant that farms could be larger, but still be run by one family.

Farmers Borrow Money From Banks

Farmers needed money to buy machines, land, and goods. They often had to borrow. When they had a bad year—perhaps because of the weather, insects, or a poor market—they could not pay back what they owed. Many farmers made it through the bad years, but others lost their farms to the Eastern bankers who had loaned them money. The bankers then sold the farms to someone else.

As farms became larger, family life changed. Women still preserved food, but they didn't have to spin or weave. They could buy cloth or nice-looking, ready-made clothes. Women were not expected to work outside the home, so many became active in church or reform groups. Farming was changing, and with it family life.

SECTION REVIEW

Can you answer these Main Idea questions?

1. What was life like on a pioneer farm?

2. What was religious life like in the Age of Homespun?

3. How did the farmers of the Northwest use the Mississippi River and the Erie Canal?

4. How did John Deere's plow and McCormick's reaper change farm life?

Can you identify these people?

John Deere, Cyrus McCormick

Can you define these terms?

pioneer, homespun, quilting and husking bees, Methodists, Baptists, camp meeting

2. INTERNAL IMPROVEMENTS

Main Ideas

Think about the following Main Idea questions as you read this section:

1. Why were canals better than early roads for transporting goods?

2. Why did railroads eventually replace canals?

3. How were roads and canals paid for?

4. Why did the telegraph revolutionize communications?

ROADS

The National Road and Local Turnpikes

In 1800, land travel was slow, uncomfortable, and expensive. Water routes were better, but did not go everywhere. The Industrial Revolution improved travel. Because these improvements in travel were inside the country, they were called "**internal improvements**." They connected places that produced goods (like New England's cloth) with people that wanted to buy these goods (like western farmers).

The first federal internal improvement was the **National Road**. Most of it was built from 1825 to 1850. For years it was the only good road across the Appalachian Mountains. The government used new technology to level and surface it. The road began in Cumberland, Maryland. When it was finally done, it went all the way to Illinois. For many years it was the most important road in the country.

Congress decided not to build other roads. In some places, private companies built good roads called **turnpikes**. They charged people who used the road. The National Road and the turnpikes helped, but in most places, trips over land remained slow, uncomfortable, and expensive.

STEAMBOATS AND CANALS

Steamboats Replace Sailboats and Rafts

In 1807, Robert Fulton's steamboat, the *Clermont*, traveled up the Hudson River. It was the first practical steamboat. Gradually, American shipping changed from using wind power to using steam power.

In 1811, steamboats began traveling on the Mississippi River. Unlike sailboats, they didn't have to wait for the wind. Unlike rafts, they could go upstream. By 1840, more than 500 steamboats went up and down the river each year. Shipping prices dropped. Western farmers took their corn and hogs to New Orleans and returned home in comfort. Missouri and Mississippi planters shipped their cotton south to New Orleans and brought back slaves, corn, and manufactured goods.

Steamboats traveled on the Hudson and Ohio rivers, too. They took goods and passengers between cities. Soon there were steamboats on the Great Lakes as well, carrying both farm and factory goods. Steamboats also traveled along the Atlantic coast. Goods from Northeastern cities were sent by steamboat to Southern cities. They returned with cotton and tobacco. By 1840, steamships were regularly crossing the Atlantic.

Building the Erie Canal

In most of America, transportation by water was quicker and cheaper than transportation over roads. But rivers did not always run in the right places. Also many were not deep enough for boats or barges, and no river cut across the Appalachian Mountains. So Americans built their own rivers, called **canals**. The most successful of these canals, the **Erie Canal**, was in New York State. Governor DeWitt Clinton supported it, and the state helped to build it. New technology, like waterproof cement, made it possible. Many Irish immigrants received high wages and three meals a day to work on it. Its 363 miles connected Lake Erie at Buffalo to the Hudson River at Albany. It opened in 1825 and was a big success.

At first, the Erie Canal carried farm products from western New York to Albany. Soon crops from the Northwest were also carried on the canal. Crops were loaded onto canal barges, which were pulled by mules that walked alongside the canal. Closed-off sections, called **locks**, raised or lowered the barge when the canal went through hills. Steamboats met the barges in Albany and took the crops to New York City.

The price of shipping dropped. Goods which cost one dollar to send by land cost only ten cents to send by canal.

Other Canals

Many other canals were built. Several connected the Ohio River to the Great Lakes. For the first time, goods from the Northwest went around the barrier of the Appalachian Mountains. Northwestern products first went to Lake Erie. They were then shipped to Buffalo, and from there through the Erie Canal. New York City took the place of New Orleans as the major outlet for Northwestern goods. As farm goods and timber went east, new settlers and Eastern factory products went west. Even things like furniture, machines, and wagons were shipped on the canal.

Another canal brought Pennsylvania coal to the Hudson River. The coal fed New York City's factories and steamboats. For about 25 years, from 1825 to 1850, canals were the most important way to transport goods in the United States.

RAILROADS AND THE TELEGRAPH

Railroads Replace Canals

After 1850, railroads took business away from canals. Railroads were easier to build. They went where canals couldn't, and they didn't freeze in winter. In 1830, the Baltimore and Ohio built the first passenger railroad. By the 1840's there were as many miles of railroads as of canals.

Most early railroads were in the Northeast, but they soon spread. Powerful railroad companies, like the New York Central, were formed when many small lines were combined into one big one. Large railroads could afford the new technology that allowed them to go through mountains, around steep curves, and across rivers. Rail lines reached further and further west. The South, too, built railroads, but not as many.

In the Northeast and Northwest, immigrants, especially the Irish, built the tracks. In the South,

A river steamboat. These boats were powered by steam generated by burning coal or wood. They were moved by one or two large paddles. These paddles looked like huge wooden asteriks [*]. *The boat in the picture had one paddle, located beneath the big round cover at its stern, or rear. You can tell that this boat was made for rivers, not the ocean, from the fact that its sides are so low above the water: ocean waves would have washed over its sides and sunk it.*

slaves were used, unless the work was dangerous. For the dangerous work, like blasting, they hired Irish immigrants or free blacks.

At first, the government left building railroads to private companies. Then, in the 1850's, Congress gave land to the Illinois Central Railroad. The railroad company sold some of the land to raise money. It then used the money to build a railroad line from Lake Michigan to the Gulf of Mexico.

Railroads opened new markets. Farm goods, often grain and cattle, were picked up at stops close to farms. The goods were taken to storage yards in larger cities. Cities like Chicago became storage and railroad centers. Chicago had only one railroad line in 1850, but by 1856 it had ten. Each day 58 passenger trains and 38 freight trains arrived in the city.

Better Communications by Telegraph

Along with better transportation came better communications. Letters and news traveled quickly on steamboats and trains. But the most important advance in communications was made possible by electricity. In 1844, **Samuel F.B. Morse** demonstrated the first practical telegraph. Messages could now be sent instantly from one place to another over electric wires.

The telegraph revolutionized communications. By 1860, most of the country was tied together by telegraph wires. News reached Chicago the same day it happened in Washington, DC. In only one more year, the telegraph reached San Francisco. From sea to shining sea, the same news was heard.

Paying for Changes

Internal improvements were expensive to build. Because these improvements served people in many places, governments were often asked to pay for them. The federal government usually would not, but state governments sometimes did.

Another way to raise money was to form a corporation. Corporations sold shares in their company to outsiders. Often foreigners and banks bought these shares. The money raised was used to build the improvement. After the improvement was built, the company made money. Then it paid those who had invested in it.

The Northwest in 1850 was very different from the frontier area it had been in the Age of Homespun of the early 1800's. People still moved west, hoping for a better life, but they had to go further to find empty land. By 1850, the Industrial Revolution had changed the Northwest. Transportation and farm machinery improved. Goods moved easily to and from other parts of the country on canals, steamboats, and railroads. By the 1850's, prosperous Northwestern farms were supplying food to the Northeast, to the South, and even to Europe.

SECTION REVIEW

Can you answer these Main Idea questions?

1. Why were canals better than early roads for transporting goods?

2. Why did railroads eventually replace canals?

3. How were roads and canals paid for?

4. Why did the telegraph revolutionize communications?

Can you identify and locate these places?

Erie Canal, Buffalo, Albany

Can you identify this person?

Samuel F. B. Morse

Can you define these terms?

internal improvements, the National Road, turnpike, telegraph

AFTER YOU READ

Discussion Questions

1. How did life in the Northwest change from 1800 to 1850?

2. How did internal improvements tie together the Northwest and the Northeast?

3. How did the Industrial Revolution change life for Northwestern farmers?

Comprehension Questions

1. Pretend you have just moved to the Ohio frontier in the early 1800's. Decide which of the following statements tell about frontier life.

   no neighbors   *large city nearby*
   hire farm workers   *grow all own food*
   hear lirrle news
   children go to nearby school

2. It is now 15 years later and many people have settled near you. Decide which of the following statements tell about life during the Age of Homespun.

   help neighbors   *welcome peddlers*
   large city nearby   *grow all own food*
   many Indians live nearby

3. It is about 1835. A canal has just been built, starting at a city 30 miles away from your farm. Decide which statements tell about your life and how it has changed since the Age of Homespun.

   grow mostly wheat   *hear little news*
   never go to city
   ship crops to New York by the canal
   bought first reaper in in area

4. It is 1850, and a railroad now stops in a town only three miles from your farm. Decide which statements tell about your life at this time.

   business farm   *send crops to train*
   no neighbors   *shop in town*
   borrow money to expand farm
   must make own clothes

5. It is a few years later, and the telegraph has just reached your town. Decide which statements tell how the telegraph changes your life.

   can send important messages to New York
   can get news about Congress
   travel is slow, so get all news from old newspapers

Writing Activity

Choose one of the time periods from the Comprehension Questions. Add more details about that time and write a story about a person that lived then. Tell about a problem they had and how they solved it. In your story include facts about how people got their food and goods and how they farmed their land. Tell what they did for fun, too. Use the story map below to help plan your story.

Characters
  Main characters
  Rest of family

Setting
  House
  Farm
  Other places

Problem
  First, say what the problem is
  Second, try to solve problem
  Third, say how you finally solved problem

TECHNOLOGY

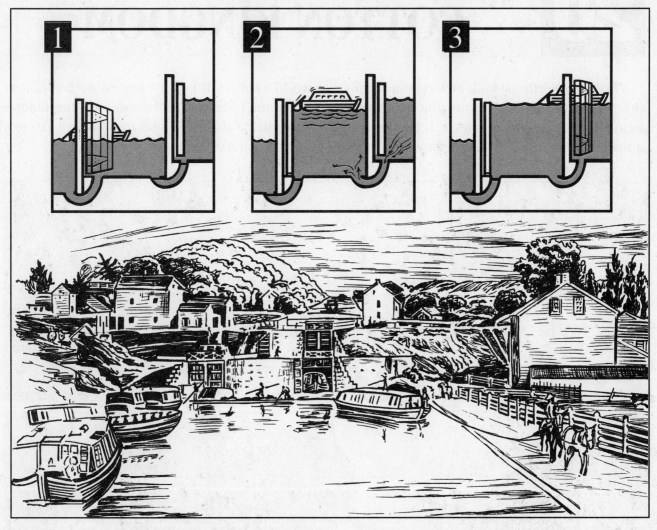

How do you connect different rivers or lakes that are at greatly different heights above sea level? You use **canal locks**.

The picture above shows a section of the Erie Canal. There's a canal lock in the center of the picture, consisting of the two walls going across the river, one above the other. The walls have big doors in them. You can see a boat just going into the lower door.

The diagram at top shows how the lock works. To go from the lower section of the canal to the higher, a boat first enters the lock and the door is shut behind it. Then water is pumped into the lock, raising the boat. When the water in the lock is at the same level as the water in the higher part of the canal, the other door opens and the boat goes on its way. If a boat wanted to go from the higher section to the lower, the process would be reversed.

The diagram shows a single lock. But when there is a great difference in water level, many locks can be used together, lifting or lowering boats many tens of feet, like a giant staircase made of water.

Many canals have locks. For example, the Panama Canal, which connects the Atlantic and Pacific oceans, has huge, tanker-sized locks.

THE COTTON KINGDOM

CHAPTER
20

While the Northeast built factories and cities, and the Northwest built farms, the South grew cotton. Large plantations and small family farms spread west. By 1860, the South grew 75% of the world's cotton. It became known as the "Cotton Kingdom." Slaves did the work on the plantations of the rich, while small Southern farmers lived much like farmers everywhere.

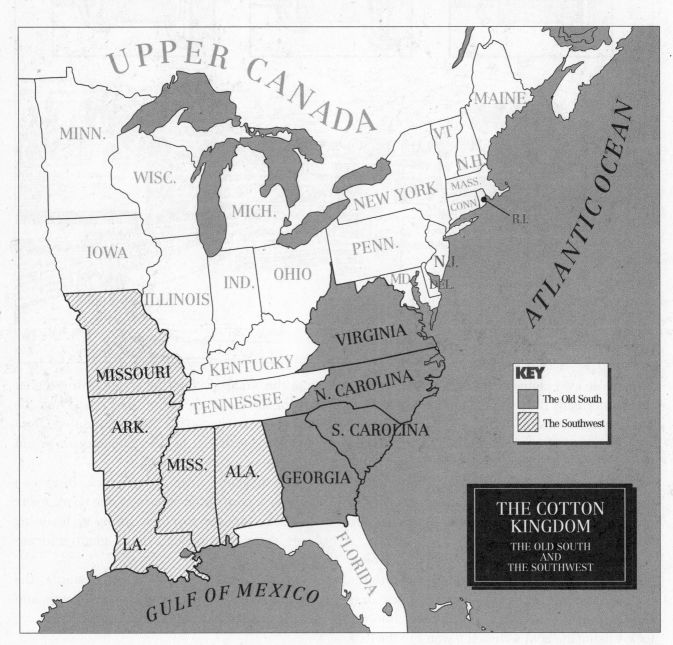

KEY
- The Old South
- The Southwest

THE COTTON KINGDOM
THE OLD SOUTH
AND
THE SOUTHWEST

248

BEFORE YOU READ

Sections in This Chapter

1. The Rise of the Cotton Kingdom
2. Life in the Cotton Kingdom
3. Slavery in the Cotton Kingdom

Reading a Map

Use the map of the South on the opposite page to answer these questions.

1. What states were part of the "Old South"?

2. What states were part of the "Southwest"?

3. What stopped the Southwest from expanding further west? Compare the map at left with the maps in Chapter 1.

Understanding a Key Concept:
CHANGING CULTURES

Under **slavery** people are used as property. Slaves are owned by other people. They are bought and sold and have no rights. Their owner made all the decisions for and about them: what work the slave would do, what they would learn, what they would eat and where they would live, sometimes even what religion the slaves could practice. During American slavery, some owners split up slave families by selling one family member to another slave owner far away. Use what you know about slavery in America to complete the following questions.

1. Because the first Spanish colonists didn't want to work hard, they would _____ .

2. In the New England and Middle Colonies some people had a few _____ to help around the house, store, or farm.

3. The triangle trade brought people from _____ to America to be slaves on Southern plantations.

4. Slaves had _____ freedoms or rights.

Making Use of What You Already Know

Throughout American history, some people have been afraid of other groups. Sometimes they had good reason to fear them, but usually they didn't. Choose the answer from the list below that best completes the sentence about people's fears.

POSSIBLE ANSWERS:

a. the English cut down trees and the wild animals disappeared.

b. their owner had complete power over them.

c. they had a different culture than the people who were already in American cities.

d. they were afraid the slaves would kill them.

e. the Indians attacked British colonists to protect the fur trade.

SENTENCES:

1. Indians feared English settlers because _____ .

2. English settlers feared the Indians who were French allies because _____ .

3. After 1845, American-born people feared immigrants because _____ .

4. Slaves feared their owners because _____ .

5. Southern whites feared slaves because _____ .

1. THE RISE OF THE COTTON KINGDOM

Main Ideas

Think about the following Main Idea questions as you read this section:

1. How did the invention of the cotton gin change life in the South?

2. Why was the South called "The Cotton Kingdom?"

COTTON BECOMES THE MOST IMPORTANT SOUTHERN CROP

Eli Whitney Invents the Cotton Gin

By the end of the 1700's, the soil on the farms of the "Old South" (Virginia, the Carolinas, and Georgia) was becoming worn out from growing tobacco. Tobacco was still the main crop, but some good cotton was grown along the Carolina coast. Cotton grew in other places, too, but it was a different kind and harder to clean. Farmers couldn't raise and clean enough to make money.

In 1793, a young Yale College graduate named **Eli Whitney** moved from Connecticut to Georgia. Whitney liked to build and fix things. In exchange for a place to live, he repaired things around Catherine Greene's plantation. She was the widow of the Revolutionary War hero General Nathanael Greene.

One night, over dinner, several plantation owners were complaining about cleaning cotton. Cotton grows in a fluffy ball with the seeds on the inside. The seeds have to be removed before the cotton can be used. Slaves did this job, but one person could clean only one pound of cotton a day. Mrs. Greene said she was sure Whitney could invent a machine to do the job.

In ten days, Whitney built the first cotton engine, called the **cotton gin** for short. The cotton gin used metal teeth to tear apart the ball of cotton and pull out the dirt and seeds. The cotton gin cleaned 50 pounds of cotton a day.

Whitney's career as an inventor did not end with the cotton gin. He later helped create the modern system of manufacturing machines and machine parts in factories.

The Cotton Gin Changes the South

The cotton gin changed the South. Cotton sold for a high price, so farmers all over the South were eager to plant it. Using a cotton gin took care of the cotton-cleaning problem. The cotton gin worked so fast that more cotton could be grown. To do this, more slaves were needed—the more slaves a planter had, the more cotton he could plant. Planters who grew a lot of cotton became very rich, and slavery became more important than ever before.

Cotton was not the only crop grown in the South. Rice was an important crop in South Carolina and Georgia. Sugar cane was grown in Louisiana. But the cotton gin made cotton the most important crop.

In some ways the cotton gin hurt the Old South by keeping it from changing. Slave owners came to depend even more on their slaves. Few new, large cities grew. The most important cities remained the old port cities, like Charleston and New Orleans. Few factories were built. The South stayed a region of farms. Cotton was king.

THE SOUTHWEST

The Settling of the Southwest

In the early nineteenth century, the "Southwest" meant the area west of Georgia, to beyond the Mississippi River. The Native Americans of this area—the Cherokees, Creeks, Seminoles,

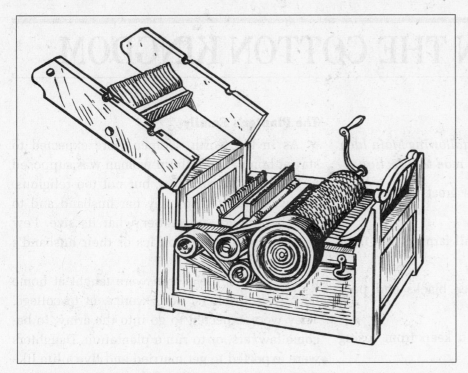

A cotton gin. Like many great inventions, the cotton gin is simple, yet ingenius. It consists of a cylinder with rows of wire teeth, similar to the teeth of a wire hairbrush, rotating in a box. The teeth comb through the cotton, catching the fibers and pulling them apart. A second cylinder, rotating in the opposite direction, then pulls the cotton off the wires. In the process, the cotton fibers are pulled away from the cotton seeds, which drop out.

Chickasaws, and Choctaws—were driven out. The government forced them to move west of the Mississippi, to Indian Territory in what is now Oklahoma. White settlers then moved where the the Indians had left, bringing slaves with them.

As the population grew, new states were formed. The states of Louisiana (1812), Mississippi (1817), Alabama (1819), Missouri (1821), and Arkansas (1836) were admitted into the Union. Because cotton was their most important crop, slavery was legal in all of them.

Pioneer Farmers, Squatters, and Planters

Pioneer farmers were the first whites to move to the frontier. They built small farms, first in Alabama, then in Mississippi. In the 1840's and 1850's, they pushed west into Texas and Louisiana. Farmers from the Old South and from Kentucky and Tennessee came with their families, slaves, and wagons filled with goods. They cleared land and planted cotton. They lived much like Northwestern frontier farmers.

Some settlers began farms on land they hadn't bought. They were called **squatters**. As the government and speculators sold land, the squatters had trouble with the new owners. Some squatters were paid off or forced to move. Some

were allowed to keep their land. Others had already left, moving even further west.

Owners of large plantations, called **planters**, also came into the new states. Some bought several small farms and put them together as a large plantation. Others bought large pieces of the richest land and had their slaves clear it and plant it with cotton.

SECTION REVIEW

Can you answer these Main Idea questions?

1. How did the invention of the cotton gin change life in the South?

2. Why was the South called "The Cotton Kingdom?"

Can you identify and locate these places?

the Old South, the Southwest

Can you identify this person?

Eli Whitney

Can you define these terms?

cotton gin, squatters

2. LIFE IN THE COTTON KINGDOM

Main Ideas

Think about the following Main Idea questions as you read this section:

1. What was life like for the great planters and their families?

2. What was life like for small farmers and their families?

3. What was life like for free blacks and poor whites?

4. What did the South do to keep from losing power to the North?

THE GREAT PLANTERS

Planters and Overseers

By 1850, the Cotton Kingdom included both the Old South and the Southwest. Life there had become very different from life in the North and Northwest. It centered on cotton farms of all different sizes.

The richest farmers, or **great planters**, owned large plantations. There were never many great planters, but they were very important. They owned most of the best land and fifty or more slaves. The planter had total say over his family and slaves. He decided many farming and business matters each day. He gave instructions to an **overseer**, who directed the daily work of the slaves. Many great planters also took part in politics.

Large plantations supplied most of their own needs. Slaves spun cotton and wove a rough cloth for their own clothes. Each plantation had a blacksmith and a cotton gin. Plantations grew some food crops, too, but not enough to feed all the slaves. The rest they bought from Northwestern farmers.

The Planter's Family

As in the North, women were expected to stay at home. A Southern woman was supposed to be pure and religious, but not too religious. She was expected to obey her husband and to run their home, no matter what its size. Few women knew about politics or their husband's business.

The planter's children were taught at home by private teachers. Sons were sent to college. They were expected to go into the army, to become lawyers, or to run a plantation. Daughters were expected to get married and live a life like their mothers'.

Planters and their families often traveled to Europe or the Northeast. They filled their home with beautiful things from these places.

Life for a planter's family was not hard, but romantic stories make it sound much easier than it really was.

SMALL FARMERS, FREE BLACKS, AND POOR WHITES

The Life of Small Planters and Small Farmers

The small planters and small farmers of the South did not live the fancy life of the great planters. Small planters might have from ten to twenty slaves working in the cotton fields. Smaller farmers might have a few slaves who worked alongside them in the cotton fields, but most had no slaves at all. Small farmers grew most of their own food and some cotton to sell. They had little money to buy goods.

Small farmers had a simple life. Most had little time for education. The Methodists, Baptists, and camp meetings were as important in the South as in the Northwest. However, in 1844, the Southern churches split away from the

Northern ones. The Southern churches believed that their religion allowed slavery. The Northern churches did not.

Free Blacks

There were some free blacks in the South. Freedom did not make their life easy, but at least they were not considered to be someone's property. They had their freedom, but not many rights. As in the North, free blacks took the same jobs as poor whites, such as building roads and working in mines. A very few owned farms, but they had to pay high taxes and could not vote.

Slave owners thought free blacks were a bad example for their slaves. They were afraid that their slaves would run away or rebel in order to be free.

Poor Whites

A small number of Southern whites were very poor. They lived on poor land that grew little. They worked just hard enough to have food to eat, but no harder. However, they were proud of their color. They thought of themselves as better than black people, slave or free, just because they were white.

THE SOUTH BEGINS TO LOSE POLITICAL POWER

The Great Planters Resist Change

The most important men in the Cotton Kingdom were the great planters. They had the most power and least wanted change. They liked the life they had. They supported slavery because it kept them rich. They didn't want factories. They didn't want to pay for roads or canals. They didn't want the government to bother them. The small planters and farmers usually followed their lead.

The South Depends on the North While Losing Power To It

But the South was not as independent as the great planters liked to think. The South needed the North. Southerners bought grain, corn, and hogs from the Northwest because they didn't grow all their own food. They used the banks, merchants, and ships of the Northeast. But they didn't like depending on these other parts of the country, and they didn't like the way the North was opposed to slavery.

At the same time, the Southern states were losing power in Congress. The North was growing faster than the South. The South tried to keep its power by making new slave states. They didn't want the North to decide if slavery would be allowed in a new state. They said slavery was a question that each new state should decide for itself. Another way the Southern states kept power was to join together and vote for the bills they wanted and against those they didn't want.

After the Missouri Compromise of 1820, slavery often divided Congress. Soon it divided the country as well.

SECTION REVIEW

Can you answer these Main Idea questions?

1. What was life like for the great planters and their families?

2. What was life like for small farmers and their families?

3. What was life like for free blacks and poor whites?

4. What did the South do to keep from losing power to the North?

Can you define these terms?

great planter, overseer

3. SLAVERY IN THE COTTON KINGDOM

Main Ideas

Think about the following Main Idea questions as you read this section:

1. Why did slavery grow in the South when it ended in the North?

2. What were some of the differences between the life of a house slave and the life of a field hand?

3. How did slave owners control their slaves?

4. What are some ways in which slaves resisted slavery?

THE LIFE OF THE SLAVES

Slavery Dies in the North but Grows in the South

In the North, slavery gradually ended as the Northern states made it illegal. This did not change life for Northern whites very much. They hired workers, sometimes free blacks, sometimes immigrants, to do the same jobs their slaves had done.

Things were different in the South. There, one third of the people were African American slaves. Life for Southern planters would change completely if the slaves were freed. Their whole way of life was based on having slaves. Although importing slaves was illegal after 1808, some slaves from Africa or the Caribbean were still smuggled into the South.

House Slave, Field Hand, Skilled Craftsman

Most of the slaves who worked on the large plantations were either **house slaves** or **field hands.** House slaves worked as servants in the planter's big house. They took care of the planter's family. They worked as cooks, children's nurses, butlers, and maids. A lucky few black children grew up in the big house and shared a white child's education. Many house slaves seemed smarter than field hands. This was because they were taught more and were better fed, and they did not have to do the tiring physical work of the field hands.

The majority of the slaves were field hands. These men, women, and children worked in the cotton fields from dawn until dark. They planted, weeded, and picked cotton.

If there was no work in the cotton fields, gangs of slaves were rented out. They built roads or railroads.

Some slaves were trained as skilled craftsmen. They did skilled work for their owners or were rented to other people who needed a skilled worker such as a blacksmith or dressmaker.

Slaves lived in small wooden cabins with only shutters on the windows to keep out the cold. Each slave was given cornmeal and pork, but they had to grow their own vegetables. Some planters allowed their slaves to hunt or fish.

Control by the Slave Owners

Slave owners controlled their slaves' lives completely. Cruel owners forced their slaves to work hard and punished them with beatings or whippings. Other owners gave their slaves enough food and warm clothes. These owners taught them to read and write, or gave them rewards for working well, like holidays or an education. A few slave owners even freed their slaves.

But whether cruel or kind, slave owners thought of slaves as property. They felt that black people were a different kind of person from whites. They believed that black people could not or would not work on their own. They were sure that black people needed whites to decide everything for them.

Slave families were often deliberately destroyed. In some states, slaves were not allowed to legally marry, although they lived in families. Slave families were often split up as family members were sold to different owners. Slaves from the Old South were often sold to slave traders, who took them to the Southwest, where they were sold to new owners.

THE SLAVES RESIST

The Hope of Religion

Black people hated slavery. In many ways they did whatever they could to resist it. Religion was one way to resist slavery. Religion gave hope to many slaves. Frequently, planters read the Bible to their slaves. The planters felt that religion would teach the slaves to be obedient to their owners. But the slaves picked up another message from the Bible—the hope that they would some day be free.

The slaves took the Christian religion and added their own music. Their religious songs, called **spirituals**, are the earliest American black music that we know about. Many spirituals mixed religious ideas and hopes with the powerful dream of freedom.

Escaped Slaves

To escape from slavery, many slaves simply ran away. When this happened, their owners sent bloodhounds and special hunters, called **slave catchers**, to search for them. Many escaped slaves were caught and punished. Others hid

Below is a family of black slaves. The slaves in this picture were field hands. Their chief work was picking cotton, which they might do for sixteen hours a day under the hot Southern sun during harvest time. The sacks slung over their shoulders are for holding the cotton which they've picked.

until they were starving and were forced to return to the only home they knew.

Most escaped slaves headed north, to states where slavery was illegal. There they could often live a free life. But even there, an escaped slave might be caught and sent back into slavery.

Some slaves who lived near Florida headed south and joined the Seminole Indians, who welcomed them.

Slave Revolts

White people in the slave states were always afraid that the slaves would revolt. They knew that slaves had often revolted on the Caribbean islands. In 1791 there was a slave revolution in a country called Haiti, on the Caribbean island of Hispaniola. The slaves killed many whites and made their country free.

Slave owners in the southern states were afraid that this type of revolt would happen to them. They had reason to fear. There were over 200 attempted slave revolts before the Civil War.

In 1800, a slave named Gabriel Prosser planned a revolt near Richmond, Virginia. But some slaves told their owners about the plan. Prosser and the other planners were captured and killed before a revolt could take place.

The same thing happened again in 1822, when Denmark Vesey, a free black, planned a slave revolt in South Carolina. Vesey and many others were killed before the revolt began.

Nat Turner's Revolt and the Slave Codes

In 1831, a slave preacher named **Nat Turner** led a real uprising in Virginia. He and his followers killed 55 whites. But Turner and his men were caught. Turner was hanged, and many of his followers killed.

Turner's uprising badly frightened Southern whites. They became so afraid that innocent blacks all over the South were also killed. They also passed new, stricter state laws called **slave codes** to control the slaves. Reading and writing could no longer be taught to slaves. A white person now had to always be at their religious services. Slaves had to have a written pass to leave their plantations. It became against the law to have anti-slavery information. Slaves couldn't buy their own freedom anymore, nor could their white owners free them. Neither slaves nor free blacks could speak against a white in court.

Slavery became more firmly fixed than ever in the life of the South.

Long before the year 1850, the South had a distinctive way of life. That way was built on cotton and slavery. While the Northeast and the Northwest were growing together, the South was going in a different direction. In the ten years after 1850, Southerners came to feel that they could no longer be part of the United States.

SECTION REVIEW

Can you answer these Main Idea questions?

1. Why did slavery grow in the South when it ended in the North?

2. What were some of the differences between the life of a house slave and the life of a field hand?

3. How did slave owners control their slaves?

4. What are some ways in which slaves resisted slavery?

Can you identify and locate this place?

Haiti

Can you identify these people?

Gabriel Prosser, Denmark Vesey, Nat Turner

Can you define these terms?

house slaves, field hands, spirituals, slave catchers, slave codes

AFTER YOU READ

Discussion Questions

1. Why was the South called the "Cotton Kingdom?" What kept life from changing in the Cotton Kingdom?

2. How did Southern farm life differ from farm life in the Northwest?

3. Describe the life of Southern slaves.

Comprehension Questions

I. Read each of the quotes below. Then choose the person most likely to have said it.

Free African American in the South

Runaway slave in the North

Plantation owner

Northern Baptist

African American slave woman

Southern Baptist

Southern Congressman

Small white farmer in South

1. "Please don't sell my children. They'll be sent far away and I'll never see them again."

2. "I might not be able to vote, but I'm not a slave anymore. I just wish those poor whites down the road would leave me and my family alone."

3. "Those Northern bankers and merchants are raising shipping prices again. They want to take all our cotton profits."

4. "The Great Planters run our state. I vote, but I don't have the time to spend at meetings or to run for political office."

5. "Slavery is not against the Christian religion. People in the Bible had slaves."

6. "I'm not rich enough to have slaves, but I wouldn't want one anyway. It's wrong to own slaves. It's against our religion!"

7. "I ran away from slavery and I'd never go back to the South again. I don't have much work in this big, bad city, and I may live in a slum, but at least I am free!"

8. "I promise you I won't let those free states in Congress force our beloved state to do things we don't want to do."

II Think about the sections of the United States described in Chapters 18, 19, and 20. Life in each section was different from life in the other sections. Pretend you're traveling through each part of the country in about 1850. Make a list for each section of the country. Include how you traveled, the people you met, and what you saw. List details about the cities and the farms.

THE NORTHEAST

THE NORTHWEST

THE SOUTH

Writing Activity

Use the lists you made in Part II above to write a paragraph describing each section. After you write these three paragraphs, write one that tells about the differences between them. In a final paragraph, tell where you'd like to live and why.

CHAPTER 21

CHANGES IN AMERICAN THOUGHT AND CULTURE

For a long time, Americans had thought of themselves as different from Europeans. Their government, their ways of life, even their language—all had changed since their European beginnings. In the early 1800's, America began to produce its own books and ideas. Americans wrote novels with American themes. They developed new religious ideas. They painted pictures in new styles. They started a system of public education and worked to reform those things that they felt were wrong with their country.

Americans in the early 1800's were filled with hope and confidence. They believed that they lived in a land of opportunity, where hard work could change any life for the better.

(1)

(2)

(3)

(4)

BEFORE YOU READ

Sections in This Chapter

1. Changes in Culture
2. Reform Movements
3. The Abolitionist Movement

Reading a Cartoon

The cartoons about drinking on the opposite page are from the early 1800's. Read them in order and use them to answer the questions below.

1. What happens to the father in the cartoon? Why does it happen?

2. What is the cartoonist's attitude about drinking?

3. Do you think the cartoonist believes that it is possible to drink responsibly?

Understanding a Key Concept:
REFORM

Many Americans wanted to improve life for other people. In order to do that, they wanted to **re-form**, or change, life in America. These people were called **reformers**. Reformers wanted to change or reform many different things. Dorthea Dix, for example, wanted to reform mental hospitals. She worked with states to reform or change how people were cared for in these hospitals.

For each item below, use what you know about life in the middle 1800's to write a sentence about what you think the reformers wanted to change.

1. Women's right to vote

2. Factories

3. Slums

4. Slavery

Making Use of What You Already Know

Read the following descriptions of subjects you have studied. For each, write the topic that the description is about. Choose from the topics below.

slums, Puritans, factories, slavery

1. People worked many hours a day, but earned little money. Many were injured by the machines they worked with. If an injured person could no longer work, they were fired.

2. These people believed that their religion and their hard work made them special to God. They wanted a government run by their religious leaders.

3. Thousands of people lived in these crowded. dirty sections of cities. Sickness spread quickly and they had little fresh water or fresh food.

4. These people were sold like property. They had no freedom and most of their life was controlled by their owners.

1. CHANGES IN CULTURE

Main Ideas

Think about the following Main Idea questions as you read this section:

1. How were the beliefs of the Transcendentalists different from the beliefs of the Puritans?

2. What ideas are Henry David Thoreau famous for?

3. How did American art change in the early 1800's?

TRANSCENDENTALISM AND OTHER NEW IDEAS

Emerson and Transcendentalism

Beginning about 1830, New England produced a number of famous writers and thinkers. One of the best known was **Ralph Waldo Emerson**, a famous writer of essays and poetry. He was also famous as a great speaker.

Emerson was a leader of the movement called **Transcendentalism**. His ideas were very different from those of the early Puritans, who had believed that people are basically sinful and could only be saved by God's mercy. Emerson believed that people are basically good, not sinful. They can become whatever they want to be by hard work and by relying on themselves.

Emerson also believed that people are part of the natural world. He believed that God can be found in the variety and beauty of nature, and that the spirit of God is in every person as well. These ideas are not unusual today, but they were new in Emerson's time.

Henry David Thoreau

The Transcendentalist who has had the most effect on the world was Emerson's friend Henry David Thoreau. In his most famous book, *Walden*,

Thoreau wrote about how he lived close to nature in a hut he built at **Walden Pond** near Concord, Massachusetts. Thoreau was one of the first people to warn that America was destroying its natural and human resources. He also wrote "Civil Disobedience," a famous essay about how to resist unjust laws. This one essay has shaped the thoughts and actions of many great people. Mahatma Gandhi, who led India to independence, and Dr. Martin Luther King, Jr., the great American civil rights leader, were both influenced by Thoreau's ideas.

People Try to Create Ideal Communities

The early 1800's was a time of hope. Some people thought they could create a perfect world. They started small communities to show how their ideas could work. Some were religious groups, like the Amana Community and the Shakers. Others, like Brook Farm in Massachusetts or the New Harmony Community in Indiana, were not. Very few of the groups lasted.

The Spread of Knowledge and Culture

Americans wanted to improve themselves. They became interested in plays and books. Shakespeare's plays were performed in large and small towns. Libraries were built. Women formed clubs to talk about new books. Emerson and other famous writers and scientists spoke at local classes for adults, called **lyceums**.

THE ARTS

American Painters

American art changed, too. Most early American painters were portrait painters. One of the best known is Gilbert Stuart, who painted the picture of George Washington that is copied on the dollar bill. Many of the early American painters had not been trained, but instead taught themselves how to paint.

In Andrew Jackson's time some painters turned to new styles. The **Hudson River Painters**, like Thomas Cole and Frederick Church, showed America's beautiful, untamed wilderness.

At the same time, in architecture, Charles Bulfinch created an American style of buildings called the Boston "Federal" style.

American Writers

American writing changed, too. Many authors wrote stories about American history.

James Fenimore Cooper wrote adventure stories about the Indians and early settlers of New York State. **Washington Irving** wrote tales of Dutch New York. His most famous tale is *Rip Van Winkle*, the story of a man who fell asleep for 20 years. Other authors wrote romantic stories, some about the South's great planters.

> It is long since I first trod the deck of this terrible ship, and the rays of my destiny are, I think, gathering to a focus. Incomprehensible men! Wrapped up in meditations of a kind which I cannot divine, they pass me by unnoticed. Concealment is utter folly on my part, for the people *will not see*. It is but just now that I passed directly before the eyes of the mate; it was no long while ago that I ventured into the captain's own private cabin, and took thence the materials with which I write, and have written. I shall from time to time continue this journal. It is true that I may not find an opportunity of transmitting it to the world, but I will not fail to make the endeavor. At the last moment I will enclose the MS in a bottle, and cast it within the sea.
>
> —From *MS Found in a Bottle*, by Edgar Allan Poe

Henry Wadsworth Longfellow's poems also told old, romantic stories. Everyone knew his *Song of Hiawatha*, about Indian legends, and his *Paul Revere's Ride*.

Edgar Allen Poe wrote many poems and stories from his wild and strange imagination. He also invented the detective story. **Nathaniel Hawthorne** wrote novels about the dark side of colonial New England life. Hawthorne's friend **Herman Melville** wrote *Moby Dick*, one of America's finest novels. It is a sea story about the chase of a great white whale by the mad Captain Ahab.

Walt Whitman tried to capture all America in his poetry, but his book of poems, *Leaves of Grass*, was not popular at first. Its poems were not in the usual poetry form. They were too strange and wild for most people. Today, however, he is known as one of our greatest poets.

SECTION REVIEW

Can you answer these Main Idea questions?

1. How were the beliefs of the Transcendentalists different from the beliefs of the Puritans?

2. What ideas is Henry David Thoreau famous for?

3. How did American art change in the early 1800's?

Can you identify this place?

Walden Pond

Can you identify these people?

Ralph Waldo Emerson, Henry David Thoreau, James Fenimore Cooper, Washington Irving, Nathaniel Hawthorne, Edgar Allen Poe, Herman Melville, Walt Whitman

Can you define these terms?

Transcendentalism, lyceum, Hudson River Painters

2. REFORM MOVEMENTS

Main Ideas

Think about the following Main Idea questions as you read this section:

1. How did reformers change prisons and mental hospitals?

2. What were the most important changes in education?

3. How did the Women's Rights movement begin?

REFORMS IN PRISONS AND MENTAL HOSPITALS

Prison Reform

The new religious thinking, like that of the Transcendentalists, said that life could be improved because human nature was basically good. To make life better, people had to "re-form" it, or change it. Reformers wanted to make the world a better place.

The first reformers worried most people. People didn't want to hear what was wrong in the world. Prisons, for example, were terrible places. Prisoners had to stay silent so that they could think about how sinful they were—an idea inspired by religion. The reformers, however, thought that crime was caused by a bad environment, like the conditions in crowded city slums. Slowly, they forced prisons to become places that tried to help prisoners as well as punishing them.

Dorothea Dix and the Reform of Mental Hospitals

The mentally ill were treated even worse than the criminals. They were often put into prisons where they were chained, beaten, and treated like animals.

One woman, **Dorothea Dix**, changed that. Beginning in the early 1840's, she traveled all over the country writing about the terrible way mentally ill people were treated. Because of her work, many states began to build special hospitals for the mentally ill and improve their care.

THE UNION MOVEMENT

An Unsuccessful Workers' Movement

Most factory workers worked long hours for low pay. Some workers joined together in **unions** to try and change this. Unions are groups of workers, usually with the same or similar jobs, who work together to improve their pay and working conditions. Unions made a few changes, but then the Panic of 1837 hit and many workers lost their jobs. Union members were usually the first to be fired. Other workers were hired to replace them for less money and for longer hours.

The unions fell apart. The union movement would not become successful until later in the century.

REFORMS IN EDUCATION

States Start Public Elementary Schools

In education, reforms were more successful. Many people wanted free public schools. They believed that everyone needed an education to take part in a democratic country. Between 1830 and 1850, most states began public elementary schools. In the South, it took longer, both because farms were more spread out, and because children had to help with the farm work.

Going to school meant that children no longer worked full time on the farm or in factories. A child's life became different from an adult's life. This was something new to many people.

High Schools and New Colleges

Most early public schools were elementary schools. High schools were usually private schools that prepared students for college. Boston had the first public high school. A few others were started, but not many.

Many new colleges were built, though. Most were small, religious colleges. In the South and West, a few state colleges were started.

Higher Education for Women

The first college to admit both men and women, Oberlin College, was founded in 1833. The first college for women only, Mount Holyoke, was founded in 1837. It was started by the remarkable **Mary Lyon**, who is said to have learned Latin grammar in only three days!

But most Americans did not feel that women needed a college education or even a high school one. Also, at this time and for many years to come, few women would be able to use their education in jobs outside the home.

Two Important Educators

Two of the most influential educators of this period were William McGuffey and **Horace Mann**. McGuffey's school books were first printed in 1837. His *McGuffey's Readers* contained stories on many subjects. They also taught religious and moral ideas to their young readers. They were the first school books to have stories followed by questions. A million copies were sold in 1843 alone. Later versions were still being used in some school systems in the 1980's.

In Massachusetts, Horace Mann trained teachers to teach new subjects and helped them teach the old ones in new ways. As head of the Massachusetts Board of Education, he raised enough money both to pay teachers better and to permit every child to go to school for at least six months each year. His ideas were soon used all over the country.

Reforms of the Early 1800's

PROBLEM	REFORM	REFORMER
Prisons were cruel places; prisoners had to remain silent.	Prisons were changed so that they tried to rehabilitate prisoners, not just punish them.	
Mental Hospitals were like cages or zoos for the mentally ill.	Special hospitals were built to treat the mentally ill, not just lock them up.	Dorothea Dix
Many people weren't **educated**. Children worked full-time.	Public schools were started in most states, to provide free education. Children no longer worked full time.	
Women didn't go to college.	Oberlin college starts admitting women. The first all-women college, Mount Holyoke, is founded.	Mary Lyon (founded Mount Holyoke)
Women didn't have the same opportunities as men.	The Seneca Falls Convention declares that men and women are equal. Several women become professionals, such as Elizabeth Blackwell (first female doctor) and Margaret Fuller (Transcendentalist writer, editor, and reporter).	Elizabeth Cady Staton and Lucretia Mott (Seneca Falls Convention)

THE TEMPERANCE MOVEMENT

The Movement Against Alcohol

In the early and middle 1800's, many people drank a lot of drinks that contain alcohol—whiskey, rum, gin, and beer. A movement to make alcohol illegal started. It was called the **temperance movement**. Religious groups joined the movement, and in 1826 a National Temperance Society was started. By 1834, it had a million members.

Many German and Irish immigrants enjoyed getting together and drinking. The Temperance Society blamed nearly all the immigrants' troubles on alcohol. They thought the immigrants were poor because they spent all their money on drink. They didn't understand how crowded slums, low factory pay, or long hours ruined people's lives and crushed their hopes.

By 1855, over 40% of the states had passed laws against alcohol. But many of these laws were later changed or declared unconstitutional.

WOMEN'S RIGHTS

Women Without Basic Rights

In the 1800's, women were expected to take care of their home, be religious, and obey their husbands. In reality, many women also worked long hours in factories or in the fields. They ran businesses and plantations when their husbands were away or died. A very few had paying jobs.

Women worked as hard as men, but they didn't have the same rights. They couldn't vote. They didn't have legal control of their children or property. They were not allowed at many public meetings.

Only a few brave women forced their way into professions. The Transcendentalist writer Margaret Fuller was Emerson's and Thoreau's editor. She later became an overseas reporter for *The New York Tribune*. In 1849 Elizabeth Blackwell became America's first female doctor.

The Seneca Falls Convention

Many women were active in their churches, and through their churches some women joined reform movements. In 1840 a Quaker women, Lucretia Mott, went to the World Anti-Slavery Convention in London. Because she was a woman, she was not allowed into the meeting. She was furious. With her friend Elizabeth Cady Stanton, she began working for women's rights.

In 1848, Stanton and Mott organized the first Women's Rights Convention. It took place in a church near Stanton's home in Seneca Falls, New York. The people at the meeting agreed that all men and women were created equal, and that women should have the same rights as men.

Many people thought something was wrong with those who wanted women's rights. The issue split other reform groups. Some men thought women should be allowed to go to and speak at meetings. Others thought that women belonged at home. For a long time, the women's rights movement made few changes. Its leaders, like Mott, Stanton, and the great organizer Susan B. Anthony, didn't stop trying, though.

SECTION REVIEW

Can you answer these Main Idea questions?

1. How did reformers change prisons and mental hospitals?

2. What were the most important changes in education?

3. How did the Women's Rights movement begin?

Can you identify this place?

Seneca Falls

Can you identify these people?

Dorothea Dix, Mary Lyon, Horace Mann

Can you define these terms?

McGuffey's Readers, temperance movement

3. THE ABOLITIONIST MOVEMENT

Main Ideas

Think about the following Main Idea questions as you read this section:

1. What was the difference between what the early abolitionists tried to do and what William Lloyd Garrison wanted?

2. How did African Americans react to the idea of abolition?

3. How did Southern whites react to abolitionist ideas?

A MOVEMENT AGAINST SLAVERY

Early Abolitionists

One reform movement changed the country more than any other. It was the anti-slavery, or **abolition**, movement. "Abolition" means abolishing, or doing away with, slavery. Those who supported it were called **abolitionists**.

Even in colonial times, some people had spoken out against slavery. Many of these early abolitionists were Southerners who were trying to reform their own way of life. These early abolitionists expected that the slaves would be freed slowly and that the slave owners would be paid for their loss.

But in the early 1800's Southern support for abolition disappeared. Nearly all Southerners believed slavery was necessary to the Southern way of life. Many also felt that there was nothing wrong with owning another human being. The center of the anti-slavery movement became the North.

The Founding of Liberia as a Homeland for Freed Slaves

One group of abolitionists in the early 1800's bought and freed many slaves and shipped them to the west coast of Africa, to a place they called "Liberia." Some free blacks were sent, too, although most didn't want to go.

About 12,000 black people were returned to Africa. Liberia later became an independent country. Many American whites at this time hoped that most American blacks would move there, but few ever did.

William Lloyd Garrison Founds *The Liberator*

In 1831 a young Boston newspaperman named William Lloyd Garrison changed the }anti-slavery movement. His newspaper, *The Liberator*, demanded immediate freedom for all slaves.

▼ *A map of Liberia, showing its location in Africa. Liberia is the oldest independent republic (a country which does not have a king, queen, prince, etc. as a ruler) in Africa.*

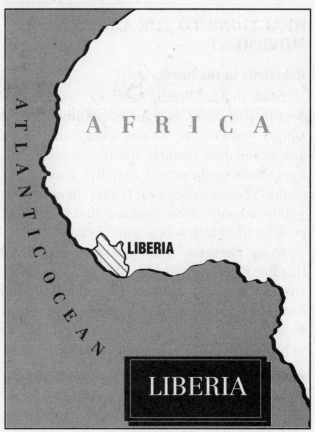

Garrison made abolitionism into a religious crusade. His writing was so powerful that others began to share his hatred of slavery.

Black Abolitionists

Free African Americans in the North were abolitionists, too. Some were born free. Others had been given their freedom or had bought it. Still others had escaped from slavery. Many worked with the American Anti-Slavery Society.

The most important African American abolitionist was an escaped slave, **Frederick Douglass**. He spoke and wrote about his life as a slave. He also owned an anti-slavery newspaper. He wanted blacks to be equal to whites in all ways, with all the same opportunities and privileges. He was a brilliant man and a stirring speaker.

Another well-known African American abolitionist was also a former slave. She gave herself the name **Sojourner Truth**. She became famous for her simple, powerful speeches against slavery and for women's rights.

REACTIONS TO THE ABOLITIONIST MOVEMENT

Reactions in the North

Even in the North, however, most white people were not in favor of abolition. Most simply didn't care. Others didn't like black people and didn't want to give them equal rights. Free blacks could vote in only five states. They couldn't become doctors or lawyers or even go to public schools. Some western states wouldn't even let free black people settle in them.

Many Northern white workers were afraid that free blacks would take their jobs. Abolitionists were attacked and their printing presses and homes were destroyed. But they continued to hold meetings, to print newspapers, and to work to free the slaves.

Reactions in the South

The South had strong reactions to anti-slavery ideas. They thought the North should mind its own business. Slavery had always been around. It was even described in the Bible.

Southern whites believed a black was much better off as a Southern slave than as a free person in Africa. They thought abolitionists wanted slaves to rise up and kill whites. That wasn't true, but the South blamed Garrison for Nat Turner's slave uprising. Southerners refused to change slavery's worst practices, like separating families. Instead, they wrote stricter laws to control slaves.

Americans in the first half of the 1800's saw a bright future ahead. They thought life could be better, and some tried to make it so. They believed Americans were specially favored by God. Everyone felt that the United States was destined to show the rest of the world how life ought to be lived.

SECTION REVIEW

Can you answer these Main Idea questions?

1. What was the difference between what the early abolitionists tried to do and what William Lloyd Garrison wanted?

2. How did African Americans react to the idea of abolition?

3. How did Southern whites react to abolitionist ideas?

Can you identify and locate this place?

Liberia

Can you identify these people?

William Lloyd Garrison, Frederick Douglass, Sojourner Truth

Can you define these terms?

abolition, *The Liberator*,

AFTER YOU READ

Discussion Questions

1. Americans wanted to create a better life than people had in Europe. How did Transcendentalists and reformers try to do that? Give examples to support your ideas.

2. Do you think that the abolition movement changed the country more than any other movement? Use facts to support your opinion.

3. How was life for women changing in America?

Comprehension Questions

1. Copy these four headings on your paper:

   ABOLITIONIST MOVEMENT

   TEMPERANCE MOVEMENT

   WOMEN'S RIGHTS MOVEMENT

   EDUCATIONAL IMPROVEMENT

2. Write each item on the following list under the movement which tried to solve that problem.

   Many men drank too much alcohol.

   People were sold as property and had no freedom.

   Most slaves worked very hard in owner's fields.

   People wanted all African Americans to have full rights.

   Women worked at home and in factories.

   Women couldn't vote and couldn't control their own property.

   People wanted to outlaw the drinking of alcohol.

   Alcohol added to the problems of the slums and immigrants.

   Teachers had few books.

   Children didn't go to school

   Better school books and ways of teaching were needed.

   Women should have the right to vote.

   Women should have a say in the control of their property and of their children.

   Women should have the chance to enter any profession.

3. Now write the following names under the reform movements to which they belonged.

   Lucretia Mott   *William McGuffy*

   Frederick Douglass   *Horace Mann*

   Elizabeth Cady Stanton

   Seneca Falls Convention

   William Lloyd Garrision

4. Add two more facts, feelings, or ideas to each of your four lists.

Writing Activity

Choose one of the lists from the Comprehension Questions. Write two paragraphs to convince someone that this is or is not an important reform to be made. Tell about life as it was, what needs or doesn't need to be changed, and why you believe as you do. Use some of your own feelings, and not just those discussed in this chapter.

AMERICANS MOVE WEST

When Andrew Jackson was elected President in 1828, the American frontier was beginning to cross the Mississippi River. Twenty years later, after a war with Mexico, the United States stretched across the whole continent. By 1850, many Americans had settled in Texas, California, Oregon and Utah. The westward movement of the United States is one of the great adventures in our history.

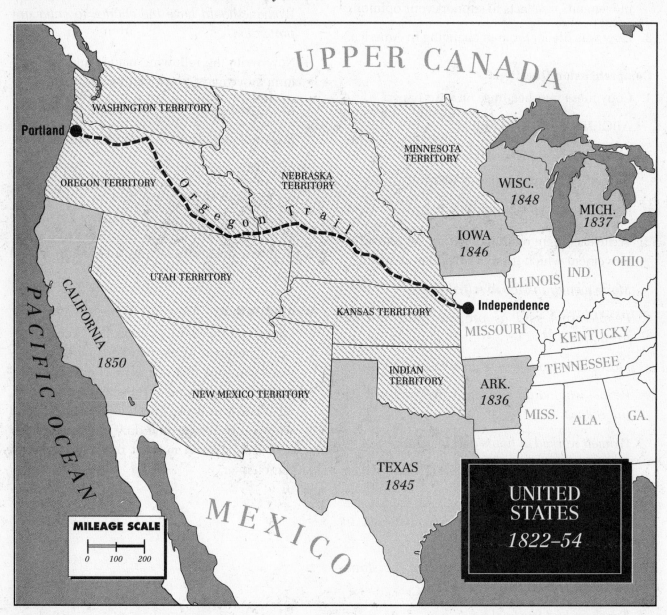

UPPER CANADA

WASHINGTON TERRITORY

Portland

OREGON TERRITORY

Oregon Trail

MINNESOTA TERRITORY

NEBRASKA TERRITORY

WISC.
1848

MICH.
1837

IOWA
1846

ILLINOIS

IND.

OHIO

UTAH TERRITORY

CALIFORNIA
1850

KANSAS TERRITORY

Independence

MISSOURI

KENTUCKY

TENNESSEE

PACIFIC OCEAN

NEW MEXICO TERRITORY

INDIAN TERRITORY

ARK.
1836

MISS.

ALA.

GA.

TEXAS
1845

UNITED STATES
1822–54

MEXICO

MILEAGE SCALE

0   100   200

BEFORE YOU READ

Sections in This Chapter

1. Explorers, Trappers, and Settlers
2. Texas and the Mexican West
3. The Pacific Northwest
4. The Mexican War
5. An American Far West

Reading a Map

The map on the opposite page shows the American West in the years 1822-1854. Use this map to answer these questions.

1. What was the main route to the Northwest called? Between what two cities did it stretch?

2. How many western states were added between 1822 and 1854? What were they?

3. How far is it from Missouri to the Pacific Coast ?

Understanding a Key Concept:
MANIFEST DESTINY

In the 1800's, many Americans believed in Manifest Destiny. "Manifest" means clear and obvious. "Destiny" means future. To these Americans, it meant that it was America's future—as if God-given—to expand as far as it could, even if that meant taking over land controlled by other people. People in other countries usually didn't agree.

Copy each statement below and write "yes" next to it if it is an example of Manifest Destiny, or "no" if it is not.

1. President Polk promised to make Texas, California, and Oregon part of the United States.

2. Very few people lived in Northern Mexico.

3. The United States government told the British government that it wanted all of Oregon from Alaska to California.

4. President Polk was afraid that his generals wanted his job.

5. The United States government offered to buy parts of northern Mexico from Mexico.

Making Use of What You Already Know

Much of the land first settled by the Spanish became the new country of Mexico. Mexico had a different culture, or way of life, than did the United States. Use what you have learned about the Spanish colonies to write a paragraph for the topic sentence below. Use at least six items from the accompanying list to describe life in Mexico.

Catholic	*ranches*	*hospitality*
fiestas	*desert*	*trade with outsiders*
adobe	*language*	*long distances*
food	*missions*	*Indians*

TOPIC SENTENCE: The life of Spanish and Mexican settlers was different from the life of American frontier settlers.

1. EXPLORERS, TRAPPERS, AND SETTLERS

Main Ideas

Think about the following Main Idea questions as you read this section:

1. Why did Lewis and Clark travel to the Pacific Ocean and back?

2. What was the life of a mountain man like?

3. Why did the mountain men's way of life come to an end?

4. Why did settlers want to move west?

5. Why didn't settlers fill up the area between Missouri and California?

EXPLORING THE LOUISIANA TERRITORY

Lewis and Clark Travel to the Pacific

The move across the Mississippi River started in 1803, when President Thomas Jefferson agreed to the Louisiana Purchase. No one knew very much about that huge piece of land. Jefferson asked his secretary, Meriwether Lewis, to explore and study it. Lewis chose an army friend, William Clark, to help lead the exploring party.

In May 1804 Lewis and Clark left St. Louis, Missouri. With fewer than 50 men, they traveled up the Missouri River, then across the Rocky Mountains to the Pacific Ocean. A young Shoshone Indian woman named Sacajawea translated for them. When they reached the mountains and could no longer travel by river, they traded with Sacajawea's people for horses.

Lewis and Clark finally saw the Pacific Ocean in November 1805. The following spring they returned east. They did not find a river route through the Rocky Mountains, but they did find passes across them. They made maps and took scientific notes about the plants and animals they saw. They even brought back two grizzly bear cubs.

Zebulon Pike Explores the Southern Rockies

Other people explored the new land, too. In 1806 Lieutenant Zebulon Pike led a group of men into the Southern Rocky Mountains. He wandered into northern New Mexico, which belonged to Spain. The Spanish took away his notes and maps and sent him back home. Luckily, Pike had an excellent memory and wrote down what he had seen when he returned east.

But the new land west of the Mississippi was so large that these explorers couldn't explore it all. Much of it remained unknown for many years.

MOUNTAIN MEN AND SETTLERS

Mountain Men Trap Beavers in the Rockies

Only a few years after the Lewis and Clark Expedition, men began trapping beavers in the Rockies. These trappers, called **mountain men**, usually lived alone or with an Indian wife. They fought hunger, thirst, snowstorms, and grizzly bears. They knew the Rockies as well as the Indians did. They were the first white men to see such famous and beautiful places as Yellowstone Park.

At first, the mountain men had to go east to sell their furs. They traveled a thousand miles, all the way from the Rockies to St. Louis, Missouri. Selling furs became easier after 1821, when Mexico became independent from Spain. Mexico allowed Americans to trade in their country. The Mexican town of Taos, in New Mexico's southern Rockies, became a fur trading center.

After 1825, traders came to the mountains. Each year they met the trappers at a different spot. At the meetings, the trappers sold their furs, had a month-long party, bought what they needed, and headed back into the wild.

The mountain men's way of life came to an end around 1840. Most of the animals were gone. In addition, silk hats had become fashionable. People no longer wanted hats made from beaver fur. Some famous mountain men, like Kit Carson, Jedediah Smith, Jim Bridger, and the African American Jim Beckwourth, guided wagon trains across the mountains or worked for the army. Most stayed near the mountains they loved.

Settlers Move West to the Pacific

As the American frontier became settled, new states were formed on both sides of the Mississippi River. Arkansas (1836), Iowa (1846), and Wisconsin (1849) became states. But the hard, dry earth of the Great Plains further west stopped the settlers for a while. Few settlers wanted it because it was too hard to farm. They called the plains "The Great American Desert" and thought it was only good for growing grass to feed the buffalo. Because they thought it was worthless, the area west of Missouri and Arkansas was set aside as "Indian Territory." Beyond the plains lay high mountains, and then came real deserts.

When Americans settlers started moving west again, most crossed these harsh lands and didn't stop. They traveled across the continent to the other side. Most settlers moved into places that didn't belong to the United States, but that didn't have many settlers: nearby Texas, and distant Oregon and California.

People moved west because they believed they would have a better chance to improve their lives, and maybe even become rich. Farmers wanted new land. Merchants wanted to trade with China and Japan, and needed ports along the Pacific Coast. There were no bosses or rich people on the frontier. But the cities, government, and army of the United States were also a long way away. Frontier life was not easy, and everyone had to work hard to survive.

SECTION REVIEW

Can you answer these Main Idea questions?

1. Why did Lewis and Clark travel to the Pacific Ocean and back?

2. What was the life of a mountain man like?

3. Why did the mountain men's way of life come to an end?

4. Why did settlers want to move west?

5. Why didn't settlers fill up the area between Missouri and California?

Can you identify and locate these places?

Missouri River, Rocky Mountains, the "Great American Desert"

Can you identify these people?

Meriwether Lewis, William Clark, Sacajawea, Zebulon Pike

Can you define this term?

mountain men

2. TEXAS AND THE MEXICAN WEST

Main Ideas

Think about the following Main Idea questions as you read this section:

1. Why didn't the Mexicans and the Americans in Texas get along?

2. What were the main events of the Texas War of Independence?

3. Why did Americans first come to New Mexico and to California?

AMERICANS COME TO TEXAS

Stephen Austin Brings American Settlers to Texas

In 1821, Mexico broke free from Spain and became an independent country. At that time, Texas was part of Mexico, but not many Mexicans lived there.

Mexico decided to let colonists from other countries settle in Texas. A settler from Missouri named Stephen Austin received a large piece of land from the Mexican government. He brought several Americans to Texas to start farms.

Other Americans received land, too. Farmers from the states east of Texas began small cotton farms. Rich planters brought their slaves and began cotton plantations. By 1830, about 16,000 Americans lived in Texas, along with only a few thousand Mexicans.

Bad Feelings Between the Americans and Mexicans in Texas

Americans and Mexicans did not get along very well in Texas. The Americans were supposed to become Catholics and Mexican citizens. Some did, but most would not follow Mexican ways. Most refused to learn Spanish. They brought their own ideas about buildings, farming, religion, and food. They also brought slaves, although slavery was against the laws of Mexico.

The United States Wants To Buy Texas

Both President John Quincy Adams and President Andrew Jackson offered to buy Texas from Mexico, but the Mexican government refused. They even sent soldiers to stop any more Americans from moving into Texas. But the Americans kept coming.

For a while, the American Texans hoped a Mexican general named **Antonio López de Santa Anna** would be on their side. When he became President of Mexico, however, he refused to make Texas a separate Mexican state. Texans began to talk about becoming a separate country or joining the United States.

Sam Houston Comes to Texas

In 1832, a famous man arrived in Texas. His name was **Sam Houston**, and he had been a general, a Congressman, and the governor of Tennessee. He had even lived for years with the Cherokee Indians. He quickly became one of the most important people in Texas.

TEXAS FIGHTS FOR INDEPENDENCE

The Fight at the Alamo

In 1836, Santa Anna and an army marched north to force the Texans to behave. The Texans resisted, and chose Sam Houston to lead them.

About 184 Texans waited in an old mission in San Antonio called the **Alamo**. Most were Americans, but 20 were Mexican Texans. Houston sent them a message telling them all to leave, but they stayed.

Santa Anna's men surrounded the Alamo. For ten days the fighting continued. More than a thousand Mexican soldiers were killed. When the Mexicans finally captured the Alamo, they killed nearly everyone in it. Among the dead were the Tennessee hero **Davy Crockett** and the famous fighter **Jim Bowie**, inventor of the Bowie knife.

Santa Anna let one woman go to tell what would happen to others who rebelled. At another post, named Goliad, the Texan soldiers surrendered, but Santa Anna's men killed them anyway.

Sam Houston Leads the Texans to Victory

Texans were furious. On March 2, 1836, they declared Texas an independent country. On April 21, an army of Texans led by Sam Houston attacked a much larger Mexican army at San Jacinto, near what is now the city of Houston. The Texans cried "Remember the Alamo!" as they charged. The Mexicans were taking an afternoon nap, a Mexican custom called a siesta. They didn't know what was happening until the Texans were upon them.

In eighteen minutes the battle was over. Santa Anna was captured. Several months later he was sent back to Mexico City. By the time he arrived, a new government had taken away his power.

An Independent Texas

Texas had won her independence. But most Texans really wanted to become part of the United States. Most Americans wanted it too, but they knew it would make Mexico angry. Since Americans weren't ready to fight a war with Mexico, the United States just recognized the new country.

Texas wrote a constitution and elected Sam Houston President. They offered free land and allowed slavery. More Southern farmers came.

▼ *The battle at the Alamo. The fighting was furious. At the end it was hand-to-hand combat, as was usual in the nineteenth century. The bravery of the defenders, who died to the last man, helped inspire their fellow Texans to victory.*

The new republic had a major problem: no money. Great Britain offered to help. The British wanted to buy Texas cotton for less than they were paying American planters. The British offer worried Southern planters, who were afraid that they would lose their British trade, or even that Britain would take over Texas. If that happened, runaway slaves could escape into a British Texas and become free.

Texas Joins the United States

The Southern states asked Congress to take Texas into the Union as a new slave state, but the Northern states refused to allow it. They kept refusing until December 1845, when Texas finally became a state—a slave state.

Mexico was angry that Texas was now part of the United States. The two countries were moving closer and closer to war.

AMERICANS COME TO NEW MEXICO AND CALIFORNIA

American Traders and The Santa Fe Trail

One reason that Mexico lost Texas was that few Mexicans had settled there. Other parts of Northern Mexico had the same problem. Santa Fe, the capital of New Mexico, was so far from the rest of Mexico that Mexican traders hardly ever came there. The stores had very little for people to buy.

In 1821, American trader William Bucknell arrived from Missouri with a load of goods. He quickly sold everything and returned with more to sell. Over the years, many wagons took his Santa Fe Trail from Missouri to Santa Fe. They brought everything from a printing press to silk.

Americans in California

California was also far from the rest of Mexico. It was like a separate country. The rich Mexican ranchers in California, called **Californios**, were famous for their skill at riding horses, their welcome to visitors, their love of dancing, and their week-long fiestas (parties). California's

government changed often as the Californios struggled with each other for power.

During the 1820's, American ships began to stop in California. They traded goods for California's cattle hides. A few Americans stayed in California. As in Texas, they were supposed to become Mexican citizens, but most didn't

Not all the new Californians came from the United States. One important settler, **John Sutter**, came from Switzerland. Sutter received a huge amount of land near Sacramento. He helped many of the first American settlers who came overland in 1841.

In 1842, a U.S. Navy commander thought America was at war with Mexico. He seized the town of Monterey. When he found out he was wrong, he apologized and sailed away.

The Californios tried to forget that the United States wanted California. But by 1845, seven hundred Americans lived in California, and many of them wanted the United States to take over.

SECTION REVIEW

Can you answer these Main Idea questions?

1. Why didn't the Mexicans and the Americans in Texas get along?

2. What were the main events of the Texas War of Independence?

3. Why did Americans first come to New Mexico and to California?

Can you identify and locate these places?

The Alamo, San Jacinto, New Mexico, Santa Fe, Santa Fe Trail

Can you identify these people?

Stephen Austin, Antonio López de Santa Anna, Davy Crockett, Jim Bowie, John Sutter

Can you define this term?

Californios

3. THE PACIFIC NORTHWEST

Main Ideas

Think about the following Main Idea questions as you read this section:

1. What white people lived in Oregon before the settlers came?

2. What was a journey west on the Oregon Trail like?

3. How did the idea of Manifest Destiny shape the way American thought about the West?

4. How did the United States finally get land in the Northwest?

WAGONS WEST ALONG THE OREGON TRAIL

Fur Traders and Missionaries in Oregon

During the 1840's, many Americans headed to the Oregon Country. At that time, "Oregon" was the name for all the land between California and Alaska. The United States and England shared control of the area.

For many years, fur traders were the only white men who lived there. John Jacob Astor's American Fur Company and Canada's Hudson's Bay Company fought over control of the fur trade. Finally, Astor sold his company to the Canadians. He believed that most of the animals were gone and that farmers would soon arrive. He was right

Missionaries and farmers first came to Oregon's Willamette Valley in 1832. They wrote letters and books about its deep forests, clear water, and rich soil. By the 1840's, many Americans had caught "Oregon Fever." They came west along a wagon route called the Oregon Trail, searching for a new frontier.

The Oregon Trail

When the frontier jumped to the Pacific Coast, the pioneers had to travel 2000 miles to reach it. The frontier was no longer just across the state line. The trip west now took six months, over plains, deserts, and mountains.

The first pioneers found out that getting to the Far West wasn't easy. They had to buy everything they needed—wagons, mules, horses, and grain—for there were few places along the way to buy supplies. Small wagons with canvas tops, called **covered wagons**, were used as transportation, house, boat, and fort. Each wagon had to be well made, for if it broke, it had to be left behind.

After buying supplies, each pioneer family waited for enough people to make up a wagon train. Wagon trains left Missouri in the spring so that they could be across the mountains before snow fell. Those that were caught in winter storms often didn't make it.

At first, there were no roads. Mountain men led the wagon trains through the mountain passes. Sometimes the pioneers ran out of food or water. Bad water made people and animals sick. Many died. Most died from sickness, but some died from overwork, and some from fights. Sometimes people didn't get along, and the wagon train split. Each part went its own way.

The Plains Indians allowed the wagon trains across their land. They might steal horses or cattle, but they didn't usually attack the wagons.

By 1849 the wagon roads were deep ruts. The trail was crowded, and everyone was in a hurry. After the year's first wagon trains, no grass was left for the animals who came later. Empty wagons and graves marked the trail. Many people paid a high price for their dream of life on the Far Western frontier.

THE UNITED STATES GETS HALF THE OREGON TERRITORY

Manifest Destiny

In 1844 **James K. Polk** was elected President. He was a friend of Andrew Jackson and had been Speaker of the House of Representatives. But he was not well known outside of Washington, D.C. He won the election because he promised to make Texas, California, and Oregon part of the United States.

Americans in the 1840's believed that the United States should stretch across the whole continent, from coast to coast. They believed that taking over the West was America's right. This belief was called **Manifest Destiny**—that is, a destiny or future that was clear and obvious to everyone. Many people were ready to go to war with Mexico and Great Britain to get the western lands that were not already part of the United States.

▲ *A wagon train heading westward. As you can see, wagon trains truly were "trains." They traveled single-file so that only the first wagon had to break a trail; the rest got to follow in its path. In the picture, they are snaking along the terrain in order to avoid rough or swampy ground, or too-steep slopes.*

Britain and the United States Divide Oregon in Half

Britain knew that the United States wanted Oregon, but had refused to divide it. President Polk told Britain that America now wanted all of Oregon, all the way to Alaska.

Britain didn't want yet another war with the United States. In 1846, Britain and America finally agreed to divide Oregon in half. They continued the United States–Canada border westward to the Pacific Ocean. The part of Oregon gained by the United States later became the states of Washington, Oregon, and Idaho.

SECTION REVIEW

Can you answer these Main Idea questions?

1. What white people lived in Oregon before the settlers came?

2. What was a journey west on the Oregon Trail like?

3. How did the idea of Manifest Destiny shape the way American thought about the West?

4. How did the United States finally get land in the Northwest?

Can you identify and locate these places?

Oregon, the Oregon Trail

Can you identify this person?

James K. Polk

Can you define these terms?

Oregon Fever, covered wagons, Manifest Destiny

4. THE MEXICAN WAR

Main Ideas

Think about the following Main Idea questions as you read this section:

1. What started the war with Mexico?

2. What were the main events of the war?

3. Why are the cadets at Mexico's Military Academy considered national heroes of Mexico?

4. What did the United States gain at the end of the Mexican War?

THE UNITED STATES GOES TO WAR

War Breaks Out

In 1845, war finally broke out over the part of Texas just north of the Rio Grande. Both the United States and Mexico claimed it. President Polk ordered General **Zachary Taylor** to move his army there. A Mexican army crossed the Rio Grande into the same area. A fight began, and several American soldiers were killed. President Polk told Congress that American blood had been spilled on American soil. He asked for war and he got it. The Mexican War had begun.

A War That Neither Side Was Prepared For

The Mexican War did not go smoothly for either side. Neither Mexico nor the United States was ready for war. Neither had enough guns or any war plans. Each side thought it was much stronger than it was. Both sides thought they'd win the war quickly.

President Polk tried to run the war from Washington. He was afraid his generals wanted his job as President. He made a mistake when he let the Mexican General Santa Anna, who was in Cuba, return to Mexico. Polk thought that Santa Anna would end the war. Instead, the General once again took over Mexico's government and led the fight against the Americans.

The Two Armies

Mexico's army was large. Rich Mexicans were officers and poor men were soldiers. The Mexican officers were not well trained, and they spent a lot of time trying to make Santa Anna happy. The army had old weapons and not enough supplies. Still, they were sure they would win quickly.

The United States had a smaller, better trained army with newer weapons, but their maps were often wrong. Sometimes American officers made plans without thinking. Many American soldiers died from sickness caused by bad living conditions. Still, President Polk was sure that the Mexicans would give up after a battle or two.

AMERICAN VICTORIES

General Zachary Taylor Takes Northern Mexico

After General Taylor was attacked, he took 5,000 men into Mexico. Santa Anna brought 20,000 soldiers through the desert to meet him. They fought several battles, but Santa Anna kept making mistakes. Soon the American army was in charge of northeast Mexico. The Mexicans wouldn't quit, though. The government and people in Mexico City still hoped to win.

Americans Take New Mexico and California

In June 1846, the American General Stephen Kearny took a small army down the Santa Fe Trail to New Mexico. New Mexico's governor surrendered without firing a shot. Kearny set up a new government, then went on to California.

At the same time, a group of Americans living in California declared it an independent country. Since their flag had a bear on it, the new "country" was called the **Bear Flag Republic**.

Less than a month later, U.S. Navy ships arrived. On July 29, Navy Commodore Robert Stockton officially said California was part of the United States. When General Kearny finally arrived in December, he found Stockton and American Army captain and explorer John C. Frémont fighting against the Californios. Kearny joined them and ended the revolt.

THE WAR ENDS

General Scott Attacks Mexico City

By 1847, President Polk realized that the Mexicans would not quickly accept peace, even though the United States had taken over much of their land. He sent an army led by General **Winfield Scott** to capture Mexico City. Scott was a brilliant general. He and his officers, like Robert E. Lee and Ulysses Grant, planned their march carefully and did not rush into battle.

Santa Anna rushed his army south across the desert. Once again, he made many mistakes and lost many battles, but his men kept fighting to protect their homes.

Los Niños Heroicos

On the hill of Chapultepec, which protected Mexico City, one of the most famous and tragic events of the war took place. Mexico's Military Academy was located on the hill. It was defended by nearly 1,000 soldiers and a group of young cadets from the school. American gunfire drove the regular Mexican soldiers away. But fifty young cadets—some as young as 13—refused to leave. They fought to the end. They are among Mexico's greatest national heroes. They are known as **Los Niños Heroicos**—the Heroic Children.

The Mexican Government Collapses

By the time the American army reached Mexico City, the Mexican government had fallen apart. No one was in control, so no one could say

that the Americans had won. It took the Mexicans several months to form a new government and to agree to a peace treaty.

The United States Gets the Mexican Lands It Wants

The peace treaty, known as the **Treaty of Guadalupe Hidalgo**, gave President Polk everything he wanted. The United States paid Mexico $15 million and in return got more than half of Mexico's territory. It got all the land north of the Rio Grande, plus New Mexico and California. In later years these lands became all or part of seven states: Texas, New Mexico, Arizona, California, Nevada, Utah, and Colorado.

Ever since the Virginia and Massachusetts colonies began, Americans had been expanding westward across the continent. After the Mexican War, they finally controlled the land from sea to shining sea. President Polk had kept his campaign promises.

SECTION REVIEW

Can you answer these Main Idea questions?

1. What started the war with Mexico?

2. What were the main events of the war?

3. Why are the cadets at Mexico's Military Academy considered national heroes of Mexico?

4. What did the United States gain at the end of the Mexican War?

Can you identify and locate this place?

Mexico City

Can you identify these people?

Zachary Taylor, Winfield Scott, Los Niños Heroicos

Can you define these terms?

Treaty of Guadalupe Hidalgo, Bear Flag Republic

5. AN AMERICAN FAR WEST

Main Ideas

Think about the following Main Idea questions as you read this section:

1. Why did the Mormons move to Utah?

2. How did people get to California during the Gold Rush?

3. What were some important effects of the Gold Rush?

4. How did the government and the white people treat the Native Americans of the West?

MORMONS FIND A HOME IN UTAH

Joseph Smith Proclaims a New Religion

The first of the former Mexican lands to be settled was Utah. It was settled by an American religious group, the **Mormons**.

The Mormon Church, or Church of Jesus Christ of Latter-day Saints, was started fifteen years before the Mexican War began. A young farmer from New York State, Joseph Smith, started it in 1830. Mormons believe that Smith was guided by an angel to discover ancient writings buried in the ground. These writings became the *Book of Mormon*. This book is sacred to Mormons, just as the Bible is to other Christians. The *Book of Mormon*, plus other messages that Smith said came from Heaven, form the basis of what Mormons believe.

The Mormons Make Enemies

The Mormon religion seemed strange to non-Mormons. In 1821 Smith and his followers were forced to move from New York State. They went to Ohio, then to Missouri, then to Illinois. Wherever they settled, they made enemies and were forced to leave. They were against slavery, which made them unwelcome in the slave state of Missouri. They voted as a group, and so people feared their political power. Their successful farms made people jealous. Mormon men were allowed to have more than one wife, and non-Mormons saw this as a sin.

In 1844, in Illinois, Joseph Smith was arrested and killed by an anti-Mormon mob. The Mormons chose a new leader, **Brigham Young**. In 1846, Young led thousands of Mormons west out of Illinois. Not even Young was sure where they were going.

Brigham Young Leads the Mormons to the Great Salt Lake

On the other side of the Rocky Mountains, Young found a home for the Mormons. He decided that they should settle in Utah, along the western edge of the Rockies, near Utah's Great Salt Lake. The land was a desert, but the soil was good. So the Mormons dug ditches and canals to bring water down from the mountains. They worked together to build Salt Lake City and many successful farms.

Some of the Mormons started small trading posts along the wagon train routes. They sold supplies to people who were moving west. The Mormon community grew. In 1850 Utah became a territory with Brigham Young as governor.

THE CALIFORNIA GOLD RUSH AND THE FORTY-NINERS

Gold Is Discovered at Sutter's Mill

In 1848, California's only government was a small American army. There were no laws, no police, and no courts. The Californios did not know exactly what land they owned, so no one knew what land was free to be settled. People began farms wherever they wanted, even in the middle of the Californios' ranches. Many Californios lost their land, even though the federal government had promised Mexico to protect the Californios' rights.

In January, 1848, at a sawmill on John Sutter's ranch in northern California, gold was discovered. Sutter tried to keep the discovery quiet. But the news soon reached San Francisco, and everyone rushed to get rich. Sutter's land was taken over by thousands of people looking for gold.

The Forty-Niners

As the news spread, people from Oregon, Mexico, Hawaii, and even South America came to California. Easterners, too, joined the rush for gold. Between 60,000 and 100,000 people arrived in 1849. They were nicknamed **forty-niners** for the year of their arrival.

Most forty-niners were men who left their homes, families, stores, or farms for the chance to get rich quick. Almost every American town lost men to gold fever.

People came to California any way they could. Some went by ship around South America, which took six months. Others took a ship to Panama and crossed the Panama jungle to the Pacific Ocean. Many got sick before they could get a ship to San Francisco. Empty ships stood in San Francisco harbor because their sailors had left to look for gold.

But most people came by land: on horseback, on foot, and by wagon train. Many tried to find a shortcut and became trapped in the desert or mountains. Those who made it usually took a mountain pass discovered by the African American mountain man Jim Beckwourth.

▲ *Men panning for gold. Looking for gold in this way was tedious, back-breaking work. For hours on end, miners would stoop, fill their pans with dirt and rocks from the bottom of the stream, and carefully try to sift the gold out. If they were lucky, a panful held a few precious specks of gold.*

Not Many Miners Get Rich

At first it was easy to pick gold out of the California streams. Miners used simple tools like a flat pan to separate the gold flakes from the pebbles in the stream bed. Everyone was equal, because everyone searched for his own gold.

But as gold became scarce and more people came, miners tried to keep newcomers out—particularly Mexicans. Mexican miners were attacked by gangs of Americans. All foreign miners had to pay an extra tax.

In the end, only a few forty-niners got rich. The average miner found about $25 worth of gold a day, but could not save much. In California, flour cost $800 a barrel and eggs were $3 each! Back East, a worker earned only $3 a day, but he paid far less for what he needed.

Food was expensive because the miners refused to stop mining long enough to hunt or farm. They all had to buy food. But because so few people farmed, there was not much fresh food to buy. Economists—people who study the economy—would say that the demand for food was much bigger than the supply of food. Whenever the demand is larger than the supply, prices go up. Therefore, it was the merchants who sold food and other supplies who became rich, not the miners. Many miners returned home disappointed or moved to Oregon or Nevada to try their luck at new gold or silver fields .

The Effects of the Gold Rush

The Gold Rush changed the West. Because so many people wanted to go California, transportation changed much faster than it would have without the rush for gold. A train crossed Panama by 1855. American ship builders built slim, fast **clipper ships** with many sails. Clipper ships cut the sailing time between New York and California to three months. In the 1850's the Butterfield Overland Stage Company ran stage coaches from St. Louis, Missouri, to San Francisco. In 1860 the famous **Pony Express** delivered mail between Missouri and California in ten days. The very next year, a telegraph line to California was completed. It sent messages across the country in one day and put the Pony Express out of business. Everyone wanted a railroad across the country, but Congress kept fighting over whether the route should be through the North or the South.

At the beginning of the Gold Rush, California was still a territory. It had no real government. Congress could not agree on whether it should be a free state or a slave state. Finally, people in California decided for themselves. In 1849 they wrote a state constitution that did not allow slaves. A governor and congressmen were elected. John C. Frémont was elected as a senator. The government couldn't start, though, until Congress made California a state. And Congress was still fighting over whether the rest of the West would be free or slave.

A Growing West

The West kept growing. People kept coming with dreams of freedom and of getting rich. The offer of free land brought settlers to Washington and Oregon. Discoveries of silver and gold brought them to Nevada, New Mexico, and Colorado. New Mexico's herds of sheep and Texas and Utah's herds of cattle grew. As the West grew, so did its businesses. Oregon farmers sent their vegetables to California. Washington's lumber was shipped to California to build new towns.

The whites who settled the West paid little attention to the rights of native peoples who already lived there. In Washington and Oregon angry groups of Indians attacked settlers. But they were soon defeated by the militia and the army, forced to sign treaties giving up their land, and placed on reservations. In California the Indians were almost wiped out by disease and by the guns of the forty-niners. In New Mexico, a revolt by the Pueblo Indians of Taos was quickly put down, but Apaches and other tribes fought against whites for 40 years after the Mexican War.

The West had changed completely from 1830 to 1850. In 1830, there were only a few Americans in Texas and only a handful of American trappers and traders in the Rocky Mountains. The land west of the Rockies either belonged to Mexico or was shared by the United States and Britain. Twenty years later, Texas had become an American state and all the western lands belonged to the United States. If Congress could ever agree on the issue of slavery, the governments in the West could begin.

SECTION REVIEW

Can you answer these Main Idea questions?

1. Why did the Mormons move to Utah?

2. How did people get to California during the Gold Rush?

3. What were some important effects of the Gold Rush?

4. How did the government and the white people treat the Native Americans of the West?

Can you identify and locate these places?

Utah, Salt Lake City

Can you identify these people?

Joseph Smith, Mormons, Brigham Young

Can you define these terms?

Gold Rush, forty-niners, Pony Express

AFTER YOU READ

Discussion Questions

1. How did the Mexicans act towards the Americans who settled in their territory? How did the Americans act towards the Mexicans?

2. What is Manifest Destiny and how did it lead to the Mexican War?

3. Discuss why Americans wanted to move to the Far West and the problems they met during their move.

4. How did the California Gold Rush affect life in the rest of the United States?

Comprehension Questions

1. Create a timeline for each set of events. First, put the events in the order in which they happened. Locate the date each happened and then place them on a timeline.

   SET 1

   Mexico becomes an independent country

   Lewis and Clark expedition

   Texas becomes part of the United States

   Santa Anna attacks the Alamo

   Texas declared an independent country

   SET 2

   A telegraph line reaches across the country

   Mormons first settle near the Salt Lake

   The Pony Express delivers mail

   Gold is discovered in California

2. Choose one of the two sets of events and write a sentence about each of the events on that timeline. Then turn those sentences into a well-organized paragraph about those events.

Writing Activity

Choose one of the situations below. List five details and events which might happen to a person living that type of life. Add some thoughts and feelings that you think such a person might have.

A mountain man in the Rockies in the 1820's.

An American rancher in Texas in 1836.

A rich Mexican rancher in California in 1842, when the U.S. Navy arrived.

An American pioneer on the Oregon Trail.

An American soldier in Mexico City during the Mexican War.

Now pretend that you are the person you wrote about and choose one event from your list. Write a letter about the event as if you were that person. Describe where you are, what is happening, and what you are feeling. Try to make your descriptions so complete that someone reading your letter could guess which person you are, even without you ever mentioning it.

BROTHER AGA
THE WAR BETV

Less than one hundred years after its birth, the United States faced its hardest, cruelest test—civil war. During the course of four years of bloody fighting, the nation's future was determined no less surely than it had been determined during the Revolution. Because the North won, we have the United States that have today: one nation, the most powerful in the world and the destination of more immigrants than any other country.

This is not to say that the United States is perfect. Far from it. And one of our most troublesome problems, the treatment of and opportunities available to our African American citizens, is the stubbornly lingering remnent of the major issue— slavery—which had nearly torn us apart in the mid-1800s.

However, consider how different history would have been had the South succeeded in seceding. Our one nation would be two, or possibly more if other sections had then gone their own way. A superpower would instead be a collection of smaller countries, perhaps with continuing hostilities between them, like the Balkans and parts of Eastern Europe. And there might still have been slavery. Nothing would have been the same.

If nations have souls, then the Civil War was a struggle for the United States' soul. Its outcome determined . . . everything, which the United States has touched. And that is nearly everything in the world.

CONFLICT AND DIVISION

For thirty years after the Missouri Compromise of 1820, the North and the South continued to grow further and further apart. In the 1850's, the split got even worse. Southerners tried to make slavery legal in the new territories and states, while Northerners tried to stop them. Old agreements were replaced by new agreements that weren't kept. Violence flared. At the center of it all was a single issue that neither side could give in on: slavery. The South thought that slavery was right and good; the North thought it was wrong and evil. On each side, people listened to those who held the strongest ideas, or who yelled the loudest. The country seemed headed towards something terrible—a time when no more compromise or understanding would be possible.

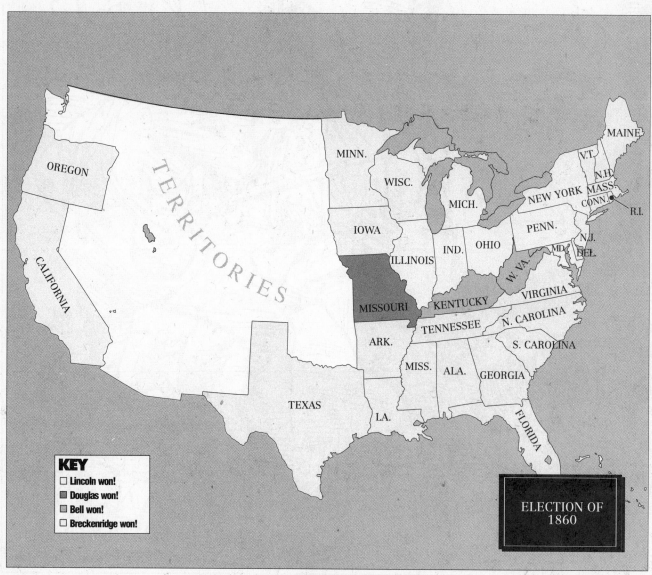

KEY
☐ Lincoln won!
■ Douglas won!
▨ Bell won!
☐ Breckenridge won!

ELECTION OF 1860

BEFORE YOU READ

Sections in This Chapter

1. Splits between North & South
2. The Breakup of the Union

Reading a Map

On the opposite page is a map showing the results of the 1860 Presidential election. Use it and the key showing what the different shadings stand for to answer the questions below.

1. What were the names of the four men running for President in 1860?

2. Think about the ideas important to each part of the country. Which candidate received the anti-slavery votes? Which candidate received the pro-slavery votes?

3. Who won the election and which parts of the country voted for him?

4. Predict how the other parts of the country will react to his election?

Understanding a Key Concept:
TECHNOLOGY AND WAR

When something happens that people don't like, they have a choice about how they will react.

- They can try and change whatever they don't like by passing new laws and electing new people.

- They can compromise, with each side giving up something to gain something.

- They can yell and scream to get their way, but they won't hurt anyone.

- They can fight and even go to war.

Each of the following events happened in United States history. Finish each question by telling the way people acted. The first is done for you.

1. When Boston colonists didn't like the British tax on tea, they <u>dumped the tea in Boston Harbor</u>.

2. Thomas Jefferson didn't like the Alien and Sedition Acts, so when he became President he_____ .

3. During Andrew Jackson's time, South Carolina didn't like the tariff laws, so it _____ .

4. When some people didn't like what Andrew Jackson was doing, they started _____ .

5. In 1820, Missouri wanted to become a state, but Congress disagreed about whether or not it would be a free state or a slave state, so it _____ .

Making Use of What You Already Know

Match each word with the phrase below which best defines it.

abolitionists   Supreme Court   Congress
federal   secede   union   territory

1. a central government made of many states

2. joining together

3. to leave a government

4. highest court in the United States

5. federal legislature

6. land belonging to a country, but not a state

7. people who wanted to free all the slaves

1. SPLITS BETWEEN NORTH & SOUTH

 Main Ideas

Think about the following Main Idea questions as you read this section:

1. What were the parts of the Compromise of 1850? How could it pass when no one supported the entire bill?

2. How did the underground railroad work?

3. Why did the reaction of the North to the Fugitive Slave Law and to *Uncle Tom's Cabin* upset people in the South?

THE COMPROMISE OF 1850 AND ITS CONSEQUENCES

Henry Clay Proposes a Compromise Over Slavery in the Territories

In the 1840's, Congress knew the Far West needed a government, but it couldn't agree on how the government should be set up. The South wouldn't allow free states or free territories, while the North wouldn't allow ones with slaves.

Finally, Henry Clay presented a compromise, known as the Compromise of 1850:

1. California would become a free state.
2. Utah and New Mexico would be organized into territories. Each would decide if it wanted to allow slaves or not.
3. Congress would pay off the money that the old Texas Republic still owed.
4. The slave trade would no longer be allowed in Washington, D.C.
5. A new Fugitive Slave Law would force people, even in the North, to return fugitive, runaway, slaves.

The Fight Over the Compromise

For a long time, Congress fought about the different parts of the compromise. President Zachary Taylor was against it, but he died suddenly while in office. His Vice-President, Millard Fillmore, became President. Fillmore was in favor of the compromise.

In the South, Senator John C. Calhoun of South Carolina attacked the Compromise. He wanted more slave territories. Other Southern Congressmen said that if the balance between the North and South in Congress changed, the South would **secede**. This means that the Southern states would leave the United States and form their own country.

In the North, people were against the Compromise for many reasons. Many were against the stronger Fugitive Slave Law. Northern farmers and workers were afraid that allowing slave labor in the territories would take jobs and money away from them. Abolitionists wanted slavery destroyed everywhere.

Since no one liked the whole Compromise of 1850, Congress voted on each part separately. All of the parts passed. Most people hoped the fight over slavery in the territories was finally over. It wasn't, and the nation's other differences did not go away, either.

The Balance in Congress Changes

When California became a free state, the balance in Congress changed. For the first time, there were more free states than slave states. This meant that there were more "Northern" senators than "Southern" ones.

The South had voted for the compromise, but it still wanted to restore the balance by adding more slave states. Southern politicians even looked outside the country to find them. They tried to buy Cuba from Spain in 1854, but were not successful.

As more Northerners turned against slavery, Southerners grew angrier. They wrote stronger slave laws and refused to listen to anyone who said their way of life should change.

THE UNDERGROUND RAILROAD AND THE FUGITIVE SLAVE LAW

The Underground Railroad Helps Slaves Escape

For many years, slaves were helped to escape by the Underground Railroad. This was not a real railroad, but a network of people who hid escaped slaves and helped them travel to freedom. Freed and escaped blacks called "conductors" led small groups of slaves out of the South.

The best-known conductor was the heroic **Harriet Tubman**. She returned to the South 19 times and led more than 300 slaves to freedom.

Other slaves came on their own, traveling north at night by following the North Star.

All kinds of people were part of the Underground Railroad. They hid and fed the runaways and helped them reach the next stop.

During the day, the runaways hid at "stations"—hiding places in the homes of friendly people. They might be barns, basements, or secret spaces under floors. The escaped slaves traveled at night, always listening for the slave catchers. Many went to Canada, where they could not be sent back to their owners.

The South called the Underground Railroad organized stealing. They wanted the Northern states to stop it, but nothing was done.

The North Resists the Fugitive Slave Law

The Fugitive Slave Law made matters worse. Southerners thought it would make the slavery system stronger. Instead, it turned more and more Northerners against slavery.

Sometimes, when escaped slaves were caught in a Northern city, people tried to keep them from being returned to slavery. Abolitionists bought their freedom, or huge crowds took them from the slave catchers. One time, it took 1100 soldiers to put one slave on a ship because so many people were trying to free him!

Because of the Fugitive Slave Laws, for the first time many Northern whites saw slave catchers chain and whip black people. They were shocked, and they felt that no human being should be treated this way. They began listening to speeches by former slaves, such as Frederick Douglass and Sojourner Truth. They read Abolitionist newspapers, like the ones published by Douglass and William Lloyd Garrison. More and more Northerners came to understand the evil of slavery.

Uncle Tom's Cabin Becomes the Most Important Book Against Slavery

One of the people upset by the Fugitive Slave Law was **Harriet Beecher Stowe**. She came from a family famous for their strong stands on slavery, education, and women's rights. Although she knew little about Southern life,

Harriet Tubman. Slave, escapee from slavery, conductor on the Underground Railroad, and later, during the Civil War, nurse, spy, and scout. Tubman was a woman of immense personal courage and conviction.

she wrote a book about called **Uncle Tom's Cabin**. The story was about a slave named Tom and the Southern whites, some kind and some cruel, who owned him and controlled his life.

Uncle Tom's Cabin came out in 1852. People everywhere read it. It quickly became the most important book against slavery. It did more than discuss slavery as an evil idea: it made readers feel the pain of the black characters. In the North, readers began to wonder if any person should be a slave.

Southerners hated the book. Some Southerners said that Stowe wrote it because she wanted to tear the country apart.

THE KANSAS-NEBRASKA ACT AND ITS CONSEQUENCES

A Compromise Over a Railroad

Now that the United States stretched from the Atlantic to the Pacific, everyone wanted a railroad across the country. Because of the cost, only one route across the country could be built. There were two possibilities: one route than ran west from New Orleans, and one route that ran west from Chicago, Illinois. Both routes had problems. The southern route, through New Orleans, ran partly through territory owned by Mexico. The northern route ran through wilderness territory west of Iowa and Missouri.

Secretary of War Jefferson Davis, who was from the South, wanted the southern route. He arranged to buy land from Mexico to make the southern route more favorable.

Senator Stephen Douglas of Illinois wanted to build the route through his own state. In order to do so, he wanted the Nebraska territory to become a state, which would make the northern route more attractive. (Originally, the area that became the Kansas and Nebraska territories was one territory.)

However, Southern politicians were against this idea. Since Nebraska was north of the Missouri Compromise line, it would become

a free state. This would give the North more power in Congress. The South didn't want this.

To gain the support of the South, Douglas proposed a compromise. He suggested splitting the Nebraska territory into two parts, Kansas and Nebraska. The question of whether each territory would be free or slave would be left to the settlers in that territory, who could vote on it. Letting the settlers in an area determine whether slavery would be allowed is called **popular sovereignty**. Douglas expected that the northern territory, Nebraska, would be free, while the southern one, Kansas, would have slavery.

Douglas hoped that by supporting popular sovereignty, he would get the support of the South. The act which would create the Kansas and Nebraska territories and give the people of each the right to vote on slavery was called the Kansas-Nebraska Act.

Northerners were against the act. They wanted a northern railroad, but they also wanted to keep the territories as places with no slavery.

Southerners were for the act. They wanted the right to bring slaves wherever they lived. They felt that the Kansas-Nebraska Act would make it easier to establish slavery in other Western territories.

There was a great deal of debate about the Kansas-Nebraska Act. It finally passed, but only because every Southern Congressman voted for it.

Northern States Pass Personal Liberty Laws

Many Northerners felt that the South had broken Congress' earlier compromises by allowing slavery to spread into the territories. For instance, the Kansas-Nebraska Act meant that the part of the Missouri Compromise that prohibited slavery in the territories was no longer in force. Some Northern states now decided not to obey the parts of the compromises that favored the South.

Eleven Northern states passed Personal Liberty Laws that protected blacks from the slave catchers. These laws were against the Fugitive

Slave Law. Some states even nullified the law, so that no one in the state had to obey it.

Twenty years earlier, South Carolina had threatened to nullify President Jackson's tariff law. This time Northern states used nullification against a Southern law.

"BLEEDING KANSAS"

Settlers Come from the South and the North

Trouble began right away in the new Kansas Territory. Settlers arrived before the government had made treaties with the Indians. There was no land for sale, but the settlers began farms anyway.

Most settlers came from nearby states. Some came from the neighboring slave state of Missouri. Others came from the free states of the Old Northwest.

A few settlers were sent by New England abolitionists. They promised the abolitionists that they would vote against slavery. This angered people in nearby slave states. Very few slaves ever lived in Kansas, but settlers from the South believed slaves should be allowed there.

An Illegal Election in Kansas

In March 1855, Kansas settlers chose between a pro-slavery government and a **free soil** (anti-slavery) one.

Thousands of pro-slavery men from Missouri crossed the border and illegally voted in Kansas. They wanted a slave state next to them. Although fewer than 3,000 men could legally vote in Kansas, over 6,000 votes were counted. The pro-slavery government won. The election was not legal, but President Pierce did nothing about it.

People all over Kansas were forced to choose sides. The pro-slavery government wrote a constitution and strict slave laws. It then asked Congress to allow Kansas to become a slave state.

The free-soil people formed another government and asked Congress to make Kansas a free state. Kansas was tearing itself apart.

Violence Explodes in Kansas

In 1856, the trouble in Kansas turned into violence. Hundreds of pro-slavery people from Missouri attacked Lawrence, Kansas, where many free-soil people lived. They destroyed a hotel and a newspaper office.

A few nights later, John Brown, a fiercely religious abolitionist, gathered a small group of free-soil men together. They murdered five pro-slavery settlers in revenge for the Lawrence raid, although none of their victims had anything to do with it.

In return, people from Missouri attacked John Brown and his family. Brown fled, but by the end of the year two hundred people had died in Kansas. Towns were burned. Neighbors fought their neighbors. The territory became known as **Bleeding Kansas**.

In 1857, Congress asked everyone in Kansas to vote on a pro-slavery state constitution. 11,300 voted against it and only 1,700 voted for it. The Kansas Territory was free, but Congress didn't admit Kansas as a state until 1861.

The Beating of Senator Sumner

Even in the U.S. Senate there was violence over Kansas. Senator Charles Sumner of Massachusetts was a strong believer in abolition. He sometimes angered people with his harsh words. In one speech about Kansas, he attacked both Stephen Douglas and South Carolina's Senator Andrew Butler.

A few days later, Senator Butler's nephew, Congressman Preston Brooks, badly beat Senator Sumner with his cane. Sumner never fully recovered from his injuries.

The beating of Senator Sumner widened the split between the North and South. Northerners saw Brooks as a brutal Southern bully. Southerners saw him as a hero and a gentleman who was defending the honor of his family and his state.

A New Political Party: the Republican Party

Feelings against the Kansas-Nebraska Act were so strong in the North and West that a new political party was formed. Northern Democrats and Northern Whigs joined together to form the **Republican Party**.

Most Republicans were not abolitionists, but they didn't want slavery to spread into the territories. Almost no one in the South joined the party. In 1856, the Republicans nominated the explorer-hero of California, John C. Frémont, for President.

The Democratic Party was the only party that had members all over the country, but it was changing. After the Kansas-Nebraska Act, many anti-slavery Democrats left the party and became Republicans. They didn't trust Stephen Douglas or the Southern Democrats.

In 1856, the remaining Democrats ran a former senator, James Buchanan, for President. They chose him because no one was against him, not because he'd make a good President. The Democrats warned voters that if a Republican was elected, the South might secede. This frightened many people, and Buchanan was elected.

SECTION REVIEW

Can you answer these Main Idea questions?

1. What were the parts of the Compromise of 1850? How could it pass when no one supported the entire bill?

2. How did the Underground Railroad work?

3. Why did the reaction of the North to the Fugitive Slave Law and to *Uncle Tom's Cabin* upset people in the South?

Can you identify these places?

Kansas, Nebraska

Can you identify these people?

Henry Clay, Harriet Tubman, Harriet Beecher Stowe

Can you define these terms?

Compromise of 1850, Fugitive Slave Law, *Uncle Tom's Cabin,* Kansas-Nebraska Act, Republican Party, popular sovereignty, free soil, "Bleeding Kansas"

2. THE BREAKUP OF THE UNION

Main Ideas

Think about the following main idea questions as you read this section:

1. Why did the Democratic Party Split?

2. What were the effects of John Brown's Raid?

TOGETHER BUT APART

The Interdependent Regions

Even as the country was tearing itself apart, there were many reasons for it to stay together. Business was growing in all parts of the country. The parts of the country were interdependent—that is, each part needed the others.

Northern textile factories bought cotton from Southern farmers. Northern ships carried Southern cotton to New England and Europe. The South bought much of its food and goods from the West and the North. If a cotton crop was bad, both Southern farmers and Northern factory owners were hurt. When people from different parts of the country met, they often found that they shared many interests.

The Issue of Slavery

But each section's ideas about slavery kept people apart. In the North, most people wished to stop the spread of slavery into the territories. A far smaller number were also calling for its abolition in the Southern states.

In the South, people believed that all Northerners were abolitionists eager to destroy the Southern way of life. They wanted the right to bring slavery into the territories. Some Southerners said that the only way to solve their problems was to leave the Union.

Other Problems

There were other problems, too. The South's population was not growing, so it was losing power in the House of Representatives. In addition, Southerners felt that their cotton was making the Northern ship owners, factory owners, and merchants rich instead of themselves. They didn't like depending on other parts of the country. They started a few factories and businesses, but most people wanted to stay cotton farmers. They had to keep importing food and other goods.

Many Southerners Want to Secede

The Constitution said that the people of this country came together to form a Union. It said nothing about states leaving that Union. Yet more and more Southerners believed it was their right to leave and start a new country. They didn't stop to think about how much they depended on other states or how the rest of the country would feel about their leaving.

THE DRED SCOTT CASE

Dred Scott Sues for His Freedom

In 1857, the Supreme Court decided an important case. A Missouri slave named Dred Scott had been taken by his owner to live in a free state, and then in a free territory. Later, he was brought back to Missouri. Now he wanted his freedom. He said that living in free areas had made him a free man. The Supreme Court was Dred Scott's last chance for freedom.

Scott lost his case. The majority of the justices said Dred Scott had returned to a slave state, so the free state's laws no longer held. He was still a slave. In addition, seven of the nine

Supreme Court justices said slaves were not citizens. Three of them doubted that any black person was.

The Supreme Court Says That Keeping Slavery Out of the Territories Is Unconstitutional

Most importantly, the Court said that the old Missouri Compromise was unconstitutional. Congress had no power to keep slavery out of any territory. Their reason was that the Constitution said that property cannot be taken away from its owner without due process (court action). Forcing a slave owner to free a slave, who was his property, was against the Constitution.

The Dred Scott Case Divides the Country

People everywhere argued about the Dred Scott case and what the Supreme Court had said. Most people, North and South, probably thought the Court was right about Dred Scott himself. They did not believe that blacks were citizens or had the same rights as whites. But Northerners were angry at the idea that Congress had no right to limit the spread of slavery. The South, on the other hand, was delighted. Southerners began to say that the government had the duty to protect slavery in all the territories.

THE LINCOLN-DOUGLAS DEBATES

Lincoln and Douglas Debate How to Keep Slavery Out of the Territories

In 1858, Illinois Democratic Senator **Stephen Douglas** ran for re-election against **Abraham Lincoln**, a Republican. Lincoln was a well-known local lawyer and politician who had served one term in Congress.

In seven famous debates, Lincoln and Douglas met and spoke at the same meetings. Both men believed that slavery should not be allowed in the territories, no matter what the Supreme Court said. Their speeches were printed in newspapers all over the country. A great many people read what they said.

Lincoln warned, "A house divided against itself cannot stand. I believe this government cannot endure permanently half slave and half free." He pushed Douglas to explain how he would get around the Supreme Court's decision.

Douglas answered that slavery needed to be protected by local laws. If a territory didn't pass those laws, slavery would disappear, no matter what Congress or the Supreme Court said. Douglas won the election, but the Southern Democrats didn't like his answer. Many refused to help him again.

Lincoln Becomes Nationally Famous

Lincoln lost the election, but he became known all over the country. People started paying attention to this poor frontier farmer's son who had challenged the great Stephen Douglas. During the next two years, Lincoln made many speeches, some as far away as New York City. People in the North liked his point of view. They remembered him.

JOHN BROWN'S RAID ON HARPER'S FERRY

John Brown Prepares to Invade the South

John Brown had been chased out of Kansas, but he was preparing another battle in his war against slavery. His ideas were so wild that some people thought he was insane. He planned to invade the South, free the slaves, and organize a new government. Rich abolitionists, who did not understand his plans, gave him money.

In October 1859, Brown and 22 men seized the government building at Harper's Ferry, Virginia. They captured weapons and took hostages. They waited for slaves to join them, but not many slaves lived nearby. None joined them.

Two days later, a force of U.S. Marines led by Colonel Robert E. Lee captured or killed most of Brown's men. Brown himself was tried, found guilty, and hanged.

John Brown. The picture above is taken from a mural in the Kansas State Legislature. Brown is pictured as a wild-haired, fiery-eyed madman, almost like a biblical prophet. He is shown standing astride the coming split in the country between the pro-slavery, secessionist South (on the right, by the Confederate flag) and those states and people that remained loyal to the Union (on the left).

John Brown' Raid Divides the Country Still Further

John Brown's raid was a small battle, but it caused big trouble. In the North, many abolitionists called John Brown a hero. The South suddenly feared a slave revolt. In some places, Northerners were arrested, beaten, or forced to leave the South.

Most Republicans spoke against what Brown did, but the South didn't listen. They continued to believe even more firmly that all Republicans were abolitionists and wanted to destroy them. Soon, more Southerners than ever believed the only way they could keep their way of life was to secede from the Union.

LINCOLN IS ELECTED PRESIDENT, THE SOUTH LEAVES THE UNION

A Strong Republican Party

In 1860, the Republican Party was strong, but only in the North and West. It was against slavery, but it took a stand on other ideas, too. It wanted a high tariff, free land for settlers, and a railroad across the country. Many people joined the party because of these stands, not because of slavery. The Republicans didn't want an abolitionist for President. They chose someone whose stand against slavery was not as strong as the abolitionists'—Abraham Lincoln.

The Democratic Party Splits

The Democratic Party split. The Southern Democrats told Stephen Douglas and the other

Northern Democrats that they must promise to protect slavery both in the South and in the territories. When the Northerners refused, many Southern Democrats left the party. The Northern Democrats nominated Stephen Douglas for President. A new, short-lived party called the National Constitution Union Party nominated a man named John Bell. The Southern Democrats nominated Senator John Breckenridge of Kentucky. Then they warned everyone that if a Republican was elected President, the South would secede.

Lincoln Wins the Election

The Republicans did little to reassure Southerners about what might happen if Lincoln was elected. The vote split along geographic lines. Lincoln received no electoral votes from the ten Southern states, but every Northern state voted for him. Abraham Lincoln was elected President by the North. The balance had changed.

THE SOUTH LEAVES THE UNION

Seven Southern States Secede

A month after Lincoln won the election, South Carolina voted to secede and left the Union. Alabama, Mississippi, and Florida left, too. Georgia, Texas, and Louisiana took longer to decide. A few important people in those states, like Sam Houston in Texas, wanted to stay in the Union. However, those who wanted to secede finally won.

By February 1, 1861, seven states in the lower South had seceded. They said they were no longer part of the United States. One week later, they met to form a government and to write a constitution for their new country.

A New Government for the South

The seven states that left the Union called themselves the **Confederate States of America**, or the **Confederacy**. They elected Jefferson Davis President and set up government offices.

Many Northerners believed that the South was just trying to get its way. They didn't think it would leave permanently. Many Southerners believed that the North would let them go without a fight. Both were wrong. The North and the South were about to begin a long and bloody war—the most costly in American history.

Many things combined to cause the breakup of the Union, but the main problem was the quarrel over the spread of slavery. The South wanted to bring slavery into the new territories and new states that were being formed in the West. The North wanted to keep slavery out. The Fugitive Slave Law, Bleeding Kansas, and the Dred Scott decision outraged Northerners. They formed a new political party, the Republican Party, to express their point of view. *Uncle Tom's Cabin*, the Personal Liberty Laws, John Brown's Raid, and abolitionist writings convinced the South that the North wanted to destroy its way of life. When a Republican, Abraham Lincoln, was elected President, the South felt that its only choice was to secede.

SECTION REVIEW

Can you answer these Main Idea questions?

1. Why did the Democratic Party Split?

2. What were the effects of John Brown's Raid?

Can you identify these people?

Abraham Lincoln, Stephen A. Douglas, John Brown

Can you identify this place?

Harper's Ferry

Can you define these terms?

Confederate States of America, Confederacy

AFTER YOU READ

Discussion Questions

1. How did attitudes toward slavery change in the North and South between 1850 and 1860? What caused these changes?

2. How did the Compromise of 1850 and the Kansas-Nebraska Act lead to the founding of the Republican Party?

3. Why was the election of Abraham Lincoln important, and what events did it cause?

Comprehension Question

The United States had many problems from 1850-1860. People tried many different solutions. Some of the results of these actions, some were what had been intended, and some were not. Below are three columns: one for PROBLEMS one for ACTIONS, and one for RESULTS. Complete the chart, so that all three columns are filled. One is completed for you.

PROBLEM	ACTION	RESULT
Far West needs government	Compromise of 1850	_Balance in Congress changes_
Slaves escape to North	Fugitive Slave Law	
No railroad across country	Kansas-Nebraska Act	
Kansas needs government to become state	Elections in Kansas	
Dred Scott wants freedom	Dred Scott decision by Supreme Court	

Election for Illinois	Lincoln-Douglas debate
South splits Democratic Party	1860 election for President

Writing Activity

How convincing are you? Below are three important issues. Choose one and decide what your stand on it would be. Then follow the directions to write an essay to convince someone of your stand

ISSUES:

People in the North should (or shouldn't) enforce the Fugitive Slave Law.

Kansas should (or shouldn't) have a slave government.

People should (or shouldn't) vote Republican in the 1860 election.

DIRECTIONS:

1. Write an opening paragraph which states where you stand.

2. Brainstorm all the details you can use to support your stand. Write another paragraph using facts to support your stand and to disagree with the opposing viewpoint.

3. Think about what might have happened if enough people had listened to your stand. End your essay with a paragraph which states how history might (or might not) have been different if people had listened to you.

CHAPTER 24

THE CIVIL WAR

The nation's leaders had not been able to work together. On a number of issues—most importantly slavery—the North and the South could not agree. All their attempts at compromise failed. And unfortunately, neither side realized just how strongly the other side felt. Neither expected a long, cruel war. Nevertheless, the country plunged into a Civil War which lasted four bloody years.

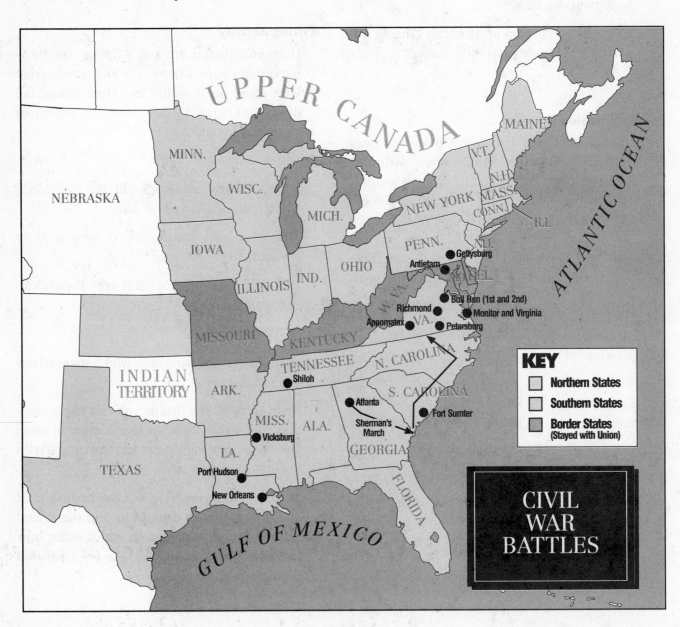

KEY
- Northern States
- Southern States
- Border States (Stayed with Union)

CIVIL WAR BATTLES

BEFORE YOU READ

Sections in This Chapter

1. At the Start of the War
2. The Early War
3. The War Draws to an End

Reading a Map

On the opposite page is map showing Civil War battles. Use this map to answer the questions below.

1. Which states joined the Confederate States of America (the Confederacy)?

2. Which slave states didn't join the Confederacy? What do they have in common?

3. In which section of the country were most of the battles of the Civil War fought? Which do you think suffered more from the Civil War—The Union or the Confederacy?

4. Washington, D.C., the capitial of the United States, is located by the border between Virginia and Maryland. Do you think that this presented a problem for the Union, and if so, why?

Understanding a Key Concept:
TECHNOLOGY AND WAR

The Civil War was the first major war America fought after the Industrial Revolution. During the Industrial Revolution, technology changed: transportation, goods, and weapons were improved, or better ones invented. Much of this technology was used to fight the war. Complete each sentence by writing how you think the new technology was used to win the war. The first is done for you.

1. Machines in shoe factories <u>made enough shoes for all the soldiers</u>.

2. Railroads helped armies _____ .

3. Better guns and bullets _____ .

4. Canned meat and milk helped _____ .

5. Iron-plated steamships _____ .

Making Use of What You Already Know

Think back to what you know about the United States before the Civil War. Answer these questions using one of the following words. Each word can be used more than once.

North   South   West   Union   Confederacy

1. In what parts of the country did most immigrants settle?

2. Which army do you think the immigrants joined?

3. Which part or parts of the country did not grow enough food to feed all its people?

4. Which part or parts of the country grew lots of food?

5. Which side had many factories to make supplies for its army?

6. Which side had more bankers, shippers, and railroads?

7. Which side felt it was protecting its way of life?

8. Which side felt it was protecting the United States Constitution?

1. AT THE START OF THE WAR

Main Ideas

Think about the following Main Idea questions as you read this section:

1. How did the South's government and trade change when it seceded?

2. How did both sides misjudge the other and the effect of the new technology?

THE CIVIL WAR BEGINS

Lincoln Takes Office

Abraham Lincoln took office as President in March 1861. In his first speech, he tried to calm the South. "We are not enemies," he said, "but friends. We must not be enemies." He said he had no right to change slavery in the South, and that he did not want to. But he insisted that the Constitution did not allow any state to secede. Most Southerners never read Lincoln's speech. They continued to believe that he wanted to end slavery and to change the Southern way of life.

The South Fires on Fort Sumter

The Confederacy took over United States forts and weapons in the South. By the time Lincoln became President, only two Southern forts still belonged to the U.S. One was Fort Sumter, on an island in Charleston harbor, South Carolina.

The U.S. soldiers at Fort Sumter were trapped and were running out of supplies. On April 12, 1861, South Carolina asked the fort's commander to surrender. He refused, and South Carolina's soldiers began firing at the fort. They kept firing for two days until the fort surrendered. Fort Sumter now belonged to South Carolina.

Lincoln Prepares for War

When President Lincoln heard that South Carolina had fired on Fort Sumter, he knew that words would not persuade the South to rejoin the Union. He told the country to prepare for war. He asked for 75,000 men to join the army. The Civil War, or the **War Between the States**, had begun.

Four More States Secede, but Others Do Not

Some slave states had not seceded. They were now forced to choose between two bad choices: they could go to war against the Confederate States or against the Union. Most thought that the lower South had acted too fast, but they also believed in the right to secede. When Lincoln called for men, they saw that the North did not agree with that right.

Virginia, North Carolina, Tennessee, and Arkansas voted to secede and join the Confederacy. But four border states—Maryland, Delaware, Kentucky, and Missouri—remained in the Union.

Part of Virginia asked to stay in the Union. It became the new state of West Virginia. Lincoln was very careful not to make the border states angry. He wanted them to stay in the Union.

THE SOUTH

The Confederate Government

The Confederacy was made up of 11 states. Both sides claimed Kentucky and Missouri, but the two states decided to stay with the Union.

The Confederates set up a government that was very similar to the U.S. government. They kept most of the same laws. Government workers kept their jobs, but now they worked for the Confederacy.

The Confederate government was not as strong as the Union government, however. President **Jefferson Davis** didn't get along with his advisors and tried to do too much himself.

Also, the Southern governors sometimes refused to follow his orders because they believed in state's rights.

Confederate Business and Trade

About nine million people lived in the South. Nearly four million of them were slaves. Most people, free and slave, grew cotton. The South had few trains, factories, machines, and ships. They didn't have many skilled craftsmen or engineers who knew how to make the things they needed, like guns and train tracks. During the war, new factories were built, but the South was never able to make everything it needed. Many things had to be brought in from Europe.

The South believed that Britain and France would help them in order to keep getting their cotton. Instead, Britain and France bought cotton from other countries. The British government said that it would not take sides, but the British secretly built ships for the South. They sent supplies, too, but refused to fight.

Because supplies from Europe were so important to the Confederacy, the Union Navy formed a **blockade** to stop Confederate ships. Some Southern ships were able to get past the blockade. They took cotton out and brought goods in. Some ships brought in medicine and army supplies. Others brought expensive goods that were not needed in the war, like silk and coffee. These "blockade runners" got rich, because fancy goods sold for much more than war supplies.

THE NORTH

The Union Government

Twenty-three states made up the North, or the Union. Northerners believed that states had no right to leave the Union. They wanted to prove that a "government of the people" worked. At first, not many Northerners thought that the war was about slavery. They thought it was about preserving, or keeping, the Union.

In the beginning, people didn't think that Abraham Lincoln would do a good job as President. But as the war went on, Lincoln gained people's respect. He made sure that he knew what was going on everywhere in the war. He listened to his advisors, but then made up his own mind. He wasn't afraid to change plans or to use new ideas. And although he had no real military experience, he was better at running the war than Confederate President Davis, who had once been Secretary of War.

Because of the war, Lincoln decided many things without waiting for Congress to pass laws. He made the army bigger and bought war supplies. He also took away some people's rights. He was careful with these powers, though, and only used them to help win the war.

After the South left the Union, most of the remaining Congressmen were Republicans. At first, Congress agreed with everything President Lincoln did. Later, some Congressmen tried to force him to agree with their own ideas about slavery, generals, or peace. He always listened carefully, but in the end he did what he thought was best for the country.

Union Business and Trade

Over 20 million people lived in the North. Most of the country's banks, factories, and trade were there. The war helped these businesses. Shoe, gun, and uniform factories grew because the army bought their products. New England shipyards built Navy ships. Trading ships continued to take wheat and wood to Europe. Textile mills changed from cotton to wool.

The North didn't want Britain to help the Confederates. President Lincoln sent Charles Francis Adams, the son of former President John Quincy Adams, to Britain. Adams worked very hard to keep the British out of the war. He knew the governments in Europe would like to see the United States' democratic government fall apart. He also knew Europe depended on American trade, wheat, and cotton. He hoped they could do without the cotton.

THE ARMIES

The Soldiers

When the Civil War began, the United States had a small army. Then some soldiers and many officers left to join the Confederate army. President Lincoln first called for 75,000 men to join the Union army for three months. Then, when he saw it would be a long war, he called for 300,000 more to join the army for three years. The Confederates called for volunteers, too. Throughout the war, each side kept calling for more men.

Soldiers joined for many reasons. Some believed in what their side was fighting for. Some joined because their friends did, or because they wanted to show off their courage. Still others joined because they got a **bounty**, or payment, and their family needed the money. On both sides, men formed units from their town or neighborhood. Some Northern units were made up of all Irish or German immigrants. Most wanted to have a good time and some did—for a while.

Most soldiers soon found out that the war was not fun and was not going to be over fast. Many soldiers didn't like army rules or army life. The camps were dirty and the marches long. Courage got them killed. Most soldiers were sick and hospitalized several times a year. As they wrote home about these problems, fewer men joined. Some soldiers deserted—that is they quit the army without permission. They saw nothing wrong about leaving a job they hated.

When men stopped joining, both sides began to **draft** men. The government picked names and told these men they had to join the army. But if the person drafted was rich, he could pay someone else to go in his place.

African Americans Join the Union Army

At first, neither side allowed black soldiers. However, some blacks helped the Union as spies, as messengers, or as part of units along the Missouri border. Their bravery impressed many people, until Lincoln finally forced the army to accept black soldiers.

Over 185,000 African Americans joined the Union Army, and 30,000 joined the navy. Some joined in groups, like the Louisiana Native Guards. Other African Americans from all over the Union joined the 54th Massachusetts Regiment. Many of the black soldiers were former slaves led by white officers. But until 1863, most of these soldiers were used as workers instead of fighting in battles.

The Generals

Many of the nation's best generals joined the Confederate army. Robert E. Lee, for example, was one of the country's finest officers. The North wanted him to take charge of the Union army, but he refused. He believed in the Union, but he was from the Virginia and refused to fight his family and neighbors. He became the Confederate Army's most important general.

The hero of the Mexican War, General Winfield Scott, age 75, was the Union's first commanding general. He warned that the war would be long and that many men would die. No one listened to him, and he soon left because of his age. The Union army would have many other commanding generals during the war.

Women in the War

On both sides, women took part in the war. They took over jobs that men used to do, like running the family farm. They sewed uniforms or worked in factories. They organized sending food to the troops. A few even pretended to be men and fought in battle.

Perhaps the most important job done by women was nursing sick and wounded soldiers. In the North more than 3,000 female nurses served during the war. Dorothea Dix, already famous for her work for the mentally ill, was put in charge of them. (There were male nurses, too; the poet Walt Whitman was one.)

Clara Barton, a clerk in Washington, D.C., became the best known of the Union army nurses.

She was called "the Angel of the Battlefield," and her courage was famous. Once, her hospital was shelled while she was helping a doctor with an operation. All the male nurses around her ran for cover. She was the only one who remained to help the doctor. After the war she founded the American Red Cross.

There were other famous women in the war. Through 19 battles, "Mother" Mary Ann Bickerdyke took care of the soldiers, rounded up food for them, cooked for them, and even did their washing—all while working to improve health conditions in the camps. In the South, nurse Sally Tompkins and her staff took care of more than 1300 wounded soldiers and saved 1260 of them. But in spite of the work of the nurses, many soldiers still died from sickness and wounds.

African American women worked for the war, too, including famous ones. Harriet Tubman, who had led so many slaves to freedom, was a nurse. The great abolitionist speaker Sojourner Truth was a spy.

THE WAR PLANS

Two Sides That Misjudged Each Other

Each side had its own plan for fighting the war. The South's plan was to protect its land until the North got tired of fighting. They didn't think that would take very long.

The Union planned to move into the South and quickly crush the Confederate government. They would need many men to do it, but they had millions who could help. They were sure that the South would have to give up if the war lasted long enough.

Neither side understood how important winning the war was to the other. If the South gave up, they would have to admit they were wrong about slavery and states' rights. If the North stopped fighting, they would have to agree to the South becoming a separate country. The Union and the Constitution would mean nothing. So neither side was willing to end the war.

A New Kind of War

The Civil War was different from all the wars before it. It was the first war to use the technology invented during the Industrial Revolution. Railroads, the telegraph, iron-covered steamships, new rifles and bullets, and even submarines and balloons were used by one side or both. The North had an advantage in that it had more factories to build these things, and more people who knew how to use them.

Most generals, however, had very little idea of how the new technology would change battles. They tried to use old ways of fighting with these new tools of war. Even though new rifles and bullets killed men a quarter mile away, generals still made their men rush toward the firing guns.

Another change was in how the public learned about the war. Reporters sent their newspaper stories back by telegraph, on the same day as the battle. Photographs showed how terrible the war was. It was the first time a war came into everybody's home.

SECTION REVIEW

Can you answer these Main Idea questions?

1. How did the South's government and trade change when it seceded?

2. How did both sides misjudge the other and the effect of the new technology?

Can you identify this place?

Fort Sumter

Can you identify these people?

Jefferson Davis, Clara Barton

Can you define these terms?

blockade, bounty, draft

2. THE EARLY WAR

Main Ideas

Think about the following Main Idea questions as you read this section:

1. Why were people shocked after the battles at Bull Run and Shiloh?

2. Why did the South's General Lee change his plans, and how were his new plans different?

3. In what ways did life in the South change during the war?

UNION FAILURES IN THE EAST AND SUCCESSES IN THE WEST

A Union Defeat at the First Battle of Manassas (Bull Run)

On July 21, 1861, the first major battle of the war took place. The Union army marched out of Washington. They expected to easily capture the railroads at the small Virginia town of **Manassas** Junction. Since the fighting was so close to Washington, many people packed a picnic and went to watch the Union win.

The armies met at a small stream called **Bull Run**. The Union army almost won, but most Union soldiers had never been in a battle before. When the Southern general **"Stonewall" Jackson** and his men began to attack, many Union soldiers turned and ran. The roads back to Washington were crowded with frightened on-lookers and scared soldiers. The Confederates won, but they did not try to take Washington.

After the Union disaster at Bull Run, the North realized both that it was going to be a long war, and that they were not prepared for it.

General **George McClellan** was put in command of the Union army. Congress gave him everything he wanted. For the rest of the year, he

trained and trained his men. He trained them well, but after a while, people began asking if he was ever going to fight.

Grant's Victories in the Mississippi Valley

The earliest Union victories were in the West. Early in 1862, Union armies moved into Kentucky and Tennessee. Boats of the Union navy worked with General Ulysses Grant and his western Union army to take Confederate forts along the Cumberland and Tennessee rivers. Then Grant and his men headed south.

But on April 6, 1862, a Confederate army surprised Grant at Shiloh in Tennessee. The Confederates gave their terrible "rebel yell" and rushed toward the Union guns. The Union line was pushed back until the second day, when more Union soldiers arrived. Then they moved forward until the Confederates finally were forced to leave. The Union army didn't follow.

Everyone was shocked at how many men lay dead and wounded. More men fell at Shiloh, in two days of fighting, than had died in the American Revolution plus the War of 1812 plus the Mexican War.

In late April, the Union navy took New Orleans, the South's most important port and business city. It seemed that Union troops would soon control the whole Mississippi River Valley and split the Confederacy.

McClellan Fails to Capture the Confederate Capital of Richmond

In the spring of 1862, General McClellan finally decided to attack the Confederate capital at Richmond, Virginia. He moved his men and supplies to the Virginia coast. But he had taken so long that the Confederates were ready for him.

The Confederates had put guns and iron plates on a wooden steamship, the *Merrimack*. They renamed it the **Virginia**. It guarded the river that

The Monitor *and the* Virginia. *These two ironclad (iron covered) ships fought for hours, often at point blank range, as shown above. Cannonballs ricocheted from their armoured sides, like hailstones off a car's windscreen. Any wooden ship would have burned-up or sunk. In an afternoon, the Age of Sail was over, and the navies of the world were obsolete.*

led to Richmond. On its first day, it easily sank two Union ships that were helping protect McClellan's army. The next morning, however, it fought an iron-covered Union ship, the **Monitor**. This was the world's first battle between iron ships. It ended with neither ship losing or much damaged. Later, the *Monitor* left the area, and the *Virginia* did not destroy any more Union ships. But it continued to protect the river that led to Richmond.

In April, McClellan started his march from the Virginia coast towards Richmond. By the end of May he was only a few miles away from the city. He was expecting help from a Union army in western Virginia.

That help never came. Confederate generals **Robert E. Lee** and Stonewall Jackson had tied up the army in several hit-and-run battles. Then Lee attacked McClellan's army. Finally, the Union army was forced back to the coast. In July, the effort to capture Richmond was called off.

LEE TRIES TO END THE WAR

Lee Takes His Army North

The Confederate leaders knew that the longer the war went on, the less chance they had to win. They would run out of men and supplies long before the North would.

General Lee changed the South's plan. He decided to take his army into the North to cut off Washington, D.C., from the rest of the country. In August a second battle was fought at Bull Run, and again the Union troops went rushing back to Washington. Lee's army moved north toward Pennsylvania.

Lee's Army Is Turned Back at Antietam

By luck, Lee's orders to his officers were captured. The information told McClellan exactly where Lee was and what he planned to do. On September 17, 1862, McClellan rushed his men to Sharpsburg, near **Antietam** Creek in Maryland, and forced the Confederates to fight.

It was the bloodiest single day of the war, but Lee's move into the North was stopped. The Confederates returned south. The Union army didn't follow. President Lincoln was pleased with the victory, but upset that the Confederates got away. He removed McClellan and put another general in charge of the army.

The Emancipation Proclamation

The Union victory at Antietam gave President Lincoln an opportunity he had been waiting for. Many people wanted him to emancipate, or free, the slaves. Congress had already freed the slaves in Washington, D.C., and those slaves who had escaped into the North. In addition, Congress had ended slavery in the territories. But Lincoln did not want to do anything more until the Union had won a major battle.

Finally, Lincoln wrote the **Emancipation Proclamation**. After the Union victory at Antietam, he announced it. The Emancipation Proclamation said that on January 1, 1863, all slaves in the rebelling states would be free. Slaves in the Union's border states weren't free, yet.

Lincoln believed that this was a step toward making it true that "all men are created equal."

African American Soldiers Join in the Fighting

1863 was an important year for the Union's African American soldiers. As news of the Emancipation Proclamation reached the Confederacy, many slaves escaped to join the Union Army.

The Confederacy warned that any black soldier they captured would be killed. But that didn't stop the Union's African American soldiers. They took part in three battles during 1863: **Port Hudson**, **Milliken's Bend**, and **Fort Wagner**.

Everyone praised their skill and bravery. By the end of the war, African Americans had taken part in 449 battles, and 23 African American

soldiers had earned the Congressional Medal of Honor, the nation's highest award for bravery.

TWO GREAT UNION VICTORIES

Grant Captures Vicksburg and Controls the Mississippi

In April 1863, Grant moved to capture **Vicksburg**, an important city built on a bend of the Mississippi River. If Vicksburg was captured, the Confederates wouldn't be able to get men and supplies from Texas, Louisiana, or Arkansas. The Confederacy would be split, and the Union would control the Mississippi River.

Vicksburg, however, had the river, swamps, and an army to protect it. To get around these obstacles, Grant made a plan that most Civil War generals would not have tried: his men circled the town and attacked it from an unexpected direction. They surrounded Vicksburg and cut it off from the rest of the Confederate army.

Grant's guns shelled the town for six weeks. The town's people had to live underground. Food ran low. Finally, on July 4, 1863, the Confederate army at Vicksburg surrendered. A week later, the Union controlled the whole Mississippi River. The Confederacy was cut in two.

The Union Wins the Greatest Battle of the War at Gettysburg

While Grant was attacking Vicksburg in the West, Lee took his Confederate army into the North again. Several battles were fought, and thousands of men died. In one of them, Stonewall Jackson was shot by his own men. It was dark, and they thought he was a Union soldier. Jackson's death was a great loss to the South. He had been one of their most brilliant generals.

The greatest battle of the Civil War began by accident. On July 1, 1863, some Confederate soldiers were shopping for shoes in **Gettysburg**, Pennsylvania. They ran into some Union soldiers and a fight began. Each side sent for help.

The 54th Massachusetts Colored Regiment attacking Fort Wagner. They charged the fort's walls, into the teeth of cannon and rifle fire. The men of the 54th Massachusetts took over forty percent casualties—almost three hundred men out of six hundred died—displaying a terrible, doomed courage. The movie Glory *commerates their bravery and sacrifice.*

The armies formed long lines and faced each other for almost fifty miles. The Confederates gave their rebel yell as they ran at the Union guns, but this time they didn't break through. Finally, three days later, Lee pulled his men back and left the North. The date was July 4, 1863, the same day that Grant took Vicksburg—and the anniversary of the United States declaring independence from Britain. Once again, the Union army didn't follow the Confederates, and a good chance to capture the Confederate Army was lost.

More than forty thousand men were killed or wounded at Gettysburg—more than in any other Civil War battle.

The Gettysburg Address

Four months after the battle, Abraham Lincoln came to Gettysburg. His great speech, the **Gettysburg Address**, reminded the Union of the liberty they were fighting for. He promised that "these dead shall not have died in vain . . . and that the government of the people, by the people and for the people shall not perish [die out] from the earth."

AWAY FROM THE BATTLEFIELDS

Life in the Union

Much of life in the Union had nothing to do with the war. Congress passed the Homestead Act, which gave western settlers free land. People went west looking for their dreams. Gold was discovered in Colorado. New land was settled. The Indians were moved once again. Many businesses grew quickly. Some, like Borden's milk and Armour's meats, sold their products to the army. A few businesses grew because they illegally sold to the South or sold poor goods at very high prices.

Decline in the South

In the South, however, the war was the most important thing, and it was not going well. Many of the South's railroads, telegraphs, and roads were wearing out or had been destroyed, and the South didn't have the materials or skilled workers to fix them. Not many ships got past the tight Union blockade, so few supplies came in and no cotton left. Most farms grew food for the army. On smaller farms, women planted, picked, and even pulled plows. They ran plantations, too. The men were all in the army.

Many Confederate soldiers were unhappy. They ate rotten food, had few clothes, and their pay was very late. Many didn't care about slavery or the Confederacy anymore. Most were small farmers who just wanted to go home. Some deserted—that is, they left the army without permission. They returned home and hid, or joined together and stole from farms and both armies. Since most men were already fighting, there were no more left to take the place of those who deserted or died.

SOUTHERNERS BEGAN TO THINK THAT THEY MIGHT LOSE THE WAR

Foreign Affairs

Vicksburg and Gettysburg showed the world that the North could win. Ambassador Charles Francis Adams warned the British that they must stop building ships for the Confederacy or the Union would fight them, too. The British didn't like slavery, so after the Emancipation Proclamation and Adams' warning, they stopped.

France took advantage of the war. They sent soldiers to Mexico and made a European, Prince Maximilian, the Emperor of Mexico. The Union demanded that they leave, but could do nothing

about it until after the war. The French were finally driven out of Mexico in 1867.

Draft Riots in New York

When the North started drafting soldiers, riots broke out in many of its cities. They were called **draft riots**, but the rioters were not just against going into the army; they were angry because the rich could pay to not be drafted. Poor men were forced to become soldiers and were killed, while richer men stayed home.

In addition, some rioters were anti-black. Many were Irish workers who had lost their jobs to free black workers who were paid less. They were afraid more jobs would be lost if thousands of freed slaves came North after the war.

New York's draft riots were the worst. Mobs burned draft offices, destroyed black homes and businesses, and killed or beat up any black people they met. Union soldiers had to be sent from Gettysburg to New York to stop the killing.

SECTION REVIEW

Can you answer these Main Idea questions?

1. Why were people shocked after the battles at Bull Run and Shiloh?

2. Why did the South's General Lee change his plans, and how were his new plans different?

3. In what ways did life in the South change during the war?

Can you identify these places?

Mananssas, Bull Run, Antietam, Shiloh, Vicksburg, Gettysburg

Can you identify these people?

Stonewall Jackson, George McClellan, Ulysses S. Grant, Robert E. Lee

Can you define these terms?

Emancipation Proclamation, Gettysburg Address, draft riots

3. THE WAR DRAWS TO AN END

Main Ideas

Think about the following Main Idea questions as you read this section:

1. How did General Grant's and General Sherman's actions lead to the end of the war?

2. How did the war both hurt and help Lincoln's chances for reelection?

3. Compare the losses suffered by the North and by the South.

GRANT AND SHERMAN

Grant Comes East and Moves Against Lee

After Vicksburg, President Lincoln made General Grant commander of all the Union armies. Grant came east and made plans to destroy Lee's Confederate army.

In May 1864, Grant marched south with a huge army to capture Richmond. On the way, they met Lee's men in battle after battle. When the Union army couldn't break through the Confederate lines, they marched around the Confederate army. Instead of short two- or three-day battles, the men of the two armies marched, fought, and died for forty days. Both armies lost many men, but the Union army replaced theirs, while the Confederate army just got smaller.

Finally, in June 1864, Lee's men entered **Petersburg, Virginia**. The Union army could not take the town, so they surrounded it. For nine months they kept Lee's army trapped inside. The Confederates refused to give up, even though they were starving.

Sherman's Destroys Atlanta

As Grant and his army marched into Virginia, General **William Tecumseh Sherman** and his army headed south toward **Atlanta, Georgia**. In August 1864 he captured Atlanta and burned it. More people in the South lost hope.

The March to the Sea

There was no Confederate army between Atlanta and the city of Savannah, on the Georgia coast. Sherman told his men to take what they needed, like food and animals, and to destroy anything the Confederate army might need. He ordered them not to hurt civilians—people who were not soldiers. Then his army began what is called **Sherman's March to the Sea**.

Not all of Sherman's men listened to his orders. Some behaved badly, and most acted as if the march was one long party. For two months, they burned crops and homes. They killed farm animals and drank stolen wine. They destroyed everything from Atlanta to Savannah. Sherman did nothing to stop them. He wanted to show Southerners that the Confederate army could not protect its own people.

After Savannah was captured, Sherman's army marched northward, burning more Southern towns along the coast.

The Election of 1864

In 1864, Lincoln ran for President again. Many people were against the way he had handled the war. Some blamed him for all the dead. A number of people wanted to stop the war, no matter what had to be done. The Democrat Party said they wanted peace. They ran General McClellan for President, even though he didn't support their peace plan.

Then, in September, the news came that General Sherman had captured Atlanta. People now thought that the war might not last too much longer, so in November they elected Lincoln again.

After the election, Congress passed the **Thirteenth Amendment** and sent it to the states for them to approve. The Amendment said there was to be no slavery anywhere in the United States.

THE WAR FINALLY ENDS

General Lee Surrenders

In April 1865, Lee's Virginia army finally left Petersburg and moved toward Richmond. Grant immediately followed. When the Union army broke through the Confederate lines, Lee was forced to surrender.

On April 9, 1865, Grant and Lee met in the village of **Appomattox Court House**. Lee was in his dress uniform, while Grant was in his favorite comfortable clothes. Grant accepted Lee's surrender. He let most of the Confederate soldiers go home with their horses and mules. Everyone now knew the war would soon be over.

The War Finally Ends

A month after Lee's surrender, Confederate President Jefferson Davis was captured. On May 26, 1865, the last Confederate army surrendered. The War Between the States had ended.

Lincoln is Shot

In March 1865, Abraham Lincoln took office as President for a second term. In a famous speech to Congress, he talked about his plans and hopes for peace and a smooth reunion.

On April 14, 1865, he was working on those plans. That night he and his wife went to **Ford's Theater** to see a play. There, **John Wilkes Booth**, a well-known pro-Southern actor, came up behind the President and shot him. President Lincoln died the next morning. Booth escaped, but he was tracked down and killed.

Booth, with several others, had planned to kill a number of government officials. Those in the plot, and some others who were not, were caught and either hanged or put in prison.

> *With malice toward none; with charity for all; with firmness in the right, as God gives us to see the right, let us strive on to finish the work we are in; to bind up the nation's wounds; to care for him who shall have borne the battle, and for his widow, and his orphan—to do all which may achieve and cherish a just, and lasting peace, among ourselves, and with all nations.*
> —Lincoln's Second Inaugural Address

▲ *Above is the speech Lincoln gave when he was inaugurated (sworn in as President) for the second time. In his speech, which is remarkable for how short and to the point it is, Lincoln says that the nation should forgive itself for the Civil War. Americans should not bear any grudges against each other, but instead should work together to heal the nation's wounds, to take care of those who suffered, and make peace.*

◀ *At left is the statue of Abraham Lincoln in the Lincoln Memorial in Washington. The sculptor has captured Lincoln's thoughtfulness and dignity in marble. Each year, millions of Americans visit the Memorial.*

During the War Between the States, over 600,000 lives were lost. The Union lost about 110,000 men in battles and another 250,000 men from disease. The Confederates lost about 94,000 men in battle and about 160,000 from disease. When the war was over, many problems remained. Much of the South had been destroyed. Many Southern cities were burned, and people had no money to rebuild. Slavery was gone, but blacks had no place to go. And the problem of how to bring the Southern states back into the Union still had to be solved.

SECTION REVIEW

Can you answer these Main Idea questions?

1. How did General Grant's and General Sherman's actions lead to the end of the war?

2. How did the war both hurt and help Lincoln's chances for reelection?

3. Compare the losses suffered by the North and by the South.

Can you identify and locate these places?

Petersburg, Atlanta, Appomattox, Ford's Theater

Can you identify these people?

Wiiliam Tecumseh Sherman, John Wilkes Booth

Can you define this term?

Sherman's March to the Sea, Thirteenth Amendment

AFTER YOU READ

Discussion Questions

1. Compare the advantages and disadvantages of each side during the Civil War?

2. How did new technology affect the Civil War?

3. How did military actions affect the people who were not in the army or navy?

Comprehension Questions

1. By looking at certain important ideas that run through the whole chapter, you can understand the war better. Some ideas were shared by both sides. Other ideas were important to one side or the other. Divide a piece of paper into three columns with the headings below. Then list each of the following phrases under NORTH if it is only about the North, SOUTH if it is only about the South, or BOTH NORTH AND SOUTH if it is about both sides. The first is done for you.

<u>NORTH</u>   <u>NORTH and SOUTH</u>   <u>SOUTH</u>

<u>Believed strongly in the Union</u>

believed strongly in the Union

believed their way of life should not be changed

had many recent immigrants

soldiers got tired of fighting the war

made most goods in their factories

many non-soldiers lost property

depended on goods bought from Europe

wanted to crush the other government

screamed a special yell when attacking

wanted to protect their land

drafted men to fight in army

changed their plan for the war

rich men paid other men to take their place in the army

changed their commanding general several times

illnesses killed many soldiers

2. Add three more details to each category. Make sure your details support the heading.

Writing Activity

Pretend you are a Civil War soldier who has just heard about or been part of one of the events below. Write a letter home. Tell your family what life is like in the army, what you think about the war, and how you feel about the ideas your side is fighting for.

First Bull Run

Shiloh

Emancipation Proclamation

Gettysburg

New York City Draft Riots

Sherman's March to the Sea

Lincoln's Death

The Gettysburg Address

Abraham Lincoln's Gettysburg Address. Lincoln gave the Address at the dedication of Gettysburg Battlefield as a Union cemetary. Interestingly, Lincoln's famous speech was almost an afterthought that day! Another man, Edward Everett, was the featured speaker, and the President had only been asked to make a few "appropriate remarks."

Lincoln's remarks were indeed appropriate, and it was his two-minute, 269-word speech which the world has long remembered, and not Everett's two-hour long one. Even the old-fashioned way he said that the country was then eighty-seven years old ("four score and seven years ago"—a score is twenty years) has become famous.

Fourscore and seven years ago our fathers brought forth on this continent a new nation, conceived in liberty, and dedicated to the proposition that all men are created equal.

Now we are engaged in a great civil war, testing whether that nation or any nation so conceived and so dedicated, can long endure. We are met on a great battlefield of that war. We have come to dedicate a portion of that field as a final resting place for those who here gave their lives that that nation might live. It is altogether fitting and proper that we should do this.

But, in a larger sense, we can not dedicate—we can not consecrate—we can not hallow—this ground. The brave men, living and dead, who struggled here, have consecrated it, far above our poor power to add or detract. The world will little note, nor long remember, what we say here, but it can never forget what they did here. It is for us the living, rather, to be dedicated here to the unfinished work which they who fought here have thus far so nobly advanced. It is rather for us to be here dedicated to the great task remaining before us—that from these honored dead we take increased devotion to that cause for which they gave the last full measure of devotion—that we here highly resolve that these dead shall not have died in vain—that this nation, under God, shall have new birth of freedom—and that government of the people, by the people, for the people, shall not perish from the earth.

A speech which the speaker thought the world would neither pay attention to nor remember has become one of the most famous, most memorable speeches ever. Why? The reason is simple: in a very few words—most pages in this book have more—Lincoln captured several very deep, very powerful truths.

The occasion was dedicating the Gettysburg Battlefield as a cemetary and monument. It was the sort of occasion at which politicians always give speeches—nowadays, we might call it a "photo op," since it is an opportunity for a politician to put himself in front of the public and get attention by saying fine things about what other people have done. Lincoln, though, realized that any speech of his would be meaningless next to what the soldiers who had fought there and died there had already said, by their willingness to die for their country and for what they believed in. Their sacrifice had, without words, said everything that needed to be said.

So that is what Lincoln told his listeners: that they could not make the battlefield any more sacred, any more special, than it already was. What they could do was to dedicate themselves instead to the country and the ideas that so many had died for. By continuing the soldiers' work, they could give their sacrifice meaning.

Consider also the overall situation at that time. The Civil War was not yet over, and Americans were still killing each other by the hundred and the thousand. There had been more suffering than during the nation's first three wars combined. Lincoln was speaking in front of an Union audience. It would have easy for him to talk about how bad the Confederates were, and to promise that they would pay for what they had done. But Lincoln didn't do that. Instead, what he talked about was the need to work together, to fix the country and make democratic government—"government of the people, by the people, for the people"—work.

CHAPTER 25 RECONSTRUCTION

In one sense, the North had won the War Between the States: the Union was saved, and the slaves were free. But in another sense, no one had won. Southern cities—American cities—and railroads were destroyed. Hundreds of thousands had died. And there were hard feelings and resentment everywhere.

The President and Congress faced two very difficult tasks: making a place for the freed slaves, and deciding how the Southern states would join the Union again. But instead of working together, they tore the government apart.

BEFORE YOU READ

Sections in This Chapter

1. At War's End
2. Reconstruction
3. The End of Reconstruction

Reading Political Cartoons

On the opposite page are three cartoons about Reconstruction. Use them to answer the questions below.

1. The man on the right side with his hands in his pockets is a veteran of the Confederate Army. Looking at him, do you think that he and his fellow ex-Confederates cooperated with the federal government after the Civil War?

2. The cartoon at bottom shows a member of the Federal Freedman's Bureau standing between a white Southern mob and freed slaves. Do you think it was drawn by a Northerner or a Southerner? What do you think Southerners felt about the Freedmen's Bureau?

3. The man in the upper left corner is called a *carpetbagger*. Were carpetbaggers well thought of?

Understanding a Key Concept:
THE UNITED STATES GOVERNMENT

To understand this chapter, you must understand how the federal government works. Review what you have learned about the United States Constitution and the United States government, then read each question and choose the best answer fom the list below. The first is done for you.

civil rights   veto   Republicans
2/3 of Congress and 3/4 of states
impeach the President   balance of powers
trial   states that remained in the Union

1. What is a change in the Constitution called?
   <u>amendment</u>

2. Who must agree to a change in the Constitution?

3. What is it called when a President refuses to let a bill passed by Congress become a law?

4. What can Congress do if it feels that the President has broken the law and must be removed from office?

5. What is it called when someone accused of breaking the law goes before a judge and jury?

6. What do all citizens of the United States have because of the Bill of Rights?

7. What makes sure that one branch of government is not stronger than the others?

8. At the end of the Civil War, which states were represented in Congress?

9. Which politicial party had power in Congress during the Civil War?

Making Use of What You Already Know

The Civil War affected the lives of Americans in many ways. Write a sentence about each change below and tell whether it affected the North or the South. Describe the change and write what you think might happen because of it.

1. Railroads were destroyed.

2. Factories grew.

3. Many farms, plantations, and homes burned.

4. Had power in Congress.

5. Whites worried that freed blacks would take their factory jobs.

1. AT WAR'S END

Main Ideas

Think about the following Main Idea questions as you read this section:

1. In what ways did the United States grow and become stronger after the Cvil War?

2. How did life in the South change and how did it remain the same after the Civil War?

3. Describe the sharecropping system and how it kept the balance of rich and poor in the South.

A BUSY, GROWING NORTH AND WEST

When the war ended, life in the North didn't change much. At first, many people were out of work because the army and the factories no longer needed them. Soon, though, most were back working. Many were hired to work on huge new projects, like the Brooklyn Bridge and a telegraph cable under the Atlantic Ocean.

The West grew quickly. Western land was opened to farmers. Scandinavian and Canadian immigrants settled Minnesota and other North Central states. Vast amounts of mineral riches, like gold, silver, copper, and coal, were taken from the earth. To help tie the nation together, Congress gave a lot of land and money to the railroads. In 1869, a railroad finally reached across the whole country—.

The country's most ambitious and able people went into business, not into politics. Some men made millions of dollars in new businesses, like John D. Rockefeller in oil and Andrew Carnegie in steel. Making money became very important to people, so important that some forgot what was right and what was wrong. They cheated or stole. Government officials cheated or stole, too.

Americans began looking at the outside world again. **Secretary of State Seward** warned the French to get out of Mexico, which they finally did. The Mexicans took back their government and killed Emperor Maximilian. Seward also bought **Alaska** from the Russians. People called it Seward's Icebox because no one thought it would be good for anything but ice. Seward had other plans, too, like buying Cuba from Spain, but the Senate would not go along with them.

A Ruined South Still Resists Change

The South did not share in the North's growth. Most Civil War battles had been fought in the South. Factories were destroyed and railroads were torn up. Fields were burned, and only chimneys stood where great houses had once been. Farm animals and tools were gone, and there were no seeds to plant. No Southern state governments were in control, either. Only the Union army had power. Slowly and with difficulty, the South began to rebuild.

What most southern whites thought about blacks did not change. They couldn't understand why black people were so glad to be free, especially since they were still so poor. They were shocked to see black soldiers. Southern whites wanted to make sure that blacks had no power and were kept "in their place," doing farm work for white people. They didn't want them to take over white jobs or tell whites what to do.

The Freedmen—Confused but Proud to Be Free

The nearly four million newly freed blacks were called **freedmen**. They were proud to be free. Many were eager to learn to read and write, to get jobs or learn skills. Volunteers from the North came South to teach them.

Some freedmen were confused by their new freedom. They thought that being free meant that they would never have to work again. Many believed they would be given free land. "Forty acres and a mule" was what they thought they had been promised.

To help the freedmen, Congress set up the **Freedman's Bureau** in 1865. It fed people, built hospitals, and helped the freedmen to find jobs. It protected them against attacks by whites. But many freedmen died from starvation, sickness, or violence anyway.

Sharecropping Continues the Plantation System

Many freedmen took jobs doing what they knew best: working in the fields. They couldn't buy their own farms, so they lived in the old slave houses. Some were hired by planters for between $5 and $15 a month. Others became **sharecroppers**. Sharecroppers were people who farmed small pieces of land that were owned by someone else. They paid a share of their crops to the landowners as rent. Often, the landowner supplied the sharecropper's farm animals, tools, and seeds. Since no one had much money, the landowner borrowed to pay for these things. The sharecropper charged goods at small stores. When the crops were sold, the landowner and the sharecropper divided the money. The landowner got half to three-quarters, and the sharecropper got the rest. The sharecropper then had to pay the landowner back for the tools and seeds. He also paid the store. Little was left to save or spend.

All over the South, both poor blacks and poor whites became sharecroppers. The system kept the landowner at the top and the sharecropper at the bottom.

SECTION REVIEW

Can you answer these Main Idea questions?

1. In what ways did the United States grow and become stronger after the Cvil War?

2. How did life in the South change and how did it remain the same after the Civil War?

3. Describe the sharecropping system and how it kept the balance of rich and poor in the South.

Can you identify and locate this place?

Alaska

Can you identify this person?

Secretary of State Seward

Can you define these terms?

freedmen, Freedmen's Bureau

2. RECONSTRUCTION

Main Ideas

Think about the following Main Idea questions as you read this section:

1. How did Lincoln's plan for Reconstruction differ from that of the Radical Republicans?

2. Why did Congress put President Johnson on trial and what was the result?

3. What were the goals of each group that helped run the Southern state governments during Reconstruction?

EARLY PLANS FOR RECONSTRUCTION

Lincoln's Plans for Reconstruction

The war destroyed the South's land, government, and way of life. The South needed to reconstruct, or rebuild, nearly everything. The time between the war's end in 1865 until 1877 is called **Reconstruction**. During this time, the U.S. government had many Reconstruction plans. Some of those plans were not carefully thought out; also, the South continued to fight changing its way of life. The Republican-controlled Congress and the white people of the South continued to work against each other.

Lincoln felt that only a generous peace could heal the wounds of the Civil War. During the war, his Reconstruction plan was followed. When the Union army took over a state, Lincoln named a governor. The governor worked to get as much local support as he could. A state government was started when 10% of the people promised to support the Union. They elected new representatives to send to Congress. Lincoln did not force the Southern states to do things that they were very much against, like giving black people the right to vote.

At first, Congress worked with Lincoln. Later, Congress refused to go along with his Reconstruction ideas. Many members of Congress—many people in the North generally—wanted to be punish the South.

President Johnson Follows Lincoln's Plans

When Lincoln died, **Andrew Johnson**, his Vice President, became President. Before the war Johnson had been a Tennessee Democrat. He didn't agree with Republican ideas and he didn't want to change the South. He also believed that black people were not as good as whites.

President Johnson followed Lincoln's generous Reconstruction plan with few changes. He worked with each state so that it could quickly rejoin the Union, naming a new governor for each Southern state. The states then changed their constitutions and elected new governments. Then each state asked Congress to let its representatives back into the Senate and the House. Johnson did all of this when Congress was not meeting, so that it had no say in his actions.

The South Tries to Return to the Past

Almost immediately, the Southern states did things which made the North angry. They chose the same men who had run the Confederate government to run their new state governments. They elected Confederate leaders to Congress. They refused to sign the Thirteenth Amendment, which freed the slaves. Most Southern states passed **Black Codes**—laws that said what blacks could and could not do. Freedmen were allowed more freedom than they had as slaves, but not nearly as much as whites. For example, they couldn't vote, and in some states, they still couldn't own land, serve on juries, or speak against a white in court. In schools and public places black people were kept segregated, or separated, from whites.

Many Northerners felt that the South hadn't learned anything from the war. They thought that the South was trying to bring back slavery in a new form. They felt that the South was still too proud, and that it still wanted things its own way.

Congress Fights with Johnson

When Congress met in December 1865, many Congressmen resented that they had not helped write Johnson's plan. They also felt that reconstruction had taken place too fast, and that Johnson's plan was too easy on the South. As a result, they refused to accept the newly elected Southern representatives.

Only the Democrats and a few Republicans firmly supported the President. Most Republicans didn't agree with him, but were willing to give him a chance. However, one small but powerful group known as the **Radical Republicans** didn't like Johnson or his plans at all. The Radical Republicans had their own Reconstruction Plan: they wanted to crush the South's pride and punish it for the war. They wanted freedmen to have more rights. They also wanted to make the Republican Party the most important party in the whole country.

Congress put together a group of men who wanted a say in Reconstruction, but who were not Radical Republicans. They suggested, and Congress passed, laws to help the freedmen. The Freedmen's Bureau was made stronger. A civil rights bill was passed to enforce the Thirteenth Amendment, which had ended slavery. The army was given the job of protecting blacks and of forcing Southern states to follow the Thirteenth Amendment. President Johnson, still believing that the best course of action was to be generous to the South, vetoed all these bills.

Johnson's angry speeches showed that he did not understand how to work with Congress. When many black people were killed during riots in Memphis and New Orleans, Johnson did nothing. Many Congressmen became disgusted with him. They began voting with the Radical

Republicans. They passed the civil rights bills again over the President's veto.

In the Congressional election of 1866, President Johnson tried to help men who agreed with him. But his speeches made the voters angry, and he kept losing his temper. Many of his supporters ended up losing.

CONGRESS AND ITS RECONSTRUCTION PLANS

Congress Passes Its Own Reconstruction Plan

In 1866, Congress was made up only of those states that had stayed in the Union. So many Republicans were in Congress that they could pass anything they wanted. If President Johnson vetoed a law, they just passed the law again over his veto. One of the first things that Congress passed was the **Fourteenth Amendment**. It said that all people born in the United States—including the ex-slaves—were citizens and had the same rights. No state could take away those rights. Johnson was opposed to the Fourteenth Amendment, and it took two years for enough states to approve the amendment. It finally became law in 1868. Two years later the **Fifteenth Amendment** was passed. It said that no state could prevent a man from voting because of his color or because he had once been held in slavery.

The Radical Republicans in Congress threw out all of Johnson's Reconstruction plans and took over Reconstruction. Congress ended the new Southern state governments and made Union Army generals the new governors. Each state had to write a whole new constitution allowing all men, black and white, to vote. Only then would a new government be elected. When a state did all that as well as signing the Fourteenth Amendment, Congress allowed its representatives back into the federal government.

The Southern states tried to resist Congress' plan. Congress simply passed other laws to force

In this cartoon, Johnson is pictured as a parrot, squawking "Constitution, Constitution." Johnson's Radical Republican opponents had no patience with Johnson or the Constitution: both were seen as obstacles in their way.

the Southern states to do what it wanted. Between 1868 and 1870, all the Southern states returned to Congress under the Radical Republican rules. But none were happy.

The Impeachment of President Johnson

The Republicans also tried to change the balance of power in the national government. They wanted to make Congress stronger and weaken the President. They passed laws which took away some of the President's powers.

One of the new laws said a President couldn't fire anyone in his cabinet unless the Senate agreed. When Johnson fired Secretary of War Stanton, a Radical Republican, Congress tried to force him out of office for breaking that law. In 1868, the House of Representatives voted to **impeach** the President. This means that they officially charged him with breaking the law. He went on trial before the Senate. Chief Justice Chase tried to make the trial fair, but Congress didn't follow the rules. They tried to stop Johnson's lawyer from presenting his case. They wanted to prove that Congress was more important than the President.

When the Senate finally voted, seven brave Republicans went against their party. They believed that Congress had no Constitutional right to keep the President from firing someone in his Cabinet. They felt that President Johnson was not guilty. The Republicans lost by one vote. They didn't remove the President from office and they didn't make Congress more powerful than the President.

Republican State Governments in the South

The Southern state governments elected under Congress's Reconstruction plan depended on three groups of people.

The first group consisted of Northerners who moved south. Southerners called them **carpetbaggers**, after a kind of cheap suitcase made of carpet. Some were Union soldiers who brought their families, built farms, and started businesses. Teachers, government workers, and businessmen came and stayed, too. Many wanted to make a life for themselves and to help their new state. Others wanted to make use of the South's bad times to make a lot of money or to gain power. Most Southern whites disliked the carpetbaggers because they were outsiders.

Another group was called **scalawags** by their opponents. They were the biggest group. They were Southern whites who worked with the Republicans. Some were rich planters or businessmen who wanted something from the government. Many had been against seceding, but had stayed with their state when it left the Union. Most of them wanted to rebuild their states as quickly as possible. Nevertheless, they were widely hated as traitors to the Southern way of life.

The freedmen were the last group. Not all blacks voted, and very few held office. Most of those who were elected to high office were smart, good men. Two black senators, fifteen black representatives, and many black state legislators were elected. Blacks held many local offices, too. But the freedmen were not used to voting, holding office, and having power. Some whites used them to get power for themselves.

People from these three groups, most of them white, ran the Southern Republican governments. They passed high taxes to rebuild roads, help the poor, start free but separate public schools—and often, to make themselves rich. They wanted Southern businesses, factories, and railroads to rebuild and grow. But many of them also put a lot of money into their own pockets. Other representatives, all over the country, were doing the same thing. The difference was that the South was poor: seeing crooked Republican politicians get rich made Southerners dislike the Reconstruction governments even more.

SECTION REVIEW

Can you answer these Main Idea questions?

1. How did Lincoln's plan for Reconstruction differ from that of the Radical Republicans?

2. Why did Congress put President Johnson on trial and what was the result?

3. What were the goals of each group that helped run the Southern state governments during Reconstruction?

Can you identify these people?

carpetbaggers, scalawags, Radical Republicans, Andrew Johnson

Can you define these terms?

Reconstruction, Black Codes, Fourteenth Amendment, Fifteenth Amendment, impeach

3. THE END OF RECONSTRUCTION

Main Ideas

Think about the following Main Idea questions as you read this section:

1. How did Southern whites regain control of their governments?

2. What made many Americans angry during President Grant's term in office?

3. How did the Compromise of 1877 end Reconstruction?

THE END OF RECONSTRUCTION

Southern Whites Change Their Governments

Most Southern whites hated the Republican state governments. They didn't like black people being part of the government, the government's protection of black rights, or high taxes. They didn't like the carpetbaggers, scalawags, and blacks who ran the state governments. In some states, whites elected Democrats who changed the government. Other states had more Republicans than Democrats. In these places, angry white Southerners forced people—especially blacks—to change how they voted or scared them until they stopped voting.

Secret groups, such as the **Ku Klux Klan**, and public ones, like the Red Shirts, were formed. They threatened and killed blacks and others who supported the Reconstruction governments. At night, men dressed in white sheets terrorized blacks, carpetbaggers, and scalawags. They whipped and killed people to show what would happen if anti-Reconstruction candidates weren't elected.

Klansmen. In the beginning, the Klan didn't wear white robes (though they wore hoods to hide their identity) and they didn't burn crosses. Those were added later. ▶

Reconstruction was America's bloodiest time that was not a war. Thousands of African Americans died in the South. In 1870, the federal government passed laws and sent the army against groups like the Ku Klux Klan. But the terror had worked. Many blacks stopped voting and Democrats took over state governments. By 1876, all but three Southern states had governments run by white Southern Democrats. Few Republicans had power in the South anymore.

President Grant and Government Corruption

In 1868, the Republicans nominated General **Ulysses S. Grant** for President. Most Northern people thought of him as a war hero. Although Grant won, other Republicans didn't. Many Democrats were elected to Congress.

Grant didn't like politics. He thought being President was his reward for winning the Civil

War. He skipped the hard parts of his job. He also failed to choose good, honest men to work with him.

During this time many businessmen and politicians did things that were not legal, but that made them rich. They didn't care whom they hurt. Men who ran railroads stole from their companies. Cities like New York, Chicago and Philadelphia were run by men who stole from the city and made secret deals to help their friends get rich. Many men like this were in the federal government, too.

People were upset with the government, but they reelected Grant in 1872. By 1874, though, the people had had enough of bad government. The country was in a depression. Banks and factories closed. Farmers couldn't sell their crops. People everywhere were out of work. Most Americans wanted Congress to work on these problems, not on Reconstruction.

In the election of 1876, the Republicans lost so many seats in Congress that the Democrats took charge of the House of Representatives.

The Compromise of 1877

In 1876, the Republicans nominated a very honest man for President, Ohio's **Rutherford B. Hayes**. The Democrats chose **Samuel Tilden**, who had reformed New York City's government. Both parties worked very hard to win.

When the voting was over, something was wrong with some of the votes for President: Republicans in three Southern states had cheated. The Democrats complained because the election was so close that the votes from those states would decide who won. A special group was chosen to count the votes because no one trusted Congress. Most voters had chosen Tilden, but the group announced that Hayes had won.

Southern Democrats were angry. They decided, however, to make a deal. They said they would not complain about the election if the Army would get out of every Southern state. Hayes agreed to the deal, which is known as the **Compromise of 1877**, and became President.

The End of Reconstruction

The Compromise of 1877 ended Reconstruction. The Army was no longer part of politics, and Congress turned to other problems. The federal government no longer tried to solve Southern problems. The Fourteenth and Fifteenth Amendments weren't enforced. Civil rights for blacks were almost forgotten for 75 more years.

White Southerners tried to keep their old way of life, while many in the North wanted to punish them. Reconstruction tore the government apart. Congress fought with the President. Republicans fought with Southern Democrats. Whites attacked blacks. When the Democrats and Republicans compromised in 1877, both black people and the white South were the losers. The North became richer, while the South remained poor for many years. More than 75 years passed before the Civil Rights Movement of the 1960's forced the federal government to pass laws ending the system that had been set up in the South after the Compromise of 1877.

SECTION REVIEW

Can you answer these Main Idea questions?

1. How did Southern whites regain control of their governments?

2. What made many Americans angry during President Grant's term in office?

3. How did the Compromise of 1877 end Reconstruction?

Can you identify this person?

Ulysses S. Grant, Rutherford B. Hayes, Samuel Tilden

Can you define these terms?

Compromise of 1877, Ku Klux Klan

AFTER YOU READ

Discussion Questions

1. Describe the changes in the lives of African Americans in the South from the beginning of the Civil War (1861) until the end of Reconstruction (1877).

2. What was Reconstruction and why were there two different Reconstruction plans? Compare these two plans.

3. How and why did the balance of power in the federal government change during the years after the Civil War?

4. Compare the people who had political power in the South during the Civil War, during most of Reconstruction, and at the end of Reconstruction.

Comprehension Questions

Americans had very strongly held ideas about what should be done during Reconstruction. The following quotes might have been said by one of the people on the list below. Match the quote to the person. One is done for you.

Northern business owner   *sharecropper*
Radical Republican   *freeman*
carpetbagger   *Ku Klux Klansman*
Southern Democrat in 1877
African American politician in the South

1. "I moved South after the war to help the area rebuild and to make a new life for my family. I know some Northerners here are doing bad things, but the people in the South treat us all— the good and the bad—the same. They hate us."
   <u>*carpetbagger*</u>

2. "I want to punish the South for causing this terrible war and killing so many of our boys."

3. "The most important thing to me now that I am free is to own my own land and to learnhow to read."

4. "If you or your black friends vote in the election, we will come back and hurt your families."

5. "My factory is growing, and I'm shipping some of my goods to other countries. I'm getting rich."

6. "I spent many years in slavery, but now I am trying to write new laws which will make the South into a place where everyone is free and has the same rights."

7. "Let's make a deal. You pull the army out of the South and don't bother us again, and we'll make sure your candidate becomes President."

8. "This year my family worked hard and raised a good crop, but after I sell it, I won't have much left. Most goes to the landowner, and some will go to the local store. Maybe I'll have enough left over to buy the children a treat, but I know I won't have enough to buy them new shoes."

Writing Activity

Many travelers in the 1800's kept a journal which told about what they had seen and the conversations they'd had with the people they'd met. Pretend you traveled in the South both before the Civil War and after, during Reconstruction. Create a chart comparing what you saw on your two trips. Several things to compare are listed below. Then use your chart to write journal entries for both trips about each of the topics.

blacks   small farms   plantations
food and shops   towns and cities

INDEX